I0128013

Reading the Dream

BOOKS BY PETER DALE SCOTT

The Politics of Escalation in Vietnam (1966, with Franz Schurmann and
  Reginald Zelnik)
The War Conspiracy (1972, 2008)
The Assassinations: Dallas and Beyond (1976, with Paul Hoch and Russell Stetler)
*Crime and Cover-Up: The CIA, the Mafia, and the Dallas-Watergate
  Connection* (1977)
*The Iran-Contra Connection: Secret Teams and Covert Operations in the Reagan
  Era* (1987, with Jonathan Marshall and Jane Hunter)
Coming to Jakarta: A Poem about Terror (1988, 1989, poetry)
Cocaine Politics: Drugs, Armies, and the CIA in Central America (1991, 1992,
  1998, with Jonathan Marshall)
Listening to the Candle: A Poem on Impulse (1992, poetry)
Deep Politics and the Death of JFK (1993, 1996)
Crossing Borders (1994, poetry)
Minding the Darkness: A Poem for the Year 2000 (2000, poetry)
*Drugs, Oil, and War: The United States in Afghanistan, Colombia, and
  Indochina* (2003)
The Road to 9/11: Wealth, Empire, and the Future of America (2007)
The War Conspiracy: JFK, 9/11, and the Deep Politics of War (2008)
Mosaic Orpheus (2009, poetry)
*American War Machine: Deep Politics, the CIA Global Drug Connection, and the
  Road to Afghanistan* (2010)
*Oswald, Mexico, and Deep Politics: Revelations from CIA Records on the
  Assassination of JFK* (1994, 1995, 2013)
Tilting Point (2012, poetry)
The American Deep State: Big Money, Big Oil, and the Attack on U.S. Democracy
  (2014, 2017)
Dallas '63: The First Deep State Revolt against the White House (2015)
Walking on Darkness (2016, poetry)
Poetry and Terror: Politics and Poetics in Coming to Jakarta (2018, with
  Freeman Ng)
Ecstatic Pessimist: Czeslaw Milosz—Poet of Catastrophe and Hope (2023)
Dreamcraft (2014, poetry)

Reading the Dream

A Post-Secular History of Enmindment

A Poem in Prose

Peter Dale Scott

ROWMAN & LITTLEFIELD
Lanham • Boulder • New York • London

Published by Rowman & Littlefield
An imprint of The Rowman & Littlefield Publishing Group, Inc.
4501 Forbes Boulevard, Suite 200, Lanham, Maryland 20706
www.rowman.com

86-90 Paul Street, London EC2A 4NE

Copyright © 2024 by Peter Dale Scott

All rights reserved. No part of this book may be reproduced in any form or by any electronic or mechanical means, including information storage and retrieval systems, without written permission from the publisher, except by a reviewer who may quote passages in a review.

British Library Cataloguing in Publication Information Available

Library of Congress Cataloging-in-Publication Data

Names: Scott, Peter Dale, author.
Title: Reading the dream : a post-secular poem in prose / by Peter Dale Scott.
Description: Lanham : Rowman & Littlefield, [2024] | Series: World social change | Includes bibliographical references.
Identifiers: LCCN 2023035849 (print) | LCCN 2023035850 (ebook) | ISBN 9781538181515 (cloth) | ISBN 9781538181522 (paperback) | ISBN 9781538181539 (epub)
Subjects: LCSH: Social evolution. | Civilization. | Postsecularism | Philosophy—History. | Poetry—Social aspects.
Classification: LCC HM626 .S438 2024 (print) | LCC HM626 (ebook) | DDC 303.4—dc23/eng/20231213
LC record available at https://lccn.loc.gov/2023035849
LC ebook record available at https://lccn.loc.gov/2023035850

Dedicated to my wife,
Ronna Kabatznick,
without whose inspiration, guidance,
correction, and support
this book would never have been finished,
written, or imagined

From where will a renewal come to us, to us who have spoiled and devastated the whole earthly globe? Only from the past, if we love it.

—Simone Weil, quoted in Czeslaw Milosz, *The Witness of Poetry*, 114

The honey of man is
the task we're set to: to be
"more ourselves"
in the making.

—Denise Levertov, "Second Didactic Poem"

Those who are alive receive a mandate from those who are silent forever. They can fulfill their duties only by trying to reconstruct precisely things as they were and by wresting the past from fictions and legends.

—Czeslaw Milosz, Nobel Prize Lecture, 1980

Get in good trouble, necessary trouble.

—Rep. John Lewis

Contents

Note about the Cover Image

The Byzantine cathedral of Hagia Sophia (Holy Wisdom) was constructed by Emperor Justinian between 532 and 537 CE and symbolizes his brief spectacular revival of the Eastern Roman Empire. Upon completion, it became the world's largest interior space. It remained the largest Christian cathedral until 1520, when the cathedral of Seville was completed.[1]

Hagia Sophia can also be seen as a product of the extreme disparity of wealth that afflicts and eventually dooms all great empires. Ironically, as this book will show, 537 CE was the second year of the long-term disruptive pandemic that led to the so-called Byzantine Dark Ages of the next two centuries, after which the Eastern Roman Empire had lost much of its territory.[2]

In 867, mosaics depicting the Virgin and Child were installed in the apse to commemorate the defeat of the Iconoclasts who, partly in response to early Muslim victories, had opposed the veneration of icons.[3] When the Ottomans conquered Constantinople in 1453, Hagia Sophia became a mosque. A century later, in the mid-sixteenth century, its mosaic depiction of Jesus and Mary was plastered over in accordance with Islamic law.

During Kemal Ataturk's program to secularize Turkey, the mosque was briefly closed. It was then reopened in 1935 as a museum and tourist attraction, with the plaster removed and the mosaics again visible. In 2020, as part of the post-secular revival of Islam under Recep Tayyip Erdoğan, the museum was again reconstituted as a mosque. In this spirit, the mosaic icons of the Virgin Mary and infant Christ are once again covered, this time only by fabric curtains. These curtains are a sign of post-secularity in Turkey, but in the West they also symbolize the conflicted relation of modernism and postmodernism to their spiritual past.

Acknowledgments, Leading to a Very Brief Note on Method

The first person I must thank is Anna Sun, professor of religious studies, Duke University, who persuaded me to write the first essay that is now chapter 1, and also encouraged me to continue as it grew slowly into a book. Thanks also to the neuroscientist Dr. Friedrich Sommer for permission to quote from his helpful emails to me.

I must thank also the many people who read and commented on my project as it developed. These include, among others, Prof. Charles Taylor; Prof. Graeme MacQueen, founder of the McMaster's Centre of Peace Studies at McMaster University; Prof. Gordon Teskey, professor of English literature at Harvard University; and my friends Daniel Ellsberg, Edwin Bernbaum, David Shaddock, Murray Silverstein, George Hammond, Brenda Walsh, Alison Jordan, Keith Eckiss, Karen Croft, Jesse Nathan, Steven Black, Freeman Ng, Suzanne Gardinier, my daughter Cassie Scott, and my granddaughter Marianna Scott. I must thank Keith Eckiss also for valuable help in revising my manuscript, and, once again, my reliable indexer, P. J. Heim.

Thanks to Google and Siri, I could write in a more holistic vein, observing my lifelong mantra that "the social sciences without the humanities are not scientific, while the humanities without the social sciences are not humane." My method, such as it was, was intuitive, leading to my original subtitle, "A Post-Secular Poem in Prose." I hope to see more books in future that will similarly move beyond the demands of "expertise," leaving space for a more generalist approach.

My greatest thanks go, once again, to my wife Ronna Kabatznick, who introduced me to Judaism, meditation retreats, and Thailand—all necessary preconditions for the conception of this work.

Introduction

(This introduction was one of the last parts of the book to be written. Those who understandably find it to be slow going should probably begin at chapter 1.)

In 2023, I published my first important book, *Ecstatic Pessimist: Czeslaw Milosz, Poet of Catastrophe and Hope*. From writing that book, I was convinced of two points. The first is that a successful revolution in politics, such as that of Solidarity which Milosz contributed to in Poland, has to be preceded by a longer-term revolution in culture. The second is that a successful revolution, unlike failures such as Stalinism, must always be securely rooted in the culture of the past.[1] Until recently, revolutions have been violent; but now, as evidenced by the victories of the American civil rights movement and of Solidarity in Poland, they can also be nonviolent—the result of persuasion rather than of coercion. America, foundering from the erosion of its democratic goals, is in a political crisis. The purpose of this book is to promote the chances that the needed response to this crisis will be, as far as possible, nonviolent and generative. More violence will mean more pain and perhaps disaster, but also a chance for greater cultural progress.

This aim is timely. The world is faced with both a pandemic and major climate change. These paired disruptions have in the past often marked major cultural shifts, including both setbacks to our mindset, defined by Webster as "outlook: set of ideas, values, and beliefs shared by a community," and the emergence of new mindsets that in the past have significantly enhanced the old.

It is possible that the current urban American and global post-Enlightenment mindset now faces the risk of radical and even violent disruption. Like past mindsets, it needs to recover its healthy origins in our dialectical cultural evolution through past creative disruptions. This need was intuited by Simone Weil almost a century ago: "From where will a renewal come to us, to us who have spoiled and devastated the whole earthly globe? Only from the past, if we love it."

Simone Weil, until recently, was an outlier in the discussion of civiliza-
tional discontents (except among poets). Her desire for a cultural renewal
marks her as what I shall call a "minder," someone who cares about defects in
our social-cultural environment and is devoted to repairing them. Perhaps the
most neglected part of our cultural development is the instructive evolution-
ary history of our culture—a more fundamental history, I believe, than our
conventional histories of political evolution.

The term *minding* is not used to cover all mental activity. For that we have
a more general term, *mentation*, "mental functioning, activity of the mind."
This includes not only thought but also dreaming by day or night, and even
the necessary activity of clearing the mind by forgetting.[2] I shall suggest in a
moment that the mental activities of thinking and dreaming correspond to the
left and right hemispheres of the human brain, respectively. For many people,
thinking and dreaming have little to do with each other. But insofar as the two
are synergistic, the result is creativity, producing great poets and other artists,
who in turn produce advances in culture.

This synergistic mentation of thought and dream is what I mean by
enmindment. This book will argue that this coalition of dream and thought
in enmindment is the source of creative evolution in the individual, and also
in the supporting culture in which we develop. It is for this reason that poets
in particular play such a large role in the evolution of culture—as Czeslaw
Milosz acknowledged in his audacious claim that "the poetic act both antici-
pates the future and speeds its coming."[3] But "poetic" here must be inter-
preted very broadly, as a spectrum from the Declaration of Independence, to
Martin Luther King's dream, to the songs of Bob Dylan or Leonard Cohen.

I will suggest that the ideals of the eighteenth-century Enlightenment, in its
current decadent phase of left-hemisphere and supposedly value-free social
sciences, have become overly rational; they need to return to the larger per-
spectives of expanded, left- and right-hemisphere enmindment. It is a symp-
tom of our somewhat skewed mindset that the definition of *mentation* in one
recent dictionary excludes such synergy and restricts *mentation* to mean only
"the process of using your mind to consider something carefully."[4]

In like fashion, Weil is sometimes referred to as an "intellectual," an awk-
ward term for someone so focused on dreaming.[5] It is a symptom of the bias
in our current science-oriented mindset that the most available terms for such
a minder or minders are "intellectual" or (in the plural) "intelligentsia." The
English noun "intellectual" was influenced by the French term *intellectuel*,
while "intelligentsia" began as a Russian term anglicized in the 1880s. Both
the French and the Russian terms connoted groups distinguished by their
alienation from their culture's spiritual and religious legacy.[6]

Social scientists have tended rather to follow Max Weber in looking to
the future rather than the past for a solution, one in which "spiritual leaders"

would heal the disenchantment (*Entzauberung*) of the modern episteme, that is, the cultural rationalization and devaluation of religion.[7]

On this point, Weber's disciple Karl Mannheim would eventually disagree—over what might sound like a technical issue but in fact involved an aporia at the very heart of this book:

> "Spiritual creativity" for Weber meant the ability to create a cultural synthesis of meaning, precisely what Mannheim rejected. Mannheim did follow Weber in dividing thought into two spheres, that of the exact natural sciences . . . and that which was "existentially connected" (*seinsverbunden*). . . . unlike Weber, he believed that this [second] sphere was not characterized by a potential organic unity, but rather by competition.[8]

This book will see these two spheres as yang and yin, corresponding roughly to the two hemispheres of the human brain: the sphere of science (yang) to the logical and analytical activities associated primarily with the brain's left hemisphere, and the less definable residual (yin) processes (or *seinsverbunden*), often thought of as "irrational," associated primarily with the right hemisphere. In this I subscribe to the view of Iain McGilchrist that "the left hemisphere tends to deal more with pieces of information in isolation, and the right hemisphere with the entity as a whole, the so-called *Gestalt*."[9]

Both Weber and Mannheim, in their different ways, recognized that the modern cultural mindset was excessively yang. It had suffered, through what Weber called "disenchantment" (*Entzauberung*), a weakening of the yin or irrational in us, what C. S. Lewis called "the longing for that *unnameable something*, the desire for which pierces us like a rapier at the smell of a bonfire, the sound of wild ducks flying overhead."[10]

This book aims to help move us again toward what has been briefly achieved at pivotal moments in our past cultural development: a better synergy of yang and yin, our analytical powers and our longings. And it will accept that these two tendencies correspond to the popular sense that "there's a distinctive analytic and verbal style of thinking associated with the left hemisphere of the brain, and a more holistic, creative style associated with the right."[11]

Karl Mannheim, whose response to the disruptions of the war was also that society needed a spiritual renewal, was convinced—I think rightly—that intellectuals were too embedded in the prevailing ethos to play that role. With György Lukács, Mannheim formed part of the postwar Sonntagskreis, for whom "the way forward was seen to be through the spiritual renewal entailed in a revolution in culture." Later Mannheim moved away from traditional social science and played a prominent role with T. S. Eliot in "The Moot," a

Christian discussion group in England concerned with the role of religion and culture in social reconstruction.

T. S Eliot's *The Waste Land* had indeed been a leading expression in poetry of the disenchantment that Weber perceived in the modernist ethos. But Eliot's prose searches for a remedy have never attracted much attention, and the same is true of Mannheim's protracted collaboration with him.[12] Eliot's *Notes towards the Definition of Culture*, the major product of this collaboration, did little to enhance his status as a cultural icon.

But there are ideas in it which, freed from their unabashedly reactionary context, have inspired this book. One is Eliot's summary observation that "culture may . . . be described simply as that which makes life worth living."[13] Culture is to the mind what the atmosphere is to the body: the ambience necessary for an active survival, and for our development into what Edmund Burke called the "second nature" of our adulthood.

Another is his claim that a culture, like an atmosphere, should be "healthily stratified."[14] In George Orwell's words, "The essence of his argument is that the highest levels of culture have been gained only by small groups of people."[15]

To extend the atmospheric analogy a little further, this book will explore how cultures, like atmospheres, are renewed both at the bottom, for example, by Christianity or blues music (cf. the oxygen of rain forests), and at the top, by canons of scriptures and classical epics (cf. atmospheric rivers).

Just as there is fresh air and stale air, good and bad air, so it is with cultures. And just as totally clean air, not fouled by smog or volcanic ash, is desired everywhere and found nowhere, so it is with pure culture, the uncontaminated aspiration of inspired minds. (When in this book I speak of cultural evolution and argue that progress in history is primarily cultural rather than political, this is the culture of which I primarily speak.)

Eliot's version of this claim was to speak of "the culture of a people as an *incarnation* of its religion." He then added, very problematically, that "it is only when we imagine our culture as it ought to be . . . that we can dare to speak of Christian culture as the highest culture . . . that the world has ever known."[16] But it was a characteristic limitation of Eliot's vision that he looked for the idea only in the past. To quote Czeslaw Milosz, in Eliot "a certain norm is placed in the past . . . the future does not promise anything good."[17]

Nevertheless, I can still endorse Eliot's wish to combat the contemporary error "that culture can be preserved, extended, and developed in the absence of religion."[18] Here his thinking aligns with the earlier efforts of both Weber and Mannheim to correct the disenchantment of modern society.

Weber's perception of *disenchantment* as a devaluation of religion affecting modern society was accurate. But many today have been slightly misled by it, failing to notice that the void created by this devaluation also acts as a vacuum to encourage its dialectical opposite—a search for *re-enchantment*. The last two decades alone have produced no less than thirteen different books with the word "re-enchantment" in their title or subtitle.[19]

These books by themselves are unlikely to achieve this dialectical change. But their numbers attest to a remarkable feature of our global culture that is explored in this book. Our culture is a self-correcting process, continuously losing old features in a zigzagging, dialectical cultural evolution that I call "ethogeny," and then beginning to compensate for what has been lost. Like so much else in the physical universe, our cultural evolution both leads to periodic crises that disrupt its orderly development and also, responding to our human psychological needs, generates what is needed to return toward the unattainable goal of cultural equilibrium.

To be conscious of this process can help each of us in our own personal moves toward an unattainable equilibrium. We can see that the world's social disruptions today are replicating those that motivated the spiritual quests of Weber and Mannheim after World War I. And it is apparent that the anxieties caused by this social and political breakdown are already generating compensatory searches in our dialectical culture.

Reading the Dream explores this transpersonal dialectic at length. It will argue that the fall of the Roman Empire emerged from the excessive disparity of wealth ("public squalor, private opulence," wrote Sallust, d. ca. 35 BCE), the widespread degradation of culturally excluded lives, and the progressive inanition of meaningful communal goals. These deficiencies energized the spread of Christianity, the new religion that more than others embraced among its members slaves and their aspirations.[20]

After the fall of Rome, the so-called Dark and Middle Ages, while suffering a millennial lapse in yang intellectual inquiry, compensated for this in such ways as reducing wealth disparity and evolving toward a more egalitarian social order. And the restoration of intellectual inquiry in the Renaissance disrupted the medieval attempt at equilibrium, only to see the revival of both old and new religious practices and inquiries, such as Rosicrucianism and later Romanticism.

This is a feature of our current discontents. Especially before World War I, liberal intellectuals tended to assume that religions were relics of a pre-enlightened era, destined to wither slowly away. Today, after the disruptions of two world wars, it is the future of Enlightenment rationalism that seems more at risk. Since the Trump campaign of 2016, newspaper headlines refer frequently to a "post-truth era."[21] On a more intellectual plane, minders, following an influential paper by Jürgen Habermas in 2008, have referred to the present as "post-secular."

Habermas distinguished between two divergent tendencies: nostalgic fundamentalism and innovative syncretism. I prefer to focus on the age-old dialectic underlying them, of coercion being supplanted by persuasion, and to contrast nostalgic violent retro-spirituality (in states like Iran and India) with the forward-looking generative spirituality of those who also seek guidance from the cultural momentum of the past.

As exemplars of those who would give this redirection shape, I would cite three recent thinkers. The first is Habermas, who anticipates that in a post-secular era a new peaceful dialogue and tolerant coexistence between the spheres of faith and reason must be sought in "an inclusive civil society in which both equal citizenship and cultural difference complement each other."[22]

The second is Charles Taylor, who in *A Secular Age* has argued that modern secularity is not a "subtraction story," an enduring residue after the disappearance of "illusions," but a transient ideology, "the fruit of new inventions, newly constructed self-understandings."[23]

The third is Czeslaw Milosz, who once wrote in a poem that,

> If there is no God, [man is still]
> not permitted to sadden his brother,
> By saying that there is no God.[24]

Like Habermas, Milosz argued that culture should be more tolerant and open-minded. As a poet, he was highly aware of two sources of thinking in his divided brain, one logical and another, extralogical and often surprising him, that was the source of his poetry. As already noted, this book will defend Milosz's claim that "the poetic act both anticipates the future and speeds its coming"[25]—a more holistic inspiration defying logic but leading, I shall argue, to enduring change.

With Milosz's twofold mode of thinking came a parallel doubleness in his personality, between a self that was secular (the Settembrini of Thomas Mann's *The Magic Mountain*) and a self that was other-worldly (Mann's Naphta).[26] Late in life, he wrote that this underlying psychological doubleness was widespread, and hence fostered an interactive doubleness in developed culture as well (what Octavio Paz once called "a tradition against itself").[27]

As a youth Milosz saw Settembrini as dominant in his personality. In his old age he had shifted towards Naphta. But consistently in his life he argued for the need to maintain balance between conflicting attitudes; and he approved a folkloric condemnation of "whoever says he's 100% right" as "a fanatic, a thug, and a rascal."[28] As I wrote in *Ecstatic Pessimist*, "Milosz's search for balance, his desire 'to retain both ends of the contradiction'"... may offer a 'way ahead'" for the needed reconciliation of conflicting elements in our sorely divided culture."[29]

And in *The Land of Ulro*, Milosz drew on the insights of the Romantic poets Blake and Mickiewicz "to trust in 'faith and love'" as the way to heal the current "dichotomy between the world of scientific laws—cold, indifferent to human values—and man's inner world."[30] This mitigation of one-sided judgment would permit us "to accept the world, not because of its order, which has been violated, but because it holds out the hope, as in the [Jewish] Cabala, that it will be followed by *tikkun*, a return to order."[31] His book closes with an appeal for tolerance and incantatory talk of "an idyllic earth where 'the hay smells of the dream.'"[32] This dream reminds us of C. S. Lewis's "longing for that *unnameable something*, the desire for which pierces us like a rapier at the smell of a bonfire." On a more practical level, I shall trace that dream also in Martin Luther King's "arc of the moral universe" that "bends toward justice."[33]

TOWARD A RECONCILIATION OF YIN AND YANG

There is a tendency today to see as inevitable and tragic the conflict in the world between two kinds of enlightenment—one through faith (yin) and one through science (yang)—or in practical terms between ISIS and the West.

To the West, China exemplifies this conflict, with the government's active oppression of Buddhists in Tibet, Muslims in Xinjiang, and the Falun Gong in the heart of China.[34] But Europe has also seen a heightening of religious tensions, exacerbated by a large influx of refugee and other Muslims. We see the same heightening in the Muslim world itself, from Algeria, Egypt, and Syria in the west to Malaysia and Indonesia in the east.

America itself is no exception to this global picture. A nation once celebrated for tolerance and nation building has seen its national consensus subside yet again into two competing epistemes,[35] each convinced of the perfidy of the other. Among the underlying causes of this conflict is a falsely imagined split between "faith" and "science." The country that united to fight against Hitler is deeply divided today over faith-related issues like abortion rights. We have also seen a return of overt racism and anti-Semitism.

This book will not go near such polemical issues. Instead it will describe the cultural origins of this current global conflict in an account which I hope will not only be readable by some on both sides but might even contribute a little to their partial reconciliation. For yang and yin mentalities are most fruitful when flourishing together and, ideally, interacting.

I hope to show that similar periods of global cultural conflict have occurred repeatedly before, in ways that have been not only seriously disruptive but also ultimately beneficial to cultural evolution. Moreover, that evolution, though diverse, has not been random and unpredictable; it has shown, I believe with Milosz, a deeper pattern of development, one that overall is mysteriously coherent if not purposive.[36]

I am struck by the analogy to the pattern in the biological evolution of the human species to which Ernst Haeckel (d. 1919) and Charles Darwin (d. 1882) gave the term *phylogeny*, "the pattern of historical relationships between species or other groups *resulting from divergence during evolution*."[37] Inspired by that analogy, I have borrowed from ethologists (people who study animal or human behavior) the term *ethogeny*, by which I mean the significant underlying pattern of human cultural development (both in an individual and, primarily, in the cultural evolution through history of the human race).[38]

I began this book (which was originally just a short essay) as what I call a poem in prose, in which I was willing to trust the yin guidance of my prosaic muse, but had no idea where, if anywhere, my writing would proceed. But finishing this first volume has convinced me that the conflict at its heart will be lessened when people accept that both faith-based and scientific searches for enlightenment are finite, fallible, and enriched by each other.

This book, as a poem in prose, is a subjective attempt to understand these yang and yin drives both in myself and also in our culture or ethos, which, as Burke wrote long ago, is the source of our "second nature."[39] Meditation on the uneasy comity between our first and second natures has persuaded me that, despite recent evident setbacks on the surface political level to the goals of peace and global cooperation (notably by election in many countries of reactionary leaders), we can still see a deeper progress toward enmindment in our slow cultural development over the centuries—progress that has increasingly been nurtured by our creativity or "third nature": our *moreness*, our human need to be more than we are. This need is universal; it is also particularly urgent today.

A clarification: versions of this moreness also characterize our first nature or *id* (the desire to befriend, to procreate, and to "best" in battle) and our second nature or *ego* (the desire to work well, to build, and to be loved, remembered, or famous). But the best in our first and second nature cherishes a third nature, colored less by id or ego than by something striving to escape id and ego—pure moreness if you will.[40]

The cumulative result of acts of moreness is positive cultural development or ethogeny. And with the cultural development of the collective mind, each of us has the opportunity to develop to a marginally higher level. Legacies of a less developed past, like lynchings in America, may not die out altogether, but they cease to define a sociocultural norm.

Thus, there is a cultural history of the mind, which builds on the much slower biological neurohistory. This book, as a yin poem in yang prose, is an example of that cultural history—sustaining the importance of our collective dreaming and also reading that collective dreaming in the light of its historic evolution.

I freely admit that it is not the only possible history. Someone else (or even I) could have written a dialectically different poem in prose from the same evidence, pessimistic where mine is ultimately optimistic. Philip Larkin once wrote an excellent poem of cynical disenchantment, "Aubade" ("I see what's really always there: / Unresting death, a whole day nearer now"). And there is really no other refutation of it than to say, as Milosz said of "Aubade," "It's a little cheap to fall into sarcasm, irony. That emptiness and cruelty, which is the basis of Larkin's weltanschauung, should be accepted as a basis upon which you *work towards something light*."[41]

I myself would give Larkin full marks as a minder. He minded the darkness, and that helps us to appreciate light. But I am tempted to say that Larkin's egotistical minding was notably deficient in moreness.

CULTURE EAST AND WEST: ETHOS AND *TIANXIA*

As I complete this volume, it is in a context of a global pandemic, compounding the chaotic U.S. presidency of Donald Trump. Modest agendas to deal with the impending crisis of climate change are barely being met. And more and more it appears that after seven decades, the so-called Pax Americana, comparable to the nineteenth-century Pax Britannica, may now be waning.

There is a prevailing sense of crisis, which at least has the advantage of increased public consciousness. Americans are more aware than before that the U.S. social structure, while conferring perhaps unprecedented social benefits on many, is also experiencing an unprecedented disparity of wealth, which (as in so many decaying cultures before it) leaves many in poverty, oppressed, and angry, both at home and abroad.

The same can probably be said of all social structures that, at one time or another, have for a while been dominant in the world and then declined. The examples of Britain, Spain, Rome, and even Athens spring immediately to mind. To say this could lead to an attitude of acceptance and resignation. There are those, however, who would like to do better than that.

One such person is the noted Chinese scholar and thinker Xu Jilin (许纪霖), a true minder who, from what I have read of him, could apparently be at home in the West. It is relevant that for six months in 2002–2003, he was a visitor at the Harvard-Yenching Institute in Cambridge. Xu has described in contemporary China the same mix of liberation and oppression that I have referred to just now in America.

And in looking forward to a better world, he begins by making the distinction that underlies this book, that between the "structure of power" (or state) that governs us and the "structure of values" that we each internalize as our ethos or second nature. The former is very fallible and in the long run ephemeral. The latter (which I would not in English call a "structure") abides and is capable of historical developments that can lead to improvements in both individuals and the state.

To his "structure of values," Xu assigns the three-thousand-year-old Chinese term *tianxia*, meaning "(all) under Heaven":

> As a value system, *tianxia* was a set of civilizational principles with a corresponding institutional system. Here, the state was merely the political order of the dynasty, while *tianxia* was a civilizational order with universal application. It referred not only to a particular dynasty or state, but above all to eternal, absolute, and universal values. The state could be destroyed, but *tianxia* could not. Otherwise humanity would devour itself, disappearing into a Hobbesian jungle.[42]

Translating *tianxia* into English is difficult.[43] Literally, *tianxia* means "(everything) under heaven." But for me there is a big difference between thinking about "everything under heaven" and thinking about "everything."

The first mode of thinking is for me closer to how most humans think, for it encompasses two elements: both everything that is, the status quo, and also *something more*—heaven—heaven being traditionally associated (in both Chinese and English) with all the values we have slowly acquired through history as aspirations yet do not fully embody. That doubleness of realized and unrealized is the world we humans live in.

(Xu anchors his vision of a China under *tianxia* to an idealized memory of China in the so-called Qing golden age of the seventeenth and eighteenth centuries,[44] when China was more tolerant of its minorities:

> When China was great in the past, China was open, not closed, and if China wishes to be great again it most adopt the same posture because civilizations by definition must be universal.[45]

Other Chinese scholars share this pacific dream.[46])

DOUBLENESS AND MORENESS

In chapter 1, I discuss this "something more," this moreness, in terms of both our individual aspirations to be "more than we are" and also the social drive to repair the inadequacy of what is now through a shared search for an otherness. The result has been religion, in two senses, both as a fact (itself in need of repair) and also in the very human need to repair.

Moreness for me builds from directional values that have already been established to others still to be striven for. This mix of immanence and transcendence in the religions of the West is what moved me to describe their evolution in time as *The Way of Moreness*, the original title of this book.

With all this in mind, what single word can we use to translate *tianxia*? "Civilization" is too specific, while "culture" is too amorphous. (Even heroin addicts have a culture.) What exists both here and in China is a kind of prevailing moral and social order, partly realized and partly aspirational. For this we sometimes use the recently anglicized word *mentalité*, dated by the *OED* to 1908. But I shall more often use, with its focus on "spirit," the older term *ethos*, defined by the *OED* as the "characteristic spirit of a people, community, culture, or era as manifested in its attitudes and aspirations" and dated by it back to 1835.[47]

Today, like many thinkers around the world (such as Jürgen Habermas), Xu envisages a "new *tianxia* that will emerge in the form of universal values"—a global ethos, in short, incorporating and transcending the best of its predecessors.

It is a thesis of this book that the goal of a global ethos has always been latent in our culture, not as a predestined outcome but as an optimal direction when established values, not under undue stress, expand to enlarged contexts. For example, a phrase like "Love thy neighbor as thyself" (Lev. 19:18) was limited at first by its context in both area and intensity of emotion. It has a different scope today, when a post from Berkeley on Facebook can be answered, empathetically, by a stranger in East Timor.

I do not wish to dispense with the useful terms *civilization* and *culture*, but I do want to use them neutrally. There was a time when *civilization* ("human cultural, social, and intellectual development when considered to be *advanced and progressive in nature*"[48]) was distinguished as being both quintessentially more urban and more advanced than *culture* ("the distinctive ideas, customs, social behaviour, products, or way of life of a particular nation, society, people, or period").[49]

Sigmund Freud disdainfully rejected the distinction. I shall retain it, but without distinguishing hierarchically between the two terms. Indeed, the thesis of this book is that both civilization (more protean and urban) and culture (more traditional and rural) are vital and progressive when active as *processes*, and already needing amendment when, as civilizations and/or cultures (plural), they lapse into mere *states*. And the deep pattern of their evolution is that, in some historical periods or shifts (including China today), there is indeed an evolution of yin rural culture toward yang urban civilization (or what I will call *urbanity*,[50] in place of the now slightly archaic *civility*). That was the trend in the nineteenth century, which celebrated this particular movement as "progress."

But in some other periods, notably but not exclusively the European Dark Age, the *progressive* evolution was in the reverse direction, from urban to rural, yang toward yin. To give just one example, "civilized" Rome, in order to harden the emotions of its warrior citizenry, staged "games" where one went to derive pleasure from watching humans kill each other or be devoured by lions. At the outset of the so-called Dark Age, rural barbarian Vandals swiftly terminated these "civilized" (urbanized) customs.[51]

The chief downside of urbanity and its leisured freedom has been slavery, flagrant in the past but still very much with us, now usually in the form of wage slavery. We must not forget that the rise of urban civilization, both in China but especially in the West, was accompanied by an *increase* in slavery. In Athens and later in Rome, both civilization and slavery reached their zeniths and then declined together. The end of this volume will describe how the gradual reduction of chattel slavery in our domestic societies has hitherto always been accompanied by the expansion abroad of its equivalent—as, for example, the slave trade—in other forms and places.

Xu Jilin's essay about *tianxia* is motivated by a concern that China's recent economic successes have once again raised China, not for the first time, to a position where it can dominate and oppress countries around it. Xu's retrospective review of the history of *tianxia* is explicitly an effort to return China to an earlier outlook when "values were universal and humanistic rather than particular"—like those of the other religions Karl Jaspers (d. 1969) grouped together as "axial [i.e., pivotal] civilizations," each of which "took universal concern for the whole of humanity as its starting point."[52] (I will argue that Jaspers's "Axial Revolution" of circa 500 BCE was only one of successive pivotal moments about every half millennium—and not even the first.)

I cannot close this section without acknowledging the parallel global importance of Chinese *poetry*, especially from the eighth-century High Tang era. That influence continues. The following poem by Bei Dao, now a poet in exile (like so many great poets before him), is clearly addressing this book's yang-yin themes of urbanity and rusticity, creation and disruption:

> a sower walks into the great hall
> it's war out there, he says
> and you awash in emptiness
> you've sworn off your duty to sound the alarm
> I've come in the name of fields
> it's war out there

I walk out from that great hall
all four directions a boundless harvest scene
I start planning for war
rehearsing death
and the crops I burn
send up the wolf-smoke of warning fires

but something haunts me furiously:
he's sowing seed across marble floors[53]

THE CHINESE AND WESTERN
ETHOS: DIFFERENCES AND COMMONALITIES

America, launched in a spirit of liberation, equality, and noninvolvement in foreign wars, is now also in a posture of global domination, increasingly at odds with China. I believe that a return to America's ethical heritage, a return not just to the nation's inauguration but to the first origins in antiquity of its ethos, would help resolve many of the serious problems besetting it both domestically and internationally.

And here we should note a difference between the traditional Chinese *tianxia*, which has been relatively centralized, continuous, and (especially in very recent years) inflexible, and the Western correlative, which has always been relatively polycentric, pluralistic, self-questioning, and above all dialectical.

By dialectical, I mean that in our ethos or culture, elements of dominance have been offset by elements of resistance, especially in our religion. I shall argue in this book that the ethos of every literate society is to some extent dialectical. This is true also of China, where the yin opening of the Taoist Daodejing ("The Tao [Way] that can be Taoed is not the true Tao") can be read as an implicit dialectical criticism of yang Confucianism.

I believe that every specific ethos or *way*, including China's, is also dialectical in that its fate, once established, is to age, lose its inspiration, become weaker and/or more corrupt, and be partially displaced and corrected by a new manifestation—as for example in the neo-Confucian revival of Zhu Xi (1130–1200) or the Protestant Reformation. In other words, the *Way*, once established, is mortal and degrades into *ways*.

Words like *culture, civilization,* and *enlightenment,* which originally referred to developmental processes, become accepted, stabilize, and eventually refer to slowly decomposing epistemes. Perhaps we should distinguish the latter (where we are now) by the terms *civilhood* and/or *enlightendom*.

In time, the decomposition becomes evident as breakdown, successful challenges, and the prelude to a new pivotal shift.

The supplanting of Han Confucianism by the Five Pecks of Rice movement of religious Taoism (ca. 140 BCE–150 CE) is one example of this dialectical transition or shift. The fifteenth-century Protestant Reformation is another. I discovered that initially these shifts, viewed in a wide historical context, were not local and episodic; each one was widespread, each one was part of a roughly contemporaneous shift in the Eurasian map, and all together they shared a deeper pattern. In this respect, one can compare, for example, the return to a simpler unsophisticated piety that one encounters in both Martin Luther (1483–1546)[54] and his contemporary, the pivotal Confucian reformer Wang Yangming (1472–1529).[55]

These shifts can be described as *pivotal* because they are revolutionary in the original sense of turning back in search of something lost. But they are also *disruptive* because each one involves the dialectical displacement, often violently, of the ethos that preceded it. Writing this book has persuaded me that these shifts between ways occur with some regularity, every half millennium or so, right across the literate world. By this calendar we may be currently due for a shift, and there is abundant evidence to confirm this. What remains to be seen is whether the shift will be relatively continuous and painless, or relatively violent, disruptive, and (as in 536 and the 1340s CE) lead to great loss of human life.[56]

More importantly, the overall pattern I see is not one of recurring loss and recurrence of different *ways*, as Arnold Toynbee seemed to suggest, but of cumulative and essentially uninterrupted evolution of one *Way* toward its latent goals, as suggested by Hegel. To be more precise, the history of states (the structure of power) is chaotic, but the underlying history of our global ethos is one of dialectical ethical evolution, or what I call ethogeny.

BIBLICAL PROPHECY AND SOCIAL PROGRESS

There is nothing in China that matches the centrality of the Jewish prophetic protests against a status quo, exemplified by the Lord's words empowering Jeremiah as a prophet:

> Behold, I have appointed you over the nations and over the kingdoms, to uproot and to crush, and to destroy and to demolish, to build and to plant. . . . And I, behold I have made you today into a fortified city and into an iron pillar, and into copper walls against the entire land, *against the kings of Judah*, against its princes, against its priests, and against the people of the land. (Jer. 1:10, 18, emphasis added)

It might perhaps seem anachronistic to invoke the spirit of Jeremiah in an age of coronavirus and global warming, but according to Martin Luther King,

> Religion, in a sense, through men like Jeremiah, provides for its own advancement, and carries within it the promise of progress and renewed power. . . . It is obvious that if we judge Jeremiah by the ordinary standards of the world, his work was a failure. He was lightly esteemed in life. He became the supreme example of what Deutero-Isaiah called the suffering servant. He was despised and rejected, a man of sorrows and acquainted with grief. But in after years his unheeded prophecies became the favourite book of the scattered Hebrew race. Many of the Psalms . . . re-echo his words, and depict scenes such as only Jeremiah could have passed through. It is for these reasons that Jeremiah came to be regarded as the greatest of them all (Matt. 16:14, John 1:21).[57]

I believe that the civil rights movement's successes against the segregationists who then dominated the American South can be attributed to its secure grounding in this centuries-old Judeo-Christian ethos, against the parochial ideology of its oppressors. This is just one example of the dialectic in our ethos that makes some causes prevailable, especially against countervailing powers, and others not.

The success of the civil rights movement in the 1960s exemplifies the way in which our ethos has evolved over time. Earlier examples include the successes of activists, marginal and even detested at first, in generating movements to outlaw first the slave trade and then chattel slavery, or to achieve women's suffrage.

In acknowledging that, at least in the West, nonviolent values have in the right circumstances occasionally prevailed over violent power, we must slightly modify for our ethos what Xu Jilin had to say about *tianxia*. In opposing the "structure of power" to the "structure of values," Xu reflected the age-old split in Chinese society between the violent world of *wu*—force, arms, violence, the army, and oppression—and the world of *wen*: civility, letters, intellectuals, and persuasion.[58] Confucian China respected intellectuals and trained them as mandarins. But their function in society was defined as to advise, not to generate policy. Western-influenced protesters in Communist China and Hong Kong, espousing a cause not yet grounded in the Chinese tradition of *tianxia*, have so far failed to overcome this dichotomy.

In the West, most demonstrably since the Renaissance, those intellectuals who choose to be minders have played a visible and increasing role in mobilizing public opinion to change policies. On occasion—as in the American Revolution—they have even created new governments. And Martin Luther King was right to see these recent secular developments as grounded in the

Jewish and Christian religions, which carry within them "the promise of progress" (cf. Exod. 23:20–23).

But values, even when embedded in mass religions, cannot change the status quo by themselves. Recently we have become more and more aware that the most significant social change is not gradualistic but disruptive and occurs after societies have been weakened by wars or environmental disasters such as earthquakes, volcanoes, or plagues.[59] I shall say more about this in chapter 9.

HOW I CAME TO WRITE THIS BOOK

Let me at this point explain how I came to write about ethogeny. I am a non-observant Christian and sometime Buddhist whose chief religious practice is now Modern Orthodox Judaism. A while ago, after getting up and before going to bed, I began reciting the Jewish Sh'ma (with part of the following V'ahavta), along with the Lord's Prayer and the Buddhist Tisarana or Three Refuges—taking refuge in the Buddha, the Dharma (practice), and the Sangha (community of practitioners).[60]

I was soon struck by their commonality: the Buddhist Threeness of alterity, practice, and community was akin to the V'ahavta's instructions to love God, follow his commandments, and teach them to your children. Less securely, I could note traces of this Threeness also in the Christian prayer for God's name, his kingdom, and the fulfillment of his will.

Encouraged by a friend to write about this, I was startled to find the Threeness also in Emile Durkheim's definition of religion as "a system of *beliefs* and practices relative to the *sacred* that unite those who adhere to them in a moral *community*."[61] I speculated that there was something in ourselves (which I called our *moreness*) that, among other things, needed to supplement the status quo (in ourselves and later also in society) with an alterity or otherness that was something more (eventually the sacred).

But the more clearly I saw that these Threenesses were shared by the Tisarana and Sh'ma, the more clearly I saw that the Lord's Prayer could not be easily reduced to the same formula. There was in it an emphasis, alien to the Sh'ma and the Tisarana, on an otherness not just now but in the future—"Thy kingdom come, Thy will be done." This dissatisfaction with the present reflected the widespread dissatisfaction in Jesus's time with the decadent priesthood of the Jewish Temple, with quarrels between the Pharisees and Sadducees and outright revolt in the case of the Essenes.

Furthermore, this Christian focus on a better future reflected parallel developments at this same time in Rabbinic (Mishnaic) Judaism, Mahayana Buddhism, and (I learned later) religious Taoism. (When I first drafted this book, I was not yet aware of the new messianic characteristics found in the Taoist Five Pecks movement of circa 140 BCE, analogous in some ways to early Christianity.)

THE IMPORTANCE OF DISRUPTIVE
MOMENTS IN OUR ETHOGENY

This evolutionary development in time led me to rethink the notion of an Axial [Pivotal] Age (*Achsenzeit*) as developed by the Swiss philosopher Karl Jaspers (d. 1969). (I prefer to speak of an axial or pivotal *moment*, drawing on the useful and not accidental ambiguity of "moment": (1) a short period of time, (2) particularly since Hegel, "a particular stage or period in a course of events or in the development of something; a turning point; a historical juncture," and (3) an essential element or significant aspect of a complex conceptual entity.

For Jaspers, the Axial Moment was a revolt against thinking in exclusively particular terms, a shift away from more predominantly localized concerns and toward *transcendence*. In the world, as Xu Jilin recognized (and as we see in the book of Isaiah), this referred to a shift beyond tribal observations toward global ideals. But there was a parallel personal shift to a more demanding level, from ritual observance to amendment—as when Isaiah (or "Trito-Isaiah") warned Jews that God was not interested in an external fast where you still "oppress all your laborers," but a fast of the spirit, where you "loose the bands of wickedness, and let the oppressed go free" (Isa. 58:3–6).[62]

The reformed religions contemporary with Christianity all saw a further cultural evolution beyond that of the Axial Moment. The earlier concern to create a purified self and immediate community had now been expanded to prepare also for the repair of a corrupt world.

The Axial Moment of circa 500 BCE, I had to accept, was not the only such shift or moment. It had been followed by what I called the Second Pivotal Moment at the beginning of the Common Era. By the time of the Second Pivotal Moment, the divergent new religions of the First, like Buddhism, had become old in ways that led to reformulated religions like Mahayana Buddhism or the replacement of temple Judaism by Rabbinic Judaism.

I see this moment of divergence, and of successive divergences like it, in Hegelian terms, with the product of an earlier dialectical divergence maturing into the dominant occasion of a new one. Thus I write of

a Third Pivotal or Disruptive Shift (Moment) of about 500 CE (with the emergence of Islam in Asia and the shift of cultural leadership in Europe from imperial cities and cathedrals to rural monks and monasteries);

a Fourth Pivotal or Disruptive Shift (Moment) of about 1000 CE (when the dominant cultural role in the West, after the revival of monetized Mediterranean trade, shifts back to cities and to friars [rather than monks] and then to laity— e.g., Dante and Chaucer—[rather than clerics]);

and a Fifth Pivotal or Disruptive Shift (Moment) of about 1500 (with the Renaissance, the Protestant Reformation, and then later the Enlightenment).

In this book I write of this pattern between twinned dominant and divergent elements in terms of yang and yin. And I write of it as not just a sociohistorical development, but also as corresponding to an internal yang-yin doubleness in our human consciousness. There are further correspondences, to the doubleness between prose and poetry and between (a) the centralizing vertical hierarchies of cities (civilization) and (b) the dispersed or more horizontal hierarchies of rural society (and culture).[63]

But my own use of the terms, although extensive, is not theoretical (yang); it is poetic (yin). What I offer in this book is not methodical or academic; it is a poem in prose. This surrender to random inspiration allows me to digress when the muse dictates into perspectives from Friedrich Hölderlin and other moderns. And I adopt this stance to question, or even challenge, what I see as our late decadent ethos of yang secular enlightenment, once open-ended and challenging an earlier decadent ethos and now dominant and increasingly one-sided.

NOETIC DEVELOPMENT AND CULTURAL DEVELOPMENT

It has taken me a whole volume to sketch this dialectical evolution through the Axial and three succeeding pivotal moments (in this volume I stop with the era of Charlemagne [d. 814] and its implications for the revived secular urbanism of the High Middle Ages—and also today). What began as a brief essay has evolved into an extended narrative, even though I say almost nothing at all about Jesus or Muhammad, two of the most important figures in this evolution. My book makes no pretensions to insights on this level.

I do however spend considerable time on what some might call the intellectual (but I prefer to call the noetic) antecedents of Pauline Christianity. For example, I ground the statement of St. Paul (a Hellenized Jew) that in Christ Jesus "there is neither bond nor free, there is neither male nor female" (Gal. 3:28) to the argument of the Stoics, against Aristotle, that women and slaves are equal by nature to free men. I then ground it also in the unprecedented sexual egalitarianism of the Song of Songs.

From this interplay between historical and noetic development, a pattern emerges: the interstitial importance of noetic cusps roughly midway between the pivotal shifts, often in the intercultural opening up of space created by cusp rulers such as Alexander, Constantine, Charlemagne, Frederick II (and/ or Pope Innocent III), and Napoleon.

Historians see the Axial (First Pivotal) Moment as "liminal," balanced between the dissolution of old structures and the emergence of new ones. But the noetic cusps midway between pivotal moments are also liminal. I shall argue that great generative authors on the cusps—I will name Plato, St. Augustine, Bede, Dante, and Rousseau—anticipate the great changes that will follow them, and as a rule tend to do their creative work at midpoints in pivotal moments. (And to this list I will add Virgil, the one great exception to the midpoint generalization.[64])

The time span of this volume will cover several noetic cusps:

the swift collapse of the Bronze Age, circa 1200 BCE, followed by the evolution of the alphabet;

the fourth century BCE passage from polis to imperial culture—Alexandria and the Song of Songs;

the gradual transition of Rome from republic to empire at the beginning of the Common Era—Virgil's *Eclogues* and the *Aeneid*;

the fourth-century CE period of the Christianized Roman Empire—St. Augustine and the *City of God*;

the eighth- and ninth-century "Carolingian Renaissance"—Bede and Alcuin; and

the Great Interregnum of the Holy Roman Empire (ca. 1250–1347) and the move of the papacy to Avignon (the "Babylonian captivity of the papacy"), 1309–1376.

Both kinds of liminal moments, the noetic and the cultural, are of immense importance to ethogeny. The ambivalent coexistence of decaying and emergent mindsets favors the appearance of generative countercultures that are seen at the time as threats to culture itself but in time come to be acknowledged as pivotal regenerations of culture.

**Among the examples of such countercultural regeneration, I shall touch on

Isaiah's redirection of religion from external rituals to a renewal, "to seek justice" (Isa. 1:17);

The Shulamite's contrast in the Song of Songs between her vineyard "which is mine" and that of Solomon which "must have a thousand (pieces of silver)" (Song 8:11–12);

Jesus Christ's redirection of faith from temple rituals to "the poor in spirit, for theirs is the kingdom of heaven" (Matt. 5:3); and

St. Augustine's call for a shift of loyalty from the earthly city, "dominated by the lust for domination," to a city of God united by fellowship in the "love of God" (*City of God*, 14.28).

INTELLECTUAL HISTORY AND NOETIC HISTORY

It is common to describe genealogies of noetic influence as intellectual history, reflecting what I see as the false and deleterious dichotomy, raised after Hegel and still unfortunately with us, between "idealist" and "materialist" conceptions of history. (There is merit in both approaches, but not after the point where each begins to deny the validity of the other.)

But I see a modern (or secular) bias in talking of "intellectual history," or "histories of ideas," because *intellect* and *ideas* are only the yang component (or what Hegel would call "moment") of healthy mental (or noetic) activity. Because "intellectual histories" are usually written by academic intellectuals, they tend, in what may be by now a decadent stage of the Enlightenment, to underplay, ignore, and sometimes attack the importance of the yin.

For example, my friend Stephen Greenblatt, in his brilliant yet vulnerable book *The Swerve*, has elegantly described the cultural shift of the Renaissance. But he describes the deurbanization after the fall of Rome (ca. 500–1000 CE), in terms reminiscent of Gibbon (d. 1794), not as a period when the ruthless slave-based social culture of Rome became marginally more compassionate, but only as a period of conflict in which, "compared to the unleashed forces of warfare and of faith, Mount Vesuvius was kinder to the legacy of antiquity."[65]

A similar argument was made in greater detail by Charles Freeman in his small masterpiece, *The Closing of the Western Mind*. And indeed, one cannot take issue with his overall argument that yang rational inquiry virtually disappeared in the European Dark Age (as opposed to the Arab world). As he points out, "The Athenian philosopher Proclus made the last recorded astronomical observation in the ancient Greek world in A.D. 475. It was not until the sixteenth century that Copernicus . . . set in hand the renewal of the scientific tradition."[66] (His argument here stands, even if we reset the date of that scientific renewal to the *Opus Majus* of Roger Bacon, d. 1292.)

And Freeman is devastating in showing how bishops, in their desire for wealth and power, used colossal bribes to determine the outcomes of church councils—in one instance, "the sum of 77,760 gold pieces—enough, it has been estimated, to feed and clothe 19,000 poor people for a year—tapestries, carpets, even ostrich eggs."[67]

But Freeman is interested only in the limited topic of his opening sentence: "the tradition of *rational* [emphasis added, i.e. yang] thought" (xv). This tradition, he argues, was destroyed in the fourth and fifth century "by the political and religious forces that made up the highly authoritarian government of the late Roman empire" (xix–xx). In this period, the effect of imperial patronage, along with huge donations, was to integrate the main body of the church with the extant imperial social structure.

However, Freeman himself makes passing reference to counterdevelopments in this era. "Instances where bishops refused the patronage of emperors were very rare," he writes, "although Martin, bishop of Tours, did decline an offer from Valentinian I."[68] Noting the new practice after Constantine of depicting Christ "as if he were an emperor" (208), he later acknowledges that "presented with a vision of Christ in majesty, Martin proclaimed that the true Christ was a sufferer and this must be Antichrist in disguise."[69]

In these small ways, Freeman recognizes that the human mind is not just rational and that the yang imperial establishment of the church in the fourth century was opposed almost immediately by a yin monastic countercurrent. The latter in his book is represented by the humble St. Martin, as described by his literate biographer Sulpicius Severus (d. ca. 425), who opens his vita of the plainspoken St. Martin with the polemical challenge, "The kingdom of God is not a matter of fine words, but of faith."

MARTIN AS AN EXAMPLE OF YIN MIND

My book gives biased attention to this yin, rural, persuasive countercurrent represented by Sulpicius Severus's *Life of St. Martin*, a very important moment in the hagiographic literature of this period. I do so because St. Martin's reported struggles as a monk and monk-bishop, with both upper-class bishops[70] and emperors, epitomize the underlying tension in this book between two types of power: unprivileged persuasive power versus dominant coercive power.[71]

Among the underlying story lines in this book is the slow modification of coercive by persuasive power in history, along with its internal correlative, the slow modification of rational (yang) by nonrational (yin) mind.[72] A corollary is the progressive redefinition of cultural notions of virtue (including the Greek *arete* and the Chinese *ren*), away from Homeric coercive prowess and

toward nonviolent persuasive gentleness and civility (including Martinian
notions, as we shall see, of humility and compassion—the old-fashioned
word *ruth*).

Reflecting my own almost utopian commitment to nonviolence, this book
reflects a biased focus on the ethogenic evolution of persuasive power. But in
fact, both coercive and persuasive power, while not morally equivalent, have
played and still play a positive function when they cooperate in the complex
moral polity of our ethogeny. Likewise, both, when in conflict, become dys-
functional. We see this dysfunctional conflict increasing today in America
and in the world.

St. Martin is a figure of enormous significance in the European cultural
shift of about 500 CE to the Dark Age. His importance can be deduced indi-
rectly from Peter Brown's magisterial *Through the Eye of a Needle: Wealth,
the Fall of Rome, and the Making of Christianity in the West, 350–550 AD.*[73]

Brown's book focuses on four very prominent literate minders of the
Fourth Century cusp: Saints Ambrose (d. 397), Augustine, Jerome, and
Paulinus of Nola.

All four were converts who distinguished themselves by surrendering
their personal wealth to the church; all but Jerome were noted poets; all but
Paulinus are remembered today with Ambrose as three of the four doctors
of the Roman Catholic Church; and all but Ambrose became a new kind of
monk, one (following the example of Martin) situated not away in the desert
but instead near the center of local society, in order to influence it.

Brown notes that, in choosing (like other modern historians) to write about
these four figures and others, he is "making a virtue out of necessity . . . the
best I can with the bad hand history has dealt us. So much *evidence* has not
survived."[74] Brown's professional dependence on documentary evidence
favors St. Augustine, furthermore, over the other three.[75] But Martin, clearly,
was an influential minder too. My global gazetteer lists eight places named for
St. Martin and only two for St. Augustine (both of them in North America).

But reliance on documentary evidence does not favor Martin, the pioneer
of the new Western monasticism, and in particular a role model for Paulinus
(as Paulinus was for Augustine).[76] Martin wrote nothing, and his exploits
while alive (as opposed to the later influence of his tomb and vita) are men-
tioned by Brown on only three pages.[77]

In contrast to Brown's figures of interest, all of whom were part of the
literati of their era (or what we awkwardly term the "intelligentsia"), Martin
instead became celebrated and remembered in southern Gaul as a worker of
miracles, usually but not uniquely among the poor. To illustrate how influen-
tial his purely persuasive work was, Brown freely admits that quasi-scientific
historical inquiry, relying on records, cannot begin to do justice to the impor-
tant Martinian achievement of his era: "The creation of a rural Christianity in

Spain, Gaul, and Italy remains the dark side of the moon in the study of the churches in this period. Yet it is one of the great changes of the age."[78]

More specifically, I shall argue, it contributed to the increasing persuasive power of the Western church in the Dark Age, with a popular base in both city and country, to offset, and occasionally overbalance, the urban-based power of secular potentates. This was not just a passing moment in the cultural development of the West. In contrast to other parts of the world, this rough balance of social power morphed into a permanent restructuring and diffusion of power in Western society.

Rationality—as opposed to self-interested cunning—is the privilege of the socially unoppressed whose power and status are reinforced by written records. Persuasive power from below, when energized, relies on myths,[79] often orally transmitted, and dreams, as vividly exemplified by the emergence of the black civil rights movement in America (and before it the slow emergence of Rabbinic Judaism).

So, from my perspective, Greenblatt's and Freeman's legitimate observations about the decline of rationality (yang) in the Dark Age are biased: they do not give equal attention to that compensating or "Martinian" (yin) countercurrent, to which I devote so much of this book. From my perspective, the age of Martin and Augustine saw not a closing of the mind but a disruptive, constructive, and valuable refocusing of it.

And, after finishing this book, I am more inclined to see the biases of Greenblatt and Freeman as not mere personal attitudes. They also reinforce what I now see as a bias toward the intelligible in the dominant *mentalité* of today's Western world—summed up by the confident dictum of J. B. Bury in 1903 that "history is a science, no less, and no more."[80] This view presents problems when discussing an era like the Dark Age, when the most important "facts" for the minders or culture shapers of that era were not events but myths, beliefs, or even dreams. (Luckily, as we shall see in chapter 9, new methods have evolved to access the irrational foundational memories of our culture: mnemohistory, reinforced by scientific archaeology.)

Bury's dictum of 1903 is still widely cited, but now usually to take issue with it. However, Chris Wickham, an excellent historian that I shall cite often, makes a point of asserting, "Above all, I have tried to avoid teleology," eliminating the "guiding principle" that the major scientist Andrei Sakharov sees as fundamental to his worldview (see chapter 14). Meanwhile, a consensus of historians today recognizes, with Geoffrey Barraclough, that "the history we read, though based on facts, is, strictly speaking, not factual at all, but a series of accepted judgements."[81]

Those accepted judgments have a history of their own, and the story of their evolution is an essential component of ethogeny. Seeing this, some historians have come to agree with the maxim of A. L. Rowse, also widely quoted, that "history is a great deal closer to poetry than is generally realised: in truth, I think, it is in essence the same."[82] In the same spirit, E. H. Carr wrote that historical facts are "like fish swimming about in a vast and sometimes inaccessible ocean." What the "historian catches will depend, partly on chance," but may also be "determined by the kind of fish he wants to catch."[83]

Four of my six chapters on the Second Pivotal Moment (or Shift) discuss its noetic antecedents: both yang (Stoics and Platonists) but also yin (the Song of Songs). The Song of Songs in particular is seen as generative on two levels: both for its valorization of erotic feelings (which the other books of the Jewish Bible had discussed at best with ambivalence[84]) and also for its enhancement of mystical language (balancing the yang virtues of clarity with the yin potentialities of mystery and ambiguity).

This contribution of the noetic element to ethical change is not nearly as dominant as the space I have given to it. As Marx once wrote, "men make their own history, but not just as they please."[85] I focus on the noetic elements in our ethogeny because I believe that what is needed right now in dealing with our historical crisis is a reassessment of them, in order to restore and advance us on what Martin Luther King called the "arc of the moral universe" that "bends toward justice."[86]

I see the constricted area of freedom in human evolution as precisely our ability to do this. By choosing which part of our past to remember, we help determine our future. And in recent years we have paid too much attention to our relation to the future, not enough to the past. However, in the words of Simone Weil I opened with, "from where will a renewal come to us, to us who have spoiled and devastated the whole earthly globe? Only from the past, if we love it."[87]

I centered my introduction on Xu Jilin's discussion of *tianxia* because, in his warning to a renascent China not to revive outmoded modes of domination, I saw an urgent political message to a hyperdominant West, even if the West may now be declining. But although political issues such as war and climate change loom large in our current cultural predicament, they are I believe symptoms of a more fundamental discomfort, less easy to define. I would awkwardly ascribe this discomfort to the mounting inadequacies of what, for want of a better term, I will call the declining Enlightenment—or modernist—mindset of eighteenth- and nineteenth-century Europe—the mindset that assumes the past in general is something to break free from.[88]

Jennifer Pitts has described how

> in the closing years of the eighteenth century, a critical challenge to European imperial conquest and rule was launched by many of the most innovative thinkers of the day, including Adam Smith, Bentham, Burke, Kant, Diderot, and Condorcet.[89]

But after Hegel, and with rising confidence that Western "civilization" (like "Christianity" before it) was a blessing to be bestowed on "backward" peoples, a later generation of liberal thinkers became active proponents of colonialism, in what Pitts has called "a turn to empire." The most prominent example of this turn was John Stuart Mill, who like his father, James Mill, did most of his writing as an employee of the East India Company and who spoke of "the native states of India" as "savage life" in which "there is little or no law." All Asia, he wrote in *On Liberty*, has "properly speaking, no history, because the despotism of Custom is complete."[90]

In 1853, Karl Marx expressed the same conviction that Indian culture, lacking historical development, needed to be replaced by that of the West:

> Indian society has no history at all, at least no known history. What we call its history, is but the history of the successive intruders who founded their empires on the passive basis of that unresisting and unchanging society. . . . England has to fulfill a double mission in India: one destructive, the other regenerating the annihilation of old Asiatic society, and the laying the material foundations of Western society in Asia.[91]

When I was a diplomat at the United Nations, more than a half century ago, a similar mindset was shared by Canadians and Americans. No one I knew then questioned the categorization of the "Third World" as "underdeveloped," a mindset that promoted opportunities for Georgia-Pacific to "develop" Indonesia by clear-cutting its rain forests and ExxonMobil to "develop" Guinea-Bissau by virtually looting its oil.[92]

To sum up, the Enlightenment began in a spirit of scientific and skeptical inquiry. Today it has frequently lapsed into the opposite mode: an aggressive certainty that liberalism and the West are good and that other cultures are to be amended on its terms, if necessary by violence. However, this is also an age of dialectical developments, some violent, like the Chinese Cultural Revolution or the American MAGA right wing, and some spiritual and non-coercive, with writers like Simone Weil and Czeslaw Milosz.

In or around the tumultuous year 1968, speaking to a small Berkeley audience of about a dozen invited guests, Herbert Marcuse described our civilization as a cage entrapping us; a new society, he argued, would require nothing less than a new language. And in a sense, as I wrote then, there is indeed "not a phrase / that has not been polluted" by past violence.[93] But language, the labyrinth in which our second nature is entrapped, is also the precious thread to our liberation from violence.

This paradox explains the ongoing importance of religion and literature in a supposed age of science. Scientific materialism, as exemplified by the "cultural revolutions" of China and Cambodia, led to large numbers of lives destroyed and people killed. But there was also a nonviolent response, as exemplified, for example, by a revival of interest in the insights of meditation.

I will close here with another quote from Weil: "The imagination is continually at work filling up all the fissures through which grace might pass." Weil, an ascetic, sought to empty her mind, a striving that might seem at first to be quite antithetical to the intention of this book. I hope that, as I develop more about what I mean by human doubleness, the reader will accept that filling and emptying, moreness and lessness, yang and yin, can both be seen as parts of the same systolic and diastolic pattern of healthy creative life.

That symbiotic doubleness, opening without prejudice (and overcommitment) to both science and the spiritual, the known and the mysterious, the yang and the yin, is what I mean by post-secularity.

PART ONE

Enlightenment

Chapter One

The Sh'ma, the Three Refuges, and the Axial Moment

The spirit brings truth, for the spirit is truth and leads humanity into truth.

—John 16:13

All great things bring about their own destruction through an act of self-overcoming.

—Friedrich Nietzsche

Religion . . . the life of the soul.

—Wendell Berry

A PERSONAL INTRODUCTION

I was baptized an Anglican Christian by my agnostic parents, but as a child I almost never went to church (except once or twice for funerals). However, in midlife, after stays at Taizé and two other Christian monasteries, I was for four decades a practicing Buddhist. Although I have never renounced Christianity, I now prefer to attend services, along with my Jewish wife, at a Modern Orthodox synagogue.

In the last year, I began on my own to recite to myself the Sh'ma and the opening of the V'ahavta (Deut. 6:4–7) on my lying down and on my rising, as is commanded there. I take this injunction in Deuteronomy to apply to what has been said up to that point, not to the following two very different verses about *tefillin* (phylacteries) and *mezuzot* (doorpost attachments), which instruct Jews how to identify themselves with these verses in writing.

Almost from the beginning I found it appropriate to follow the V'ahavta with the Lord's Prayer. The former has strengthened my old age; the latter had helped guide me through a rocky adolescence and youth. For reasons I shall partly develop later, I recite the verses from Deuteronomy in the original Hebrew and the Lord's Prayer (as found in the Byzantine version of Luke 11:2-4) in Koine Greek. Later, I am not sure why, I decided to add also the Three Refuges that I had, during my Buddhist middle years, often recited in Pali before taking the Buddhist precepts at retreats.

To my surprise, the recitation together of all three root passages from these religions greatly enhanced the meanings for me of each of them. They *resonated* together. The more I repeated them, the more I found myself meditating on their compatibilities, their similarities, and their differences. I still do.

This contemplation could be viewed as syncretistic; it has no secure base in any single religion. But what I am saying here is categorically *not* a syncretistic case for bringing together these three religions into one. I see religion as a way to ground oneself in whatever is one's cultural past in order to live more securely in the cultural present.

I need to be clear about this. I am not interested in the notion of systematically practicing more than one traditional religion at a time. I believe that to function in a culture, one must be embedded in a practice and a community, not just consciously picking and choosing from it like an unaccompanied guest at a buffet.

I once quoted Thomas Merton in a poem, "Confession," to say, "I am a Christian . . . in the spirit of Merton's *I am a Jew and a Moslem*," and I am not now rescinding that.[1] But Merton remained faithful to the rigorous demands of his adopted monastic Catholicism, to which he was a convert—like his friend Denise Levertov, who converted to Catholicism because, she said, the Anglicanism of her birth was not demanding enough to meet her religious needs.

At the same time, one can be interested in enlarging the frontiers of one's practice. As Thomas Merton wrote shortly before he died,

> I think that we have now reached a stage of (long overdue) religious maturity at which it may be possible for someone to remain perfectly faithful to a Christian and Western monastic commitment, and yet learn in depth from, say, a Buddhist or Hindu discipline or experience.[2]

Another sign that we have reached this stage of religious maturity is the fact that the three greatest English-language poets of the twentieth century, Yeats, Pound, and Eliot, all independently sought inspiration for their most serious poetry from the religions of the East. (So did two of the greatest postwar

American poets, Allen Ginsberg and Gary Snyder. This may have been partly in protest against the worship of Mammon/Moloch in America. See below.)

It is becoming more and more usual to describe our current situation as post-secular.[3] But perhaps we can see two divergent post-secular developments: one regressive (the revival of militant religious hatred) and one forward-looking (the slow expansion of critical religious consciousness to a more global awareness).

The latter development has again been well expressed from a Christian perspective by Thomas Merton: "If we want to bring together East and West, we cannot do it by imposing one upon the other. We must contain both in ourselves and transcend them both in Christ."[4]

I am certain that my immersion in Merton a decade ago was a major factor in developing my current prayer practice.

THREEFOLD PATTERN IN THE
REFUGES AND THE V'AHAVTA

The first striking similarity in the texts I recite is the threefoldness of their internal compositions (which is unrelated to the accidental fact that I am comparing just three texts). This is most strikingly asserted in the Three Refuges that a lay Buddhist recites before taking the precepts, after first reciting the Namo Tassa three times:

Homage to Him, the Blessed One, the Worthy One, the Perfectly Enlightened One!

Here is the entire English text of the Tisarana or Three Refuges (the Buddha, his teachings, and his community). There is no better exemplar of threeness:

I go to the Buddha for refuge.
I go to the Dharma for refuge.
I go to the Sangha for refuge.

For the second time I go to the Buddha for refuge.
For the second time I go to the Dharma for refuge.
For the second time I go to the Sangha for refuge.

For the third time I go to the Buddha for refuge.
For the third time I go to the Dharma for refuge.
For the third time I go to the Sangha for refuge.

Three is not the only number prominent in Buddhism. There are also the Four Noble Truths, the last of which consists of the Eightfold Path; and the precepts taken by laymen after the Three Refuges are known as the Five Precepts. But the threeness is obvious in the Tisarana or Three Refuges or Triple Gem, following the triple recital of Namo Tassa, which celebrates the Lord Buddha by naming his three attributes.

Why this threeness? Commentaries point to the connected development between them. In the past, the *Buddha* became enlightened; he recorded the path to this enlightenment in the *Dharma* we have now; and the Dharma in turn creates and continues to strengthen the *Sangha* into the future. It is a synecdoche for cultural evolution. We shall say more about this.

Somewhat to my surprise, I have come to discern a comparable threeness in the Sh'ma and the V'ahavta. The Sh'ma, unlike the Namo Tassa, is repeated only once, but its three pairs of words—

Sh'ma Yisrael, Adonai Eloheinu, Adonai echad [Hear Israel, the Lord our God, the Lord (is) One]—

can be read as one, two, or three ideas. And these words, and these diverse readings of them, could be said to suggest an underlying threeness of the *people* Israel, the *Lord* God, and the *truth* of His oneness. As usually translated—"Hear, O *Israel*: the *Lord* our God, the Lord *is one*"—these three elements conform with the three elements of the Triple Gem—Buddha, Dharma, Sangha—except that the Sangha is here not in last but in first place.

In the three sentences which follow (Deut. 6:5–7), this threefoldness becomes harder to ignore:

And thou shalt love the *Lord* thy God with all thy heart, and with all thy soul, and with all thy might.

And these *words*, which I command thee this day, shall be upon thy heart.

And thou shalt teach them diligently unto thy *children*, and shalt talk of them when thou sittest in thy house, and when thou walkest by the way, and when thou liest down, and when thou risest up. (King James Version)

Unmistakably the key nouns in these three sentences (Lord, words, children) form a threeness analogous in both content and order to the threeness of the nouns in the Triple Gem (Buddha, Dharma, Sangha), and for the same reason, the underling unity of the process uniting them.

This should not surprise us: the three elements in the process here are the basic constituents of religion as the sociologist Emile Durkheim (in Robert Bellah's translation) defined it: "a system of *beliefs* and practices relative to the *sacred* that unite those who adhere to them in a moral *community*" (a secular, nondoctrinal version of Dharma, Buddha, and Sangha).[5]

Religion is not just a system, however; it is a dialectical process. Whether we are talking about a cargo cult or Zen Buddhism, the root process is the same: dissatisfaction with this imperfect world as we know it forces a search for something else that is better (the *sacred*). And a shared search for a better alterity that does not exist in our world leads to something that does: to religious *beliefs*. And the continued sharing of beliefs creates and consolidates a *community*. This three-step process, from A, to non-A, to A + non-A, matches the dialectical triad that Hegel saw in logical reason (*Vernunft*), operating both in the individual and also in history.

In more concrete terms, the Buddha was born into the world, withdrew from the world to receive enlightenment, and then returned to share his enlightenment with the world through dharma. The Hebrews were reportedly living in a world of enslavement, proceeded to the desert where they received the Ten Commandments, and then as Jews created a new community in Canaan shaped by Mosaic law. The threefoldness of the Refuges and of the V'ahavta thus mirror the threefoldness of the process that led to their creation.

THE THREEFOLD PROCESS AND THE AXIAL MOMENT

The underlying threeness of the two texts can be generalized as a transition in time from *authority* to *language* to *community*—a process so obvious and commonplace that most of us give no thought to it today. However, these two ancient incantations date back to a period in cultural evolution (or what I like to call ethogeny) where they represented something new, even revolutionary.

This period, the so-called Axial (versus earlier pretextual shifts) Moment, occurred at various times in the middle of the first millennium BCE, resulting in major changes to religion and thus to civilization. The philosopher Karl Jaspers, who invented the term, wrote that "a strange veil seems to lie over the most ancient cultures" before this shift, "as though man had not yet really come to himself."[6] That condition, I like to think, is still true: we are still far short of our potential for development.

In the preceding or so-called Archaic Era, divine authority tended to be either vested in kingship or else expressed through it. Hammurabi's so-called code of law, for example, was received and transmitted in King Hammurabi's name. (The epilogue to the code adds, "I am indeed the good shepherd who brings peace, with the just scepter. My benevolent shade covered my city.")

But the relationship between royal and divine authority was weakened and problematized by the Axial Moment, or what I prefer to call the First Pivotal Shift. To quote the sociologist of religion Robert Bellah, "new insights appeared, such as the idea that rule is conditional on divine favor and may be withdrawn from wicked rulers."[7]

Bellah points to the contrast between pre-Axial rulers like Hammurabi, who were the source of divine law, and the Israelite kings whose authority, according to the Deuteronomy of circa 550 BCE, was subordinate to divine law. He quotes in particular Deuteronomy 17:18–20 ("That's all . . . the Torah has to say about a king"):

[18] And it shall be, when he sitteth upon the throne of his kingdom, that he shall write him a copy of this law in a book out of that which is before the priests the Levites:

[19] And it shall be with him, and he shall read therein all the days of his life: that he may learn to fear the Lord his God, to keep all the words of this law and these statutes, to do them:

[20] That his heart be not lifted up above his brethren, and that he turn not aside from the commandment, to the right hand, or to the left: to the end that he may prolong his days in his kingdom, he, and his children, in the midst of Israel.[8]

This revolutionary thought can be discerned in writings from Confucius to Plato. But other scholars have highlighted different features of Axial Judaism. S. N. Eisenstadt, for example, focuses on the emergence of a "'new type of intellectual elite' concerned with the possible restructuring of the world in accordance with the transcendental vision."[9] I myself, in a couple of pages, will point to the late Axial Age prophets' emphasis on internal practice of ethical self-improvement and devotion to care of others, rather than on the Torah's external practice of bloody communal sacrifice.

These features, along with others, all rose during the period of extreme stress on the Jewish community that climaxed with the Babylonian Captivity (587–538 BCE). For two centuries, starting with the Assyrian conquest of the northern kingdom of Israel in 722 BCE, Judaic temple worship was first menaced and then for a period obliterated. Other religions, such as the Hittite, disappeared under such pressures. The Jews, already more close-knit than most contemporary peoples, responded constructively, with both the yang reforms recorded by the so-called Deuteronomist of this era and the yin prophecies (in particular those attributed to Isaiah) which challenged them.[10] Both of these changes responded to, and intensified, the emergent role of literacy.

THE AXIAL MOMENT, WRITING, AND JUDAISM

The main feature of the first Axial Moment (versus earlier pivotal shifts) is that it reflected the emergent emphasis in religion on scripture rather than ritual.[11] Literacy, according to Robert Bellah, "goes back as far as 3000 BCE," but in the Archaic Era it "remained largely a craft literacy, confined to small groups of scribes, until well into the first millennium." Then literacy became a more general feature and now united societies, thanks often to the replacement of elitist hieratic with more demotic alphabetic scripts.[12] Shared texts began to define and strengthen *peoples*, the Jews in particular.

In the case of Judaism, there is an increasing consensus among philologists that the text of Deuteronomy dates, along with the major prophets Isaiah and Jeremiah, from the era of the destruction of the kingdoms of Israel (722 BCE) and Judah (586 BCE).[13] At this time, the destruction of the First Temple, and the interruption of Temple rituals, led the Jews to find their identity increasingly in the texts of the Jewish Bible (Tanakh). Starting then, and especially after the destruction of the Second Temple (70 CE), the Bible and its various commentaries have replaced the Temple at the center of Jewish religion. But even the V'ahavta in Deuteronomy, which is probably pre-exilic, shifts from its original focus on loving God to external manifestations, the need to write these words "upon thine hand" in phylacteries and "upon the posts of thy house" in *mezuzot* (Deut. 6:8–9).

I myself identify late Axial Age Judaism with the prophets' emphasis on internal practice rather than on such external practice. Especially after the sixth-century exile of the Jews to Babylon, Jews were forced to reconceive a new worship, not based on the Temple, that emphasized "a more individual relationship with Yahweh that involved individual responsibility, morality and justice."[14]

There is no better example of this changed emphasis than in the post-exilic closing chapters of Isaiah (often attributed to an unidentified "Trito-Isaiah"), whose contrast between external fasting (conformity to a ritual) and internal fasting (amending one's behavior) is read every year in Jewish Yom Kippur services:

> Why, when we fasted, did You not see? When we starved our bodies, did You pay no heed? Because on your fast day you see to your business and oppress all your laborers! Because you fast in strife and contention, and you strike with a wicked fist! . . . Is such the fast I desire, a day for men to afflict their soul? . . . Is not this the fast that I have chosen? to loose the bands of wickedness, and let the oppressed go free to undo the heavy burdens and break off every yoke? (Isa. 58:3–6)[15]

There is too much ambiguity about the meaning and history of the Pali word *Dhamma* (Dharma) for me to comment on it here. But we can say of the Hebrew word *devarim* (words) that in the V'ahavta they are first discussed as spoken, then written. The book of Deuteronomy where it occurs begins, "These are the words (*devarim*) which Moses spoke (*devar*) to all Israel," and the passage in the V'ahavta is in the same spirit—"And these words (*devarim*), which I command thee this day, shall be upon thy heart." But only two verses later, the *devarim* are no longer spoken; they are written:

> You shall bind them as a sign on your hand, and they shall be as frontlets between your eyes. You shall write them on the doorposts of your house and on your gates. (Deut. 6:8–9)

The V'ahavta was written at a pivotal (axial) moment in Jewish history, when public writings were emerging, in the temporary absence of both the Temple and the kingdom, as the central focus uniting the Jews and also preserving their culture.

A NECESSARY DIGRESSION: THE IMPACT OF WRITING ON THE HUMAN MIND

With the development of writing, the search for moreness reached a higher level—not just for better crops but for better authority, better rules of conduct, and a better alternative community. This feature of a pivotal moment was often in response to violent disruptions (such as the Babylonian Captivity of the Jewish people or the Time of Troubles responded to by Confucius) and was marked by the development of literate monotheisms from Confucius (d. 479? BCE) to Jeremiah (d. ca. 570 BCE). (Both Confucius and Jeremiah experienced exile.)

According to Robert Bellah, "new insights appeared, such as the idea that rule is conditional on divine favor and may be withdrawn from wicked rulers."[16] This revolutionary thought can be discerned both in Confucius and in the Jewish Torah. The insight that writing established codes by which to judge rulers is only one of the dramatic changes introduced by writing. Two others in particular need to be mentioned. One was the enlargement of our human spatial environment, enabling language to travel securely beyond the more limited range and means of speech. Another was a more clearly developed sense of time, as records of the past, first transmitted orally, as in the mysterious Old English poem *Widsið*, could now be preserved more permanently.

For me the significance of both enlargements is illustrated by the stark difference between the *Iliad* and the *Odyssey*. Both works as we have them are probably the products of oral transmissions that became fixed in writing at an early time when oral culture was still strong, perhaps in the late eighth or early seventh century. But the *Iliad* is very much narrower than the *Odyssey* in both space and time, and thus also in the mentalities of its heroes, who live very much in their psychological present.

As Bruno Snell argued long ago, Iliadic heroes do not even possess mental identities as we think of them today. They are essentially creatures of the moment, dominated by drives of lust or rage as the occasion and immediate environment dictate. If they have different characters, it is because some are more courageous, others more wily, others more effeminate. As a rule, they do not control their emotions; their emotions control them. And if they do control them, it is not on their own initiative but because a divine voice tells them to.[17]

Thus Agamemnon, inquiring if angry Achilles is now ready to leave his tent and join his companions in the battle, adds, "Or does anger still possess his proud spirit [thumós]?" (*Iliad* 9:675),[18] not "Does he still not constrain his anger?" as would be the expected phrase today. The very first line of the *Iliad* announces that in the epic the Muse will not sing of "Achilles" (an abstraction) but of the rage of Achilles, a reality.

How different is the Odysseus of the *Odyssey*! When we first meet him (in book 5), he is, years after the Trojan War, bereft by shipwreck of his Iliadic equipment and comrades, being cared for instead by an earth goddess. She loves him and promises him immortality if he will stay, but he is still set on returning to his wife and homeland, despite not having seen them for two decades.

Shipwrecked again, he emerges naked from the waves to start life anew. He is awakened by a princess and her maids who, in a scene of completely un-Iliadic compassion, take him to their court. There he finds himself among a friendly but un-Iliadic people, the Phaeacians, who confess, "We are not faultless boxers or wrestlers, but . . . ever to us is the banquet dear, and the lyre, and the dance . . . and warm baths" (*Odyssey* 8:246, 248–49).

At the court, a bard sings an Iliadic song of how Odysseus himself had once inflicted death and fate on the Trojans. And Odysseus's response after his sufferings is to weep, as a woman weeps when seeing her fallen husband before being led off to captivity by the enemy (*Odyssey* 8:523–30).

There are other signs that we are dealing with a changed and more capacious and compassionate Odysseus. In a battle with the one-eyed giant Polyphemus, Odysseus, declaring himself to be "Noman" (Outis; i.e., "no man"), is said to have bested the giant "by guile [dolós] and not by force [bie]" (*Odyssey* 9:366, 408). The episode thus anticipates the denouement of the epic, when Odysseus, back home in Ithaca and deceitfully disguised as a beggar, is able with two companions to defeat twenty-two suitors for his wife Penelope.

Odysseus is prepared for this prodigious victory by advice from a blind seer in the underworld, advice emblematic of a major shift in cultural development: "You may reach home . . . if you will curb your own spirit [thumós] and that of your comrades" (*Odyssey* 11:105–6).[19] Odysseus follows the advice, endures all kinds of insults without response, and will not even respond when his old dog recognizes him after an absence of twenty years (17:292–300). His companions do not: when hungry they devour the sacred cattle of Helios (12:398), and in consequence they are drowned.

The *Iliad* and the *Odyssey*, between them, frame a step in the evolution of mind. More specifically, they illustrate the progressive liberation of mind from its impulses that is represented by the First Pivotal Shift, and the consolidation of this second nature when supported by language in an expanded and more literate culture.

The revision of the Iliadic ethos in the *Odyssey* presages a continuous evolution in what I see as the sequence of generative epics at the center of Western civilization. In the *Argonautica* of Apollonius of Rhodes (third century BCE), we shall encounter a similar subordination of a Homeric ethos (represented by Jason) to an erotic one (represented by Medea). In the *Aeneid* of Virgil (d. 19 BCE), both the erotic ethos and the Homeric ethos will be meticulously subordinated to a contrasted Roman ethos of *pietas*. And in the *Comedy* of Dante (d. 1321), the limitations of Virgil's rational ethos will be presented by way of comparison with the spiritual ethos of Beatrice.

Epics based on earlier epics, and rooted like them at a high culture's core, become the poetic spine or backbone of that culture.[20] As a sequence, they thus contribute to and epitomize the changes in our developing ethos through each pivotal shift. The development in the *Odyssey* of emotional self-restraint is one striking example, but so are the progressive expansions of compassion from the *Iliad* to later epics and their spin-offs.[21]

The five epics listed above, read together in sequence, illustrate the development of the human mind through history. In other words, they epitomize our ethogeny, the subject of this book.[22]

A PERSONAL CODA: MORENESS

There is one more obvious threeness to be discussed here, the one that first gave rise to all these meditations. It is in the first verse of the V'ahavta, which tells us to love God "with all our heart and all our soul and all our might" (Deut. 6:5). But the Hebrew word translated here as "might" (meod, מְאֹד) defies translation.

Jesus, calling these words "the great and first commandment . . . said to the lawyer, 'You shall love the Lord your God with all your *heart*, and with all your *soul*, and with all your *mind*.'" Jesus then linked this commandment to love God to the verse in Leviticus to "love thy neighbor as thyself" (Lev. 19:18), saying, "On these two commandments depend all the Law and the Prophets" (Matt. 22:37–40). (Slightly earlier, Rabbi Hillel [fl.

60 BCE–30 CE] had phrased the "love thy neighbor" commandment nega-
tively and given it similar importance: "What is hateful to you, do not to your
comrade; this is the whole Torah in its entirety; the rest is commentary."[23])

It is unlikely, however, that *meod*, when Deuteronomy was written, meant
what we mean by "mind." *Meod*, uncommon as a noun, is common as an
adverb, meaning "very." *Lev* is the word translated as "heart," but Rashi
(1040–1105 CE), the important commentator on Torah and Talmud, inter-
preted *lev* in Deuteronomy to have meant "mind" as well as "heart." This
reading fits well with the notion of Bruno Snell and others that the distinction
between "heart" and "mind"—so obvious to us—only really began about the
beginning of the Common Era.[24]

Citing the Midrashic Sifrei Devarim, Rashi defined *meod* in this verse as
"property," "means," or "possessions." Strong's Bible Concordance defines
the noun *meod* as "muchness, force, abundance,"[25] and this is the sense
offered to me by each of the two rabbis I consulted. And when, after reflec-
tion, I asked these rabbis whether they would accept the word "moreness" as
a translation, they, also after reflection, each said yes.[26]

In a poem, which cites the V'ahavta, I write of "Our need as humans—/ to
be more than we are." And in *Poetry and Terror* I wrote,

> Our nature is given an initial determination by our genes at birth, but also slowly
> evolves towards what Edmund Burke called our "second nature," shaped by
> our cultural environment.[27] Burke's view of second nature was conservative,
> because he ignored the natural evolution [ethogeny] of cultures. My own is
> dialectical. . . . One might even say . . . that our cultural ontogeny recapitulates
> our cultural ethogeny.[28]

I have since written to a friend:

> Our first nature is biological; what we inherit when we are born. Our second
> nature is what we become as we assimilate the ethos of the social environment
> in which we are embedded. Our third nature is the creative part of us that needs
> go beyond our first and second natures.

All three of our natures expand through moreness; but the third is the least
embedded in what already exists.

Our first nature does not disappear as the second develops but is in most
individuals at least partially subordinated to it. The inevitable result is an
internal doubleness: a contention depicted by theologians as between our
worse and better angels, and by Freud as between the id and the ego.

Freud, for most of his life, was a child of the Enlightenment who cham-
pioned the ego as the fulfillment of maturation: "Where id was there ego
shall be."[29] He also acknowledged a third element in the human psyche, the

superego, which "becomes the vehicle of tradition and of all the time-resist-ing judgments of value which have propagated themselves in this manner from generation to generation."[30]

Freud did not champion the superego, because for him it was too uncon-scious. But in the face of the Nazi challenge to the frail Weimar Republic, Freud's faith in reason was shaken. This might have led to his reconsidering the role of the superego and of art, but it did not.

This nisus toward moreness exists not only in ourselves but, I believe, in the culture that molds us. Culture is not a settled state but a continuous dialectical process, with some elements looking back and others forward. As Czeslaw Milosz wrote, our culture is (at least in part) eschatological, by which he meant that at its core it "rejects the present inhuman world in the name of a great change."[31]

In the period of contemplation I spend each morning, I continue to see body, soul, and moreness—the threeness of the V'ahavta, as a better guide for both my poetry and my prose. That sense of moreness has grown on me. It did so at first when I began to recite the V'ahavta and related texts every day. But it did much more when, inspired by that practice, I began to write this book's poetic meditation.

The more I wrote, the more clearly I saw that my own developing inner sense of moreness was visible in the writings of others who, cumulatively, have created a kind of collective moreness. And that process of collective moreness, I have come to see, is nothing else than the cultural evolution, or ethogeny, that I have pointed to in my last two books. The moreness of others has contributed to our second nature. And now, through this book, I would like to give something back.

ONE YEAR LATER

After first drafting this chapter, I have acquired a much stronger sense of how my daily practice of incantation has changed me. In particular, as I recite, I am far more conscious that many of my utterances are *performative*—that is, I am actively fulfilling by my speech what the sentence in question wishes for.

For example, if I say "hagiastheto to onoma sou [ἁγιασθήτω τὸ ὄνομά σου]" (Hallowed be thy name), I am actually fulfilling the wish that the Lord's name be venerated. And with respect to myself, if I say, "Buddham saranam gacchami" (I seek refuge in the Buddha), I am actually for that moment venturing beyond the trenches and barbed-wire defenses of my own ego and trusting instead in the gift of what the Buddha offers.

The cumulative power of these performative sentences induces an overall effect of what I might call enchantment. I feel as if, in reciting "genetheto to thelema sou [γενηθήτω τὸ θέλημά σου]" (Thy will be done), this too is performative, and I am at this moment actually fulfilling, in an infinitesimal way, God's will. And I feel even more altered when I chant, rather than merely repeat, the Tisarana and the Sh'ma.[32] In short, by these incantations (which I would not now think of skipping), I have over the years acquired a much stronger identification with what I repeat, which means in practice a stronger commitment to the intentions of my words.

And I have come to see over the year that this increasing identification has been for me a process of personal ethogeny, or cultural development. By this I mean that my practice has embodied in me (or in my second nature), more securely than before, the values, ideals, and purposiveness of our collective *tianxia*.

In the last year, I also became more convinced that the diverse faiths and cultures of our world are not discrete phenomena but participants in an overarching dialectical process of ethogeny—one in which the nouns *faith*, *culture*, and *civilization* must be contemplated in the singular. I now see civilization from the perspective of what Teilhard de Chardin called the *noosphere*, a coherent activity on the mental level both analogous to and the culmination of the *biosphere*—which, according to the Gaia philosophy, is regulated by all organisms on a life-giving planet in such a way as to promote the biosphere's habitability.[33]

RETHINKING DANTE FROM A NOOCENTRIC PERSPECTIVE

Rethinking our culture from a noocentric perspective has forced me to reconsider notions I once took for granted. I am now deeply embarrassed to recall how, in my early days as a self-taught medievalist and teacher of Dante, I so uncritically accepted the academic consensus of memes prevailing then about the "medieval vision of cultural unity," mentioned interchangeably (as if the two were the same!) with "the spiritual, linguistic, and cultural unity of medieval Christendom."[34]

Dante was supposed to exemplify that unity, but it would be truer to say that he exemplified some of medieval Christendom's limitations. Of course, he also expanded the realm of Western culture by including, among the non-Christian "great spirits" in Limbo, the Muslims Saladin, Averroës, and Avicenna. In Paradise he also included Joachim of Fiore (d. 1202), some of whose radical ideas had already been condemned at the Fourth Lateran Council in 1215. (Joachim had predicted that the age of the church and the New Testament was about to be succeeded by a Third Age with a new, egalitarian "Eternal Gospel.")

But the church's chief enemy at that time, Muhammad, was placed by Dante in Hell, as one of the "sowers of scandal and schism" (*Inferno* 28:35), with his body split open and his entrails showing. Dante's attitude toward the Jews, meanwhile, is more complicated.[35] There are no Jews along with the Arabs in Limbo, and indeed no Jews at all in the *Comedy*, except five from the Old Testament and Apocrypha. These are two brave warriors (Joshua and Judas Maccabaeus; *Paradiso* 18:37–40), two just rulers (David and Hezekiah; 29:37–51), and only one prophet (Moses; 32:130–32).

Moses indeed is in the very highest circle of heaven, the penultimate canto of *Paradiso*, and the very last male to be identified there, before four ladies: Mary's mother Anna, Lucy, Beatrice, and Mary herself. But Moses is not named and is described only as

> quel duca sotto cui visse di manna
> la gente ingrata, mobile e retrosa.
> that leader under whom lived on manna
> the thankless, fickle, and stiff-necked people.

> (*Paradiso* 32:131–32)

In the 14,233 lines of Dante's *Comedy*, this is the one reference to the Jewish people. It is true that Moses himself, in the penultimate canto of Deuteronomy, addresses the Jews he was leaving as "a generation crooked and perverse. . . . They are a nation void of counsel, and there is no understanding in them" (Deut. 32:5, 28). But Jewish self-criticism is hardly comparable to Dante's condemnation. Dante's line is more in the spirit of Pope Innocent III, who in 1205 "censured Alfonso the Noble [King of Castile, d. 1214] for the protection granted by that monarch to his Jewish subjects."[36]

In my Dante classes, which ended twenty-five years ago, it never occurred to me to speak of Dante's limitations. It seems important to do so now, after a year of reciting the Sh'ma and the Lord's Prayer together, sometimes with a few lines from the Quran. (The change introduced by these brief recitations has been reinforced by attendance at a synagogue, and even more by the inspiring example of my wife's dedicated commitment to Judaic practice.)

Reviewing what I have written in the last year, I see that in perceiving and pursuing patterns inherent in our ethogeny, I have both gained a particular insight but also lost, at least for a while, a larger perspective. In pursuit of the knowable past, I have neglected, indeed almost forgotten, the unknowable present. In terms of our ethos or *tianxia* ("everything under heaven"), I have plunged eagerly into the "everything" below; but I have been drifting away from what Lama Surya Das calls the ineffable "awareness, love, and power of the Buddha within [us]." So I have adapted my meditation practice to contemplate, besides "the open space ahead," "the open space within."

A PERSONAL POSTSCRIPT: WHAT I CHANT

WHAT I CHANT	TRANSLATION OF TEXT
1. *Buddhist chants*	
1.1	

Namo Tassa	นะโม ตัสสะ (Thai Script)
Namo Tassa Bhagavato Arahato	I pay homage to the Blessed One, the
Samma Sambuddhassa (3 times)	Perfected One, the fully Enlightened One.

1.2

Tisarana (Triple Gem)	
Buddham saranam gacchami	I take refuge in the Buddha
Dhammam saranam gacchami	I take refuge in the Dhamma
Sangham saranam gacchami	I take refuge in the Sangha
Dutiyampi Buddham saranam gacchami	For the second time, I take refuge in the Buddha
Dutiyampi Dhammam saranam gacchami	For the second time, I take refuge in the Dhamma
Dutiyampi Sangham saranam gacchami	For the second time, I take refuge in the Sangha
Tatiyampi Buddham saranam gacchami	For the third time, I take refuge in the Buddha
Tatiyampi Dhammam saranam gacchami	For the third time, I take refuge in the Dhamma
Tatiyampi Sangham saranam gacchami	For the third time, I take refuge in the Sangha.

2.1

Sh'ma (Deut. 6:4)	
Sh'ma Yisrael, Adonai eloheinu, Adonai echad	4 Hear, O Israel: the LORD our God, the LORD is one

2.2

V'ahavta (Deut. 6:5–7)	
V'ahavta et Adonai Elohecha, b'chol l'vavcha uv'chol nafsh'cha uv'chol m'odecha	5 And thou shalt love the LORD thy God with all thy heart, and all thy soul, and all thy might.
V'hayu had'varim haeileh asher anochi m'tzav'cha hayom al l'vavecha.	6 And these words, which I command thee this day, shall be upon thy heart;
V'shinantam l'vanecha v'dibarta b'am b'shivt'cha b'veitecha uv'lecht'cha vaderech uv'shochb'cha uv'kumecha.	7 and thou shalt teach them diligently unto thy children, and shalt talk of them when thou sittest in thy house, and when thou walkest by the way, and when thou liest down, and when thou risest up.

3.

Our Father or Paternoster (Luke 11:2–4, Byzantine rite)	
[2] Pater hēmōn, ho en tois ouranois,	[2] Our Father which art in heaven,
hagiasthētō to onoma sou;	Hallowed be thy name.
elthetō hē basileia sou;	Thy kingdom come.
genethetō to thelēma sou hōs en ouranōi,	Thy will be done, as in heaven,
kai epi tēs gēs	so on earth.
[3] ton arton hēmōn ton epiousion	[3] Give us day by day
didou hēmin to kath hēmeran	our daily bread.
[4] kai aphes hēmin tas hamartias hēmōn	[4] And forgive us our sins;
kia gar autoi aphiomen panti opheilonti hēmin	for we also forgive every one that is indebted to us.
kai mē eisenenkēis hēmas eis peirasmon	And lead us not into Temptation
alla rhusai hēmas apo tou ponērou	but deliver us from [the] evil.

CODA

Since beginning this book, on my morning walk, I have occasionally restored, from my past practice:

(1) the opening of the Daodejing:

Dao ke dao	The Tao that can be Taoed
Fei chang dao	Is not the true Tao.
Ming ke ming,	The name that can be named
Fei chang ming	Is not the true name.

(2) part of the first sura from the Quran, 1.6

> Ihdinā -ṣ-ṣirāṭa -l-mustaqīm(a)
> Guide us in the straight path
> The path of those whom You have blessed,
> not of those who have earned your wrath,
> or of those who have gone astray.

(3) two lines from the Mahayana Heart Sutra, recited as do the Japanese: the first in Buddhist Japanese and the second in Buddhist Hybrid Sanskrit:

> Shiki soku ze ku, ku soku ze shiki.
> Form is emptiness, emptiness is form.
> gate gate pāragate pārasaṃgate bodhi svāhā
> Gone gone, gone beyond, gone utterly beyond, Enlightenment hail!

Chapter Two

The Lord's Prayer: A Second Pivotal Shift

THREEFOLD PATTERN IN THE LORD'S PRAYER

To sum up the previous chapter, there are significant similarities between the Three Refuges and the V'ahavta. But there are also significant differences between them, and in the case of the "children" in the V'ahavta and the "Sangha" in the Refuges, we can think of them almost as opposites. Children are born into their family relationship, whereas Buddhist *sanghas* began (and in the West often still begin) with a monastic renunciation of the familial and lay material world and acceptance of an alternative community. Temple Judaism, in contrast, was at first deeply rooted in the existing world.

We shall discuss in this chapter how, about the beginning of the Common Era, both Judaism and new branches of Buddhism developed an increasing focus on changing the present status quo rather than just responding to it. Mahayana Buddhism (about the first century CE) developed an increasing emphasis on the enlightened bodhisattva's role of returning to and improving the world. And after the destruction of the Second Temple (70 CE), Rabbinic Judaism developed a similar emphasis on restoring the world and making it better, *tikkun ha-olam* (the first known use of the phrase *tikkun olam* is in the Mishnah, ca. 200 CE).

The underlying process, however—source → language → community—remained the same in both religions. This raises the question of whether this process also underlies root texts in other religions. Or is it just found, for whatever reason, in Judaism and Buddhism?

From my practice of reciting the Lord's Prayer as my third daily text, I am now very aware that it too is composed of the same threenesses, twice in fact. The first threeness consists of prayers for the Lord and His will:

45

> Our Father which art in heaven,
> Hallowed be *thy name*.
> *Thy kingdom* come.
> *Thy will* be done, as in heaven, so on earth. (Luke 11:2–4, KJV)

Greek, unlike English, is inflected, and so the threeness of the three verbs is emphasized by their rhyming:

> Pater hemon ho en tois ouranois
> *hagiastheto* to onoma *sou*:
> *eltheto* he basileia *sou*:
> *genetheto* to thelema *sou*, hos en ourano kai epi tes ges:

> Πάτερ ἡμῶν ὁ ἐν τοῖς οὐρανοῖς
> ἁγιασθήτω τὸ ὄνομά σου
> Ἐλθέτω ἡ βασιλεία σου
> Γενηθήτω τὸ θέλημά σου ὡς ἐν οὐρανῷ καὶ ἐπὶ τῆς γῆς.

The first expresses optatively the honoring done affirmatively in the Namo Tassa of Buddhism ("I pay homage to the Blessed One"), the Om Namo Narayana of Hinduism ("I praise, with devotion, the All-pervading"), and given as a commandment in the V'ahavta ("Thou shalt love the Lord thy God with all thy heart"). In this it is like the Kaddish of Judaism, expressed in Aramaic (Yitgadal v'yitkadash sh'mei raba, "Glorified and sanctified be God's great name"). All of these formulas encapsulate one of the great shifts in the Axial Moment: instead of just praying primarily to benefit oneself, one prays first of all to honor and submit to a higher presence.

This use of internal rhyme in the Lord's Prayer can be compared with the terminal rhyming of both the Three Refuges and the V'ahavta. Every word in the Refuges is repeated three or more times, according to three different repetitive patterns. The ceremonial effect of this repetition reinforces the psychological content of the chant, as the chanter directs his own will to that of the Buddha/Dharma/Sangha.

All five verses of the full V'ahavta (not just the three verses that I recite) rhyme with the second-person plural ending *-echa*. The repetition is even more intense than this, for the five verses repeat *-echa* seventeen times in all, thirteen times in the three verses I repeat. The effect of the end rhymes is further enhanced by the initial *V* ("and"), which begins the same five verses; here too the incantatory repetitions reinforce the submission of the reciter to the commands (love/commit to heart/teach) of the speaking authority.

There is a repetitive pattern also in the second half of the Lord's Prayer, centered on three inflected forms (*hemon, hemin, hemas*) of the pronoun "us," which are used a total of eight times (hemon//hemon/hemin//hemin/hemon/

hemin//hemas/hemas) in the three verses. Both in content and in style, the verses focus on "us" in a submissive role, praying for three verbal actions (give/forgive/deliver) from a quasi-parental Father.

"BUT DELIVER US FROM THE EVIL" IN THE LORD'S PRAYER

Thereafter the comparison is less easy. I said earlier of the process authority → language → community that it was temporal, leading from past to present to future. The next two lines of the Lord's Prayer seem to look energetically to the future ("thy kingdom come") and also to the process as a whole ("thy will be done"), but without any reference to past or present.

But let us look now at the second threeness—the requests for ourselves:

> *Give* us day by day our daily bread.
> And *forgive* us our sins; for we also forgive every one that is
> indebted to us.
> And lead us not into temptation; but *deliver* us from [the] evil.

There is a threefold process here, whether or not it is comparable to the earlier one. The first wish is to take care of the present. The second is then to remedy the past, by forgiving and being forgiven. The third, I believe, includes a messianic expectation of a better future. (The idea that Christianity represented a pivotal moment toward a better future was clearly expressed in the late Gospel of St. John: "For the law was given by Moses, but grace and truth came by Jesus Christ" [John 1:17, KJV].)

The Greek in this verse of the Lord's Prayer—alla rhusai hemas apo tou ponerou, ἀλλὰ ῥῦσαι ἡμᾶς ἀπὸ τοῦ πονηροῦ (Matt. 6:13)—translates literally as "But deliver us from the evil." I find it a symptom of the revolutionary implication of this line that, to my knowledge, no English Bible translates it fully as it clearly reads in Greek.

By contrast, the "the" is reproduced in French, German, Dutch, Danish, Italian, and Spanish versions of the Lord's Prayer, though not in Czech, Polish, or Russian. Most of these translations were the work of lay humanist reformers of the Renaissance, in opposition to the Catholic status quo.[1]

The difference is significant. In "from evil," the evil is undefined, even hypothetical, as in the tepid translation of the Contemporary English Version: "And keep us from being tempted." In "from the evil," the evil is present and threatening. In the words of St. Paul, "we wrestle . . . against principalities, against powers, against the rulers of the darkness of this world, against spiritual wickedness in high places" (Eph. 6:12). After Christendom itself became a power, this radical alienation itself became muted. But we still live in a world of intolerable poverty and injustice, enhanced now by the threat of nuclear warfare. Beyond the social and political improvements we all should work for, some will see a need for deliverance, one we can only pray for.

But for centuries the tone for English Bibles has been set by the King James Version, "deliverance from evil," omitting the word *the* (τοῦ).[2] In the current era of revisionist scholarship, the New King James Version now reads, "But deliver us from the evil one." "The evil one" is now also named in the text of the New International Version, the Christian Standard Bible, the International Standard Version, the American Standard Version, the World English Bible, and others.

This is a possible extrapolation of the Greek, perhaps even an obvious possibility. But it is not a necessary extrapolation, certainly not a literal one, and in my view regressive rather than sympathetic. Early Christians saw themselves as "a remnant chosen [eklogen, ἐκλογὴν] by grace" (Rom. 11:5), defined by their awareness of the need for personal change to escape from an evil world. The "tou ponerou" (τοῦ πονηροῦ, the evil) of the Lord's Prayer was echoed in an Epistle of John: "oidamen hoti ek tou theou esmen, kai ho kosmas holos ek you ponerou keitai" (οἴδαμεν ὅτι ἐκ τοῦ θεοῦ ἐσμεν, καὶ ὁ κόσμος ὅλος ἐν τῷ πονηρῷ κεῖται; And we know that we are of God, and the whole world lieth in wickedness [to ponero, τῷ πονηρῷ; literally, "the evil"]) (1 John 5:19).

Oppression by a brutal pagan empire, perceived as evil, explains the rapid early spread of Christianity, just as a similar oppression and perception help explain the rapid early spread of religious Taoism and Islam. Apparently it is more difficult for anglophone Christians to perceive the status quo as containing evil when they have played such a dominant role in shaping it.

Of the twenty-nine English Bibles translated on the internet website Bible Hub, *not a single one* translates Matthew 6:13 (Luke 11:4) the way it clearly reads in Greek: "But deliver us from the evil." Yet since World War II and the Holocaust, many religious writers, such as Thomas Merton and Czeslaw Milosz, have had to struggle in their faith with the omnipresent evil in (many would say "of") the world.[3]

THE WORLD AS TRANSIENT AND IN NEED OF APOCALYPTIC CHANGE

"But deliver us from the evil." A half century later, the book of Revelation would give a more vivid and ominous description of the evil threatening the chosen, as the beast of the sea:

And I stood upon the sand of the sea, and saw a beast rise up out of the sea, having seven heads and ten horns.

And it was given unto him to make war with the saints, and to overcome them: and power was given him over all kindreds, and tongues, and nations. . . .

He that leadeth into captivity shall go into captivity: he that killeth with the sword must be killed with the sword. Here is the patience and the faith of the saints. (Rev. 13:6–7, 10)

Later we learn that the vision is an allegory: the seven heads and ten horns of the beast, whose number is 666 (Rev. 13:18), are kings (Rev. 17:9–12).

These shall make war with the Lamb, and the Lamb shall overcome them: for he is Lord of lords, and King of kings: and they that are with him are called, and chosen [eklektoi, ἐκλεκτοί], and faithful. (Rev. 17:14)

Numbers in Greek, Latin, and Hebrew were all expressed by letters (as in the Roman numbers we still use). Early Christian allegorists had no trouble calculating the letters of the 666 beast as the Roman Empire (perhaps under Nero, the first of the persecuting emperors). Using different calculations, the beast in the Middle Ages was identified as Islam, and later in the Protestant Reformation as the papacy. What did not change was the identification of the beast as a violent earthly power already in place and at war with the chosen followers of the Lamb.

The apocalyptic messianism at the time of Jesus (echoed also in Virgil's fourth eclogue[4]) was nourished by an ineluctable awareness of historical calamity and the impending close of an era. This mood flourished not just among Christians (Matt. 16:28, 1 Cor. 15:23, 1 John 2:18) but also in Judaism (the book of Enoch, the Essenes, the revolt of Simon bar Kokhba, 132–35 CE), in early religious Taoism, and in Mahayana Buddhism. (The cult of Maitreya, the future successor to the present Buddha, apparently dates to the first centuries CE.) The heightened expectation of the early Christians, and their imitators since, was not just for moral propriety but for deliverance.

This look to the future is also more evident in the original Greek of the line "Thy will be done on earth as it is in heaven" (Matt. 6:10). The Greek— genetheto to thelema sou, hos in ourano kai epi tes ges, γενηθήτω τὸ θέλημά σου, ὡς ἐν οὐρανῷ καὶ ἐπὶ γῆς—should perhaps be translated, "May Thy will come, as in heaven, so on earth."[5] The original temporal order of heaven and earth, reversed in translation, allows for a view of divine will in terms of process theology: as emerging along with, *pari passu*, its implementation on earth. This sense of an emergent will is further reinforced by the original verb, "May Thy will *come*" (literally, "be born," *genetheto*, from the same root as

Genesis), rather than *"be done,"* which I suspect implies for most Christians fulfillment of a will as it already exists in heaven.

The idea that God's will is emergent, evolving relationally to human wills rather than preexistent, is central to process theology. Like the notion of our condition as moreness, it is dependent on the vision of the actual universe in Alfred North Whitehead's *Process and Reality*: as not a fixed assembly of Newtonian *objects* in motion (what Whitehead calls the "Fallacy of Misplaced Concreteness"),[6] but a process of *events* in the course of becoming. In this process, "'becoming' is a creative advance into novelty."[7]

I believe the fixation of the Lord's Prayer on the future explains why the threenesses in it are only obliquely akin to what we saw before—the process authority → language → community. The difference arose because Christianity was a later religion, closely contemporary with the parallel development of Rabbinic Judaism, Mahayana Buddhism, and (I realized later) religious Taoism. All of these newer religions see a further cultural evolution beyond that of the Axial Moment: the earlier concern to strengthen an existing community has now been expanded to preparation for an impending repair of a corrupt world, often in anticipation of apocalyptic change.

The shift is illustrated by the difference between Psalm 145:13, "Your kingdom is an everlasting kingdom," and the Lord's Prayer, "Thy kingdom come" (Luke 11:2).[8] But the evolution was a continuous one, traceable back to the messianism in Isaiah, which survived the Jews' return to Jerusalem. Consider for example Zechariah 14:9 (ca. 520 BCE), repeated by Jews during the Musaf service: "And the Lord shall be king over all the earth: on that day shall there be one Lord, and his name one" (in contrast to the seventh-century BCE Sh'ma: "the Lord is one").

This cultural resistance to political oppression

> was found among all the larger nations of the ancient Near East: the Babylonians and Egyptians under the Persians and the Egyptians and Persians under the Greeks who, in turn, developed a preponderantly cultural resistance under the Romans. The eastern pattern, however, was religious: foreign conquest destroys the sacred and just world order by which native king, cult, nature, and people function under the ruling god, a belief which was strengthened by the frequent misrule of the conqueror. A future cataclysmic reestablishment under a kingly redeemer must therefore right all wrongs. Meanwhile, a hereafter would punish or reward the individual. This apocalyptic scheme existed throughout the Near East: e.g., the *Oracle of Hystaspes* and the later *Bahman Yasht* (Persian), Sesostris and Ramses legends, *Demotic Chronicle*, *Oracle of the Potter* (Egyptian), *Babylonian Chronicle*, Ninos-Semiramis legend (Babylonian). Archaizing styles (e.g., script and literature, cf. Coins, Dead Sea Scrolls), clerical organization, and proselytism were also aspects of resistance.[9]

Both Christianity and Rabbinic Judaism, which flourished after the loss of the Judaean kingdom and Second Temple, had obvious reasons to regard their contemporary era of loss and persecution as a world in need of repair.

(We see an additional variation in Buddhism as well. The Buddha's original teaching was how to become an Arhat and escape from the world, which Theravadan Buddhists still formally adhere to. For this the Mahayana Buddhists substituted the goal of becoming a bodhisattva to change the world. This may be an oversimplification of the change, but the core difference is there.[10])

APOCALYPTIC LIBERATION THROUGH MARTYRDOM

A sign of the Second Pivotal Shift was the emergence of voluntary alternative communities—the Essenes, Christians, and, especially after the destruction of the Second Temple in 70 CE, Jewish synagogues. These were ascetic but not monastic; both sexes participated and perhaps raised families. All three represent a new emancipation of bottom-up power: the empowerment of the individual to choose an alternative to the status quo, in a cause not diminished but enhanced by the possibility of resulting martyrdom. In this early contest between persuasive and violent power, the cause of the nonviolent, invigorated by the energy of their moreness, was in most cases ultimately victorious.

The new social phenomenon of martyrs can be traced to the Essene communities (second century BCE–first century CE). As described by Josephus, the Essenes (who "addict themselves to virtue") ascribed all things to God and taught that the soul was immortal and that righteousness must be fought for nonviolently (including by martyrdom).[11]

Early Christians believed, as the book of Revelation says, that the "slain from God" were promised heaven.[12] Martyrdom became something to be not just risked but admired, and by some desired. Reading early saints' lives like *The Passion of Perpetua and Felicity*, narrated largely in Perpetua's own voice, one is struck by the happy confidence of the martyrs themselves, in contrast to the discomfort of those around them.[13]

Perpetua's father, for example, is at first furious with his daughter's choice of religious rebellion; but he leaves, defeated, and returns later, weeping from his concern. The saints' cheeriness in prison disconcerts their guards:

> After a few days, Pudens, the military adjutant, who was in charge of the prison, began to show us considerable respect, recognizing that there was some great power [magnam virtutem] in us.[14]

(Let us note here the dramatic dialectical reversal in meaning of the Latin word *virtus* [which we will see developed in Dark Age saints' lives or vitae]. It originally signified the active prowess of a man [vir] in dominating others in war, as in the *arete* of Homer's *Iliad*. Here it designates the self-control of a woman, not in action, but in suffering—*passio*, the Latin word that became the standard term for martyrdom. The noble sufferings of the early Christian martyrs—*marturoi* in Greek means witnesses—became a significant element in the gradual ethogenic transvaluation of emotion—*pathos* in Greek, *passio* in Latin, from being seen as negative, as in the English terms *pathetic* or *pathological*, to a positive.)

The hostile mob in the arena were "stunned" by the comportment of Perpetua and her companions:

> The day of their victory dawned, and they marched from the prison to the amphitheatre, joyously, as if going to heaven, their faces radiant; and if by chance they trembled, it was from joy and not from fear. Perpetua followed, with a shining face and a calm step, as a wife of Christ and darling of God, and the intensity of her stare caused the spectators to look away. (*Passion of Perpetua* 18)

Today we are not likely to believe every detail of this hortatory tale. But there is no denying that the early Christian church, inspired by its martyrs, became after the Second Shift an unprecedented example of successful bottom-up persuasive power. The church steadily gained in steadfastness and cohesive strength, while by comparison the declining Roman Empire was dissipating into factions and rival armies, looting when underpaid.

APOCALYPTIC RESISTANCE IN THE FAR EAST

But was this spread toward apocalyptic resistance a universal development across the written world? To answer this question, we must look at China. And here I must confess I was originally blinded to the Chinese evidence for a comparable development.

My initial error was to focus too exclusively on written texts, which meant relying on the Confucian history of China as recorded by Sima Qian (ca. 145–ca. 86 BCE). I forgot to take into account the profound warning from the Daodejing that I sometimes repeat to myself as I start out on my morning meditation walk: "The Tao that can be Taoed [i.e., expressed, acted on, or embodied] is not the true Tao (Daodejing 1).

But because what developed in both the Chinese and the Roman Empires was dialectical—a tension between the empowered and the disempowered, between the flawed and its correction—it is still important to begin, as I first did, with contemporary changes to Confucianism, which in this era became China's official imperial doctrine.

CONTEMPORARY CHANGES IN CONFUCIAN CHINA

**Confucius (Kongfuzi; ca. 551–479 BCE) had emerged in a "Time of Troubles" between two traditionally recognized eras of Chinese history. Cultural historians have often described his teachings as a dialectical response to the collapsing of civilization around him, "as multiple states and factions within them fought for control of China."[15] Robert Bellah, however, stresses that the transition to axial culture in China, at the time of Confucius, had been relatively continuous.[16] Thus the evolution of Confucianism in China is quite different from the evolution of Judaism in response to the catastrophic displacements of the seventh and sixth centuries.

Confucius was able to take guiding concepts from his era, such as *li* (rites), and give them a new and ethical meaning, so that *junzi* (originally "son of a lord") now became what we translate as "gentleman" or "superior person," as in *Analects* 4:11: "The superior man thinks of virtue; the inferior man thinks of possessions." This achievement marks the axial transition: from blind fealty to a hereditary ruler to the ability to judge and criticize a ruler and his subjects by moral standards.

For this very reason, Qin Shihuang, the first emperor who united China in 221 BCE, preferred the philosophy of the competing Legalist school, which based authority not on principle but on naked enforcement of existing practices (*fa*). Accordingly, in 212 BCE, he ordered that Confucian books be burned and Confucian scholars murdered (buried alive, according to the historian Sima Qian).[17] In this the emperor followed the advice of his prime minister, Li Si, who advised, "Anyone referring to the past to criticize the present should, with all the members of his family, be put to death."[18]

> This conflict of principles between the Qin Emperor and Confucius was revived by a Maoist scholar in 1972, in order to condemn Confucianism as reactionary and thus justify the Cultural Revolution. The title of his essay was "The Struggle between 'Emphasizing the Present While Slighting the Past' [i.e., Qin] and 'Using the Past to Criticize the Present' [i.e., Kong]."[19]

However, Bellah observes that when Li Si "chided his Confucian teacher Xunzi

> for relying on humaneness [*ren*] and righteousness [*i*] when what was needed was a strong army . . . Xunzi replied that such a view was shortsighted and such a regime could not last long. As it turned out, Li Si was executed in 208 BCE

> [about a decade later] as a result of factional conflicts . . . by having him cut in half.[20]

The Qin dynasty itself soon fell to the same internecine conflicts; and one cannot avoid observing that the Cultural Revolution, though catastrophic, was also short-lived. However, the ongoing conflict in China between warriors and intellectuals, with their competing cultures of *wu* (force) and *wen* (civility), has endured from before the Qin era to the present, and the outcome is not yet decided.[21] (It is hard to avoid seeing analogues to developments in the former Soviet Union and indeed in America today.)

What is inescapable is the dramatic change in the nature and status of Confucianism around the time of the Herodians and Jesus, especially after it was established by the emperor Han Wudi (141–87 BCE) as "the ideology in which the state's officials should be trained."[22] For the first time a class of scholar-officials, often called literati, was established to perform the day-to-day governance of the state, as they would do until the collapse of the last Qing dynasty in 1912 CE.

The Confucian vision of history also changed. The transmission of rites from dynasty to dynasty, celebrated by Confucius as a peaceful process requiring occasional renewal (*Analects* 2.23), was now seen by Sima Qian as involved in dialectical violence, on a par with Roman persecutions and the destruction of the Herodian kingdom.

What Sima Qian had not yet developed was this awareness of history as a continuous, dialectical, disruptive process in which religion participates.

TAOISM AS A CONFIRMATION OF
A SECOND PIVOTAL SHIFT

However, I failed to consider, in writing the preceding section, how the official empowering of Confucianism, as a state-backed ideology, disempowered all other Chinese schools of thought—above all Taoism, whose root text, the Daodejing, could be read as an implicit criticism ("The Tao that can be Taoed is not the true Tao") of all public ideologies.

One could almost predict that the elevation of Confucianism to be the doctrine of the empowered would be followed by the debasement of Taoism in particular to become a doctrine of the lowly and disempowered. Indeed, one can read the puzzling second section of the Daodejing as a prediction of just such a dialectical development:

> When all in the world know beauty as beauty, there arises the recognition of ugliness. When they all know the good as good, there arises the recognition of

evil. . . . So it is that existence and nonexistence give birth the one to the other. . . . Therefore the sage manages affairs without doing anything [wei wu wei], and conveys his instructions without words. (Daodejing 2)

especially as further developed:

> The best quality/character is like water. The water's goodness is that it benefits the myriad things but does not quarrel, and it willingly goes to where others hate. Thus it is almost like the Dao. It is good to be/live on the ground, to deepen a heart, to love people while associating with them, to keep one's word while talking, to be peace while governing, to do what one is capable of, to act at a fit time. Because of the non-fighting-over, there will be no problem. (Daodejing 8)

While these words may have been originally composed as advice for the exercise of power (through *wu wei*, not acting), they could also easily serve as a consolation and rallying point for those to whom power is denied.

And this seems to have happened. Taoism, originally a philosophic school of thought, produced in the second century of our era a popular apocalyptic movement. This was the Five Pecks of Rice movement, later known as the Tianshidao or Taipingdao (Celestial Masters movement or Supreme Peace movement), the first organized Taoist cult.

According to a later mythicized account, a deified Laozi appeared in 142 CE on a mountain to a Taoist hermit, Zhang Daoling, and bestowed upon him the title Celestial Master (Tianshi). He warned that plagues, beasts, and the demons of the Three Offices and Six Heavens of the underworld were due to be released upon humankind and that only 240,000 people would be chosen as survivors and "seed people" to populate the new golden age of Supreme Peace.[23] The chosen were to commit themselves by donating five pecks of rice and should worship only a pantheon of Taoist deities transmitted by Laozi to Zhang, not the public pantheon of the Chinese state.[24] The Tianshidao spread among non-Han subjects of the empire, as did Mahayana Buddhism, first recorded in China in 65 CE.

In other words, the establishment of Confucianism as an imperial doctrine by the Han emperor Wu was followed by a popular apocalyptic movement of chosen people rejecting public observance. It is hard not to see an analogy with the Roman deification of first Julius Caesar and then his imperial successors, followed swiftly by another popular apocalyptic movement of chosen people refusing this observance.

Perhaps the dialectic of pivotal shifts can be summarized this way: A religion concentrates the collective moreness of a people who reject the status quo and empower this religion as an alternative, an other. But all power corrupts, and this religion, as it is more and more empowered, becomes part of the corrupt status quo. This leads to the empowerment of a new religion or sect in rebellion, and with it a new pivotal shift. The details of this dialectic will vary from shift to shift, but the underlying energy of moreness, the dissatisfaction with corrupt things as they are, has powered our cultural development or ethogeny from the beginnings of literate time.

To sum up: the example of China, which I initially thought was at odds with the notion of a Second Pivotal Shift across the written world, instead confirms it.

THE SECOND PIVOTAL MOMENT AND SHIFT

In all these various and roughly contemporary developments across a wide geographic span, a common feature is an increased attention to time, change, and alterity, focusing on an escape from the status quo toward a better world to come. This shared shift of attention I now see as a Second Pivotal Moment, at about the beginning of the Common Era, leading to a Second Pivotal Shift.

I am using the word *moment* here in its dictionary sense of a historical turning point. But I am mindful also of its Hegelian sense: an essential but partial stage of a dialectical triad, in which the synthesis of an earlier triad merges into the thesis of a new one. This Hegelian sense of *moment* is exemplified by the fact that both Christianity and Tianshi Taoism, after beginning as alternatives to established secular power, eventually acquired secular power themselves.

A second feature, of no less importance, was the bifurcation of a religious culture into two elements, one preserving authorized texts and the other deviating from them. The two elements were repeatedly distinguished by class, and the traditionalists sided with the status quo. Buddhism itself had first evolved as a casteless spin-off from Hinduism, and the Buddha's suttas or sutras were spoken and later recorded first in local languages (sometimes loosely grouped as Prakrit),[25] and later their refinement Pali, rather than the Vedic Sanskrit of the dominant Brahman caste, which the Buddha himself once rejected as an obsolete and archaic language.[26]

But when Buddhism became associated with the post-Alexandrian Mauryan Empire under Aśoka, Pali itself became an established rather than deviant language. Thus, at the time of the Second Pivotal Shift, Mahayana Buddhism (as we have already seen) emerged as a future-oriented alternative to the older Theravadan and Sarvastivadan versions of Buddhism, writing its sutras in what is now recognized as the alternative Buddhist or Buddhist Hybrid Sanskrit.[27]

We also see conflicts within Judaism at this time between the more aristocratic Sadducees, who held to a stricter dependence on the words of Torah alone, and (according to Josephus) the more plebeian and popular Pharisees, who relied also on the authority of the later biblical books of the prophets, etc. With the destruction of the Temple came a later tension between the halachic rabbis of Talmudic Judaism and mystical alternatives such as Merkabah (מרכבה) or Chariot mysticism, eventually evolving into Kabbalism.

This pairing of twinned dominant and divergent elements, sometimes thought of as yang and yin, is not just a sociohistorical development; it also corresponds to an internal yang-yin doubleness in our human consciousness. And we see this splitting repeated in a Third Pivotal Moment of about 500 CE (with the emergence of Islam in Asia and the shift of cultural leadership in Europe from imperial cities to rural monks and monasteries), a Fourth Pivotal Moment of about 1000 (when the dominant cultural role shifts back to cities and to friars and then laity rather than monks), and a Fifth Pivotal Moment of about 1500 (with first the Protestant Reformation and then later the Enlightenment). We shall return to these topics in subsequent chapters.

Both in the East and in the West, we see a dialectic whereby a popular alternative to established power (the Pharisees, the Taoists) first gains power itself, becomes a new established authority, and then is opposed by a new popular power. In various ways we can see this as a recurring and perhaps predictable pattern, in the histories of Christianity, Islam, and the breakaway Protestant churches of northern Europe. These successive disruptions of the status quo can be interpreted as adjustments of the human cultural environment to irreversible progressions in the historical evolution of the human mind.

I believe it is worth studying the successive twists and turns of this dialectic in the West because of its relevance to the cultural situation (perhaps crisis) we are in today.

Chapter Three

Yang and Yin: Torah, Psalter, and Disruption

YANG AND YIN

In the last chapter we saw history as a progressive dialectic between the status quo and an alterity generated beyond it. In the first stage or moment, religions, responding to a human craving for moreness, supplied that beyond. But in a second stage or moment, when religions themselves had become part of the status quo, new religious adaptations evolved in reaction to them.

There is a parallel to this sociohistorical process on the literary level, between the definite and the indefinite, the understandable and the mysterious, or what we loosely call the yang and the yin. A complex, nonhostile synergy emerges between organized attempts to codify the knowable, such as the Four Books of Confucianism or the Jewish Torah (Pentateuch), and organized poetry, which does not. Thus the Confucian prose classics and the Jewish Torah define the negative space that is filled by poetry: the classic Confucian Book of Odes and the Judaic book of Psalms.

It is a complex dialectic in which the oldest written texts are poetry (such as some of the Psalms or the Song of the Sea in Exodus), but the oldest codifications are of prose (the organization of Torah precedes the organization of the Psalter).

Yang and yin are also relative terms, like right and left, or light and dark. The Daodejing, for example, is definitely yin when compared to the yang of Confucian books, but yang when compared to Zhuangzi. In like manner, the book of Psalms is yin compared to Torah but yang when compared to the Song of Songs.

An underlying assumption in this chapter, already stated, is that the cultural evolution we shall look at traces a parallel development in this period of human consciousness. The period between the First and Second Pivotal Shifts (ca. 500 BCE–1 CE) is the period when the first books emerge about reasoning (e.g., Plato and Aristotle, a yin-yang pair of sorts) and also about love (the Kama Sutra and the Song of Songs).

Today neurologists distinguish between the rational or yang functions of the intelligence in the language-dominant left hemisphere, associated usually with our right hand, and the more mysterious functions of our nondominant right hemisphere, which can in conjunction with language contribute to higher functions of intuition and insight: "The co-association of language along with other novel module combinations to the nondominant hemisphere may precipitate development of emergent higher-order cognitive functions."[1]

This means that in all of us, not just those who are commonly recognized as left-handed creative people, is a doubleness of consciousness grounded in our two cerebral hemispheres, a doubleness of which scientists are slowly making us more aware:

> Over the last few years, a number of studies have concluded that it's not which hand is dominant that matters—it's the degree of dominance. According to researchers, very few people are truly entirely left- or right-handed; it's more of a spectrum. We use our left hands for some things and our right hands for other tasks.

> These experiments have found that people toward the middle of the spectrum are more flexible thinkers. They seem to be more empathetic and better able to view things from other people's perspectives.[2]

What is true of our psyche is also true of great literary art. The greatest literature, I have always believed, comes from the center of the spectrum between the yang of intelligibility and the yin of enchantment. This is true also of both great prose, which appeals primarily to the left or yang hemisphere of our brain, and great poetry, which appeals primarily to the yin or right hemisphere.

In this way, great art responds to both aspects of a deep pattern found not just in our brain but in our sociocultural environment: to the yang of dawn and the yin of nightfall, the yang of empires and the yin of disruptions.[3]

YANG AND YIN, THE KNOWN AND UNKNOWN, IN GENESIS AND THE *ILIAD*

This doubleness is found both in great prose and in great poetry. Even the book of Genesis, though yang compared to the prophecies of Isaiah and

Jeremiah, is problematically yin in many ways—particularly so in the intimate interactions between God and men.

In Genesis 18, for example, Abraham dares challenge the justice of God's decision to destroy the city of Sodom. Yet when God orders an older Abraham to sacrifice his own innocent son (Gen. 22), Abraham prepares to do so without hesitation. Rabbinic Judaism focuses on the loyal commitment of the older Abraham. But we should also focus on the younger Abraham, the spiritual ancestor of Job, Pascal and Milosz.

These scenes of intimate interaction between man and the divine have their counterpart in the roughly contemporary *Iliad*, a polytheistic poetic work where heroes are guided in their decisions by gods or goddesses who speak to them. The topic of the *Iliad* is the great anger of Achilles, but Achilles controls that anger in book 1 not by himself but only after the goddess Athena grabs him by his yellow hair and tells him not to strike Agamemnon (*Iliad* 1:197, 206–21). In this, Achilles's unthinking obedience is like that of the older Abraham.[4]

In book 1, Athena is acting on behalf of Hera, not as the avatar of wisdom she later became. In book 4, at the urging of Zeus, she incites a Trojan to launch an arrow and thus end the pause in the Trojan War (*Iliad* 4:85ss). Even Zeus's reluctant interest in violence, which he saw as a threat to his marriage, was aroused by an earth goddess, Thetis, who had "laid hold of his knees with her left hand, while with her right she clasped him beneath the chin" (*Iliad* 1:500–501). And Thetis in turn was acting on behalf of her son Achilles, who out of rage wants to get back at Agamemnon (*Iliad* 1:407–12).

These gods, as remembered from before the First Pivotal Shift, are almost as unprincipled and labile as the humans they control.[5] How different are this Zeus and this Athena from their Roman counterparts in Virgil's *Aeneid*: the "Juppiter omnipotens" who enforces fate and the Minerva who represents artistic skills! It appears that not only has the human mind developed between Homer and Virgil, but so also have the gods they depict.

The first steps in this process can be seen in the last two (possibly later) books of the *Iliad*. The gods now take steps to reduce the conflict they helped stir up in Book 1; chaos is channeled into ritual; and the heroes' impulse to outdo in battle is slowly subdued in heroic games. Thetis, obeying Zeus, has Achilles reconcile briefly with his enemy King Priam of Troy: and after the two heroes eat and lament their losses together in compassion (*Iliad* 24.510-11), the body of Hector is returned for a sacred burial.

In an ambitious seminal but controversial work, *The Origin of Consciousness in the Breakdown of the Bicameral Mind*, the psychologist Julian Jaynes argues that the *Iliad* was composed at the cusp in time when literacy was slowly (ca. 3000–800 BCE) giving rise to conscious decision making.

Originally, he suggested, humans lived in a hallucinatory state, where they responded without reflection to voices issuing from their bicameral mind.

This condition is remembered and reproduced, he claims, in the *Iliad*:

> The characters of the Iliad do not sit down and think what to do. They have no conscious minds such as we say we have, and certainly no introspections. . . . It is a god who . . . whispers low to Helen to sweep her heart with homesick longing [*Iliad* 3:139–40], . . . a god who tells Glaucus to take bronze for gold (6:234ff) . . . who debates and teaches Hector what he must do. . . . In fact, the gods take the place of consciousness.[6]

Jaynes also sees an attempt to return to this condition in the appeal of Homer (and of innumerable poets ever since) to the "goddess" (*Iliad* 1:1), later identified as the Muse (Mousa; *Iliad* 2:761, *Odyssey* 1:1), to sing the poetry that eventually will be written in the form that we know it. Jaynes interprets this appeal to poetry in terms of the bicameral mind:

> Speech, as has long been known, is a function primarily of the left cerebral hemisphere. But song . . . is primarily a function of the right cerebral hemisphere. . . . More specifically, ancient poetry involved the posterior part of the right temporal lobe, which I have suggested was responsible for organizing divine hallucinations, together with adjacent areas which even today are involved in music.[7]

Jaynes's treatment of poetic inspiration must be seen in the light of his account, while struggling in Boston with a problem in writing his book, of "a firm, distinct loud voice from my upper right which said, 'Include the knower with the known.'"[8]

YANG, YIN, AND RECENT NEUROSCIENCE

Here is Jaynes's argument as summarized by the scholar poet Julie Kane:

> Jaynes (1976) observed the absence of individual "free will" and the puzzling presence of external, godly voices uttering mandatory commands to humans in ancient literary works such as the *Iliad* or the oldest books of the Old Testament. He hypothesized that signals arising in the temporal lobe of the brain's *right* hemisphere could have travelled to the auditory area of the *left* via the small *anterior commissures* connecting the two lobes—that is, bypassing the need for interhemispheric transfer via the *corpus callosum*. Significantly, from our perspective, Jaynes further argued that the hallucinated voices spoke in *poetic verse*, and that they disappeared with the rise of writing in the second millennium BC.[9]

Kane's article, with its suggestive title "Poetry as Right-Hemispheric Language," seemed to me to be a wish-fulfillment of everything I had wanted to believe about yang, yin (two terms Kane did not use), and poetic (or prophetic) inspiration.[10] So I submitted the article to a neuroscientist friend at Berkeley, Fritz Sommer, a man whom I knew to be cautious about lateralizing theories of the brain.

It took a few weeks, but his answer when I received it was even more of a wish fulfillment:

> I am not at all an expert in brain lateralization, but a recent work that made my attention threshold is by my friend Robert Miller from Dunedin [New Zealand]. In his book he puts forward the hypothesis that the proportion of thin fibres with long axonal delays is larger in the left versus the right hemisphere. According to the theory, the bigger temporal dispersion in the left hemisphere benefits the understanding and production of speech patterns. Conversely the right hemisphere is able to make faster associations and *by this trait can dominate the left hemisphere*—maybe this supports "magic thinking."[11]

His email referred me to Robert Miller's book, *Axonal Conduction Time and Human Cerebral Laterality*. Though I found the book excruciatingly difficult to read, I was grateful for this summary of it on Amazon:

> This book takes a new and up-to-date look at the prominent theory that the left hemisphere is specialised for representing patterns extended in time whereas the right hemisphere represents simultaneous or "spatial" patterns. What makes it unique in the field is that it looks at this theory from a neurobiological basis. It suggests that the difference resides in the range of conduction times in the axons connecting different regions of the cortex in each hemisphere.

And in the book itself I found a question that I could barely understand, followed by an answer that again left me, almost literally, breathless:

> When the cerebral cortex deals with non-linguistic sensory programming and motor control, can it deal with such complex temporal structure . . . as it does when processing language? In answer to this question, it can easily be pointed out that musical sequences, musical performance and many other distinctively human motor functions can also have such a fine temporal structure. However, these motor functions are also lateralized, which may be a reflection of some more fundamental difference between hemispheres in humans which leads to lateralization of language as well as other functions.[12]

My excitement was still further increased by a detail that Fritz Sommer had not shared with me:

In 1961 [Miller] started as a medical student at Oxford University, and commenced serious study of brain physiology, focusing especially on the integration of scientific information from many sources. However, at this period he experienced increasingly severe psychiatric problems, which led, in 1967 to a serious psychotic breakdown.[13]

(Editing this passage years later, I searched Wikipedia in vain for a corroborating detail about Jaynes. And then, while meditating, I recalled that Jaynes heard "a firm, distinct loud voice from my upper right" dictate to him. This experience, too, in a secular society, would not be considered by "normal" people to be "normal.")

Miller experienced a break from normal rationality before his discoveries, just as T. S. Eliot suffered a nervous breakdown while writing *The Waste Land*. As in society, so in the individual, disruption precedes creative development.

After reading all this, I sat for two hours at the breakfast table in a kind of trance. So many things now seemed clear. Miller's research, like Jaynes's, was not only controversial now (as Sommer had told me) but might continue to be, because some yang neuroscientists were simply not capable of momentary or psychotic yin domination.

But I myself, like both Jaynes and Miller, knew about yin domination at firsthand and had already written about it in poetry, from my experience of the ineffable (in *Coming to Jakarta*, I.i–II.iv, III.vii) to that of the merely hallucinatory (in *Listening to the Candle*, I.ii).[14]

And late in life, here I am experiencing it again, right now, writing this crazy yet perhaps somehow predetermined poem (yin) in prose (yang).

THE SHIJING AND THE BOOK OF PSALMS

To repeat: the yang-yin doubleness of human nature is reflected not only in the yang-yin doubleness of coercive and persuasive power but also in the yang-yin doubleness that all written cultures exhibit between prose and poetry—the latter, at least in its origins, usually the older of the two and at first expressed in song. This is considered to be true of both the Chinese Book of Odes (Shijing), traditionally said to have been collected by Confucius, and the Hebrew book of Psalms.

Both collections include songs dealing with love, but with a sharp and consistent difference. The Book of Odes deals with a wide range of topics drawn from everyday life, including what we think of as love songs, along with songs about farming, war, and politics. The Psalter, on the other hand, is very sharply focused on the human relationship to God. To quote Robert Alter,

The two preponderant genres in the book are songs of thanksgiving, which over-lap significantly with psalms of praise [Tehilim, the Hebrew word for Psalms], and supplications, but there are more supplications than psalms of thanksgiving.[15]

In the psalms of thanksgiving, which include some of the oldest in the book, we find talk of love. But it is of God's love for God's people, or their love of God.

The same is true of two of the oldest texts elsewhere in the Bible. One is the thanksgiving Song of Deborah after she and Barak have defeated the Canaanites:

> may all who love you be like the sun
> when it rises in its strength. (Judges 5:31)

The other is the Song of the Sea, sung by Moses after the Israelites have escaped across the Red Sea:

> You stretch out your right hand,
> and the earth swallows your enemies.
> In your unfailing love you will lead
> the people you have redeemed. (Exod. 15:12–13)

Love in these Hebrew songs is a relationship with an altogether Other Being; the analogous feeling in the Book of Odes is of this world. And when a song there deals with humans and the divine—

> Dignified, dignified are the many officers,
> Holding fast to the virtue of King Wen.
> Responding in praise to the one in Heaven
> They hurry swiftly within the temple.

> ("Clear Temple," *Qing miao*)—

it is clearly from a more mundane perspective. Contrast the tone of Psalm 104:

> Who maketh his angels spirits; his ministers a flaming fire:
> Who laid the foundations of the earth, that it should not be
> removed for ever.
> Thou coveredst it with the deep as with a garment: the waters stood
> above the mountains.
> At thy rebuke they fled; at the voice of thy thunder they
> hasted away.

> (Psalm 104:4–7)

These differences between the Chinese and the Hebrew reflect the relatively more secure geography of the Han people.

> China's heartland is bound together by two long navigable river systems in rich alluvial valleys (the Yangtze and Yellow rivers), and it is joined from north to south by relatively easy connections between these two river systems. As a result, China very early became dominated by two huge geographic core areas of high productivity, which gradually fused into one.[16]

The state of Chu was in the south, and *Chuci* is sometimes translated as "Songs of the South."

> Scholars agree that the "southern" culture of China, roughly identifiable with the state of Chu during the period between 700 and 200 B.C.E., is of great importance in the subsequent development of Chinese culture. Early Han artists and writers from the first century B.C.E. were encouraged to preserve "exotic" and "barbaric" Chu images and songs as an antidote to the harsh laws of the [northern] Qin.[17]

PERSONAL LOVE LYRICS

The Shijing and the Psalter were each followed in due time by more intimate and personal collections of shorter songs: The Songs of Chu (Chuci; ca. 200 BCE) in China and the Hellenized Hebrew Song of Songs (Shir Hashirim, third or second century BCE).[18] Both of these are dialectically complementary (yin) to the earlier longer and more rational (yang) texts. But the Songs of Chu diverge from the Book of Odes in their exploration of the magical and shamanistic, while the Song of Songs is of course one of the world's most famous love songs.

It is relevant that a roughly similar complementarity appeared in other cultures at the same time. The great Hindu war epic, the *Mahabharata* (ca. 400 BCE), was followed by the *Ramayana*, which narrates the travels and travails of the god Rama and his wife Sita, before his ultimate return to Ayodhya to be crowned king. Likewise, the Greek *Iliad* was complemented by the *Odyssey*, focusing on the travails of Odysseus before his return to his faithful wife Penelope.

In the wake of these specific epics, collections of shorter songs proliferated, including songs of love. Notable among these are the prosimetric Kama Sutra in India and the Archaic Greek songs of Sappho (d. ca. 570 BCE). Sappho was so preeminent among the lyricists that in the *Anthologia Palatina*, Plato was alleged to have honored her as the Tenth Muse. Others from his era called her "the poetess," to match the practice of referring to Homer as "the poet."

Only 670 of Sappho's reputed ten thousand verses have survived. But of these, one extended fragment, Sappho 31, deserves to be considered a root text of all Western love poetry. Here it is, in Anne Carson's superb translation:

> He seems to me equal to gods that man
> whoever he is who opposite you
> sits and listens close
> to your sweet speaking
>
> and lovely laughing—oh it
> puts the heart in my chest on wings
> for when I look at you, even a moment, no speaking
> is left in me
>
> no: tongue breaks and thin
> fire is racing under skin
> and in eyes no sight and drumming
> fills ears
>
> And cold sweat holds me and shaking
> grips me all, greener than grass
> I am and dead—or almost
> I seem to me.
>
> But all is to be dared, because even a person of poverty . . .[19]

Even the most superficial reading of this poem reaches into a realm beyond where words can easily perform. It is even more difficult, and perhaps irrelevant, to analyze the poet's emotion in the presence of a "he" and a "you" (female, we know from other fragments). Is the poet so shaken from love of the "you"? From jealousy of the "he"? From the shock that the "he" can listen while she herself is deafened? Does the poetess herself have no clue? Or does the reader learn in this presence not to ask such mundane questions?

Something like the last reaction persuaded the first-century Greek critic Longinus to include what we have of the poem in his essay *On the Sublime* (Peri Hypsous, Περὶ Ὕψους; literally, *On Heights*, or *On Depths*). Of the poem specifically, he asked,

> Are you not amazed at how at one and the same moment she both freezes and burns, is irrational and sane, is terrified and nearly dead, so that we observe in her not a single emotion but a whole concourse of emotions?

More generally, he observed that

the Sublime leads the listeners not to persuasion, but to ecstasy: for what is wonderful always goes together with a sense of dismay, and prevails over what is only convincing or delightful, since persuasion, as a rule, is within everyone's grasp: whereas, the Sublime, giving to speech an invincible power and strength, rises above every listener. (*On the Sublime* 1.4)

Let me suggest a more contemporary word for this transcendence of rational discourse in both the speaker and the reader: ego loss. The mood of my morning incantations, when I take refuge in the Buddha and love God, with all my heart and moreness, is akin to what is happening here. Longinus himself, to illustrate the sublime's combination of strength and simplicity, wrote (surprisingly, if he himself was not actually Jewish),

A similar effect was achieved by the lawgiver of the Jews—no mean genius, for he both understood and gave expression to the power of the divinity as it deserved—when he wrote at the very beginning of his laws, and I quote his words: "God said,"—what was it?—"Let there be light, and there was. Let there be earth, and there was." (*On the Sublime* 9.9)

THE SONG OF SONGS

This combination of directness and depth is perhaps the predominant feature shared by Sappho 31 and the Song of Songs. The feverish alienation and loss of both sense and ego is central to the love expressed in the Song as well:

Stay me with flagons, comfort me with apples: for I am sick of love. (2:5)

(The scholarly translation by Chana and Ariel Bloch suggests, "Let me lie among vine blossoms, in a bed of apricots! I am in the fever of love.")

My beloved is mine, and I am his: he feedeth among the lilies. (2:16)

The development between Sappho and the Song moves us even further away from the merely rational. For one thing, as we see here, images, many of them pastoral and some of them baffling, are omnipresent in the Song, and their repetition enhances the sense that they are not literal but metaphorical. Indeed, the song itself insists that we read its imagery allegorically:

A garden inclosed is my sister, my spouse; a spring shut up, a fountain sealed.[20]
Thy plants are an orchard of pomegranates, with pleasant fruits; camphire, with spikenard,

Spikenard and saffron; calamus and cinnamon, with all trees of
frankincense; myrrh and aloes, with all the chief spices:
A fountain of gardens, a well of living waters, and streams from
Lebanon.
Awake, O north wind; and come, thou south; blow upon my garden,
that the spices thereof may flow out. Let my beloved come into his
garden, and eat his pleasant fruits. (Song 4:12–16)

Another difference, more subtle, is even more revolutionary. Sappho's
poem reflects a doubleness in the speaker, with the speaker providing
a clinical diagnosis of her own fever. The love in the Song of Songs is
single-mindedly sensual, and the speaker, sometimes male and more often
female, celebrates it from within its power. This leads the Blochs to comment:

> Despite the brothers and watchmen, the Song has none of the dark complication
> of many familiar love stories. For Romeo and Juliet, love is wedded to loss and
> death; for Tristan and Isolde, or for Heathcliff and Catherine, love itself is a
> form of suffering. The word "passion" comes from the Latin *patior*, "to suffer,"
> and passionate love is often regarded as a consuming disease, its symptoms
> being (in Sappho's diagnosis) a fluttering heartbeat, a burning sensation, a
> drumming in the ears, a cold sweat, paleness, and trembling. But apart from one
> episode of rapid heartbeat (5:4) ["my heart beat wild," in their translation],[21] the
> lovers in the Song exhibit few of the usual symptoms. They don't suffer love,
> they savor it.[22]

The point made here is immensely important. It reflects the fact that the
Song of Songs is one of the last biblical books to be composed, situating it
on the cusp between the First Pivotal Shift and the Second. Erotic love here is
not reproved or regretted but taken seriously, as a source of exaltation.

THE SONG OF SONGS AND THE
SECOND PIVOTAL SHIFT

The word for "love" here is from the same root (*ahav*, אָהַב) as the word "love"
in the V'ahavta repeated after the Sh'ma: "Thou shalt love [V'ahavta, וְאָהַבְתָּ]
the Lord thy God with all thy heart and all thy soul and all thy might" (Deut.
6:5). The "heart" ravished in the Song ("Thou hast ravished my heart, my
sister, my bride"; 4:9) is from the same root (*leb*, לֵב) as the heart in "with all
thy heart."

Many cultures have dealt with the link between erotic and spiritual love,
but usually by first differentiating them. In Plato's *Symposium*, the prophet-
ess Diotima speaks of the "heavenly ladder" of love, in which "love with the

beauty of one individual body" leads gradually upward "to the special love that pertains to nothing but the beautiful itself."

> And . . . it is when he looks upon beauty's visible presentment, and only then, that a man will be quickened with the true, and not the seeming, virtue—for it is virtue's self that quickens him, not virtue's semblance. And when he has brought forth and reared this perfect virtue, he shall be called the friend of god, and if ever it is given to man to put on immortality, it shall be given to him. (*Symposium* 210a–212b)

Recently Christian theologians, following Plato's lead, have distinguished between *eros* (self-serving) and *agape* (self-sacrificing) love. But the Song does not just ignore this distinction; it annihilates it. For this reason, many objected, after the destruction of the Second Temple, to adding the Song to the canon of the Jewish Bible. Rabbi Akiva (d. 135 CE) successfully argued for its inclusion:

> For the whole world is not as worthy as the day on which the Song of Songs was given to Israel; for all the writings are holy but the Song of Songs is the Holy of Holies. (Babylonian Talmud, *Yadayim* 73a)

Both Jews and Christians saw the Song as an expression of the holy love between the Lord and his believers, either the Jewish people (Rabbi Akiva) or the Christian Church (Origen, d. 253 CE). This interpretation is reflected in the Gospel of John's allusion to the passage in the Song just quoted:

> He that believeth on me, as the scripture hath said, out of his belly shall flow rivers of living water [hydatos zōntos; echoing the Septuagint version of Song 4:15: "Thou art a fountain of gardens, a well of living waters (hydatos zōntos), and flowing streams from Lebanon."] (John 7:38)

This perhaps inevitable elaboration of the Song's text illustrates for me how the Song anticipates the Second Pivotal Shift. As we saw earlier, this was a time (about the beginning of the Common Era) when religion shifted from a focus on purifying the present to a focus on preparing for a better future.[23]

The Song celebrates on a personal level the importance of change that we saw on the collective. Its verses repeatedly voice the *altered* state love puts us in—"I am sick of love" (2:5; cf. 4:9, 5:1, 5:8, etc.)—as a condition not regretted but celebrated. Thus the Song is important to both Jewish notions of *t'shuvah* (repentance; literally "return") and the related Christian notion of conversion ("turning back or returning"; *OED*).

FROM THE CANTICLE TO THE APOCALYPTIC

It is common for Jewish exhortations to *t'shuvah*, or "the journey from devastation to renewal," to cite Song 6:3 as understood numerologically:

> The Babylonian name of the month of Elul has been thought of as an acronym for Ani L'dodi V'dodi Li (I am my Beloved's and my Beloved is mine) which is a line from Shir HaShirim (The Song of Songs). As we prepare ourselves for the High Holy Days, we spend the month of Elul repairing the very foundation of our connection to the Great Mystery.[24]

The outstanding example of conversion among Jesus's followers, the reformed prostitute Mary Magdalene (who "had been healed of evil spirits and infirmities"; Luke 8:2) was specifically identified by Origen with the Bride in the Song of Songs.[25]

Calls for repentance in the Jewish Bible (the Christian Old Testament) are a call to *return* to Mosaic law, as in Ezekiel 14:6: "Thus saith the Lord GOD; Repent, and turn yourselves from your idols." The Messiah of Deutero-Isaiah (interpreted as referring to King Cyrus the Great of Persia) is also a restorer of the past: "And the Redeemer shall come to Zion [Jerusalem], and unto them that turn [ul'shuvah] from transgression in Jacob, saith the LORD" (Isa. 59:20).

But according to Philo (d. ca. 50 CE), repentance for the Essenes meant *abandoning* traditional Jewish society for a new ascetic liberated life in spiritual fellowship (*koinonia*, κοινωνία) and brotherly love:

> And a proof of this is to be found in their life of perfect freedom; no one among them ventures at all to acquire any property whatever of his own, neither house, nor slave, nor farm, nor flocks and herds, nor any thing of any sort which can be looked upon as the fountain or provision of riches; but they bring them together into the middle as a common stock, and enjoy one common general benefit from it all.[26]

For Jesus, too, repentance was not a return but the opening to a new and different life. Echoing the apocalyptic message of John the Baptist (Matt. 3:2), the very first preaching of Jesus to the public began, "Repent ye: for the kingdom of heaven is at hand" (Matt. 4:17).[27] The Greek word for "repent" here (Metanoieite, Μετανοεῖτε) is from the noun *metanoia* (μετάνοια), meaning a "change of mind" rather than a "return." And for the first Christians, as for the Essenes, repentance did not mean restoration of traditional life but abandonment of it.

A new fellowship (*koinonia*, κοινωνία; Acts 2:42) was contemplated, whose ideal (like that of the Essenes) was to be classless. Thus St. Paul:

> For as many of you as have been baptized into Christ have put on
>   Christ.
> There is neither Jew nor Greek, there is neither bond nor free, there
>   is neither male nor female: for ye are all one in Christ Jesus.
>
>   (Gal. 3:27–28)

And to implement this ideal, the very first Christians reportedly transferred their private wealth to the community:

> And all that believed were together, and had all things common;
> And sold their possessions and goods, and parted them to all men,
> as every man had need. (Acts 2:44–45)[28]

Such extreme renunciation, I believe, was contingent on imminent apocalyptic expectations. For over a century, scholars have argued that the Essenes lived by the apocalyptic book of Enoch, a book prophesying a Messiah—and not Isaiah's Messiah of restoration but a Messiah inaugurating a new millennium.

The Dead Sea Scrolls from Qumran include references, like other late Jewish texts such as the "book of Zohar," to two different Messiahs, a prophet and a warrior.[29] In one text, the "War Scroll," the Messiah (distinguished today as the Messiah of Israel) is a prophet who ignores the war between the "sons of light" and the "sons of darkness." In others, the Messiah (the Messiah of David) is a liberator who will struggle against the "sons of Belial," who are identified with the pagan rulers who "counsel together against the Lord" (Psalm 2:2).[30]

More and more scholars link the Dead Sea Scrolls to the Essenes, and they point to the Qumran texts, from which they conclude:

> The Essenes were an apocalyptic sect that believed the end of the world was near with its epic battle between the "Sons of Light" (themselves) and the "Sons of Darkness" (pretty much everyone else).[31]

The Essenes were thus an early example of a community eschewing earthly pleasures in order to prepare for a radical historical change.

The book of Enoch is also quoted in the New Testament:

> And Enoch also, the seventh from Adam, prophesied of these, saying, Behold, the Lord cometh with ten thousands of his saints, To execute judgment upon all, and to convict all that are ungodly among them of all their ungodly deeds which they have ungodly committed, and of all their hard speeches which ungodly sinners have spoken against him. (Jude 1:14–15)[32]

In the Christian New Testament, the yang teachings of the Epistles are primarily balanced by the yin book of Revelation, much as the Torah in the Jewish Bible is balanced by the Psalms and Song of Songs. And the book of Revelation, in addition to imitating the Song's use of imagery, has been shown to echo the Song of Songs (in its Septuagint Greek version) in at least four places. One example is Revelation 3:20:

> Behold, I stand at the door [thuran, θύραν], and knock [krouo, κρούω]; if any man hear my voice [phones, φωνῆς], and open the door, I will come in to him, and will sup with him, and he with me,

echoing Song 5:2 in the Septuagint:

> I sleep, but my heart is awake: the voice [φωνὴ] of my kinsman knocks [κρούει] at the door [θύραν], saying, Open, open to me, my companion, my sister, my dove, my perfect one: for my head is filled with dew, and my locks with the drops of the night.

Perhaps the most seminal example is the description of the New Jerusalem, developing the river of living water image already echoed from the Song (4:15) by the Gospel of John (7:38):

> And I saw a new heaven and a new earth: for the first heaven and the first earth were passed away; and there was no more sea.

> And I John saw the holy city, new Jerusalem, coming down from God out of heaven, prepared as a bride adorned for her husband. (Rev. 21:1:2)

(This image of the city adorned "as a bride" parallels a similar apocalyptic vision in the apocryphal book 2 Esdras, another text shared by both Christians and Essenes.[33]

> And he shewed me a pure river of water of life [hudatos zoes, ὕδατος ζωῆς], clear as crystal, proceeding out of the throne of God and of the Lamb

> In the midst of the street of it, and on either side of the river, was there the tree of life. (Rev. 22:1–2)

YIN DISRUPTION AND ETHOGENY

Though this chapter began by extolling the right balance of yang and yin, the preceding paragraphs have been steeped in yin wildness, as if violent imperial oppression had alienated both Essenes and Christians from normal civic life and forced them into living in accordance with poetic prophecies that made no literal sense whatever. (Also, as noted in the last chapter, religious Taoism, inspired by the apocalyptic Taipingjing, emerged in the millenarian peasant uprisings at the end of the Han dynasty in 220 CE.[34])

But if we pull back from this close-up view, we can perhaps see that the yang of the First Pivotal Shift, which provided laws and customs to the peoples of the world, was balanced by the wild disruptions of the Second Pivotal Shift with its glimpses of a freer and more egalitarian society.

This is perhaps the time for me to explain why this book is a study in ethogeny, which I have defined in *Poetry and Terror* as "the slow evolution of both our culture and our second nature." I added that "disruptions of established order contribute to cultural evolution (ethogeny)," and described this evolution as dialectical, a process in which "traumatic experience can produce poetry, which in turn can contribute to social change."[35]

I regard the socioreligious innovations of the Second Pivotal Shift, inspired in part by poetry, as a good example of this dialectical process. Without wishing to diminish all apocalyptic literature to the status of poetry, we can still see that (like poetry) it appeals less to the dominant left hemisphere of the brain than to the nondominant right.

Histories of cultural development, such as Stephen Greenblatt's *The Swerve*, have up to now tended to be histories of ideas, which is to say, narratives of the yang. But histories of ideas alone, without giving full account of their yin counterparts, miss the dialectic whereby the irrational disruption of ideas provides for the creative innovation of new ideas. This is why I have chosen, in place of the yang term "Enlightenment," to write of the more inclusive term "Enmindment" (in other words, a process from both hemispheres, not just the left).

From the crucible of Roman violence at the beginning of the Common Era came glimpses of ideal social societies that some people still hope to implement today.

Chapter Four

Yang and Yin in the Polis: The Pre-Socratics and Plato

A BRIEF OVERARCHING PREFACE

This is a book about ethogeny—the simultaneous interactive evolution of our global ethos or culture on the one hand and the human mind on the other. In the following chapters, the comparative study of two rich generative sources, the dialogues of Plato and the Song of Songs, gives us evidence of the way the brain has evolved dialectically since antiquity and also how the social interaction of dominant and subservient cultures has contributed to the evolution of individual consciousness.

As we have seen in earlier chapters, initial doctrines from the First Pivotal Shift were enlarged through the Second, but only after prose doctrines had been complemented by counteracting poetry. Where the prose had provided rational or yang precepts for maintaining social order, the poetry added yin dimensions of mystery, social change, and intrapersonal love.

The Jewish Tanakh (the Christian Old Testament) gives us a stratified record of increasing attention to erotic love. The word *love* (*ahava* or *ahabah*) carried as many meanings in Hebrew as in English, but its most common use by far in the Tanakh, from Deuteronomy to the later prophets, is to express the interactive feelings between the Lord and the people of Israel.

From the beginning, it described love on the human level as well. The "love" in "love thy neighbor as thyself" (Lev. 19:18), part of a list of practical instructions,[1] is presumably akin to that of a putative slave who says, "I will love my master, my wife, and my children" (Ex. 21:6). But erotic love could also be strong, as when "Jacob served seven years for Rachel; and they seemed unto him but a few days, for the love he had to her" (Gen. 29:20), or when "Jonathan made a covenant with David, because he loved him as his own soul" (1 Sam. 18:3).[2] And David's son Amnon "fell sick" with "love" for his sister Tamar, but this love was a deranging sexual urge that led him to rape her and then throw her out on the street (2 Sam. 13:15 et al.).

Before the Song of Songs, the only biblical book to take heterosexual love seriously as a topic was the late collection of Proverbs. There the overall tone was didactic and admonitory, to warn against adulterous love with strange women. But on occasion its imagery for marital (as opposed to adulterous) love was Song-like:

Drink waters out of thine own cistern, and running waters out of thine own well.

Let her be as the loving hind and pleasant roe; let her breasts satisfy thee at all times; and be thou ravished always with her love.

And why wilt thou, my son, be ravished with a strange woman, and embrace the bosom of a stranger? (Prov. 5:15, 19–20; cf. 7:18–23)

Nothing else in the Tanakh approaches the reverent attention to heterosexual love in the Song. As noted in the last chapter, an analogue is found in Plato. In this chapter, Plato's dialogues will be discussed further for their correspondence, in *yang*-yin prose, to the Song's *yin*-yang poetry.

This chapter and the next will also focus on the generative importance of Plato's dialogues and the Song of Songs—how they both resemble and completely outclass the writings of contemporaries like Zeno the Stoic, Epicurus, Theocritus, Callimachus, and Apollonius of Rhodes.

What distinguishes Plato and the Song from their contemporaries, I believe, is an admixture in their work of sacred or yin mysteries, linked to the past, with a progressive, rational, yang movement away from the past. The resulting fusion of yin and yang in this era reached its peak achievement in the metropolitan culture of Alexandria, where a dominant Greek culture and a subservient Jewish one coexisted for a brief period harmoniously under the Ptolemies.

The signal achievement of the Song of Songs in melding these cultures calls to mind the master-servant dialectic outlined by Hegel, in which two disparate consciousnesses, one dominant, one subservient, each acquire self-consciousness through recognizing the consciousness of the other.[3]

In Hegel's dialectic, it is the *Knecht*, or servant, who is subservient (in this case, the Jew), not the *Herr* or master (the Greek), who is alienated by his social status and thereby knows that he is not what society takes him to be. For Hegel this fuller consciousness is the key to liberation: "The humankind has not liberated itself *from* servitude [Knechtschaft], but *by means of* servitude."[4]

It is time to note how closely the interaction between yang (what is rational or explicable) and yin (what is not) mirrors the interaction between what used to be stereotypically called the *dominant* (or male, or "digital") left brain and the *minor* (or female, or "analog") right brain.[5]

According to a widely circulated internet summary of the research of Nobel Prize winner Roger W. Sperry, the left or dominant hemisphere of the brain (which governs the right hand) is "more verbal, analytical, and orderly," while the right or minor hemisphere is "more visual and intuitive . . . more creative and less organized." These easy stereotypes have inspired an entire genre of self-help pop literature.[6]

Unfortunately, this attractive description of the right brain is not supported by science. Neuroscientists agree that two areas in the temporal lobe of the left brain (Broca's and Wernicke's) are responsible for the production and comprehension of speech. Most agree further that the left hemisphere is "quite dominant for major cognitive activities, such as problem-solving."[7] However, few today call the left hemisphere, as a whole, "dominant," and some now even attribute this role to the right hemisphere.[8] The more neuroscience advances, the more nearly all of the brain's higher activities are seen as bicameral, not lateralized.

In particular, neuroscientists have much more difficulty attributing specific characteristics to the right brain. There, there are no clearly definable areas like Broca's and Wernicke's in the left brain. As a result, the current state of neuroscience tends to treat the left brain as in some ways definable and the right brain as not. Perhaps we should expect such limits to language, generated as we now say in Broca's area of the left brain. This treatment of the brain, better than the pop stereotypes, fits the correspondence I see with my shorthand descriptions of yang (what is explicable in words) and yin (what is not).

I hope that, by the end of the following three chapters, the reader will see another correspondence: that a dialectic between a dominant yang and a minor yin in our culture corresponds not only to our left-right brain but also to Hegel's phenomenological dialectic between a dominant *Herr* and a subservient *Knecht*.

FROM TRIBE TO IMPERIAL CITY: MULTICULTURALISM AND LITERATURE

We have already seen how the Second Pivotal Shift occurred after the establishment of dominant empires in Rome, China, India, and Egypt (and also Parthia). Each of these empires spawned a new kind of city: a multicultural metropolis. In the next chapter, we shall look at the role of the first great

Western metropolis, Alexandria, which was founded in 331 BCE, in the interstitial or cusp period between two pivotal shifts.

But key features of this new social unit, the multiethnic metropolis, can already be seen in Athens by the late fifth century BCE. As Thucydides has recorded, Athens in its last decades of dominance in the fifth century had expanded from a polis or city-state to a small but locally powerful and ruthless empire. This led to major changes in the city itself.

At the time of the First Pivotal Shift, Athens, like Jerusalem, was essentially peopled by an ethnically and culturally homogeneous tribe. By the time Athens (and its local environs of Attica) had fallen to Sparta in 404 BCE, it had perhaps tripled in size, with an estimated population of 40,000 male citizens, 100,000 family members, 70,000 *metics* (resident foreigners, many engaged in foreign trade), and 150,000 to 400,000 slaves (the most of any city in Greece).

At the same time, many of its soldiers, most notably the Athenian author Xenophon (d. 354 BCE), served in times of Greek peace as mercenaries in Persian armies. By the end of the third century, according to Sylvain Levy, Buddhists and Brahmans were to be found in Athens.[9]

But Athens was not the only Greek city to expand in this way. In 415 BCE, the population size of Syracuse in Sicily, a Corinthian colony founded in the eighth century BCE, "was probably similar to Athens."[10] But Syracuse in that century, though visited by Pindar (d. 438 BCE), left no cultural heritage comparable to the great tragedians, historians, and philosophers of fifth-century Athens. This suggests that literary genius is not solely a private matter and that certain social circumstances are more conducive to it than others (a truth underlying Eliot's attack on what he called the "mute inglorious Milton" fallacy).

Why this should just have been true of fifth-century Athens is not really clear to me. But as this is just poetic prose, I will speculate. Athens, a functioning democracy as late as the 460s BCE, saw its social political processes increasingly disrupted by Athens's almost inevitable evolution from a polis into an imperial city with multicultural diversity. The result (then as now in America) was a shared concern for lost social values, above all an anxiety that the traditional respect for the "golden mean" ("nothing in excess," meden agan, μηδὲν ἄγαν) of the Delphic Oracle and the "moderation is best" (metron ariston, μέτρον ἄριστον) of the sixth-century sage Cleobulus, was being lost.

The theme that *hubris* (excess) is followed by *nemesis* (vengeance, downfall) is explored in such tragedies as Aeschylus's *Persae* (the *hubris* of Xerxes and Darius in bridging the Hellespont) and Sophocles's *Antigone* (the *hubris* of King Creon in decreeing that the body of the warrior Polynices would not be buried). But the same theme underlies Thucydides's careful analysis in his *History of the Peloponnesian War* of why Athens lost that war (431–404 BCE), particularly in his long description in book 6 of the Athenians' hubristic and disastrous expedition against Syracuse. It is also, as we shall see, a theme explored by Socrates and Plato in Plato's *Gorgias* and elsewhere.

Thus disruption, as throughout this book, was for Athens a time of both political disaster and creative opportunity. Significantly, the last of the great tragedies in Athens, Sophocles's *Oedipus at Colonus*, was produced in 401 BCE, just three years after Athens's defeat and the loss of its empire.

MULTICULTURAL DIVERSITY AND
ATHENIAN PRODUCTIVITY

Not surprisingly, Athenian authors in this period began to write about the customs and values of other contemporary cultures. An early example is Aeschylus's *The Persians*, a tragedy about the Athenian defeat of the Persian navy at the Battle of Salamis in 480 BCE, first performed eight years later.[11] The play still continues to be produced, I believe, because of the vibrancy of its doubleness;[12] as Wikipedia notes, "Interpretations of *Persians* either read the play as sympathetic toward the defeated Persians or else as a celebration of Greek victory within the context of an ongoing war."[13]

But to make the Persians sympathetic to an Athenian audience, "Aeschylus attributes actions and speech normally associated with Greek women to the Persian elders in order to characterize them as Persian—that is, foreign, Eastern, and not Greek."[14] Thirty years later, the *Histories* of Herodotus (d. 425 BCE) *contrast* the behavior and values of the Persians with those of the Greeks, with the Persians, in the eyes of some, "seeming to come off more favorably."[15]

> The customs which I know the Persians to observe are the following: they have no images of the gods, no temples nor altars, and consider the use of them a sign of folly. (Herodotus, *Histories*, 1.131)

An enlarged point of view was hardly surprising for a Greek who had been born under Persian rule (in what is now Turkey) and whose application for Athenian citizenship had been unsuccessful.

We see a still greater sympathy for the exotic in the *Medea* of Euripides (431 BCE), where "Jason's cold-hearted [Greek] rationality contrasts unfavourably with Medea's [foreign] emotionalism."[16] In this tragedy, deplored by Nietzsche for its "Socratic" separation of the Dionysian (yin) from the Apollonian (yang), the two lovers on stage both exhibit tragic flaws. But

Euripides's play also raises enduring moral questions, not just about Greek civilization but indeed about civilization itself.

This enlargement of both consciousness (yang) and sympathy (yin) reflects the era's increasing awareness that one's own community and history are part of a larger ordered world (or cosmopolis),[17] in space and also in time.

A measure of this slow evolution is that the Roman word for universe (*seculum*) acquired a temporal as well as a spatial meaning; the Greek word for universe (*cosmos*) did not. In the same period, conversely, the Hebrew word *olam* (עוֹלָם), which in Psalm 89:2 is temporal (forever, all generations), acquires in the Hellenistic era the spatial meaning of "world" (Eccles. 3:11: "He hath set the world in their heart"). This anticipated the time dimension that the cultural status quo would fully acquire in the Second Pivotal Shift.

THE ALTERITY OF THE SOPHISTS, SOCRATES, AND PLATO

As the minds of Athenians expanded beyond the traditional limits of their city's culture, alternative modes of thinking emerged. Perhaps the first example of this as a social phenomenon would be the emergence in fifth-century BCE Athens of the sophists, professional educators who wandered through Greece offering instruction in a wide range of subjects. They responded to a felt need:

> The increasing wealth and intellectual sophistication of Greek cities, especially Athens, created a demand for higher education beyond the traditional basic grounding in literacy, arithmetic, music and physical training.[18]

According to Plato, Protagoras (d. 411 BCE) claimed to be the first to call himself a sophist, distinguishing himself from the itinerant rhapsodes who taught *arete* (ἀρετή, virtue) from heroic examples in Homer, and instead teaching *arete* in more civil terms, as "how to make the most effective contribution to the affairs of the city by word and action" (*Protagoras* 317b, 319a).

Protagoras today is chiefly remembered for his aphorism that "man is the measure of all things [panton chrematon metron estin anthropos, πάντων χρημάτων μέτρον ἐστὶν ἄνθρωπος], of those things that are, that they are, and of those things that are not, that they are not." Both Plato and Aristotle criticized this relativistic statement, seeing it as a denial of objective truth. Plato has Protagoras contend that "whatever seems right and honorable to a state is really right and honorable to it, so long as it believes it to be so" (*Theaetetus* 167c).

Many have commented that the sophists' challenge to traditional Greek morality is mirrored in the postmodern challenge to the Enlightenment. As Roger Scruton observes, "many of today's gurus are sophists: Derrida, Foucault, Heidegger, Lyotard, Rorty, to name but five."[19] The celebrated classicist Bernard Knox has written,

> It is often said that the importance of Socrates in the history of Western thought is that he brought theory down from the skies, from cosmological speculation, to the human world, to the moral and political problems of mankind. But this was in fact the achievement of the Sophists, who created an education designed for the first great democracy. . . . It was Plato, of course, who made the word "Sophists" into a term of abuse and also, though this aspect of his work is seldom mentioned, tried to suppress the new humanities.[20]

But Knox's yang attitude to Plato, common in today's universities, fails to notice what I think explains history's millennia of preference for Socrates and Plato over the sophists. This is the yin element in their thought, not fully definable: an extra dimension to their thinking distinguishable by Socrates's reference to a guiding voice within him, at odds with his own thinking:

> Perhaps it may seem strange that I go about and interfere in other people's affairs to give this advice in private, but do not venture to come before your assembly and advise the state. But the reason for this, as you have heard me say at many times and places, is that something divine and spiritual [daimonion] comes to me [hoti moi theion ti kai daimonion gignetai phone, ὅτι μοι θεῖόν τι καὶ δαιμόνιον γίγνεται φωνή], the very thing which Meletus ridiculed in his indictment. I have had this from my childhood; it is a sort of voice that comes to me, and when it comes it always holds me back from what I am thinking of doing, but never urges me forward. This it is which opposes my engaging in politics. (*Apology* 31c–d)

Xenophon's slightly later account of Socrates's *daimonion* was that it was not the instruction but the divinity communicating it, and that this divinity urged him "to do," as well as "not to do," certain things (Xenophon, *Apology* 12, *Memorabilia* 1.1.4).

The skeptical agnosticism (yang) of the sophists is not known to have led to their persecution in Athens.[21] But the *daimonion*, or "spiritual something" (yin), that Socrates claimed to possess was seen, perhaps rightly, as a dangerous threat to the older civic religion based on the boisterous Olympian myths. This yang-yin difference was and remains hugely important.

For example, it underlay, I believe, the issue at stake in the 1971 debate about human nature between Noam Chomsky and Michel Foucault. In this debate, Foucault referred our sense of justice to the social struggle; and

Chomsky to some "highly organised and very restrictive schematism" within us, tending "towards the creation of a better society and also a better system of justice."[22]

It also anticipates the distinction the brilliant Chinese thinker Xu Jilin makes (in the words of Ian Johnson) between "two elements" of modern civilization: the defense of values and the pursuit of wealth and power. While China has assiduously pursued the latter, it has failed to engage with the former.

> Chinese today are like nineteenth-century Europeans, bursting with ambition, industrious and thrifty, full of greed and desire; they believe that the weak are meat for the strong and that only the apt survive—they are vastly different from traditional Chinese, who prized righteousness over profit and were content with moderation. What kind of victory is this?[23]

Xu's critique of a power-obsessed China also recalls the Platonic Socrates's critique of the transgressive pursuit of wealth and power by Athenian leaders (like Pericles). Socrates asked instead how Athens could be made not greater but better:

> We know of nobody who has shown himself a good statesman in this city of ours. . . . I consider [former statesmen] have shown themselves more service-able than those of our time, and more able to procure for the city the things she desired. But in diverting her desires another way instead of complying with them—in persuading or compelling her people to what would help them to be better . . . that is the only business of a good citizen [agathou politou, ἀγαθοῦ πολίτου]. But in providing ships and walls and arsenals, and various other things of the sort, I do grant you that they were cleverer than our leaders. (Plato, *Gorgias* 517b–c)[24]

His discomfort with new affluence is pervasive in this period. We see it again in Socrates's choice to refuse payment for his teaching, to live a life of poverty (penia, πενία; *Apology* 31c), go barefoot, and wear a simple cloak of Spartan austerity.[25]

We can think of both Socrates and Xu as minders who are trying to link the traditional past with the investigative future. In the *Euthyphro*, for example, we see Socrates defend the spiritual enlightenment of piety from the past with the intellectual enlightenment of free inquiry for the future. In like manner, Xu uses liberal notions of free inquiry to make a case for Confucian values which China has abandoned.[26] The cultural challenge he addresses is not specifically Chinese but global. It stems from the challenge to consensual piety (an accepted *tianxia*) from a rapidly expanding global environment, analogous to that of Athens in the fifth century BCE.

We see this discomfort with affluence and power again in Plato's ideal *Republic*, where the lower chrematistic class pursuing the acquisition of wealth is subordinated to the philosophic goal of making the city just (*Republic* 434c). This perspective is further reinforced by Plato's allegory of the cave, where most see shadows only and should be governed by those philosophers who through knowledge have seen the good (*Republic* 519c–520a).[27]

SOCRATES ON LOVE AND DIVINITY

The *Republic*, with its vision of enlightenment through intellectual knowledge, presents the yang Plato that I was taught at university. Only later did I learn that Xenophon and Plato each wrote a yin *Symposium* in which Socrates, having drunk a little wine but not too much, discoursed on how love also could transcend our realm of shadows.[28]

Both of these dialogues establish that Socrates could be a yin as well as a yang thinker. Plato's *Symposium* in particular is fascinating: it both shows Plato at his most brilliant and generative and simultaneously supplies evidence that even one of the greatest minds of Greek antiquity was less developed in some ways than that of an average rock musician today.

In Xenophon's more conventional *Symposium*, Socrates distinguishes between "Vulgar" (i.e., sexual) love and "Heavenly" (i.e., chaste) love (8.9–10).[29] The same distinction is made in Plato's *Symposium*, first by Pausanias (180d) and then in Socrates's report on his dialogue with Diotima, a priestess and sorceress. Diotima also distinguished between two kinds of love—of procreation and of being renowned—but love of a beautiful body was for her the beginning (as we saw in the last chapter) of a process where one rises to the love of true virtue.

Let us look more closely at Diotima's description of the lover's gradual steps to true virtue:

> Beginning from obvious beauties he must for the sake of that highest beauty be ever climbing aloft, as on the rungs of a ladder, from one to two, and from two to all beautiful bodies; from personal beauty he proceeds to beautiful observances, from observance to beautiful learning, and from learning at last to that particular study which is concerned with the beautiful itself and that alone; so that in the end he comes to know the very essence of beauty. (*Symposium* 211c–d)

In the end, "his contact is not with illusion but with truth (ate ouk eidolou ephatomeno, alla alethe; ἅτε οὐκ εἰδώλου ἐφαπτομένῳ, ἀλλὰ ἀληθῆ). So when he has begotten a true virtue (areten alethe, ἀρετὴν ἀληθῆ) and has reared it up, he is destined to win the friendship of Heaven; he, above all men, is immortal" (212a).

Diotima's account parallels very closely the escape of the philosopher from
the reflections in the cave to the vision of the good in the Republic:

> And at first he would most easily discern the shadows and, after that, the like-
> nesses or reflections [eidola, εἴδωλα] in water of men and other things, and later,
> the things themselves, and from these he would go on to contemplate the appear-
> ances in the heavens and heaven itself, more easily by night, looking at the light.
> ... "It is the duty of us, the founders, then," said I, "to compel the best natures to
> attain the knowledge which we pronounced the greatest, and to win to the vision
> of the good [idein te to agathon, ἰδεῖν τε τὸ ἀγαθὸν]. (*Republic* 518a, 519c)

What Diotima promises through love exceeds the reward to the philosopher
escaping the cave, especially because the latter's duty, like that of a bodhisat-
tva, is to return to those not liberated and harmonize the community (*Republic*
519c–520a). And yet Plato has Socrates endorse Diotima's remarks, going so
far as to call love "the best helper that our human nature can hope to find"
(*Symposium* 212b).

The exalted tone of the *Symposium* is broken at this point by the arrival of
Alcibiades, "very drunken and bawling loud." Alcibiades was an Athenian
general notorious for both his beauty and his perfidy, having in the war with
Sparta defected to the enemy. Plato has Socrates tell the assembly both that
he loves Alcibiades and that he fears his amorous frenzy (manian te kai phil-
erastian, μανίαν τε καὶ φιλεραστίαν).

Many have seen in this abrupt return to the realm of earthly love an
intended contrast in praise of the heavenly. But Hölderlin, amid the violence
of the French revolutionary wars, read it differently, as if Beauty had "at last"
transcended Wisdom:

> "Warum huldigst du, heiliger Sokrates,
> diesem Jünglinge stets?
> Kenntest du Größeres nicht?
> Warum siehet mit Liebe,
> wie auf Götter, dein Aug' auf ihn?"

> Wer das Tiefste gedacht, liebt das Lebendigste,
> hohe Jugend versteht, wer in die Welt geblickt,
> und es neigen die Weisen
> oft am Ende zu Schönem sich.[30]

> "Why do you favor, holy Socrates,
> Always this youth? Have you no greater aim?
> Why do you fix, with love,
> As on gods, your eyes on him?"

Who most deeply has thought, loves the most living,
High virtue discerns, who has beheld the world,
And the wisest bow down
Often at last to the Beautiful.

If I am permitted (at this point I am ninety-four), I hope to write how Hölderlin is a guide for those today who are seeking to overcome the limits of modernism.

Meanwhile, another analogy is with Czeslaw Milosz's argument that our inborn search for an "eternal moment" (or "a mystical state . . . *beyond the boundaries of speech*")[31] should not be pursued by withdrawing from our present imperfect reality but by immersing ourselves in it.[32]

THE GREATNESS AND LIMITATION OF
PLATO AND THE *SYMPOSIUM*

Great authors in the interstitial or cusp eras between pivotal shifts, like Plato, Virgil, Dante, or Blake, tend both to anticipate the next shift and to be hobbled by the past one. In the case of Plato, we can say that he is the only philosopher, perhaps the only author, whose name, spelled without a capital (as in "platonic love"), has entered everyday discourse in the English language.[33] (In contrast, according to the *OED*, "Socratic," "Ambrosian," "Dantesque," "Marxist," and "Freudian" all still require capitals.)

It is impossible to overestimate the generative influence of Plato's dialogues on subsequent Western intellectual development. Alfred North Whitehead once noted that "the safest general characterization of the European philosophical tradition is that it consists of a series of footnotes to Plato."[34] Plato and his disciple Aristotle have been the poles of a yin-yang dialectic through subsequent ages, with Aristotle providing structure for stable systems in power, as notably in the *Summa Theologica* of St. Thomas Aquinas, and Plato inspiring the disruptive energy to challenge those stable systems.

With this in mind, I looked to see if Plato helped inspire Copernicus (d. 1543) in his challenge to the medieval model of the geocentric Aristotelian-Ptolemaic universe. And I learned that André Goddu indeed believes that "Plato's advice in *Parmenides* about how to treat hypotheses provided Copernicus with methodological guidelines."[35] (Goddu adds that "I also think it likely that [Cardinal] Bessarion's *In calumniatorem Platonis* inspired Copernicus to appreciate Plato's dialectical method of inquiry."[36])

The same generativity can be attributed to Plato's *Symposium* in particular. In Western thought at least, I think it is safe to say that Plato is the first to have acknowledged in yang or left-brain discourse the importance of love at a higher level. His notion of the *daimonion*, as "halfway between god and mortal . . . interpreting and transmitting . . . the things of gods to men" (202e), helped normalize and secularize a notion of inspiration that has gradually become commonplace, from Dante to Czeslaw Milosz.

Having said all this, I believe that, after we consider the *Argonautica* and the Song of Songs in the next chapter—two great works following Plato's by only a century or so—we will see more clearly that Plato, in contrast, was comparatively hidebound, at least in one respect. This was the disparaging attention he gives to heterosexual love.

In this respect, Plato is a man of his age. Only men converse in the *Symposium* (a flute girl, who arrives as was customary to entertain with music, is told to go away and play to "the women who are within"[37]).

Even the climactic speech of Diotima is spoken by Socrates, and she, like the others, praises pederasty over heterosex:

> So when a man by the right method of boy-loving ascends from these particulars and begins to descry that beauty [hotan de tis apo toned dia to orthos paiderastein epanion ekaste to kalon archetai kathoran, ὅταν δή τις ἀπὸ τῶνδε διὰ τὸ ὀρθῶς παιδεραστεῖν ἐπανιὼν ἐκεῖνο τὸ καλὸν ἄρχηται καθορᾶν], he is almost able to lay hold of the final secret. Such is the right approach, or induction to love-matters [ta erotica, τὰ ἐρωτικὰ]. (211b–c)

An earlier speech given to Pausanias, and unrefuted, is more blatantly sexist:

> Does anyone doubt that [Aphrodite] is double? Surely there is the elder, of no mother born, but daughter of Heaven, whence we name her Heavenly; while the younger was the child of Zeus and Dione, and her we call Popular [pandemon, Πάνδημον; i.e., "of all the people, common, vulgar"]. . . . This is the Love we see in the meaner sort of men; who, in the first place, love women as well as boys; secondly, where they love, they are set on the body more than the soul; but the other Love springs from the Heavenly goddess who, firstly, partakes not of the female but only of the male; and secondly, is the elder, untinged with wantonness: wherefore those who are inspired by this Love betake them to the male, in fondness for what has the robuster nature and a larger share of mind. (180d–181c)[38]

In practice, both Aphrodite Pandemos and Aphrodite Urania were worshiped traditionally in Athens as equals; the demeaning of the popular Aphrodite here (which as we saw was repeated later by Xenophon) is Plato's innovation:

> Pausanias's description of the love associated with Aphrodite Pandemos as dedicated only to sensual pleasure and therefore directed indifferently to women

and boys, and that associated with the Ouranian Aphrodite as "altogether male" and dedicated to the education of the soul of the beloved is actually an innovation—for Aphrodite Ourania was served in Corinth by prostitutes and Aphrodite Pandemos was the goddess as worshipped by the whole community.[39]

Like the male and female voices in Socrates's long monologue, their author Plato can be described as having two minds here. On the one hand he gives the climactic words of the *Symposium* to Diotima. This may be out of respect for the authority of Sappho, for in the *Phaedrus* (235c), Plato has Socrates acknowledge "the beautiful [kales] Sappho" as one of two influences, along with "the wise [sophou] Anacreon," on his thinking.

But on the other hand, as if to reinforce Diotima's authority in this all-male *Symposium*, Plato has her speak like a man. There has long been a scholarly debate about whether or not Diotima (the name means "honored [or honoring] Zeus") was, like the other speakers, a real contemporary of Plato's in Athens. We can judge very clearly the Diotima who speaks in the dialogue, however: she is Plato in drag.

Platonic love is remembered for its exaltation of spiritual over sexual love; its exaltation of pederasty over heterosex we can rightly attribute to the limitations of Greek culture and even language.[40] It is no more specific to the speaker himself than was Aristotle's assertion that some are by nature marked out as slaves (*Politics* 1254a21–24). But today the exaltation (as well as enjoyment) of heterosexual love is as much part of most people's second nature as is the repudiation of defenses of slavery.

Indeed, only a century or so later, one of the world's greatest exaltations ever of heterosex, the Song of Songs, would be written. It will be time then to consider the difference in consciousness between Plato, who wrote in the dominant Greek language of Hegel's *Herr*, and the anonymous author of the Song, who wrote in the subservient language of Hebrew.

Chapter Five

Yang and Yin in Hellas: The Post-Socratic Philosophers

THE EVOLUTION FROM CITY TO METROPOLIS

A major development preceding the Second Pivotal Shift in the West was the permanent subordination of the old Hellenic polis, after the brief but irreversible empire building of Alexander (323 BCE), to the new Hellenistic metropolis. The division of his empire among his generals led to successor Hellenistic capitals for the Seleucids of Persia, the Antigonids of Macedonia, and the Attalids of Pergamon. But none of these cities could compare with the metropolis of Alexandria, the capital of the Greek Ptolemaic Empire in Egypt. It flourished partly by conquest and tribute, but also by trade with the other new great empires in India and even China.[1]

The capital of each of these empires became a large multiethnic metropolis. In particular, the Han capital Chang'an (today Xi'an), the Mauryan capital Pataliputra (now Patna), and the Ptolemaic capital of Alexandria (founded 331 BCE) became multinational trade marts and were soon the largest cities in the world, with populations estimated from 150,000 to 400,000.[2]

All three cities were enlarged culturally by influences from each other. Buddhism was spread with the missionaries of King Aśoka (d. 232 BCE) to Egypt and also Chang'an, where Buddhist temples (one of which still stands intact) were eventually the tallest buildings in the city.[3] (Aśoka's missionaries to Egypt have often been linked, controversially, to the rise of the Essenes and eventually of Christian monasticism.[4])

This change in urban milieu was reflected in a change in modes of thinking. The polis-oriented philosophy of Socrates and Plato, which we saw was an exaptation for new functions of rhetoric in the polis, became the gateway to a whole new noetic class of ethical philosophers in fourth-century classical Greece: Diogenes the Cynic, Zeno of Citium the Stoic, Epicurus the Epicurean, and Pyrrho the antecedent of Skepticism.

At the same time, an influential new noetic class emerged also in Alexandria, a small class, however, not of philosophers but of poets— Theocritus, Callimachus, and Apollonius Rhodius (third century BCE). I shall argue that all these philosophers and these poets, who wrote about individuals rather than affairs of state, were influential for over a half millennium. In particular, the philosophy of Zeno was Latinized by Cicero (d. 43 BCE) and Marcus Aurelius (d. 180 CE), that of Epicurus by Lucretius (d. 55 BCE).

The bucolics of Theocritus and the feminized epic of Apollonius gave a determining shape to the *Eclogues* and *Aeneid* of Virgil. In particular, the coldhearted Aeneas and the overly passionate Dido in *Aeneid* 4 are both stereotypes where Virgil imitated the Euripidean figures of Jason and Medea in Apollonius's *Argonautica*. And the elegiacs of Callimachus, a genre not to be confused with the modern genre of elegy, were extensively used and developed by Ovid.

I will claim, however, that while these philosophers and poets were both influential in Rome, the poets in particular were more generative. The influence of the Greco-Roman philosophers survives today among intellectuals, our modern minders, but the Romans' philosophy is remembered as more derivative than original.

Perhaps the most generative of the Greeks was the least yang philosopher of them all—Pyrrho, who as we shall see has been alleged to have met Buddhists in Gandhara (northwest Pakistan). Scholars attest to the influence of Pyrrho on the skepticism of David Hume (d. 1776), and through Hume in turn on that most generative scientist, Charles Darwin (d. 1882).[5]

The most original pagan philosopher of the Roman Empire, Plotinus (d. 270 CE), was by contrast born (of uncertain race) in the Egyptian delta, studied and settled in Alexandria, and wrote in Greek; his so-called Neoplatonism has continued to evolve in Christian Europe through the innovations of the fifteenth-century Florentine Academy to Rosicrucianism and present-day theosophy.

Perhaps even more influential has been the influence of Plato and Plotinus on the Muslim mysticism of Sufism and the Jewish mysticism of the Kabbalah.

> There are extraordinary parallels between the Kabbalistic notion of *Ein-sof* and the Platonic "Form of the Good," and, especially, the Neoplatonic "One," which was conceived by Plotinus and his followers in "negative theological" terms as absolutely transcendental, ineffable, and devoid of all predication.[6]

However, scholars of Judaism have recently suggested that Plotinus not only influenced Jewish thinkers but was influenced by them. They argue that the notion of *unio mystica*, so important to both Plotinus and to medieval Kabbalists like Abraham Abulafia (d. 1292), may in fact derive from a Platonic gloss in Greek by the Alexandrine Jewish philosopher Philo (d. 45 CE) on Genesis 2:24 ("Therefore shall a man leave his father and his mother, and shall cleave unto his wife: and they shall be one flesh").[7]

An influence like that of Plotinus, which continues not just to replicate but to evolve, is what I mean by generative. And I hope to show in the next two chapters that the influence of the post-Socratic poets of Alexandria, in contrast to the post-Socratic philosophers of Greece, was more generative.

More audaciously, I shall propose that the Song of Songs, though written in Hebrew by a Jew who was probably a native of Judaea, shows enough similarity to earlier Egyptian love poetry, as well as to both Theocritus and Apollonius, to be considered a poem in the Alexandrian tradition—and by far the most generative of them all.

My argument, if persuasive, will lead to two questions:

1. Why, in the fourth century, are *all* of the memorable philosophers from mainland Greece, and nearly *all* of the memorable known poets, inhabitants of Alexandria?
2. Why are the generative writers from this period, as opposed to the merely influential ones, all from Alexandria—none of them from Greece, which had been the site of so much poetic and philosophic generativity just one century earlier?

The answer to both questions, I shall argue, will return us to the distinction Hegel made between the consciousness of the servant (*Knecht*) as opposed to the relatively nonconscious master (*Herr*). But the second question, rephrased more narrowly as, "Why did Greek creativity decline so precipitously after Socrates and Plato?" is one that returns us to the insight of both Hegel and Nietzsche, that Socrates and Plato both wrote at what they called a "turning point" in world history.

A DIGRESSION: LOCAL CULTURE, YIN-YANG CULTURE, AND ETHOGENY

A digression here: The Greco-Jewish culture of Philo and Plotinus in multicultural Alexandria, so clearly different from that of the predominantly yang philosophers in this chapter whose culture was almost purely Greek, shows features that in the next chapter we shall explore in the Song of Songs. It is a moment to reflect on the double meaning of the word *culture* itself. The relevant definition of it in the *OED* is "The distinctive ideas, customs, social behaviour, products, or way of life of a *particular* nation, society, people, or period" (emphasis added); and many modern thinkers, such as Xu Jilin, contrast the *culture* of disparate societies with the more universal city-generated civilization of the world as a whole:

> What China hasn't grasped, Xu writes, is the distinction between civilization and culture. The new world civilization, he argues, embraces common values for all of humanity. Culture, by contrast, is specific, but need not come into conflict with those common values—the concept of rights, for example, can be found in Chinese tradition. Xu holds that China's behavior resembles that of nineteenth-century Germany, which believed that its *Kultur* was superior to Anglo-Saxon *Zivilisation*, a view that led German elites to justify their country's slide toward militarism and fascism.[8]

But in my view, the asymmetry I noted earlier between yang and yin—that yang is what is discernible to reason and the left brain and yin is what is not—is true here of their analogue terms *civilization* and *culture*. Just as *yin* can mean either (a) what is opposed to yang or (b) what embraces both yin and yang, so *culture* can either mean what is local and subordinate to the spreading influence of rational civilization, or in some larger indefinable way it can refer to a larger synthesis of both local culture *and* civilization.

It is the evolution of culture (or ethos) in this larger sense, illustrated here by the fruitful interaction of Greek and Jewish local influences, that, along with the concomitant evolution of our human "second nature" or presentational selves, that is the subject of this book. It is, in short, what I mean by human ethogeny.

According to the Liddell and Scott Greek Lexicon, the Greek word *paideia* (παιδεία; from *pais*, παίς, child), which originally meant "childhood" and then "training and education," was in this very period first used by Democritus (d. 361 BCE) in the relevant sense of training's "result, mental culture, learning, education." In his monumental study *Paideia*, Werner Jaeger showed how "through the changes initiated by Socrates the concept and meaning of paideia took on a broader and deeper spiritual significance and that its value for man was raised to the highest point."[9]

The ancient Greeks, in short, developed a clear notion of individual culture. I believe, however, that there was as yet no clear idea of culture in the larger sense above. (According to Liddell and Scott, the modern Greek word for collective culture, *politismos* [πολῑτισμός], occurs first with Diogenes Laertius [third century CE], where it is translated as "administration of public affairs.")

I have seen fit to digress here in this way because I believe the two senses of culture, along with their relations to distinctions between yang and yin, are well illustrated here at this point.

THE POST-SOCRATIC EVOLUTION OF
YANG MIND AND YIN MIND (POETRY)

Both Hegel and Nietzsche, seeking the origins and limits of eighteenth-century Enlightenment thinking, saw Socratic thinking as a revolutionary turning point (or as we might say, pivot) in our noetic evolution. Hegel saw as progressive Socrates's insight, which he acknowledged learning from Anaxagoras, that "Nature is an embodiment of Reason; that it is unchangeably subordinate to universal laws." For Hegel, "such a thought," clarified by Socrates, "makes an epoch in the annals of human intelligence."[10]

On the other hand, for Nietzsche, a far more profound critic of the Enlightenment than Hegel, Socrates's influence here was detrimental:

> Socrates corrupts mankind by teaching that the world is rational and that reason should rule in the soul and in the city. Socrates' dialectical way shows the traditional gods and laws of all nations to be inconsistent and therefore defective. By elevating reason, Socrates succeeds in subordinating the nobler irrational instincts to the baser instinct of reason ([Dannhauser,] pp. 212–13). While characterizing Socrates in this manner, Nietzsche often seems to condemn Socrates.[11]

In *The Birth of Tragedy*, Nietzsche's first, and for me his best, least problematic book, Nietzsche indeed condemns both Euripides and his friend Socrates for splitting into separate components the Dionysian (yin) and Apollonian (yang) unity of earlier Greek Pre-Socratic philosophers and poetical tragedians. Thanks to Euripides and Socrates, the deeper truth of the Pre-Socratics, he believed, was replaced by mere philosophy and science, that is, the "Apollonian clarity that obstructs access to the Dionysian vision of the world."[12] This Dionysian vision is what Nietzsche later called "gay science" (fröhliche Wissenschaft) (from the Provençal *gai saber*, the art of poetry), a uniting, as Heidegger observed, of passion with reason.

For Nietzsche as for Hegel, Socrates is the "one turning point and vortex of so-called world history."[13] Very important in my own analysis is this recognition of the dialectical shift represented by the passage from the fifth-century dialogues of the tragedies and Plato to the fourth-century expository philosophy, or yang mind, of the Stoics, Epicureans, and Skeptics that I shall touch on in a moment.

But I see this as a noetic shift in the history of ideas, not a pivotal shift in society comparable to that of the spreading influence of Christ's Sermon on the Mount. In this it is comparable to the noetic dialectic of the yang-minded Hegel and the yin-minded Nietzsche in the nineteenth century, both of whom, in my view, underestimated the poetic complexity of Socrates and Plato.

When I came to recognize a noetic shift in this interstitial or cusp period between the First and Second Pivotal Shifts, this complicated the pivotal shift sequence as I first outlined it. But I then saw that succeeding interstitial or cusp periods between later pivotal shifts were also accompanied by noetic shifts—Augustine in the fourth century, Bede and Alcuin in the eighth, the Provençal poets and Dante in the twelfth and thirteenth, and then (among many others) Newton, Rousseau, Hölderlin, Wordsworth, and Marx. When I acknowledged this, the dialectical interplay of mental (noetic) and social (cultural) development became more clearly defined for me.

However, I see the turning point attested to by Hegel and Nietzsche as less climactic than they presented. I shall argue in this chapter that, after the yang-yin equilibrium in Socrates and Plato, there was continuous as well as disruptive development in the cultural evolution of the West in the fourth and third centuries BCE.

1. There were yin elements in the yang philosophers of classical Greece: Zeno of Citium the Stoic (d. 263 BCE; not to be confused with the Pre-Socratic Zeno of Elea), Epicurus (d. 269 BCE), and Pyrrho the Skeptic (d. ca. 270 BCE). Recently some scholars have even argued that, thanks to a cultural contact made by Alexander's army, one or more of these philosophers may even reflect the influence of the Buddha.
2. These philosophers were not only complemented but overshadowed by the more generative yin-yang poets associated with Alexandria—Theocritus (d. after 260 BCE), Callimachus (d. ca. 240 BCE), Apollonius Rhodius (third century BCE), and above all the anonymous author of the Song of Songs.

IS THERE A CASE FOR BUDDHIST INFLUENCE IN POST-ALEXANDRIAN GREECE?

Two generations ago some scholars speculated that Plato, who died before Alexander's journey to India, developed his ideas about the reincarnation of souls from Buddhist teachings; but this notion is now often discredited. However, there is now emerging support for the possibility that Buddhism reached the West through the philosophers who are said to have accompanied Alexander to Taxila in Gandhara (Pakistan) in 326 BCE.

Two contemporary scholars in particular attach great importance to this meeting. Richard Stoneman, in *The Greek Experience of India: From Alexander to the Indo-Greeks*, claimed that

> Pyrrho of Elis also accompanied the expedition and, according to one report at least, sought out the company of Gymnosophists. After Alexander's death in 323 BC, Pyrrho returned to Greece and became a teacher of the doctrines that collectively bear his name, Pyrrhonism, also referred to as Skepticism. Pyrrho's radical mistrust of sense perception and rejection of all dogmatism and claims to knowledge have often been traced to Indian teachings. . . . [Richard] Stoneman is . . . supportive of a Buddhist origin for Pyrrhonism.[14]

Christopher Beckwith makes an even broader estimate of Pyrrho's spread of Buddhist influence in Hellas:

> Returning to Greece after Alexander's death, [Pyrrho] became a teacher of ethics, specifically of the way to escape suffering, *pathe*, and to achieve *apatheia*, "freedom from suffering" [the goal of Stoic philosophy], and hence *ataraxia*, "untroubledness, calm" [the goal of Epicurean philosophy].[15]

Such speculations are welcome after centuries of a narrow classicist focus on classical Greek texts at the expense of their cultural context. But most of the relevant data has not survived, and I suspect that these scholars, especially Beckwith, may be claiming too much from the little that remains.[16]

Both scholars, for example, point to Pyrrho's mendicant and peripatetic cultivation of poverty. Stoneman even speculates that Pyrrho's solitary, wandering way of life after he left India—including a curious habit of murmuring to himself—came about in imitation of Buddhist ways. Noting that Pyrrho explained his murmurs as a way of "training to be good," Stoneman writes, "This looks suspiciously like a description of a man engaged in meditation, murmuring a mantra."[17]

But, as we already saw, the sophists were also peripatetic, and Socrates chose to live a life of poverty (*Apology* 31c). Diogenes the Cynic (d. 323 BCE) was already making a virtue of mendicant poverty before Alexander's entry into India.

In general, the recent increase of wealth, and disparity of wealth, was associated with the subordination of the old polis to the new imperial reality. As later in the declining years of imperial Rome, the possession of wealth was now problematic, and some minders chose to eschew it.

IMPERIAL PATRONAGE AND THE EXPANSION
OF GREEK CONSCIOUSNESS

The new imperial environment meant a new status for the Greek author. He was now less a citizen than a courtier:

> Unlike in fifth-century Athens, the creative artist in Alexandria did not have to rely on popular support and public visibility: instead Alexandrian literati, mostly Greek outlanders with ties just to the court, constituted a court-sponsored enclave.[18]

(We have already seen that China, with the consolidation of the Han dynasty by Han Wudi in the same period, also saw a similar shift to a court-supported noetic class of scholar-officials, also known in the West as literati.)

To a lesser degree, the same shift involved other Hellenistic capitals. Theocritus and Callimachus were supported by Ptolemy II Philadelphus in Alexandria and wrote panegyrics to him. Theocritus was rewarded for celebrating the incestuous pharaonic marriage of Ptolemy II to his older sister Arsinoë. Zeno of Citium, even though he settled his new school of Stoics in Athens, was still supported, along with other philosophers, by the Macedonian monarch Antigonus II Gonatas in Pella.

In this expanded realm of consciousness, Greeks, dominant in the West, began to think of themselves as inhabitants not just of a polis but of a larger *oecumene* (οἰκουμένη): the known, inhabited world. Diogenes the Cynic is alleged to have said, when asked where he came from, "I am a citizen of the world [cosmopolites, κοσμοπολίτης]."[19] The Greek language itself evolved from a multitude of local dialects (Attic, Ionic, etc.) into a new Koine Greek, shared by Greeks in Europe, Asia, and Africa.

A new kind of literature emerged to record this expanded consciousness. We can see the shift by contrasting the *political* concerns of Socrates and Plato (d. ca. 347 BCE) with the *ethical* concerns of Zeno and Epicurus. In the fifth century BCE, both Socrates and Plato served as critics of the dominant Athenian mindset. But they did so as concerned citizens of the polis; both, for example, served in the Athenian army.

In marked contrast, Zeno of Citium was a Phoenician from Cyprus by birth and a resident alien in Athens. Far from being a citizen-soldier, he is said to have been first a wealthy international trader. Zeno's *Republic*, a rebuttal to Plato's *Republic*, has been called the first cosmopolitan text; it summarized the ethical Stoicism that later served as the ideology of the pagan Roman Empire. Though it is now lost, it was apparently cosmopolitan in outlook, saying that all human beings are our fellow citizens, having equal rights. It initiated the idea of natural law, as a product not of the polis but of the cosmos.[20]

And its concern was the topic of *arete* or goodness—no longer the heroic *arete* of a Homeric warrior (*arete* is cognate with the war god Ares, just as the Latin equivalent *virtus* derives from the word *vir*, "man"), nor the civic *arete* of Plato's "good citizen," but goodness pure and simple, like natural law, a feature of the cosmos.

In Zeno's utopian *Republic*, as reconstructed by a modern scholar,

> Men and women were completely equal in society's eyes and there was no injustice because all actions proceeded from reason. There were no laws necessary because there was no crime and, because everyone's needs were taken care of in the same way that animals are in nature, there was no greed, nor covetousness nor hatred of any kind. Love governed all things and everyone living in this cosmopolis understood they had what they needed and wanted for nothing more.[21]

Unquestionably the Athenian Stoics developed the concept of a *kosmopolitês* (κοσμοπολίτης), a citizen of the world (*kosmos*).[22] But they never fully effaced the older Greek contrast between a Hellene and a barbarian. Rather, they tended to imagine a cosmopolis in which Athenian virtues would be acknowledged worldwide.

Stoics as a rule extended the notion of human equality to include women and slaves, rejecting Aristotle's view that some people are slaves "by nature" and are better ruled by others (*Politics* 1254a21–24). According to the Greek biographer Diogenes Laertius (third century CE), Stoics regarded the ownership of slaves, by either capture or purchase, as morally wrong (*phaule*, φαύλη; *Lives of the Eminent Philosophers* 7.121–22).

Stoicism at one point became the prevailing ideology among the Roman ruling class and was espoused by the emperor Marcus Aurelius (d. 180 CE). Nevertheless, it never produced anything like a movement to press for slavery's abolition. Likewise,

> although the Stoics throughout history asserted that women possessed the same capacity for virtue as men, they never inferred from that or any other premise that women deserved treatment equal to that of men in any sphere except perhaps education. More importantly, they never argued that women should participate in civic life.[23]

Something similar can be said about the other dominant philosophical school, the Epicureanism of Epicurus (d. 269 BCE). Although most of his works have been lost, we know that, in searching for the best means to a happy life free from fear (*ataraxia*, untroubledness), he sought natural rather than theological explanations for both *moral behavior*, which was naturally rewarded by freedom from guilt (stories of punishment in the afterlife he thought ridiculous), and

natural phenomena, such as earthquakes (which he attributed to the movements of atoms, not the whims of the gods).[24]

Epicurus was not an atheist; he believed that gods existed and that humans could have awareness of them. But he regarded them as perfect, remote from our world, and uninterested in human prayers or behavior. He totally rejected the traditional legends of the anthropomorphic Olympian gods with their lusts and jealousies.[25]

The ideas of both Zeno and Epicurus were recovered in the Renaissance, helped to inspire the Enlightenment, and continue to be espoused today as integral to modernism.[26] But while they prevailed intellectually among the Roman elite for half a millennium, they did very little to change the social structure and religion of Roman society as a whole.

In the end, of course, they lost out, for almost a millennium, to a different kind of outlook, that of Christianity. We can, however, see Stoic influence in the famous dictum of St. Paul, a Hellenized Jew: "There is neither Jew nor Greek, there is neither bond nor free, there is neither male nor female: for ye are all one in Christ Jesus" (Gal. 3:28).

But St. Paul also argued in 1 Corinthians that both the blind authority of the earliest Judaism and the yang wisdom of the Greek philosophers fell short of the yin-yang unity of Christ's teaching:

[17] For Christ sent me not to baptize, but to preach the gospel: not with wisdom of words, lest the cross of Christ should be made of none effect.

[18] For the preaching of the cross is to them that perish foolishness; but unto us which are saved it is the power of God.

[19] For it is written, I will destroy the wisdom of the wise, and will bring to nothing the understanding of the prudent.

[Note that St. Paul here is echoing Isaiah 29:14:

"Therefore, behold, I will proceed to do a marvellous work among this people, even a marvellous work and a wonder:

For the wisdom of their wise men shall perish, And the understanding of their prudent men shall be hidden."]

[20] Where is the wise? where is the scribe? where is the disputer of this world? hath not God made foolish the wisdom of this world?

[21] For after that in the wisdom of God the world by wisdom knew not God, it pleased God by the foolishness of preaching to save them that believe.

[22] For the Jews require a sign, and the Greeks seek after wisdom:

[23] But we preach Christ crucified, unto the Jews a stumblingblock, and unto the Greeks foolishness;

[24] But unto them which are called, both Jews and Greeks, Christ the power of God, and the wisdom of God. (1 Cor. 1:17–24)

I hope to show that St. Paul's admixture of Judaic irrationality and Greek wisdom echoes the cultural achievements of Alexandria and the Song of Songs.

Chapter Six

Yin and Yang in Alexandria: The Song of Songs

to fault enlightenment
>   for its lack of kinship with the dark
>   is to think critically once again

—Scott, Minding the Darkness, 14

THE GRECO-JUDAEAN-EGYPTIAN
CULTURE OF ALEXANDRIA

In all of the post-Alexandrian cities of Hellas, the public language was Greek. But Alexandria, in contrast, was multicultural as well as multiethnic. At least three languages were used by its "mixed population of natives, settlers, and itinerants: Egyptians, Jews, slaves of various ethnicities, as well as diverse Greeks."[1]

Greek was the official language in Alexandria but a limited one. Somewhat like Anglo-French[2] in the Middle Ages, it was the language of occupiers, used for government business, and by those dealing with the occupiers. But in the streets, one would also hear the prevailing Demotic Egyptian of the masses and also an intermediate class of Jews speaking Aramaic.[3]

Egyptians, though mostly undocumented in this era, were probably the largest element of the population. However, it is probable that the well-organized Jewish community in Alexandria, which grew in time to be the largest Jewish community in antiquity, with its own *politeuma* or self-government, eventually outnumbered the Greeks.

At least one of the city's five divisions was reserved for Jews, who had been arriving in Egypt, often voluntarily, from as early as the destruction of the kingdom of Judah in 587 BCE (cf. 2 Kings 25:26, Jer. 43:7).[4] The Hellenized Jew Philo (d. ca. 50 CE) wrote in *Against Flaccus* that in his day the Jews of Egypt numbered no less than a million. The total population of Egypt in this era has been estimated at from 3 to 4.5 million, of whom Greeks (in another shaky estimate) constituted from 5 to 10 percent (i.e., from 150 to 450 thousand).[5]

What matters here is less the relative numbers than the central fact that in Alexandria, two powerful literate cultures, for the first time in Western history, were surviving, coexisting, and interacting in the same relatively peaceful environment.[6] Over 90 percent of the Egyptians, in contrast, were illiterate, and the quite sparse literary heritage in Demotic Egyptian from this era is said to be remembered for three minor antimonarchic and apocalyptic texts: the Oracle of the Lamb, the Oracle of the Potter, and the Demotic Chronicle.[7]

The chief literature of Ptolemaic Alexandria taught today is the work of three Greek poets, none of them native to the city. Theocritus (d. after 260 BCE), a native of Sicily (possibly Syracuse), initiated the genre of pastoral that led to imitations by such authors as Virgil and Milton. Callimachus (d. ca. 240 BCE), a native of Cyrene in Libya, initiated the genre of elegiacs that were so popular later in Rome. Apollonius Rhodius (third century BCE), from the island of Rhodes, created the genre of romanticized (i.e., feminized) epic that, directly or indirectly, influenced such later works as Virgil's *Aeneid* and Dante's *Comedy.*

For these Greek contributions alone, Alexandria would occupy a central place in this stage of cultural development or ethogeny. But I see the same limitation in them that I noted earlier in the achievements of Zeno and Epicurus. All of these relatively yang products of the dominant Greek culture were ultimately far less influential in human history than the Gospel accounts in Greek of Jesus, an impoverished Jewish *tekton* or woodworker (Mark 6:3).[8]

Meanwhile, as I argued in chapter 3, the radical breaks with tradition in the Second Pivotal Shift, represented by first the Essenes and then Christianity, were anticipated and prepared for by the radically innovative yin-yang prosody of the Song of Songs. I wish here to strengthen the case that the Song was a product of Alexandrine Greco-Judaean culture by showing the connections of the Song to ancient Egyptian love poetry on the one hand and to both Theocritus and Apollonius on the other.

THE STATUS OF JEWS IN THE HELLENISTIC MIDDLE EAST

To appreciate the complex status of Jews in Egypt and elsewhere, let us consider what life could be like for occupied peoples under the Ptolemies (as under other rulers and occupiers). According to the monumental universal history of Diodorus Siculus (*Bibliotheca historica*, ca. 60–30 BCE),

> Ptolemy [I] son of Lagus had in 312 taken severe measures against the native populations in Cyprus and northern Syria. These included the destruction of cities and deportations ([Diodorus Siculus,] XIX.79.4–6). The inhabitants of Mallus in Cilicia were even sold into slavery, and the region was pillaged (79.6). The concurrent violent struggle in Cyrene (79.1–3) indicates that the occupied population was outraged over its treatment by Ptolemy. As to Coile Syria and Phoenicia, it is reported that immediately after the battle of Gaza Ptolemy won over the Phoenician cities, partly by persuasion, partly by besieging them (85.5). On his retreat a few months later, in 311, he razed the four "most important cities"—Acre, Jaffa, Samaria, and Gaza (93.7).[9]

As the Bible records, the Egyptian oppression of Coile Syria (including Jerusalem and Palestine) dated back to the Battle of Megiddo in 609 BCE, when Pharaoh Necho II defeated and killed King Josiah and converted Judah into a client state paying exorbitant tribute (2 Kings 23:29–35). The subsequent destruction of Jerusalem and the First Temple by Babylonia in 587 BCE was only one of an endless series of calamities in which Jewish history was often a footnote to the larger conflicts between Egypt, Assyria, Babylonia, and later Macedonia and Rome.

Even the brief quasi-independent Jewish Hasmonean kings ("Maccabees," 167–37 BCE) became in the end proxies for the Parthian Empire, until they were overthrown in 37 BCE by the Roman client Herod. Taxation to pay for all these wars left most of the Jews of the homeland more and more oppressed.

But this was not at all the condition of the Jews in Alexandria under Ptolemy II Philadelphus (d. 246 BCE). While the Jews in the homeland suffered under successive invasions, taxations, and punitive repressions of revolts, most of the Jews of Alexandria led a relatively wealthy, calm life, neither dominant nor repressed.[10] (Babylonian Jews in this period were also numerous and wealthy; like the Jews of Alexandria, they sent large amounts of silver and gold to the Temple in Jerusalem.[11]) Simon Schama tells us that

> in the [Egyptian] upper country Jews frequently occur as tax-collectors: many were soldiers, on garrison service or in the field army, and many others were engaged in agriculture. At Alexandria the Jews seem mostly to have been

occupied in commerce or industry, as merchants or tradespeople, as artisans, jewelers, smiths, and so forth.[12]

Jews as well as Greeks came to Egypt as occupying soldiers. The substantial fifth-century Jewish military settlement at Elephantine on the upper Nile was established under Persian occupation.[13] According to Schama, it was this

> Hellenistic-Jewish world that invented the synagogue—created to serve the needs of Jews who lived far from Jerusalem . . . in Cyrenaica, in Krokodilopolis, Schedia . . . Alexandria . . . Sparta.[14]

Like Plato's Academy, the synagogue was a home for a culture outside that of the larger city. But while the Academy was still part of the dominant Greek culture, the synagogue preserved an alien and subservient Jewish one. We see this subservience in Egyptian synagogue dedication stones routinely thanking Ptolemies II or III, the oldest synagogue fragments found anywhere in the world. (Like the word *synagogue* itself, they are in Greek.) But the Jews of the synagogues of Egypt were relatively privileged compared to those in Palestine, successively dominated and taxed by the Babylonians, Persians, Seleucid Greeks, and Romans.

In this period, different strains of Jewish literature developed, ranging from pro-Hellenic to anti-Hellenic. At one extreme were syncretists like Aristobulus (fl. 181–124 BCE) and Philo (15 BCE–45 AD), both of Alexandria, both writing in Greek, who maintained that celebrated Greek thinkers, like Plato, had acquired most of their wisdom from ancient Jewish sources.[15]

Meanwhile, Jews outside Egypt, supported by the other great Jewish diaspora capital, Babylon, developed a culture and literature, some of it in Aramaic, that tended to be anti-Hellenic. The best examples of this literature are the four books of Maccabees, describing how Hellenistic suppression of Jewish law led to a successful (if largely fictionalized) revolt.

These two cultures overlapped and interacted, partly because (it is important to recognize) the relative wealth of the Alexandrine Jews made them a presence in Jerusalem as well.

> A certain Nicanor of Alexandria offered the Temple the most famous of its portals, that of the Sanctuary itself on the East. Long after the destruction of the sanctuary, the Talmud still evokes with amazement the miraculous circumstances by which this portal escaped a shipwreck when it crossed from Alexandria. The children of the donor were themselves buried in the Holy City.[16]

This strength of the Greco-Hellenic culture is reflected in a significant paradox. In Jewish practice today, the victory of the Maccabees is celebrated annually at Chanukah, just as the Jews of the eastern diaspora are remembered at Purim; but nothing is remembered of Jewish experience in Alexandria. Nevertheless, when the twenty-four-book canon of the Hebrew Bible (Tanakh) was established after the Temple's destruction, the two Hellenized books of the Song of Songs and Ecclesiastes were included.[17] The largely fictional books of Maccabees, celebrating a military victory of the Jews over Hellenization, were relegated to the Apocrypha.

It is time to consider the ways in which the Song of Songs is one of the greatest works in any language from this period. (The only competitors I see for this honor are also mystical and mystifying: the writings of Zhuangzi [late fourth century BCE] and the poem "Li Sao" by Qu Yuan [d. ca. 278 BCE]. But those works are for highbrows; the Song is for humanity.)

THE STATUS OF WOMEN IN PTOLEMAIC LIFE AND LITERATURE

Joan Burton describes how the decline of traditional male roles in the Alexandrian metropolis created a new space for women.

> Masculine power in the old Greek world was closely linked with the ideal of a citizen-soldier. But in a mobile Hellenistic world, citizenship was losing its appeal as a measure of masculine power. Further, the rise in state wealth, resulting in part from Alexander's conquests in the East, enabled reliance on mercenaries in armed forces. . . . As male political life faded, the scope of female public life expanded. Strong queens, such as Olympias [of Macedonia] and Arsinoe II [of Egypt], were setting new levels of visibility for Greek women, and the horizon of possible social roles was expanding for less elite Greek women as well.[18]

Burton's remarks precede her study of the strong women in Theocritus's *Idylls*. In *Idyll* 17, for example, Theocritus compared the marriage of Ptolemy II and his sister Arsinoë II to the incestuous sacred marriage (*hieros gamos*) of Zeus and Hera (*Idylls* 17.128–32).

In Theocritus's *Idyll* 15, two women walk though crowded streets berating men, including their husbands. (Keep in mind that, at the time, Alexandrian households were quite likely to include one or more female slaves to serve husbands as concubines.) The speakers are on their way to the Adonia, a festival instituted by Queen Arsinoë to celebrate the love of Aphrodite and Adonis. The Adonia in Attica had been an unofficial women's festival; in Alexandria it was made an official cult with state patronage. According to Christine Havelock, "Theocritus allows us to imagine that it might be Arsinoe herself in the guise of Aphrodite who is lying in the arms of her lover Adonis."[19]

Arsinoë was not just the consort of her younger brother Ptolemy II Philadelphus; she was also a full pharaoh in her own right.[20] She thus recreated for the Ptolemies an Egyptian tradition of incestuous female pharaohs going back to Hatshepsut (d. 1458 BCE), considered by the Egyptologist James Breasted to be "the first great woman in history of whom we are informed."[21]

After her death, furthermore, Arsinoë was further deified by order of her husband-brother, and all temples in Egypt were required to include a cult statue of her. Her incarnation of an aspect of Aphrodite may explain the proliferation in Ptolemaic sculpture of naked women, including naked representations of the most famous Ptolemy, Cleopatra VII.[22] (Consider that all nudes in Greek art had been male before the post-Socratic sculptor Praxiteles [d. 330 BCE] and his contemporary, the painter Apelles.)

In this atmosphere, it is not surprising that women received enhanced status in the works of court-supported poets like Theocritus. Women are also given enhanced status and attention in Callimachus's epyllion *Hecale* and above all in the *Argonautica* of Apollonius Rhodius. The latter opens in the first two books with the mock-heroic and quasi-Homeric travel narrative of Jason in pursuit of the Golden Fleece. But this plot is subordinated in book 3 to the romantic narrative of Jason's involvement with, and dependence on, the powerful sorceress Medea, a mortal with divine ancestry (she is the granddaughter of the sun god Helios and niece of the dangerous demigoddess Circe).

The first two books concern the dealings of the ineffective Jason ("a great warrior only with the help of magical charms, jealous of honour but incapable of asserting it"[23]) with Heracles. They open with an invocation to Apollo, the god of sun and light, but then Heracles disappears to search for his abducted beloved squire Hylas. Books 3 and 4 then open with an invocation to Erato, the muse of erotic poetry (*Argonautica* 3.1; cf. *Aeneid* 7:37), and the theme shifts to "how Jason brought back the fleece to Iolcus aided by the love of Medea."

Book 3 is perhaps closer in some ways to the Song than anything in Theocritus. Much of it, like the Song, is from the heroine's point of view and uses subtle similes to convey her inner perplexity:

> And fast did her heart throb within her breast, as a sunbeam quivers upon the walls of a house when flung up from water, which is just poured forth in a caldron or a pail may be; and hither and thither on the swift eddy does it dart and dance along; even so the maiden's heart quivered in her breast. (*Argonautica* 3:765ss; cf. *Aeneid* 8:18–25)

She famously gives what has been called the first interior monologue in Western literature,[24] speaking as one wholly caught up in her passion (in contrast to Sappho, the accurate analyst of her sufferings): "Poor wretch, must I toss hither and thither in woe? On every side my heart is in despair; nor is there any help for my pain; but it burneth ever thus" (*Argonautica* 3:772–74).

Medea is complaining of a love that will isolate her, leading her to betray those around her, before being betrayed in turn. In this way Apollonius, while imparting to heterosexual love a driving epic energy (in contrast to Heracles's homoerotic digression with Hylas), still preserves the traditional view of love as destructive.[25]

Medea's soliloquy merits comparison with the Song of Songs, where the main speaker is the Shulamite, who at times also seems to be singing to no one but herself. But where the *Argonautica* demythologizes an ancient kingdom, the Song elevates one. This may reflect the difference in status between Apollonius at the court of Ptolemy and the disempowered Jewish author of the Song. At the summit of the Ptolemaic Empire, one could hardly be awed by the tiny kingdom of Colchis. But a subservient Jew was remembering the glory of a once great Jewish kingship under Solomon that was now essentially lost.[26]

This may help explain his or her choice to preserve and revive a partially archaized Hebrew, dating from the age of Jewish power, rather than write in everyday Aramaic. It also explains the desire to preserve and indeed enhance Judaism's most precious and enduring legacy, a yin-yang link to the sacred in everyday life.

To conclude: the position of women in Alexandrian society and literature, as I have described it, stands in dramatic contrast, indeed dialectical opposition, to what we have seen earlier in either Jerusalem or Athens. I know of no evidence to suggest that this was a conscious dialectic at the time. But was there perhaps a coherent dialectical process working at some deep level?

Others have thought so. Bruno Snell observed a dialectical shift at this time, from the yang rationalism of Athens and Hellas in the fourth century BCE to the yin of Alexandrian poetry in the third:

> Callimachus . . . stood on the threshold of a new age. After more than a century of enlightenment in the course of which the ancient religious beliefs had been dissolved, they had finally become weary of the spirit of rationalism. A new important era of poetry was about to begin.[27]

On the other hand, Gianni Barbiero describes the dialectic as a response to the new and unfamiliar environment of the third-century deracinated metropolis: "The decadent life of the city gives rise to nostalgia for a life that is simpler and in contact with nature."[28]

THE SONG OF SONGS AS A YIN-YANG
RIGHT-BRAIN MASTERPIECE

I need to demonstrate that the Song of Songs emerged from the Judeo-Hellenic-Egyptian culture of Alexandria, and in the end contributed to the dialectical disruption of the yang-yin mentality of the post-Socratic philosophers. But more central to this book is the Song's synthesis not just of Jewish and Greek and Egyptian cultural elements but of clarity (yang) and mystification (yin) in a higher yin-yang experience.

There is a strong inclination in our modern/postmodern mentality to read the Song quite differently. The elegant and learned translation by Chana and Ariel Bloch, which has been called "quite simply the best version in the English language,"[29] presents a much simpler picture of the Song, as "a poem about the sexual awakening of a young woman and her lover."[30]

(This secular reading of the Song, though controversial, is not original. Theodore of Mopsuestia (ca. 350–428 CE) saw the Song as "love poetry composed by Solomon to justify his marriage to the daughter of Pharaoh [1 Kings 11:1] and concluded that it should not be in the canon."[31])

The Blochs wish to liberate the Song from two millennia of allegorical readings, which they argue arose because for rabbis and Church Fathers, "the very fact of sexuality had become problematic."[32] In their view, "allegories that reconstructed the intimate passion of the lovers as political or religious history now seem particularly misconceived."[33]

But the Blochs also acknowledge that "the Song fared better at the hands of the mystics, Jewish and Christian, who honored its literal meaning as symbolic of the Jewish longing for union with God." Citing the *Zohar* of the Kabbalists, St. Bernard, and St. John of the Cross, they conclude that "the mystics read the Song allegorically, to be sure, but they remained true to its intensity and passion, its emotional power."[34]

The Blochs cite the example of the Kabbalistic *Zohar*'s speculations "about intercourse between the male and female aspects of God," which indeed stands in sharp contrast to the arithmetic allegorizing of the prominent commentator Rashi (d. 1105), for whom the Shulamite's two breasts ("Thy two breasts are like two young roes that are twins"; Song 7:4, cf. 4:5) are "the two Tablets. Another explanation: the king and the high priest."

Despite claiming to know that the Song actually describes a "sexual awakening," the Blochs concede that "the Song is in many respects an enigma." They concede further the role of fantasy in the Song: "It is often hard to tell what is real and what imagined; for that reason, many readers have found the poem to be dreamlike, with a freedom of movement, a dizzying fluidity, that conveys the intoxication of the senses."[35]

The Blochs' distinction between rationalizing allegory and imaginative play is real and important. St. Augustine acknowledges a similar distinction in his *City of God*:

> The Song of Songs voices a kind of spiritual delight felt by holy minds in the marriage of the king and queen of that city, namely, Christ and the Church. But this delight is wrapped up in allegorical draperies, so that it may be *more eagerly longed for*, and that its uncovering may *afford more pleasure*.[36]

I regret a kind of inverted modernist puritanism that would deny readers that pleasure. Neuroscientists acknowledge that it is real and associate it with the right (yin) hemisphere of the brain. Professor Tania Lombrozo describes their discovery that (as all good poets know) "green book" makes for a more complex neural reaction than "interesting book":

> To our surprise, it was the *right* hemisphere that elicited imagery-related brain activity to "green book" compared to "interesting book." Thus, although the left hemisphere is clearly important for language processing, the right hemisphere may play a special role in creating *the rich sensory experience* that often accompanies language comprehension . . . and *that makes reading such a pleasure*.[37]

What follows is a plea to read the Song less as an artifact to be understood and more as it traditionally has been, as a poem to be contemplated and enjoyed, like music, for inspiration and exaltation. Let me begin with a non-Freudian explanation for the Song's vast legacy of allegorical readings. The Song is dense with metaphor:

> A garden inclosed is my sister, my spouse; a spring shut up, a fountain sealed. . . .
>
> A fountain of gardens, a well of living waters, and streams from Lebanon. (Song 4:12, 15, KJV)

Allegory is defined as "extended or continued metaphor." The metaphors in the Song are conspicuous, indeed mutually contradictory, defying a systematic allegorical translation. But on a higher level they create a sustained sacral space behind the carnal lovers.

They do so by repeatedly echoing language and imagery from the Bible, above all from Isaiah. Wordsworth wrote of "spots of time, that with distinct pre-eminence" raise us above "the round of ordinary intercourse" (*Prelude*, 12.208–9, 12–13). These intermittent allusions (or "spots of scripture") in the Song similarly work together to supply a background of moreness behind the lovers' actions. These are of course enhanced by the author's decision to compose the Song in Hebrew, by then primarily the language of scripture and ceremony, rather than in his or her normal Aramaic.

From this perspective, we can see the foreground of the Song as a collage of fragments from lost earlier songs, with sometimes quite striking discontinuities. But on a higher level, we see the same kind of archetypal tension between rural and urban that we saw in Theocritus.

It is true that the metaphors in the Song are unsystematic and characteristically contradictory ("I am a wall," sings the Shulamite in Song 8:10). Thus I understand (though I do not endorse) the Blochs' rejection of systematic allegories to explain the Song, such as the "Allegorical Rendering Following Rashi," which in my bilingual Jewish Bible (the Stone Tanakh) replaces the literal text of the Song.

But I submit that readers and hearers respond to the Song not as a narrative but as a rich sensory/noetic experience that can evoke (and always has evoked) meditation on meanings at many levels.

THE SONG OF SONGS, EGYPT, THEOCRITUS, AND THE BIBLE

In language, style, and content, the Song of Songs, though it probably incorporates older materials, is an Alexandrine poem. That its Hebrew is from the Hellenistic era is shown by the signs of Mishnaic Hebrew and Aramaic influence and by the presence of Greek and Persian loan words in the text (e.g., פַּרְדֵּס, *pardes*, "orchard," cognate with Greek *paradeisos* and English "paradise"; Song 4:13).[38]

Scholars have tended to focus on similarities of content between Theocritus's *Idylls* and the Song, notably the image of foxes raiding a vineyard (Song 2:15; *Idylls* 1.48–49, 5.112–134) and the comparison of a graceful woman to a horse (Song 1:9; *Idylls* 18.30–32).[39]

The Shulamite's self-description as beautiful though black (*s'hora*), because "the sun hath looked upon me" (1:6), which has been interpreted as identifying her as the Queen of Sheba (1 Kings 10:1–13) or the daughter of Pharaoh (1 Kings 11:1–2), has also been compared to Theocritus's description of "Fair Bombyca" as "sunburnt" (haliocauston) and "honey-brown" (melichloron; *Idylls* 10.26–27, quoted in Virgil, *Eclogues* 10.38–39).[40]

Now that the Song is generally recognized to be composed from a collection of shorter love songs,[41] we can perhaps see a stronger analogy. Both the Song and the *Idylls* are anthological compositions, whose unity is reinforced at times by repetitions. Both compositions consciously interweave and ultimately contrast the innocence, authenticity, and spontaneity of the countryside with the opulence and structure of the city.[42]

In Theocritus, the basic contrast is between the urban idylls I have already mentioned and the better-remembered bucolic idylls through the *prosopa* (Latin *persona*; literally a mask) of a *boukolos*, or herdsman, "smelly, uneducated, often a slave, the fit companion of the beasts with whom he spends most of his time."[43]

The *Idylls* begin with the bucolic, such as the picture of the poor giant Cyclops ("Wheel-Eye," who in the *Odyssey* was a menace to Odysseus and devourer of his men), recast in *Idyll* 11 as a comically demented lover, "sick at heart" for the unattainable sea nymph Galatea. They proceed to the urban, such as the celebration we saw in *Idyll* 17 for the sacred marriage of Ptolemy to Arsinoë ("than whom no better wife embraces her young husband in all the halls, loving with all her heart her brother and her husband"; *Idylls* 17.129–30).

The Song of Songs, confusingly episodic throughout, nonetheless balances both bucolic and urban moments, while following a curve from initial clarity to ultimate mystery and moreness. This curve is framed by the introductory picture of the Shulamite as a field-worker: "black, because the sun hath looked upon me: my mother's children were angry with me; they made me the keeper of the vineyards" (1:6).

But soon she "goes about the city in the streets," in a setting of jewels, gold, and frankincense, seeing "king Solomon with the crown wherewith his mother crowned him" (3:11). In the end, however, she prefers her own vineyard to the riches of Solomon (8:11–12).

As Michael Fox has clearly demonstrated, there are Egyptian as well as Jewish and Greek influences in the Song.[44] Of these, perhaps the most striking is the Egyptian genre of *wasf*: a downward praise (as opposed to visual description) of specific body parts.[45] Such catalogs later became a stock-in-trade of Petrarchan and later love poetry, down to Shakespeare's parody in Sonnet 130: "My mistress' eyes are nothing like the sun." Take, for example, the praise of the Shulamite in chapter 4:

> Behold, thou art fair, my love; behold, thou art fair; thou hast doves' eyes within thy locks: thy hair is as a flock of goats, that appear from mount Gilead.
> Thy teeth are like a flock of sheep that are even shorn, which came up from the washing; whereof every one bear twins, and none is barren among them.
> Thy lips are like a thread of scarlet, and thy speech is comely: thy temples are like a piece of a pomegranate within thy locks.
> Thy neck is like the tower of David builded for an armoury, whereon there hang a thousand bucklers, all shields of mighty men.
> Thy two breasts are like two young roes that are twins, which feed among the lilies. (Song 4:1–5)

Fox cites as precedent an Egyptian lover's song one thousand years earlier:

> One alone is (my) sister, having no peer:
> More gracious than all other women.
> Behold her, like [the star] Sothis rising   52
> at the beginning of a good year;
> Shining, precious, white of skin;
> lovely of eyes when gazing
> Sweet her lips (when) speaking:
> she has no excess of words.
> Long of neck, white of breast,
> her hair true lapis lazuli.
> her arms surpass gold,
> her fingers are like lotuses.
> Full(?) (her) derrière, narrow(?) (her) waist,
> her thighs carry on her beauties.[46]

(On a higher level, if I am right to read the Song as a celebration of earthly eroticism with sacred overtones, then one might also point to a haunting similarity with the important Egyptian Middle Kingdom poem "The Story of Sinuhe." I would point in particularly to the shared plot motif of ambivalence to royalty and the literary technique of word choices that together form "a web of association."[47] But apparently no scholar has made this connection, and I shall not press the point.)

Prof. Robert Graves has suggested that "the writer who assembled the Canticles in their present form is likely to have been an Alexandrian jew acquainted with Meleager's poems; also with those of the Sicilian Theocritus and other Greek pastoral poets."[48]

I personally believe that the author, while Alexandrian in culture, came from Palestine. As the Blochs observe, the geography of the poem "reaches from the mountains of Lebanon to the oasis of Ein Gedi, from Heshbon in the east to Mount Carmel on the sea." (The comparison of the woman's head of hair to the densely forested peak of Carmel (7:6) suggests familiarity with the landscape.)

But it could have been as Alexandrian for a Jew to write there of his native Judaea as it was for Theocritus to write there of shepherds in his native Sicily. It was traditional to write songs of love in Egyptian and Greek, while, as the Blochs observe, the Song "is the only example of secular love poetry from ancient Israel that has survived."[49] As noted earlier, the closest approach in the Tanakh is a brief praise of marital love in the course of Proverbs' austere warning against adultery (5:15, 19–20; cf. 7:18–23).

To discern sources in the Song of Songs is to risk under-recognizing the Song's stunning originality, even if its composition is indeed partly a collage.

To begin with, as Phyllis Trimble has persuasively demonstrated, the Song affirms and celebrates, as no poem ever before it, mutuality of the sexes; in it "there is no male dominance, no female subordination, and no stereotyping of either sex."[50]

The Song breaks in other ways with both Egyptian and Greek tradition. Its reticence, tact, and mystical ambiguity contrast starkly with the frankness of Egyptian songs, which (in hieroglyphics replete with phallus and vulva pictographs) refer to the woman's "cave" and the man's loins, where something "is longer than broad."[51]

And as noted earlier, the Song converts the traditional Greek *complaint* of being lovesick, as with Sappho, the Theocritan Cyclops, and the Apollonian Medea, into an affirmation. At a minimum, the Shulamite sings of her sickness to celebrate, enjoy, and enhance the intensity of her love.

> I am the rose of Sharon, and the lily of the valleys.
> As the lily among thorns, so is my love among the daughters. . . .
> He brought me to the banqueting house, and his banner over me
> was love.
> Stay me with flagons, comfort me with apples: for I am sick of love.
> (2:1–2, 4–5, KJV)[52]

A YIN-YANG READING OF THE SONG OF SONGS

As noted earlier, I see more than merely sexual exultation in this. Here and throughout the poem, the Shulamite is voicing the altered state that love puts us in, which liberates her from oppression (the anger of her brothers in 1:6, the beatings inflicted by the watchmen in 5:7, and her brothers' threats in 8:9) to a higher fellowship with her beloved, in which she becomes (in the Bloch translation) "a city of peace" (8:10). (The difficult verse 8:10 is variously translated, but undoubtedly in the Hebrew the last word is *shalom*, peace.[53])

Far from being estranged like Sappho from her beloved, her surrender to him lifts her, like no lover before that we know of, to a unity in ego loss: "My beloved is mine, and I am his" (2:16, cf. 6:3). This loss of ego in transcendence, which later will be celebrated by the Provençal troubadours and Dante, is even clearer in the Hebrew.[54]

This transcendent view of the Song was enhanced by the Septuagint and Vulgate translations of the disputed verse 2:4 above. Instead of "his banner over me was love," translated by Michael Fox as "his intent toward me was love," the Septuagint has "taxate ep'eme agapen" (τάξατε ἐπ' ἐμὲ ἀγάπην), echoed by Jerome's "ordinavit in me caritatem" (he has ordained [set in order] charity in me).[55]

The idea that the disordered sickness of love could be a step to "ordered charity" (*caritas ordinata*; a concept derived by St. Augustine and others from verse 2:4) received much attention in the Middle Ages from authors such as Bede, St. Bernard, and Dante.[56] Indeed, Dante's vision of Beatrice in the *Vita Nuova*, which abstracted him from the bitter family feuds of Florence, which "never allowed Love to govern [him] without the faithful counsel of reason" (*Vita Nuova* 1), and which indeed inspired him to write "things never said of any woman" (*Vita Nuova* 31), can be seen both as a by-product of the Song of Songs and as a sympathetic recreation of its exalted mood.

I believe that such expanded readings of the Song are as appropriate today as they were when the Song was written, and when the primary meaning of "love" (*ahava*) in biblical Hebrew was the emotional bond between the Jewish people and God. To revive a word that has fallen out of favor, the Song of Songs is *sublime*, and the sublime (as I quoted earlier from Longinus, first century CE) "leads the listeners not to persuasion, but to ecstasy" (*On the Sublime* 1.4)—that is, to the expansive pleasures enjoyed in enmindment by the yang-yin mind.

The mark of truly great literature, such as the dialogues of Plato, is that it is an irresoluble mix of yang (what is explicable) and yin (what is not), and the greater such a work, the more its meaning will be what it suggests to the reader. The greatness of the Song, I believe, lies in its unique admixture of the straightforward—

> For, lo, the winter is past, the rain is over and gone;
> The flowers appear on the earth; the time of the singing of birds is
> come, and the voice of the turtle is heard in our land; (2:11–12)—

with the prophetically opaque—

> We have a little sister, and she hath no breasts: what shall we do for
> our sister in the day when she shall be spoken for?
> If she be a wall, we will build upon her a palace of silver: and if she
> be a door, we will inclose her with boards of cedar.
> I am a wall, and my breasts like towers: then was I in his eyes as
> one that found favour. (Song 8:8–10)

This admixture makes it for me an undeniably yin-yang poem, and is I believe the key to its generative greatness. The Song's historical influence is perhaps best epitomized by its inevitable stimulation of a new mode of extra-rational (poetic) thinking and allegorical exegesis among both Christian and Jewish thinkers.[57]

Here, for example, is an example of how the Song inspired the writer of 4 Ezra (2 Esdras), an apocalyptic text said to have been written in the late first century CE:

"O Lord my Lord, out of all the woods of the earth and all the trees thereof thou hast chosen thee one vine; out of all the lands of the world thou hast chosen thee one planting ground; out of all the flowers of the world thou hast chosen thee one lily; out of all the depths of the sea thou hast replenished for thyself one river; out of all the cities that have been built thou hast sanctified Sion unto thyself" (4 Ezra [2 Esdras] 5:23–26a).

The figures allegedly taken from the Song of Solomon and interpreted allegorically are the lily (Cant[icle; i.e., Song] 2:2); the dove (Cant 2:14); and the stream (Cant 4:15).[58]

This new mode of enlarged thinking helped prepare the world for the anti-Greek theology of St. Paul, for whom "the letter killeth, but the spirit giveth life" (2 Cor. 3:6). And that same spirit has survived wherever people acknowledge that to survive, prose is not enough; poetry is also needed.

The Song is ambiguous, indeed mysterious, in other ways as well. It contains pastoral elements, as when the beloved is presented as a shepherd (1:7), the woman as a sunburned vineyard worker (1:6), conceived and born under an apricot tree (8:4).[59] But the Song also mentions the woman's jeweled necklace, golden earrings, and expensive spices (1:10–11). Whether as a sobriquet for the male lover or in person (a debated point, even among literal readers), a king, indeed King Solomon, is also in the poem, especially in what can be read as a crucial epithalamic moment:

Go forth, O ye daughters of Zion, and behold king Solomon with the crown wherewith his mother crowned him in the day of his espousals, and in the day of the gladness of his heart. (3:11)

A PERSONAL READING OF THE SONG

The Song is as polysemous as a Rorschach blot, in which we can each see our own preferred patterns of development. What I personally see is the following:

1. An idealized pastoral opening in chapters 1 and 2, in which the poem is a dialogue, reflecting their intimacy ("My beloved is mine and I am his"; 2:16). The lovers use nature imagery to describe themselves ("I am the rose of Sharon, and the lily of the valleys. . . . As the apple tree

among the trees of the wood, so is my beloved among the sons"; 2:1–3). They feel the energy of springtime ("The fig tree putteth forth her green figs. . . . Arise [kumi] my love, my fair one, and come away"; 2:13).

2. A dramatic shift to an urban and courtly setting in chapter 3 ("I will rise now, and go about the city in the streets. . . . The watchmen that go about the city found me"; 3:2–3), with admiration for King Solomon and his riches (3:7–11). Dialogue verges into monologue and at times soliloquy, with the Shulamite essentially the speaker of chapters 3, 5, and most of 8, and her lover of chapters 4, 6, and 7. Nature imagery ("A garden inclosed is my sister, my spouse"; 4:12) is now complemented by new images drawn from urban power ("Thy neck is like the tower of David builded for an armoury"; 4:4; cf. 5:14, 7:5).

3. This more complex milieu leads to alienation and the first violent discord ("The watchmen that went about the city found me, they smote me, they wounded me"; 5:7), and then a contrast between the opulent promiscuity of a Solomon ("There are threescore queens, and fourscore concubines, and virgins without number"; 6:8) and the lovers' modest but committed monogamy in the next verse ("My dove, my undefiled is but one; she is the only one of her mother"; 6:9).

4. A call to return ("Return, return [Shuvi, shuvi], O Shulamite; return, return, that we may look upon thee" (7:1 [6:13 in KJV]) is reinforced by the male lover: "Come, my beloved, let us go forth into the field. . . . Let us get up early to the vineyards" (7:12–13; cf. 8:14). This is followed by the great paean to love, "as strong as death," as something which cannot be bought (8:6–7), followed by a rejection (as noted above) of King Solomon's wealthy vineyard in favor of "My vineyard, which is mine" (8:11–12).

ECHOES OF THE PROPHETS IN THE SONG

My reading is personal, but not, I think, idiosyncratic; it follows the biblical allusions I see to the great prophets, especially Isaiah. In this respect, my method of reading is somewhat akin to Rashi's—except that, time and again, where I see an allusion to the prophets, Rashi reads the same verse in the light of the Pentateuch, the Five Books of Moses.

For example, a choral flourish from the daughters of Jerusalem with biblical solemnity: "Who is this [mi zot, מִי זֹאת (f.)], that riseth up [עֹלָה, 'olah] out of the wilderness" (3:6; repeated at 8:5), echoing prophetic (some would say messianic) passages in Isaiah 63:1 ("Who is this who cometh from Edom") and Jeremiah 46:7 ("Who is this [mi zeh, מִי־זֶה] like the Nile that riseth up ['olah]").

The Song is elevated by such biblical echoes, analogous to the Homeric allusions and echoes in the *Argonautica*. Some might seem to be momentary. "Thy lips are like a thread of scarlet" (4:3) echoes (as Rashi duly noted) the "line of scarlet thread" (Josh. 2:18) which the harlot Rahab hung in her window as a prelude to the destruction of her city of Jericho.

Some are more archetypal. In "A garden inclosed is my sister, my spouse; a spring shut up, a fountain sealed" (4:12), the repetition "garden inclosed ... spring shut up" is more emphatic in Hebrew: "gan na'ul ... gal na'ul" (גַּ נָעוּל ... גַּל נָעוּל). Exactly the same repetition, "gan na'ul ... gal na'ul," is found in Isaiah 58.11: "You will be like a well-watered garden, like a spring that flows with never-failing waters." (This is the reward promised in the admonitory chapter about internal fasting that is read at the Yom Kippur Torah service, discussed earlier in chapter 1.)

The Song's reference to Solomon's vineyard seems more sustained:

> Solomon *had a vineyard* [kerem hayah, כֶּרֶם הָיָה] at Baal-hamon; he let out the vineyard unto keepers; every one for the fruit thereof was to bring a thousand pieces of silver. (8:11)

This echoes Isaiah 5:1,

> beloved a song of my lover about his vineyard. My beloved had a vineyard [kerem hayah li-ydidi, כֶּרֶם הָיָה לִידִיד] on a fruitful hill,

where Isaiah himself explained that the vineyard was part of an allegory, for the destruction of Israel because of its iniquities:

> I will lay it waste: it shall not be pruned, nor digged; but there shall come up briars and thorns: I will also command the clouds that they rain no rain upon it.
> For the vineyard of the Lord of hosts is the house of Israel, and the men of Judah his pleasant plant: and he looked for judgment, but behold oppression; for righteousness, but behold a cry. (Isa. 5:6–7)[60]

There are other key echoes of Isaiah in the Song that reinforce Deutero-Isaiah's mood of expectancy. In "Rise up [kumi], my love, my fair one, and come away" (2:10, 2:13), the verb *kumi* recalls its use in verses of Isaiah like "Awake, awake, stand up [kuma], O Jerusalem" (Isa. 51:17) or "Arise [kuma], shine, for thy light is come, and the glory of the LORD is risen upon thee" (Isa. 60:1).[61]

There is also a powerful biblical echo in

שׁוּבִי שׁוּבִי הַשּׁוּלַמִּית שׁוּבִי שׁוּבִי וְנֶחֱזֶה־בֵּךְ
Shuvi, shuvi, ha-Shulammit

Shuvi, shuvi, ve-nehezeh bach
Return, return, O Shulamite; return, return, that we may look upon
thee. (Song 6:13 in KJV; 7:1 in Masoretic Hebrew text)[62]

The Hebrew for "return"—here *shuvi*, שׁוּבִי, in biblical Hebrew, *shuvah*,
שׁוּבָה—is a major word in Judaism: in the cognate form *t'shuvah*, it also means
repentance. It is central to the biblical accounts of Israel's transgression and
return. In this sense we find it in Isaiah 44:22: "I have blotted out, as a thick
cloud, thy transgressions, and, as a cloud, thy sins; return [shuvah, שׁוּבָה] unto
Me, for I have redeemed thee."

We find *shuvah* also in Psalm 126, which Jews sing after Shabbat meals:

Turn again [shuvah] our captivity, O Lord, as the streams in the
south.
They that sow in tears shall reap in joy.
He that goeth forth and weepeth, bearing precious seed, shall doubt-
less come again with rejoicing, bringing his sheaves with him.
(Psalm 126:4–6)

And again in Hosea 14:2:
Return [shuvah], O Israel, unto the Lord thy God; for thou hast
stumbled in thine iniquity. (Hosea 14:2)

This verse introduces the Haftorah reading for Shabbat Shuvah (Shabbat of
Return), the special Shabbat that falls in the Days of Awe (Yamim Noraim)
between Rosh Hashanah and Yom Kippur.[63]

A LATE INTERPOLATION AFTER
FINISHING THIS BOOK

A belated full disclosure: In insisting on the biblical overtones of the appeal
to the Shulamite,

Return, return, O Shulamite; return, return, that we may look upon thee. (7:1)

I am reprising a debate I had years ago over this verse with my dear
friend the late poet Chana Bloch. For me the meaningfulness of the Song
is enhanced rather than obscured by the natural desire to interpret its mys-
teries. Here for example is the grandiloquent translation and gloss in the
eighth(?)-century Midrash Tanchuma (commenting not on the Song but on
the book of Numbers [Bamidbar]):

The nations said to them (in Cant. 7:1), **"Return, return, O Shulammite** (i.e., O Israel). Cling to us and come to us; then we will make you sultans, generals, and commanders."** . . . **"Return, return that we may look upon you."** . . . Then Israel said to them, **"What will you see in the Shulammite?"** And what grandeur are you giving to us? [It is] perhaps (ibid., cont.) **"like a dance of the camps?"** Can you possibly give us anything like the grandeur which the Lord our God gave us in the desert? [There he gave us] the standard of the camp of Judah, the standard of the camp of Reuben, the standard of the camp of Ephraim, the standard of the camp of Dan [cf. Num. 2:3–25]. . . . Are you able to do so for us? (Cant. 7:1), "What will you see in the Shulammite?" It is perhaps (ibid., cont.) "like a dance (*meholat*) of the camps"; [in] that when we sin, He pardons [mohel] us and says to us (in Deut. 23:15 [14]), "and your camp shall be holy?"[64]

Compared to this, I find the pared-down version (it is not a translation) of the Blochs—

> Again, O Shulamite,
> Dance again,
> That we may watch you dancing. (7:1)[65]

to be both inaccurate and anticlimactic.[66]

The Blochs' willingness to rewrite the poem to suit their interpretation[67] explains my reluctant decision to replace the beautiful Bloch translation in my text with the sometimes erratic King James Version. An unreliable translation that is open to many meanings is ultimately far closer to the Song's mysterious tone than one that is philologically enhanced but sometimes falsifies the text to sustain one "true" meaning.

I have gone on so obsessively about this verse ("Return, return, O Shulamite") because, in retrospect, I see how clearly it illustrates a point made by Charles Taylor about secularity:

Taylor has argued at length in his magnum opus, *A Secular Age,* that the crucial mistake is to interpret the emergence of modern secularity in terms of a "subtraction story" which suggests that in the course of their history Europeans have managed to gradually rid themselves of old illusions and confined horizons so as to finally gain a clear view of the perennial features of human nature. Against this, Taylor maintains that secularity is to be viewed as "the fruit of new inventions, newly constructed self-understandings."[68]

The Blochs sincerely believed they had gained a "clear view" of the Song by blocking the old temptation to read it allegorically. But in fact their translation, albeit beautiful, was at times a newly constructed invention, and at these points, in my view, a diminished one.

(End for now of this late interpolation, to be resumed below.)

THE CLOSING CHAPTERS OF THE SONG OF SONGS

Is there any support in the context of this verse ("Return, return, O Shulamite") for reading *shuvi* as "return"? Not in the next verse—"How beautiful are thy feet with shoes" (7:2; 7:1 in KJV), which initiates a scan of the beloved's body. But unquestionably in the last three verses of chapter 7,

> Come, my beloved, let us go forth into the field . . .
> Let us get up early to the vineyards; let us see if the vine flourish, whether the tender grape appear, and the pomegranates bud forth: there will I give thee my loves.
> The mandrakes give a smell. (7:12–14)

there is indeed a belated return to the vineyards and natural seasons in chapters 1 (1:6) and 2 (2:10–13).

From this secure vantage point, the Shulamite can (as mentioned earlier) now recall the wealth of Solomon with a kind of scorn:

> "My vineyard, which is mine, is before me: thou, O Solomon, must have a thousand [pieces of silver, 8:11], and those that keep the fruit thereof two hundred. (8:12)

This verse is translated more vividly by the Blochs as

> My vineyard is all my own.
> Keep your thousand, Solomon! And pay
> Two hundred to those
> Who must guard the fruit.

The last verse of the Song—

> Hurry [barah], my love! Run away,
> My gazelle, my wild stag
> On the hills of cinnamon. (8:14; Bloch)—

leaves us expecting. Like the end of the book of Genesis, or the Tanakh itself, it is an open closure; instead of resolving the poem's actions, it can be read as opening to a prospect of something more. The dictionary translation of *barah* is "escape, flee, run away," as we see in the Stone Tanakh's "Allegorical Rendering Following Rashi" of 8:14: "Flee, my Beloved, from our common exile . . . and rest Your Presence among us on the fragrant Mount Moriah, site of your Temple."

Modernist commentators who reject such allegories have a problem with a love song ending in hasty departure. Michael Fox, after speculating that the verse may not be a closure at all ("Perhaps the end of the song, which would be exposed on a rolled-up scroll, was lost"), has this suggestion:

> Since "the mountains of spices" . . . seem to represent the perfumed breasts of the girl . . . her entreaty here that he be like a gazelle on the mountains of spices is best understood as an appeal that he leave his listening companions and come to her by himself to spend the night between her breasts.[69]

To Fox's "appeal . . . to spend the night," or the Blochs' "to run away before sunrise so that he will not be caught,"[70] I prefer a sense that sustains the mood in the poem that love exalts us. I see this in Rashi's reading of the "hills of cinnamon" ("This is Mount Moriah and the Temple, may it be built speedily and in our days, Amen."[71]). And that is indeed how the verb *barah* is used in Isaiah 58:20: "Go ye forth from Babylon, flee ye [barah] from the Chaldeans; with a voice of singing declare ye, tell this, utter it even to the end of the earth; say ye: 'The LORD hath redeemed His servant Jacob.'"

THE SONG OF SONGS IN MODERN TIMES: A BRIEF PERSONAL DIGRESSION

Such anticlimactic conclusions (I could cite others) do not explain the Song's survival through two millennia. Indeed, my immersion for two months in the Song and its commentaries has made me more aware than ever before of a pervasive limitation to contemporary culture. Whether modernist or postmodernist, I see it as still in the spirit of the Enlightenment's needed, but wildly overreactive, response to the corrupt state of the eighteenth-century Catholic Church.

The more I read, the more I see around me a needless post-Enlightenment prejudice that would limit the contemporary imagination to the down-to-earth and secular. For example, I could not have written this prose poem without the aid of a very intelligent book on the new topic of neurohistory, *On Deep History and the Brain*, by Daniel Smail. I am immensely grateful to Smail's book for introducing me to neurohistory, a field so new that the term is not yet in the *OED*.

Concerned by the efforts of some local school boards to teach so-called creation history, Smail hopes to achieve a continuity between written history and the earlier, unwritten "deep history" of paleoanthropologists. While I entirely approve of his project, I do not care at all for his characterization of it as "building a human history that *shakes free from the grip of the sacred*."[72]

I myself am less oppressed by a few local school boards than by the idiolects of poststructuralists and their kind—even when I agree with their foundational principles. In my experience, our age on the whole is no longer suffering from "the grip of the sacred." Smail's own words suggest the opposite: that he, like many of us, is in the grip of the secular.

A LATE INTERPOLATION

I loved and admired Chana Bloch, who was in a poetry workshop with me for over thirty years. And I know and sympathize with some of the reasons for her resolute decision (by no means unique) to be culturally and not religiously Jewish. But now, having finished this book, I need to express stronger personal reservations than before with the secularism that inspired her to translate "Shuvi, shuvi" (Song 7:1) as "Dance again," rather than a straightforward "Return, return."

I myself am all for the *secularity* that in the U.S. Constitution separated church from state, thus liberating religion from what had become in the eighteenth century an apparatus of oppression. But this contribution to the opening of our collective minds must be contrasted with the *secularism* that attempts to close it, the secularism that tries to cleanse our minds and our culture of residues of spirituality.

This comment does not belong in my final chapter, which ends with an appeal for tolerance and double-mindedness. My hopes are for a post-secular era in which spirituality and secularity coexist with mutual tolerance and respect, one where all of us can enjoy the urban vistas of culture in all its recherché forms, and the open spaces where we are free to contemplate and listen to the stars.

[End of interpolation.]

CONCLUSION (OR ENVOI)

As I said, this is a personal reading. It is not offered to displace Chana Bloch's reading but to complement it and many others, and thus sustain the prevailing tone of puzzling ambiguities in the original.[73] For there are kingly references in the pastoral context of chapter 1, and urban references in the rural context of chapter 8. In 4:9 the lover addresses the Shulamite as "my sister, my spouse." Why then does she lament, wistfully, "O that thou wert as my brother" (8:1)?[74] These paradoxes and antinomies mirror those found elsewhere the Bible.[75]

I submit that my reading of the Song, though personal, is in keeping with the messianic readings of the Song we saw in the books of Enoch and Revelation, and indeed the whole tradition represented by Rashi. The insistence of some modern critics on breaking with that tradition is in my view symptomatic of our prevailing post-Enlightenment "disenchantment of the world" that Max Weber attributed to modernism.

The Song's pregnant ambiguities, securely grounded in sacred tradition, make it a uniquely *generative* poem. Somewhat like *The Waste Land* in the 1920s, its defiance of rational order, at a time of rapid social change, struck a responsive chord with its subservient audience.

I mentioned earlier that the Greek poets under Ptolemy II—Theocritus, Callimachus, and Apollonius—all produced generative works, each with a major influence on the later literary canon, but none contributing to social change. The *Idylls* and the *Argonautica* of the dominant Greek culture are today read almost exclusively in academies alone. In contrast, the Song of Songs, violating yang standards of intelligibility, and with its recurring verses of both affliction (5:7) and expectancy (2:10, 8:14), stirred the hearts of those suffering under the Greek imposition of order.

As we saw in chapter 3, fragments of the Song of Songs, particularly from the Greek Septuagint version, found themselves into both the Gospel of St. John (7:38) and the apocalyptic texts of 2 Esdras (e.g., 10:4) and Revelation (3:20, 21:1–2). These readings of the Song, as a text for disruptive social change, appear (along with the emergence of anti-Semitism) in Egypt under the later Ptolemies.[76]

The Song of Songs is still with us, in both Jewish and Christian services, at weddings, and in popular imitations. More importantly, it permanently affected how the greatest poets of the West in future would teach the rest of the world how to feel, and speak, about love.

Chapter Seven

Virgil as Prophet of the
Second Pivotal Shift

PROEM: LEISURE, FREEDOM, AND THE GOOD LIFE

In the last two chapters, we looked at the transition from the actively engaged Greek civic audience of Athens to the leisured Greek audience of Alexandria. We might say that *schole*, the Athenian notion of active leisure (from which is derived the word "school") was on its way to becoming *otium*, the imperial Roman notion of unencumbered leisure (from which is derived the word "otiose").

In Plato we find the notion that the best use of *schole* (free time) is "education [paideian, παιδείαν] in goodness, which makes a man eagerly desirous of becoming a perfect citizen, understanding how both to rule and be ruled righteously." Anything else would be "vulgar and illiberal [aneleutheros, ἀνελεύθερος, 'not free'] and utterly unworthy of the name 'education'" (*Laws* 643e–644a).

A generation later, Aristotle recognized "a form of education in which boys should be trained not because it is useful or necessary but as being liberal [i.e., for free men] and noble [eleutherion kai kalen, ἐλευθέριον καὶ καλήν]" (*Politics* 1338a, 30). However, illustrating the changed role of free men in an empire rather than a republic, Aristotle downplayed "politics and war," though "preeminent in nobility and grandeur," as unleisured [ascholos, ἄσχολος, not-leisured] and directed to some further end, not chosen for their own sakes, whereas the activity of the intellect is felt to excel in serious worth, consisting as it does in contemplation (*Nicomachean Ethics* 1177b, 7).

Roger Scruton has explained what Aristotle meant by *ascholos*, "not leisured":

Ascholia was Aristotle's term for business, and it has its equivalent in Latin (*neg-otium*). . . . What purpose is served by business, and when is that purpose fulfilled? For Aristotle the answer was clear: you work in order to free yourself for leisure, and in leisure you are truly free: free to pursue the contemplative life which, for Aristotle, was the highest good.[1]

We see that both Plato and Aristotle agree on the relevance of leisure to liberty, and of both to the good life—assumptions still embedded in our notions of "free time" and "liberal arts."[2]

Their differing views of liberty are, I would say, poorly reflected in the modern distinction made by Benjamin Constant (d. 1830) between the Athenian or active notion of liberty—"the sharing of social power among the citizens of the same fatherland"—and the modern (or passive) notion of liberty—the guarantees to our "enjoyment of security in private pleasures."[3]

For Aristotle, contemplation was not just an activity but indeed the highest activity, an approach to the contemplative activity of God:

Such a life as this however will be higher than the human level: not in virtue of his humanity will a man achieve it, but in virtue of something within him that is divine.[4]

(I do not remember noticing this passage when I read Aristotle as a student. I relate to it intensely in my old age, as I write this book about human moreness. On one level, I link it to the scientific paradox attributed to Albert Einstein: "The most incomprehensible thing about the Universe is that it is comprehensible."[5] But more relevantly to my present purpose, I read it as an unanticipated corroboration, from an even more unanticipated source, of what I have been writing about: our "third nature" that seeks a new level, our moreness, "our need to be more than we are."[6])

According to Leah Kronenberg, the Roman poet Lucretius (d. 55 BCE) "was the first to use an image of pastoral *otium* to connote the epicurean ideal of a life according to nature (Lucr. 2.20–36)."[7] And after him the depiction in his epic *De Rerum Natura* (*On the Nature of Things*), of a world energized and exalted by the cosmic force of love—

> Before thee, Goddess, and thy coming on,
> Flee stormy wind and massy cloud away,
> For thee the daedal Earth bears scented flowers,
> For thee waters of the unvexed deep
> Smile, and the hollows of the serene sky
> Glow with diffused radiance for thee!
>
> (Lucretius, *De Rerum Natura* 1.7–12)—

would in turn energize and exalt the *Eclogues* of Virgil (d. 19 BCE).

LEISURE, SLAVERY, AND LOVE

We must not forget however this major gap between the Greek and Roman thinkers of antiquity and ourselves: that the notions of liberty and leisure they wrote of were both supported by chattel slavery.[8] To quote Perry Anderson, "The solstice of classical urban culture always also witnessed the zenith of slavery; and the decline of one, in Hellenistic Greece or Christian Rome, was likewise invariably marked by the setting of the other."[9]

Athens, once taught as the exemplar of liberty in antiquity, was also preeminent in slavery. Becoming, as Thucydides reported, a ruthless mini-empire, it acquired by far the largest slave population of any Greek city-state, with as many as eighty thousand in the sixth and fifth centuries BCE, and an average of three or four slaves per household.

The resulting availability to the leisured class of casual sex on demand, a commodity like sweetmeats or wine, had a considerable effect, especially in the Roman Empire, on the meaning of *amor* or love. Thus Theocritus's one-eyed Cyclops pining for unfulfilled love for the sea nymph Galatea (and regretting that he was not born with fins to swim with her) may have seemed even more of a comic figure to Alexandrian upper-class males with one or two concubines.[10]

If we jump forward to the end of the Roman Empire, we can read a perspective on this availability in the poetic memoir of a Christian, Paulinus of Pella, remembered in some manuscripts of his verse as *Saint* Paulinus of Pella (d. ca. 461). In extraordinary language, he records that he took a vow of strict sexual continence—to have sex only with his slaves:

> Howbeit, so far as wilful wantonness could be curbed and bridled with prudent restraint, lest I should heap heavier offences on my faults, I checked my passions with this chastening rule: . . . that I should be satisfied with servile amours in my own home.[11]

The Latin for "satisfied with servile amours," *inlecebris famulantibus uti*, is more literally "to use [*sic*] servile attractions"—the verb *uti* being a workaday verb, as in using a fork or a cane.

Typically, among most Latin poets other than Virgil, the poetry of *amor* celebrates fulfilled rather than unfulfilled love. The paramount example is Catullus 5, *Vīvāmus mea Lesbia, atque amēmus*:

> Let us live, my Lesbia, and let us love . . .
> Give me a thousand kisses, then a hundred,
> then another thousand, then a second hundred,
> then again a thousand then a hundred.

But a better illustration of Catullan *amor* is the difference between Sappho's anguished self-examination that we looked at in chapter 3—

> and sweat pours coldly over me, and all
> my body shakes, suddenly sallower
> than summer grass, and death, I fear and feel,
> is very near—

and Catullus's world-weary addition to his translation of Sappho in Catullus 51, blaming *otium* for his discomfort:

> otium, Catulle, tibi molestum est:
> otio exsultas nimiumque gestis:
> otium et reges prius et beatas
> perdidit urbes.

> Idleness, Catullus, is bad for you:
> You exult in idleness and play too much.
> Idleness in the past has undone kings
> And wealthy cities.

The status of the last stanza, not found in the fragments of Sappho we have, is unclear. What can be said safely, however, is that Catullus (d. ca. 54 BCE) writes it philosophically, far from total immersion in Sappho's agony. And it presages the purposelessness we find in the *Amores* ("Loves," a significant plural) of Ovid (d. ca. 18 CE), where the gift of *otium* becomes associated with boredom and the need for diversion.

The strength of the Roman love elegists lies in their exploration of the complexities into which we are led by love. This was epitomized memorably in Catullus 85 (and Pound's translation):

> Odi et amo. Quare id faciam fortasse requiris.
> Nescio, sed fieri sentio et excrucior.

> I hate and I love. Why? you may ask but
> It beats me. I feel it done to me and I ache.

and expanded on by Ovid:

> Odi, nec possum, cupiens, non esse quod odi;
> heu, quam quae studeas ponere ferre grave est!

> I hate, and though I want to, I can't stop being what I hate.
> Alas, how it hurts to carry something you long to drop!

(Ovid, *Amores* 3.4.5–6)

The corresponding weakness is that their experiences and sympathies are narrowly constrained to members of their own privileged class, with the result, to quote Czeslaw Milosz, "we learn more of everyday life in the Roman Empire from the Gospels than from the Latin poetry of the Golden Age."[12]

The limits of their sensibility are well illustrated by Ovid's linked elegies 2.7 and 2.8, in which Ovid successively addresses his lover Corinna, and then her slave girl Cypassis.

> The poet-lover first hotly denies the charge of having betrayed Corinna by sex with her slave-hairdresser, and then blackmails the unhappy girl into more sex on pain of exposure to all too real slave punishments.[13]

The multitude of books still written on Ovid will never exhaust the ways in which he still speaks to us. Yet hopefully the modern reader is more likely to be concerned at the sexual exploitation of the slave Cypassis and not just *enjoy* it as a witty joke.

Ovid is a very great poet; his epic *Metamorphoses* can be considered in some ways wiser and deeper in its outlook than Virgil's *Aeneid*. He himself dismisses his elegies as "light" (levis; *Amores* 2.1.12); but Elegy, personified as a woman competing with Tragedy for his attention in 3.1, is able to point out, "'Twas I who first made swell the fruitful seeds of your mind" (felicia semina mentis; 3.1.59).

> Ovid is implying, and expecting his readers to understand, that being a Roman love elegist had come to mean something comparable on some level to what it meant in this culture to be a philosopher.[14]

The overall limitation of most Latin love elegy after Catullus, and in particular of Ovid, is its need to be *clever*. The affect of love, so exalted in later love poetry, tends to be belittled by Ovid. When he writes of his own tears, it is because his lover's husband has locked him out (*Amores* 1.14.61; cf. 1.6.18); his beloved's tears are written up after a cosmetic disaster from dying her hair (1.14). One self-questioning exception is *Amores* 1.7, when Ovid guiltily laments his madness [*furor*] of having struck his weeping girl with raging blows. But even this moment of introspection quickly digresses into urbane comparisons with the anger and guilt of Greek mythic figures. (The Latin word *urbanitas*, "perhaps coined by Cicero," was used by Cicero to refer to this kind of "refined wit."[15] And Dryden used the English word *urbanity*, "or well-manner'd Wit," the same way.[16])

The liberating folly of love would later be celebrated as a source of positive energy by troubadours, beginning with Guillaume d'Aquitaine (d. 1127): "ferei un vers de dreit rien" (I will make a poem about nothing at all).

Ovid sees his folly as nothing to rejoice in; what he celebrates instead is his having overcome it.[17]

This limitation of sensibility afflicted the whole era, not just Ovid in particular. Four centuries later, when Rome had been nominally Christianized, the commentator Servius will say of Dido's love and suicide in *Aeneid* 4, "It's all about schemes and subtleties, so that it is virtually in the comic style—no wonder, as it deals with love" (paene comicus stilus est; nec mirum, ubi de amore tractatur).[18] This critical verdict by Servius shows

> how different an ancient point of view may be from ours. . . . The ancients . . .
> hardly conceived of love as a proper theme for tragedy: witness the abuse that
> Euripides incurred for his innovations with such dramatic subjects; and Servius
> is probably voicing the traditional critical feeling in this matter.[19]

I will have more to say about Servius's judgment when dealing with Augustine. Meanwhile, we should keep all of this in mind as we turn to consider Virgil.

VIRGIL'S *ECLOGUES*: AN OVERVIEW

In the midst of a prolific outburst of witty and slightly world-weary love poems, from Catullus, Tibullus, and Ovid, we find something qualitatively different—the *Eclogues* of Virgil (d. 19 BCE). Though these echo and emulate Theocritus, particularly in the mélange of rustic and urban themes, the whole is also spectacularly new.

These shepherds are not Sicilian; they are literary, inhabiting an idealized Arcadia: "a spiritual landscape set . . . half-way between myth and reality; it is also a no-man's land between two ages, an earthly beyond, a land of the soul yearning for its distant home in the past."[20] These shepherds are able to quote from their forebears in Theocritus (e.g., *Eclogues* 8.23–25; cf. *Idylls* 3.3–5), even while they are rubbing shoulders with Virgil's Roman patrons (*Eclogues* 10.19–20) or singing of them (*Eclogues* 4.11, 9.26–29).

Shepherds and goatherds with Theocritan names discuss themes of concern to "the city they call Rome" after decades of civil war, from the displacement of peasants by war veterans to hopes for a new age of peace and ease (*otia*) at war's end. They are also, like the Song of Songs, both easy to read at the outset and also baffling, a mixture of yang and yin, especially toward the end.

Horace said of these eclogues that they were *molle et facetum*, itself a much-discussed ambiguous phrase for which a typical translation is "tender and highly finished."[21] Later the pagan grammarian Aelius Donatus (ca. 350 CE) would praise Virgil for his *astismos*: "a varied trope with many virtues. It describes what is free of *rustic simplicity* and is polished by a rather witty *urbanity*" (quiquid simplicitate rustica caret et faceta satis expolitum est; Donatus, *Ars maior* 3:6, emphasis added).[22] A century later, the pagan grammarian Servius (ca. 450 CE) would define *astismos* as "urbanity without resentment" (urbanitas sine iracundia).

A DIGRESSION: THE DIALECTIC OF
URBANITY VERSUS RUSTIC SIMPLICITY

Donatus's pupil St. Jerome, along with other church leaders, would pivotally reverse this valuation of urbanity over rustic simplicity. In *Epistola* 52, Jerome identified urbanity with "the detestable wit of Roman comedy";[23] while in *Epistola* 57 he wrote that he had always venerated the apostolic virtue of *sancta simplicitas*.[24] In this way, Jerome, though himself far from a paragon of holy simplicity, did anticipate the ethos of the Dark Age.

An example of this ethos was Pope Gregory I (d. 604), who denounced Rome's schools of pagan rhetoric "for their perverse urbanity, which confounds truth with falsehood."[25] For the rest of the Middle Ages, "exegetes would appeal to the authority of Gregory against the humanists who took Donatus as their authority."[26]

We shall see that Dark Age poets from Fortunatus (d. ca. 600) to Alcuin (d. 804) also exhibit in their verse a poetics of rustic simplicity. (Alcuin, however, a cusp figure, also revived for the oncoming Middle Ages the notion that *urbanitas* [i.e., correct classical Latin] was desirable in prose.[27])

Like the cusp figure Dante after him, Alcuin's sensibility melded aspects of both urbanity, represented in Dante's *Comedy* by the "ornate speech" (parola ornata) of Virgil praised by Beatrice (*Inferno* 2:67), and rusticity, the "sweet plain speech" (dir suave e piana) of Beatrice praised by Virgil (*Inferno* 2:56).[28] As mentioned before, it is this admixture of yang and yin, urban and rustic, ordered and extra-ordinary, that makes cusp figures from Plato to Rousseau and Wordsworth great generative figures in our ethogeny.

The dialectical opposition of urbanity to rustic simplicity continues in modern times, usually today to the detriment of the latter. The *OED* records one meaning of *rustic* to be "unrefined, vulgar; rough; crude," while *sancta simplicitas*, according to the *Oxford Dictionary of Foreign Terms*, is used for "expressing astonishment at a person's *naïveté*." Though it is easy to find critiques of hyper-refinement in Eliot's poetry and elsewhere in our literature, I do not find a negative view of urbanity encoded in our dictionaries. In this respect, the modern sensibility, and still more the postmodern sensibility, has declined in both poetry and criticism from the creative dialectic of our ethogeny.

URBANITY AND RUSTICITY IN VIRGIL'S *ECLOGUES*

Virgil himself was a similar cusp figure, despite the anomaly of his dates. A model of polished urbanity for the pagan grammarians preserving the sophistications of Theocritus, he was also an *anima naturaliter Christiana*[29] ahead of his time for Tertullian (d. ca. 220 CE) and other Christian Fathers. This praise was primarily for Virgil's prediction in *Eclogue* 4 of a golden age of anarchic rural peace, inaugurated by a child.

But that vision is carefully balanced and undercut by Virgil, first in his ironic (one might say astismotic) exaggeration (e.g., grapes from brambles, honey from oaks) toward the eclogue's close. More seriously, we see a pattern of rise and fall in the *Eclogues* as a whole, in what is called a ring structure of composition. Just as in the Song of Songs, there is a curve of development in the sequence of the *Eclogues*, from rural concerns to lofty urban-rural celebrations and back again.

Like a sine curve, or curve for a pandemic, the apex that concerns us here is in the middle:

1–2 Political injustice, the dementia of love

    3 Theocritan poem contests on human matters

        4 Prophecy of anarchic peace (*Saturnia regna*)

           5 Apotheosis

        6 Mythology (*Saturnia regna*, universal history)

7–8 Theocritan poem contests on human matters

9–10 Political injustice, love-dementia (with divine involvement).[30]

The Cyclops of Theocritus had been an eccentric buffoon. The self-demeaning Corydon of Virgil in *Eclogue* 2 ("rusticus es, Corydon"; 2.56), even when quoting the Cyclops, is quite different, a representative lover acknowledging, as had Lucretius, the cosmic power of love in the universe. This puts him in an empathic relation not just to the reader but to his pastoral landscape. The lovers in Theocritan *Idylls* 3 and 11 sang only to their isolated selves; Corydon, however, sings "to the hills and woods" (2.5). So does the singer in *Eclogue* 10, "not to deaf ears; the woods echo every note" (respondent omnia silvae; 10.8).

But both sing of the *dementia* of love. The yin of folly here is not a source of joy and inspiration, as it would become for the troubadours a millennium later. Love does not elevate Corydon to the rhythms of the cosmos; it separates him from them, in the equilibrium of twilight:

> Look, bullocks yoked drag home the hanging plough;[31]
> Love burns me still, what limits does love know? (*Eclogues*
> 2.67–68)

It is important to be mindful of this context when thinking about the fourth eclogue, which can be seen as an episodic epiphany of the paradisal followed by a return to the earthly.

The same ring structure writ large underlies Virgil's *Aeneid*, where a revelation to Aeneas in the underworld (in book 6 of twelve) is granted a revelation of Rome's transcendent and unprecedented destiny, to "impose" (an ambiguous verb) the custom of peace, to spare the humbled, and to tame in war the proud (pacique imponere morem / parcere subiectis et debellare superbos; *Aeneid* 6:852–53).

But in the end of book 6, Aeneas returns to earth through the ivory gateway of false dreams (*Aeneid* 6:896–98). And the historical arc of the *Aeneid* ends, like its beginning, in warfare. Aeneas is able to humble his opponent, Turnus. But instead of sparing Turnus, an infuriated Aeneas kills him (*Aeneid* 12:938–52), in circumstances that very closely replicate Achilles's killing of Hector near the end of Homer's *Iliad* (22:322–30).

In this way the *Aeneid* brings an Isaian vision of peace and justice back to the world in which we all live, where humans are torn between two conflicting forces: *pietas*—religious observance, corresponding to what I have treated as "second nature"—and *furor*: rage, insanity, possession by our id or first nature.

In the twenty-first century, still dominated by visions of progress we either endorse or attack, it is frustrating to be presented with a process that appears at first to be progressive but in the end is more cyclic—like an *ouroboros*, a serpent eating its own tail. And yet this process recurs widely in the lead-up to the Second Pivotal Shift.

I see it also in the Song of Songs, in which the song of the Shulamite, a woman shepherd and vineyard keeper (Song 1:6–7, 8:12), is elevated in the middle to a biblically epithalamic sequence, possibly involving King Solomon and the Queen of Sheba (3:6–11). The climax also reads a little like an epiphany: "Go forth, O ye daughters of Zion, and behold king Solomon with the crown wherewith his mother crowned him in the day of his espousals, and in the day of the gladness of his heart" (3:11).

But in the end the Shulamite turns away from the wealth of King Solomon (Song 8:11–12). In the same way the peaceful vision of the fourth eclogue, in which we are told "Apollo [god of the sun, light, and reason] now reigns" (iam regnat Apollo; 4.10), is undercut by the tormented lament of the lover in *Eclogue* 10. This lover is not a shepherd in Arcadia but Virgil's Roman friend and patron, the poet Gaius Cornelius Gallus (d. 26 BCE), although we are told that to console him, "the shepherd came . . . the swineherds came . . . Menalcas came," even "Apollo came, [saying] 'Gallas, what madness is this?'" (10.18–22).

Gallus responds, singing first of his "mad passion [insanus amor] for the stern god of war," and then of the cruelty of love (amor) itself. No singing can appease his frenzy (furoris) (10.60); "no toils of ours can change that god" (10.64). The famous last line of Gallus's lament—"Love conquers all; let us too yield to love" (Omnia vincit Amor; et nos cedamus Amori; 10.69)—is a line of defeat and surrender, not the triumphant Christian boast of easy victory to which, by exaptation, it has been pivotally converted. This is not quite the last line of the *Eclogues*: in a nine-line closure, Virgil concludes that he has sat and sung enough: "Let us rise [Surgamus];[32] the shade oft brings peril to singers" (10:78). Virgil is ready to move on.

VIRGIL'S FOURTH ECLOGUE

With this context in mind, let us now consider *Eclogue* 4. The sixty-three-line eclogue, which has had more impact on history than any other of its length, is, let me repeat, both easy to read and baffling, a mixture of yang and (especially toward its end) of yin.

> Sicilian Muses, let's elevate our song.
> Not all are pleased by shrubs and apple trees.
> If we sing woods, let the woods befit a consul.
> Now comes the last age of the Sibyl's song;
> The great order of ages begins anew.   5
> Now Justice returns, Saturn's Age returns;
> Now a new generation descends from the lofty sky.
> Chaste Lucina, favor this child's birth
> With whom the iron race shall cease, and the race of gold
> Arise through the world; now your Apollo reigns.   10
> And with you as consul, Pollio, shall this great age
> Begin, and the glorious months begin their march.
> If any traces of our guilt remain,
> With you as guide, they will be annulled
> And earth released from never-ending fear.   15
> He will be deified, be seen by gods
> And rule a world his father pacified
> [pacatumque reget patriis virtutibus orbem].

And for you, child, shall the untilled soil
Pour gifts, the errant ivy vine
Mixed in with foxglove and Egyptian bean.   20
Uncalled, will goats bring their swollen udders home
And herds afield nor fear the mighty lions.
Your cradle emit blossoms for your pleasure.
And the snake will die, and the false poison-plant
Will die; Assyrian spice will spread.   25
But as soon as you can read of glorious heroes
And your father's deeds, and can grasp what virtue is,
Slowly the fields will turn gold with waving grain,
Unpruned vines will hang with blushing grapes
And rugged oaks will sweat a dewy honey.   30
Yet traces will abide of ancient wrong,
Driving some to cross the sea, build city walls,
And carve into the patient soil with furrows.
Then a new Tiphys will appear, with a new Argo
Bringing new heroes; and there will be new wars   35
Again a great Achilles will be sent to Troy.
And then, when time has made you fully man,
The merchant shall quit the sea, nor shall piny ships
Trade products; all earth shall bear all things.
The soil will not feel a plow, nor the vine a knife;   40
The plowman shall release his ox from its yoke;
Wool will no more deceive with concocted dyes
But the ram himself in the fields will change
His fleece, now blushing purple, and now gold;
Of itself will scarlet swathe the grazing lambs.   45
"Such times, flow on," the Fates sang to their spindles
In concord with the will of Destiny.
"Enter your honors" (the time will soon be right)
Dear child of gods, great increment of Jove!
Behold the earth made convex with this weight: 50
Earth, and the tracts of sea, and the depth of sky!
Ah, that for me will remain a stretch of life
With the inspiration to recount your deeds!
Thracian Orpheus will not best me in song,   55
Nor Linus, though their parents aid them:
To Orpheus, Calliope; for Linus, fair Apollo.
Even Pan, in a contest with Arcadian judges,
Even Pan, Arcadia would judge, had lost.
Begin, small child, to acknowledge with a smile   60
Your mother, whom ten laboring months have tired:
For he, on whom his parents have not smiled,
Merits no god's table, nor a goddess' bed.[33]   64

Most of this is *molle et facetum*. Is Virgil seriously prophesying a world of peace to end Rome's long history of foreign and civil war? Or is he ridiculing such a vision by parody—"the ram teaching his fleece to shine with diverse colors" (*Eclogues* 4.42–45)? Much modernist scholarship has strenuously rejected earlier attributions to Virgil of any kind of seriousness, let alone prophetic insight. Morton Smith, for example, has described the fourth eclogue as "a delightful nonsense poem for a child's birthday," adding that "to suggest that he [Virgil] took it seriously would equate him in stupidity with his interpreters."[34] There are reasons to think this—at times Virgil is clearly echoing the Alexandrian genre of "childish play" (paizein; Callimachus, *Epigrams* 16.1) found in Callimachus and Theocritus.

Virgil tells his Theocritan muses in *Eclogue* 4, however, that he intends to sing at a more serious level. And there is no doubt, moreover, that his poem was taken very seriously when it was written, as well as for centuries afterward. The *Eclogues* were composed at a turbulent and pivotal moment in Roman history, the fragile truce between the warring civil factions of two heirs to the recently assassinated Julius Caesar (d. 44 BCE): Octavian (later Augustus; d. 14 CE) and Mark Antony (d. 30 BCE).

This truce between the two warriors would be confirmed, though not for long, by the Treaty of Brundisium of 40 BCE, arranged in part by the diplomacy of Virgil's patron Gaius Asinius Pollio (d. 4 CE), to whom *Eclogue* 4 is dedicated.

The lines—

> now your Apollo reigns.
> And with you as consul, Pollio, shall this great age
> Begin, and the glorious months begin their march (4.10–12)—

may allude to the grave political events of this period, "though there is uncertainty regarding whether Virgil composed the poem in anticipation of Pollio's consulship or to celebrate his part in the Treaty."[35] (Pollio had been appointed as a consul in 43 BCE, but with a designated installment date of 40 BCE.)

Taking the long view, however, one can think of Virgil as being attuned to the spirit rather than the details of this war-weary period, above all the understandable longing for peace—much as Bob Dylan in the 1960s was attuned to the deep antiwar sentiments of American and global youth and sang, "The times they are a-changing."

THE HISTORIC CONTEXT TO THE FOURTH ECLOGUE

**This may have made Virgil, like Dylan, accidentally prophetic, even if not divinely inspired. Take, for example, line 10, "Now your Apollo reigns" (tuus iam regnat Apollo), written at a time of a growing Roman cult of Sol Invictus. The sun god Apollo was a Greek rather than Roman deity, but already associated with both Antony and Octavian, the two dominant rulers (not yet antagonists) in the Second Triumvirate (43–33 BCE). Virgil's allusion to Apollo was therefore a safe bet.

The Second Triumvirate was a brief and bloodstained alliance of convenience, launched (as Virgil chose not to mention) with the execution of 4,700 opponents, including Cicero. In 15 BCE, as Octavian (now Augustus) slowly bestowed more and more imperial powers upon himself, he also elevated Apollo to a higher status in the Roman pantheon.[36]

Prior to this, the Triumvirate, in 42 BCE, had helped persuade the Senate to deify Julius Caesar. (Because Octavian was Caesar's adopted son, he then assumed the title *Divi filius*, "son of God.") Virgil duly celebrates the arrival in heaven of Daphnis (usually assumed to refer to Caesar), a peace-loving leader, in *Eclogue* 5—

> Kind Daphnis loves peace. . . .
> The very groves ring out the song: "A god is he, a god, Menalcas"
>
> amat bonus otia Daphnis. . . .
> Ipsa sonant arbusta: deus, deus ille, Menalca (5.63–64)—

a miraculous death and resurrection to match the earlier miraculous birth in *Eclogue* 4 of a savior child.

Just for a moment, Virgil's shepherd imagines Daphnis's exaltation in heaven:

> Daphnis, in radiant beauty, marvels at Heaven's unfamiliar threshold, and beneath his feet beholds the clouds and the stars. Therefore [ergo] frolic glee seizes the woods and all the countryside, and Pan, and the shepherds, and the Dryad maids. The wolf plans no ambush for the flock, and sets no snare for the stag; kind Daphnis loves peace [amat bonus otia Daphnis]. (5.56–61)

This openness of spirit, this crazy transcendence of logic in the mood of moreness, is a momentary foretaste of what love will become in the Middle Ages. But Virgil does not sustain it. And for good reason.

Dio Cassius (d. ca. 235 CE) tells us that the Triumvirate deified Caesar "in expectation of someday being themselves thought worthy of like honours."[37] And indeed Augustus, on his death in 14 CE, was declared a god. The context of Caesar's deification, so exalted in Virgil's rendering of it, was less exalted in fact. After the defeat of the republican army at Philippi (42 BCE), their supporters were dealt with at home.

Those murders by proscription which Sulla had once indulged in were once more resorted to and the whole city was filled with corpses. Many were killed in their houses, many even in the streets and here and there in the fora and around the temples; the heads of the victims were once more set up on the rostra and their bodies either allowed to lie where they were, to be devoured by dogs and birds, or else cast into the river. (Dio Cassius, *History of Rome* 47.3.1–2)[38]

Hints by shepherds in *Eclogues* 1 and 9 have suggested to some that Virgil may himself have originally been a republican sympathizer. The first eclogue refers to the singer's changing lovers and then achieving *libertas* in Rome, after being rescued by a god ("It is a god who has wrought for us this peace [deus nobis haec otia fecit]"; 1.6; cf. 19–35). *Eclogue* 9 refers more directly to the perils of that time, and the need to adjust:

Amid the weapons of war, Lycidas, our songs avail as much as, they say, the doves of Chaonia when the eagle comes. So, had not a raven on the left first warned me from the hollow oak to cut short, as best I might, this new dispute, neither your Moeris here nor Menalcas himself would be alive. (9.12–16)

THE FOURTH ECLOGUE AND THE PROPHETIC TRADITION

The *Eclogues'* mixture of near-tragedy and hope would be repeated in Virgil's *Aeneid*. (It would be repeated much later in the great wartime poems of Czeslaw Milosz with their pastoral insert "The World.") The shepherds' allusions to their vulnerability lend poignancy and urgency to the great prophecy, or fantasy, of peace in the fourth eclogue.

Eclogue 4, written circa 40 BCE, writes of a virgin, and of a saving child who in his lifetime will inaugurate a new era of peace. The flocks will no longer fear the lion; the serpent itself will die. No one today believes, as St. Augustine did, that Virgil, writing one of the poems that gained him security and the patronage of Augustus, was also a divinely inspired predictor of Christ's birth.[39]

But even if Virgil lacked divine foreknowledge, can we at least accept that he knew of the messianic prophecies in Isaiah 7:11 ("Behold, the virgin shall conceive and bear a Son, and shall call His name Immanuel") and 11:6:

The wolf also shall dwell with the lamb,
The leopard shall lie down with the young goat,
The calf and the young lion and the fatling together;
And a little child shall lead them.[40]

Eclogue 5—"The very rocks / The very groves ring out the song: 'A god is he, a god, Menalca'"—might also seem to echo Isaiah 55:12–13:

> For you shall go out with joy,
> And be led out with peace;
> The mountains and the hills
> Shall break forth into singing before you,
> And all the trees of the field shall clap their hands.
> Instead of the thorn shall come up the cypress tree,
> And instead of the briar shall come up the myrtle tree.

A century ago, scholars accepted that Virgil must have known Isaiah, either directly through the Jews in Rome or indirectly through Pollio, who "in this very year accompanied Herod to deposit in the Capitol the decree which the Senate had passed naming Herod king."[41] And there are scholars today who believe that parts of the Old Testament were translated into Latin even before Jesus Christ.[42]

Another theory is that Virgil read Isaiah's prophecies in the Judeo-Greek Sibylline Oracles from Alexandria (as opposed to the Cumaean prophecies from Italy, which were destroyed in Rome in 83 BCE). Although the versions we have are post-Virgilian, *Oracle 3* contains, like *Eclogue 4*, Isaiah's maiden, wolf, lamb, and neutralized serpent:

> Of honey and trees shall give their fruit,
> And fatted sheep and cattle there shall be,
> Young lambs and kids of goats; earth shall break forth
> With sweet springs of white milk; and of good things
> The cities shall be full and fat the fields;   v.935
> Nor sword nor uproar shall be on the earth;
> No more shall earth groan heavily and quake;
> Nor shall war longer be on earth, nor drought,
> Nor famine, nor the fruit-destroying hail;
> But great peace, shall be upon all the earth. . . .
> Be of good cheer, O maiden, and be glad;
> For he who made the heaven and earth gave thee
> Joy in thy age. And he will dwell in thee;
> And thine shall be immortal and wolves
> And lambs shall in the mountains feed on grass   v.980
> Together, and with kids shall leopards graze. . . .
>   This end of all things God
> Shalt consummate, whose dwelling is in heaven.
>
>   (*Sibylline Oracle* 3.931–40, 976–82, 1001–2)[43]

If Virgil indeed mined this *Sibylline Oracle* for material, as some think, it may have intensified the ambivalence toward power that undoubtedly underlies Virgil's work. For the Oracles as a whole, and *Oracle* 3 in particular, are anti-imperial in general, and anti-Roman in particular.[44]

Another likely explanation is that the fourth eclogue, already famous in Virgil's lifetime, is a source for emendations in the *Oracle* rather than vice versa. An earlier Christian reference to the arrival of "a holy Lord" and to three men (presumably the Second Triumvirate) who "shall by piteous fate / Endamage Rome" (vv. 48, 62–63) is suspected of being a Christian interpolation. More central to the *Oracle* is a history of "dire war" through nine kingdoms. The last of these is Rome, described as "many-headed, from the western sea" (vv. 185–214; cf. Dan. 7:6, "The beast also had four heads, and dominion was given to it"). Rome's destruction is also predicted, as retribution for her "destructive outrage" (vv. 436–37).

It is irrelevant for our purposes which of these two texts inspired the other. Both, like so many other apocalyptic texts from this era, see their moment in time as a pivotal one. And that is the importance for me of the fourth eclogue. What mattered then and still does is not whose child or whose marriage was being celebrated (uncertain from the outset, perhaps deliberately so) but its expression of a widespread yearning for pivotal change—in the context of this book, a Second Pivotal Shift.

Am I denying to Virgil the prophetic powers so long attributed to him by pagans and Christians alike? Not at all. Among the *OED* meanings of the word "prophet" (from Greek προ- (before) and -φήτης (speaker; from φάναι, "to speak") is listed (between more divine and more secular senses of the term) "an inspired bard or poet. *Obsolete*." Four examples of this use are given from a span of five centuries. Of these four, two are to "the prophet Virgil" (1788 and 1897), and a third (before 1387) to Satiricus—that is, Horace, who in his sixteenth epode also played with the aspirations of the fourth eclogue.

I am deadly serious when I say that some writers have the power to foresee, and even to some extent influence, events in the near future. To unpack the full meaning of the *Eclogues*, one has to read carefully the whole of the *Aeneid*, which itself contains two spoken prophesies. The first is that of Jupiter at the time of the Trojan War, after Aeneas and his crew are shipwrecked, promising Aeneas's mother Venus that Aeneas's fate, to found a city in Italy, remains unchanged (immota; 1.257). At the end of his rapid summary, Jupiter predicts that under "Caesar" (i.e., Augustus), "wars will cease," the Gates of War to the Roman Temple of Janus will be closed, and "impious Furor" will be constrained behind them (*Aeneid* 1:291–93).

As the *Aeneid* was composed between 29 and 19 BCE, Virgil (unlike Jupiter) is not altogether predicting here. The Gates of War were indeed closed by Augustus in 31 BCE, in a symbolic act commemorating that Rome was not at war for the first time in two centuries, since 235 BCE. This closure was only the third in Roman history. Although it would not be the last (there were two more in Augustus's lifetime), it nonetheless marked a hugely important shift, from the last of the civil wars in the dying Roman Republic to the onset of the bloody, repressive, but relatively stable Roman Empire.[45] (Gibbon judged its peace in the second century CE to be, without doubt, "the most happy and prosperous" period in human history.[46])

AN AMBIGUOUS PROPHECY: "TO IMPOSE THE CUSTOM OF PEACE"

I consider both the *Eclogues* and the *Aeneid* to be genuinely prophetic about the Second Pivotal Shift, if we see that their true concern is about the evolution not of politics but of culture. That is my reading of the second long prophecy in the *Aeneid*, that spoken in Hades to Aeneas in book 6 by his father Anchises:

> Remember, Roman: your empire will rule nations
> And these will be your arts:—to impose the custom of peace,
> To spare the downfallen and bring down the proud.
>
> tu regere imperio populos, Romane, memento
> hae tibi erunt artes: pacique [pacisque] imponere morem,
> parcere subiectis et debellare superbos. (*Aeneid* 6:851–53)

"To impose the custom of peace" (or "for peace") is clearly an ambiguous phrase, almost oxymoronic. Whether for philosophic or merely diplomatic reasons, it epitomizes the underlying doubleness of the entire *Aeneid*. By itself, it could easily be used in a yang argument to justify the U.S. invasion of Afghanistan or Iraq.

But these lines should be considered in context—above all the prophecy of Jupiter in book 1, that after Augustus dies,

> Then shall wars cease and the rough ages soften.
> Aspera tum positis mitescent saecula bella. (*Aeneid* 1:291)

What is being predicted in books 1 and 6 are goals for Rome rather than achievements. And the ambivalence toward power and wealth throughout the poem, in which Matthew Arnold could see "an ineffable melancholy,"[47] marks the *Aeneid* as less an homage to fallible Roman emperors than an epic breakthrough in that great arc of cultural history that, as Martin Luther King said, "bends toward justice." The rough ages did soften after Augustus; in a sense, Jupiter's memorable prophecy has continued down to the present. But this claim can only be made of our cultural development (ethogeny). On a political level, today's most dominant nation, like European nations before it, has gratuitously invaded others, notably Iraq.

In Anchises's faint echo of Isaiah,[48] one can see Virgil, speaking as Anchises, indicating how Roman rulers after Augustus should be different from the rulers of Troy and the generals (*imperatores*) of the republic in his own day: they should be men of peace not war, and they must learn to "impose peace" on many peoples, not just the citizens of the Roman city.[49]

And indeed, as the *Aeneid* became required reading in schools for Roman leaders, the Roman rule of law, not its tenuous imperial power, became Rome's enduring legacy—to Europe first and eventually most of the world. The popularity of the fourth eclogue contributed to that solid legacy. It also contributed indirectly, through Dante and others, to a vision of a still greater Isaian justice ahead, beyond that established in the *Institutes* of Justinian (d. 565).

Tertullian (d. ca. 220 CE), one of the more doctrinaire Christian Fathers, nonetheless was able to recognize in Virgil an *anima naturaliter Christiana* (*Apologeticus* 17.6). Whether one is a theist or an atheist, one should be able to see in this homage a firm indication of a major cultural change, evolving simultaneously from both pagan and Christian sources.

In a series of lectures at Harvard after receiving the Nobel Prize, Czeslaw Milosz remarked, "The poetic act both anticipates the future and speeds its coming."[50] It is ironic that in the same series Milosz should have noted his personal quarrel with classical authors like Virgil for their remoteness from the common people. I see Virgil's *Eclogues* and *Aeneid* as exemplifying Milosz's extravagant claim for the "poetic act," more securely perhaps than any other poet since Isaiah himself.

Admiration of Virgil, once widespread, has become more controversial with the decline of trust in government since about the time of the Vietnam War. We saw earlier how the fourth eclogue has been dismissed as a "nonsense poem," but recently the visionary prophecy of Anchises in the *Aeneid* has come in for more severe treatment.

Seamus Heaney, perhaps the greatest English-language poet of his generation (and an admirer of Milosz), wrote that *Aeneid* 6 is "the best of books and the worst of books. . . . Worst because of its imperial certitude, its celebration of Rome's manifest destiny and the catalog of Roman heroes."[51]

Back in 1976, the excellent scholar Ralph Johnson dismissed the possibility that Virgil could have attached any credence to what he had written in Anchises's prophecy. Instead this was "a witty and understated *recusatio* . . . throwing doubt on the value and validity of the artistic process."[52]

A LATE DIGRESSION: SEAMUS HEANEY
AND CZESLAW MILOSZ

In this book, perhaps the most telling mark of the contemporary episteme we all live in is Seamus Heaney's failure to acknowledge the pregnant ambiguity in Anchises's seminal vision of imposing peace, his writing it off as banal "imperial certitude." Not only was Heaney (d. 2013) perhaps the very greatest English-language poet of his generation, but also of extreme relevance here are his clear love for the rest of *Aeneid* 6, his overall astuteness as a critic, and his profound decency as a man.

One can attribute Heaney's remark about "imperial certitude" to his understandable antipathy to empire after having experienced the British efforts to "impose peace" on troubled Ireland. A clearer picture of how affected he was by that misguided policy occurs in his magnificent poem sequence "Station Island."

Heaney regarded Milosz as "the Master" and also praised his work as ethogeny: "the embodiment of a loyalty to the ancient dream that human beings are on earth to transcend their worst selves, to create civilisation, to build the new Jerusalem in spite of all."[53]

But in "Station Island," Heaney's response to Ireland's troubles was the opposite of Milosz's to Poland's: not engagement, but escape. The poem is enhanced by Heaney's own doubleness. In the poem's purgatory, we hear first from the ghost of a shopkeeper who in the middle of the night opened his shop door to provide pills for a sick child and for this rash act of kindness was promptly murdered by the IRA.[54] But later we hear also from one of the IRA hunger strikers who died in their protest at being treated as common criminals. He thus empathizes with the feelings of both the enforcers of power from above and also those of the oppressed.

> At that stage, the IRA's self-image as liberators didn't work much magic with me. But neither did the too-brutal simplicity of Margaret Thatcher's "A crime is a crime is a crime. It is not political." My own mantra in those days was the remark by Milosz that I quote in "Away from It All"; "I was stretched between contemplation of a motionless point and the command to participate actively in history."[55]

Heaney's response to Milosz's dilemma in "Station Island" is to heed the advice of Simon Sweeney at the opening of the poem, "Stay clear of all processions!" as reinforced at the end by the ghost of James Joyce:

> "What you do you must do on your own.
> The main thing is to write
> for the joy of it."[56]

The value system or ethos expressed here underlies Joyce's *Finnegan's Wake.* It is much more wide reaching, however, than a response to the dilemma of Irish civil strife; it is, I believe, the underlying motif of most contemporary poetry, from Ashbery in America to Larkin in England.

It is, however, antithetical to the response of Milosz. Both early and late in life Milosz distinguished his goal for poetry as both more ambitious and more traditional than that of most contemporary poets—no less, in effect, than collective salvation:

> What is poetry which does not save
> Nations or peoples?
> A connivance with official lies.[57]

And in *Native Realm*, where he formulated the dilemma of the timeless versus the ephemeral, he added, "Right or wrong, I considered my poetry a kind of higher politics, an unpolitical politics."[58]

In his short epic "A Treatise on Poetry," he addressed this dilemma at some length, and his choice was unequivocal, not "contemplation" but "to be of use."[59] Offered the chance to write poetry as an exile in America on a farm, he declined: "It would mean to isolate oneself from the affairs of the twentieth century and from the political and philosophical commitments of Polish poetry."[60]

Milosz's daring claims for his poetry's function on a higher level, which I explore elsewhere,[61] not only exemplify what I am stating in this book about ethogeny; they helped inspire it. In his aspirations for a poetry "of use," he broke with the limiting mantras of his generation, such as Auden's "poetry makes nothing happen." In his despair at the Irish crisis, Heaney did more to exemplify them, much as the Blochs did when they cleansed the Song of Songs of its potentially apocalyptic patina.

It's no accident that both Heaney and Milosz came from marginal areas where class distinctions were strong and reinforced by strong differences between contesting nationalities and languages (Polish and Lithuanian for Milosz, English and Irish for Heaney). In both these milieus of division, Virgil was taught with a biased emphasis on his role in a culture of enforced pacification from above, provoking the two poets' criticism of him.

Yet in his "Quarrel with Classicism" (including Virgil), Milosz noted that the tension between power from above and power from below in society was mirrored by "a quarrel . . . between classicism and realism" in literature, adding that "these two opposed tendencies usually also coexist within one person."[62] Milosz faults Virgil for exhibiting only the first tendency in his work. In this, I believe, Milosz was wrong.

In a moment, I shall discuss how the classicist dream of order and *pietas* in the *Aeneid* is undercut at the end by the realism of "pious Aeneas"'s merciless slaying, in a moment of *furor*, of his victim Turnus. Here I wish to observe that, even in the sixty-three crowded lines of *Eclogue* 4, there are two opposed subjects with opposing points of view: the otherworldly and the this-worldly, the unreal and the real.

The first subject is the vision of order imposed by heroes from above or outside this world, not only the child who will inaugurate a golden age but also the mythic "chosen heroes" of the Argo (including Orpheus), whose *gubernator* or helmsman was Tiphys.

Far less noticed today are the last eleven lines of the poem, with a change of tone, content, pacing, and above all subject and perspective. Virgil now sings of his own powers and the inspired poem he will write of the grown child's deeds. And he dares to predict, in a manner without precedent in Greek or Latin poetry, that he will "vanquish in song" the divinely inspired and parented Orpheus and Linus.[63] The one heavy repetition in the poem—

> Pan etiam, Arcadia mecum si iudice certet,
> Pan etiam, Arcadia dicat se iudice victum.
>
> Even Pan, in a contest with Arcadian judges,
> Even Pan, Arcadia would judge, had lost. (4.58–59)—

stresses that a contemporary mortal can best those whose partial divinity has been accepted. And the closing couplet about the child's need for human approbation reaffirms this perspective that humanity and divinity can be intermingled from this world below, not just ordained from above.

To say this is to see *Eclogue* 4 in terms of what I spoke of in my introduction to this book: the traditional and classical mode, of imposing order and justice in society from above through enforcement, being (very slowly) challenged and displaced by a contrary movement from below of human power, through cultural development (ethogeny) and its empowerment.

At least one Greco-Latin poet, the first-century CE Roman fabulist Gaius Julius Phaedrus, alluded to, and imitated, this second or counter-classicist movement of *Eclogue* 4 rather than the first:

In 3. *Prol.* the fabulist [i.e., Phaedrus] names himself for the first time (*Phaedri*, 1); uses the first person pronoun *ego* three times . . . and boasts of his literary pedigree (*ego litteratae qui sum proprior Graeciae* [I am a literate person who belongs to Greece], 54; *Linoque Apollo sit parens, Musa Orpheo* [And let Apollo be the parent to Linus, the Muse to Orpheus], 57; cf. 16–23).

[This] recalls Vergil's *Eclogue* 4.57 (*Orphei Calliopea, Lino formosus Apollo*) with remarkable precision: both Phaedrus' allusion and Vergil's original passage appear in the fifty-seventh line of sixty-three-line poems.[64]

Phaedrus emphasizes his following in Virgil's footsteps in order to accept that he would be no Virgil, "that his [own] inventiveness and sophistication would ultimately do nothing to improve his position on the margins of Roman literary culture."[65] But Phaedrus was right, I believe, to read *Eclogue* 4 as a poem of authorial empowerment. The messianic vision it contains is in the end correctly identified as a human artifact, generative because of its correspondence to an underlying human need.

In a recent book on the novel use of the first person in classical Latin lyric poetry, Kathleen McCarthy refers to the dimension of a poem that focuses on the characters as the "storyworld" and the dimension that consists of the words communicated to the reader as "discourse."[66] Virgil's "discourse" at the close of *Eclogue* 4, claiming that his poetry would approach and surpass previously divinely inspired works, anticipates the romantic and post-romantic claim, exemplified by Milosz in particular, that "the poetic act both anticipates the future and speeds its coming."[67]

[End of this long but relevant digression.]

VIRGIL'S WORKS AS A DEMONSTRATION OF CULTURAL DEVELOPMENT (ETHOGENY)

The response of Heaney and Johnson to Virgil reflects the ambivalence in contemporary culture about white male domination. But in terms of the reception of Virgil through the ages, they are outliers. Over and over, in times of major disruption and chaos, major writers, like Dante, have returned to Virgil for guidance.

During World War II, Bruno Snell, to combat the shadow of Nazi barbarism, wrote in German his short masterpiece, *The Discovery of the Mind*. In it, he summarized very well Virgil's closeness to his age's longing for peace and a home.

> And in the fourth eclogue, where this political yearning is even more prominent, it straightaway reaches out into the golden age and immerses itself in eschatological hopes. These dreams of the poet place an interpretation upon history which answered to a good many expectations of the age. After the disastrous anarchy of the civil wars the desire for peace was paramount, especially among the better minds of the day. Thus Virgil's poetry reflects a genuine political reality, and it is not without significance that Virgil, at a time when Augustus was

only just beginning to make his authority felt in the affairs of Rome, had already voiced that yearning for peace which Augustus was fated to satisfy. . . . In this sense Virgil may be said to have determined to a considerable extent the political ideology of the Augustan age, and his *Eclogues* did indeed exercise an important political and historical function.[68]

And to emphasize the *Eclogues'* huge generative role in the Western literary canon, Snell claimed that the modern poet "who in the stillness of nature surrenders himself to his feelings . . . did not exist until he saw the light of day in Virgil's Arcadia."[69]

Snell's whole book, as its title indicates, is a study in ethogeny or cultural development. Its final chapter on Virgil emphasizes how poetry in particular has contributed to the creative evolution of culture:

> Hesiod, pasturing his flocks and composing his songs on . . . Parnassus, does not exert his imagination, but obeys the inspiration of a deity. . . . Even Plato, who in his *Ion* refers to the enthusiasm of the poet as a divine gift, a *theia moira* [*Ion* 534 c], regards his enthusiasm as a means of rousing the audience and transmitting the passion of the poet, not as a creative process in which the objects of the poem are themselves given life. . . . In Virgil . . . the ancient gods . . . are deprived of their ancient mysterious power, and . . . have taken on a Utopian quality, embodying the spiritual truths which are not to be found in this world.[70]

Snell's argument can be advanced still further by a glance at the second or Iliadic half of the *Aeneid* (complementing the Odyssean first half, where Aeneas, like Odysseus, develops from a Trojan ethos to a new ethos, in this case a Roman *pietas*). I mentioned earlier that at the close of the *Aeneid*, Aeneas, despite his new character, becomes infuriated (furiis accensus et ira terribilis; 12:946–47) and kills his enemy Turnus in a close replica of Achilles's killing of Hector.

So Aeneas in book 12 fails the high standard set for him in book 6 by his father in Hades. Many critics, accepting this dénouement as Virgil's concluding verdict, talk of Virgil's pessimism in both the episode and the poem.[71] I however see the second half of the *Aeneid* as Virgil's strongest affirmation that Roman *pietas* represented a clear advance over the violent ethos of *arete* promoted in the Homeric *Iliad*.

In book 7, Aeneas, with his followers, arrives in southern Italy (Latium) and first encounters the Latin race he is fated to embrace, by marrying their princess Lavinia. Her father, king Latinus, tells Aeneas that "the Latins are Saturn's race, righteous not by bond or laws, but self-controlled of their own free will and by the custom of their ancient god" (*Aeneid* 7:202–4). From a second king, Evander, whose city was on the site of future Rome, Aeneas heard a conflicting and less idealistic account of this Saturnian golden age: that Saturn had come to Latium and given its people laws:

> Under his reign were the golden ages [aurea . . . saecula] men tell of: in such perfect peace he ruled the nations [populos]; till little by little there crept in a race of a worse sort and duller hue, the frenzy of war, and the passion for gain [et belli rabies at amor successit habendi]. (*Aeneid* 8:322, 324–27)

(Evander here speaks like a precursor of Rousseau. Or, more sensibly, we should see Rousseau as in the tradition of Evander.)

The arrival of Aeneas shatters what remains of this peace. Juno, implacably opposed to the fate Jupiter has designed for him, vows: "If Heaven I cannot bend, then Hell I will arouse." Though she cannot prevent Aeneas from marrying Lavinia, "yet to put off the hour and bring delay . . . that I may do"—by stirring up a futile war between Aeneas (whom she calls a "second Paris") and the Latin people. To this end, she summons up a Fury, Allecto, "whose heart is set on gloomy wars, passions, plots, and baneful crimes [crimina noxia]."[72]

(The actions of Juno and Allecto in *Aeneid* 8 echo those of Hera and Athena in *Iliad* 4, but with a crucial difference. In the unprincipled heaven depicted in the *Iliad*, Zeus not only consents to his wife Hera's demand for war, but he himself orders Athena (centuries before she became associated with wisdom) to initiate it [*Iliad* 4:68–72]. In the *Aeneid*, where Jupiter now personifies fate, the war Juno initiates is doomed in advance, as Juno herself acknowledges [*Aeneid* 7:310–17].)

At Juno's bidding, Allecto visits first the Latins and then Turnus to implant the "first shafts of frenzy" (primos . . . furores; *Aeneid* 7:406) and again "the accursed frenzy of war" (scelerata insania belli; *Aeneid* 7:461). Virgil could hardly have framed more starkly the futility and sheer madness of the Iliadic bloodshed that ensues in his poem, often imitating specific scenes in the *Iliad*. The *Iliad* for Homer's audience, as for public schools in nineteenth-century imperial Britain, had been a textbook of heroic *arete*, or virtue. But in the *Aeneid*, such matters are now viewed from an alien perspective as *furor*, not akin to Roman *pietas* but a threat to it.

That Aeneas, already inspired to a higher calling, could lapse from anger into an act of furious revenge illustrates the short-term influence of Juno, or counterfate (as in the recent past of Virgil's Rome, beset by almost a century of civil war). One can still hope that a truer picture of the future, both inside and outside the *Aeneid*, will be found in the prophecies of first Jupiter and then Anchises, even though we have not yet succeeded in subordinating violence to the goal envisioned by Anchises—"to impose the custom of peace" (paci[s]que imponere morem; *Aeneid* 6:852).

VIRGIL AS A PROPHET OR MINDER

Already in the *Argonautica*, Apollonius had shifted the focus of epic and of virtue away from male prowess. His Argonaut Idas (the "mightiest of men on earth" in the *Iliad*, 9:557–58) was now depicted as a "hot-headed arrogant" (to quote George Mooney), an ugly parody of the Homeric hero.[73] Medea at the center of the narrative is not an exemplar of Homeric *arete*; she is more like a victim of it.

But never before Virgil had anyone depicted war in epic as so unequivocally antithetical to human destiny and (in his word) *pietas*. After nearly a century of bloodshed, Virgil voiced a sentiment that would, soon after his death, become embodied in a new social movement—Christianity, the most influential sign and product of the Second Pivotal Shift.

So would Virgil's related condemnation of not just destructive war but greed (et belli rabies et amor successit habendi; *Aeneid* 8:327).[74] Jesus's subsequent warning, "It is easier for a camel to go through the eye of a needle, than for a rich man to enter into the kingdom of God" (Matt. 19:24), would in the later empire help to convince a significant number of Romans to sell all that they had and give to the poor.[75]

Anticipating St. Paul's condemnation of money as "the root of all evil" (1 Tim. 6:10), a tag from Virgil, "auri sacra fames" (the accursed greed for gold; *Aeneid* 3:57), became a commonplace of Christian homiletics, and later the title of a major economic text by John Maynard Keynes. (It is quoted also in Italian—"sacra fame de l'oro"—by Dante's Statius in *Purgatorio* 22.40–41.)

Because of his prophecy of a new golden age introduced by the birth of a child, Virgil, as noted above, was accepted as a prophet by some of the Christian Church Fathers. Thus Dante chose to have his fictional guide Virgil speak prophetically in the opening canto of the *Inferno*. And Dante later describes Virgil's teaching influence in *Purgatorio* 22, where the Roman poet Statius (d. 79 CE), who in Dante's unfounded account was a secret Christian, says that it was Virgil's fourth eclogue that converted him:

> You were the first to send me
> to drink within Parnassus' caves . . .
> when you declared: *"The ages are renewed;*
> *justice and man's first time on earth return;*
> *from heaven a new progeny descends."*   *Eclogues* 4.5–7
> Through you I was a poet and, through you,
> a Christian.

> (*Purgatorio* 22.64–73)

In this way Dante, like Virgil, preserves and projects what Milosz called a "sense of open space ahead."[76] So, before the French Revolution, did Jean-Jacques Rousseau (d. 1778), celebrated by Hölderlin as a "yearning man" who

> . . . flies as the eagles do
> Ahead of thunder-storms, preceding
> Gods, his own gods, to announce their coming.[77]

Among these visionary cultural pathfinders or minders, I would list Milosz himself, whose works in poetry and prose helped keep alive the flame of poetry in postwar Poland behind the Iron Curtain. In the 1950s, exiled from Poland, Milosz translated into Polish the writings of the French left-wing Catholic Simone Weil and thus contributed to the left-wing Catholic coalition Solidarity that liberated Poland nonviolently two decades later.[78]

The undeniable influence of such pathfinders means that human history is more than a conflict between blind Darwinian forces. History, which has helped shape the evolution of the human mind, reflects generative human minds among its influences.

This is particularly true, I believe, during pivotal shifts, when past social systems are collapsing. Virgil, even before Jesus, was a generative pathfinder for the Second Pivotal Shift.

And Augustine, I shall suggest later, was similarly a generative pathfinder for the third.

PART TWO

Endarkenment

Disruption and Creativity in the Dark (Yin) Age

Chapter Eight

Disruptive Shifts in the Evolution of Culture

THE ROLE OF VIOLENT DISRUPTIONS IN PIVOTAL SHIFTS

It is now widely accepted that a pivotal shift in the evolution of Eurasian culture and history occurred at various times toward the middle of the first millennium BCE. Denoted by the emergence of spiritual leaders, from Confucius to the Buddha and Isaiah, their belief systems attached new importance to the authority of written texts, which could be used as a criterion by which to judge and even oppose established political authority. The new sense of identity in a moral community was accompanied also by a heightened sense of individual ethical responsibility.

These are only some of the features of the so-called Axial (i.e., Pivotal) Age, when most of the great world religions first came into being. It was a shift that in many cases was a response to major violence at the end of a historical era. Confucius, for example, lived at the end of the so-called Spring and Autumn period of Chinese history, Isaiah and Jeremiah during the extinction of the kingdoms of Israel and Judah. There is no consensus on when Zoroaster lived, but some place him in the seventh and sixth century BCE, when Cyrus the Great replaced the Median, Babylonian, and Lydian Empires with the new Achaemenid (Persian) Empire.

The Second Cultural Shift was also a response to violent disruptions. Both early Christianity and Mishnaic (i.e., Rabbinic) Judaism arose as responses to the end of Judaean independence and the permanent destruction of the Second Temple in Jerusalem. They were also profoundly affected by the Roman destruction of the Hellenistic kingdoms in the Levant in a series of internecine campaigns by competing Roman generals.

A by-product of these campaigns was the de facto end of the self-governing Roman Republic, already weakened by plagues "at least once a decade."[1] Its replacement, what we remember as the Roman Empire, disrupted regional social structures and thus unwittingly also facilitated the rapid spread of both Christianity and post-Temple Rabbinic Judaism.

What Karen Armstrong has called a second axial age, the Renaissance,[2] also arose partly in response to plague (as we shall see), but also calamitous violence. After the fall of Constantinople in 1453, a wave of immigrant refugee scholars contributed to Greek scholarship in the Florentine Academy and elsewhere. Before that, the great flowering of urban middle-class culture in Florence, at the time of Dante, emerged after weakened imperial courts ceased to attract poets as they had under Emperor Frederick II (d. 1250).

Finally, the dawn of the scientific era was overshadowed by the Thirty Years' War (1618–1648), which weakened the papal restrictions on science, and by the Treaty of Westphalia (1648), which definitively ended the last imperial pretenses of the Holy Roman Empire, inaugurating the modern international system of sovereign states.

In other words, the erosion and collapse of moribund systems under pressure made space for the emergence, stabilization, and eventual erosion of new ones. The history of our cultural evolution, which I believe to be progressive, has not been continuous on its surface: catastrophic disruptions of outmoded social structures have played a major part. But these surface disruptions contribute, I believe, to a deeper continuity in which recurrent constructive expansions and disruptive recisions, like the diastole and systole of a healthy heart, both contribute to organic growth toward greater peace.

VIOLENCE AND NONVIOLENCE IN THE
THIRD PIVOTAL SHIFT, CA. 500 CE

I hope to argue here that there was one such creative disruption or pivotal shift in the middle of the first millennium CE, coinciding with the fall of Rome and ensuing yin or Dark Age in the West and the emergence of an expansive Islam in the East. At this time the creative link between cities and civilization, the key to yang-dominated periods of history, was essentially broken in western Europe (as it had already been to a lesser extent in China).

We are conditioned to see this Third Shift (to deurbanization) in terms of negative causes: barbarian irruptions (much less causative than commonly thought), the military exhaustion of Byzantium and Persia (a factor in the rapid spread of original rural Islam), or (as I am about to discuss) natural violence in the form of devastating plagues and/or climate change.

But writing this book has led me to attach more importance to a positive feature, a new phase in the generative evolution of our culture: the rise to cultural leadership in northern Europe of intentional, nonviolent communities, at all levels of society. I am referring to the well-known fact that in northern Europe, particularly in Ireland and northern Britain, cultural and educational leadership was spread by missionary monks and housed in rural monasteries. This energetic movement can be traced back to the proselytizing efforts of St. Martin in the fourth century.

This in turn was preceded by the emergent nonviolent power of the newly dominant Catholic episcopal church. The eminent historian Peter Brown tells how in 386 the nonviolent persuasive power of St. Ambrose, the bishop of Milan (then the Western imperial capital), was victorious over the imperial troops of the Roman emperor, Valentinian II:

> Throughout 386, Ambrose would show his power in his inimitable manner. In February, the Emperor's mother, Justina, had ordered Ambrose to surrender a church for use by the Arian[3] members of the court. . . . With studied deference, he flatly refused to give up the church. It became an issue of "court" against "city," with Ambrose making little effort to check the hatred of the Milanese for their Gothic garrison. The leading courtiers were placed under a curfew lest they join this "usurper"; and, as the Gothic troops surrounded the basilica in which Ambrose stood with his congregation, it seemed as if a general massacre might ensue. But the court lost its nerve and gave way. . . . The boy, Valentinian [Justina's son], rounded on his followers, saying that "If Ambrose gave you word, you would hand me over in chains to him." "We priests," Ambrose had said [quoting St. Paul], "have our own ways of rising to Empire. Our infirmity is our way to the throne. For *When I am weak, then am I powerful.*"[4]

The anecdote needs some qualifications. The emperor, Valentinian II, was only fifteen at the time of this incident. The Arianism of his mother had lost official imperial support after being denounced at church councils in 325 and again in 361. (The last Arian emperor, Valentinian's uncle Valens, had died in 371.) While Catholic unity was increasing, the Roman imperial power was weakening; in 384 the two official emperors (Theodosius and Valentinian) had reluctantly agreed to a peace agreement (negotiated in part by Ambrose) in which they accepted a rebel general, Maximus, as their coequal emperor in Gaul.

This list may help illustrate the social change and above all confusion of this cusp period before the Third Shift, including the growing power of Ambrose, the dissipation of imperial unity, the increasing distaste for worldly wealth, and St. Martin's imitation of Eastern monachism in the West.

	Imperial and Church Events of the Late Fourth Century
350(?)	St. Hilary, "The Hammer of the Arians," is elected bishop of Poitiers, secures excommunication of Arian bishop Saturninus of Arles.
356	at the Synod of Biterrae (Béziers), summoned by the Arian emperor Constantius II, Hilary is banished to Phrygia for four years.
357	Constantius removes Altar of Victory from Roman curia.
360(?)	St. Basil modifies Pachomian monasticism by advancing a coenobial (communal) or heremetical (hermit) ideal.
361	Constantius dies and is succeeded by the last pagan emperor, Julian "the Apostate." St. Hilary returns to Poitiers. St. Martin, a disciple of Hilary of Poitiers, establishes at Ligugé the first monastery in France, imitating the Desert Fathers of Egypt.
362(?)	Julian restores Altar of Victory to curia.
363	Julian dies; succeeded for eight months by Jovian, who restores Catholic Christianity to privileged imperial status.
364	Jovian dies, and Valentinian becomes emperor.
	Valentinian attacks the increasing wealth and worldliness of the clergy; issues edict forbidding the grant of bequests to Christian clergy.
370(?)	Valentinian takes as second wife Justina, an Arian.
371	Martin elected bishop of Tours, despite episcopal opposition.
372(?)	Martin establishes monastery of Marmoutiers near Tours.
374	Valentinian, to reinforce tolerance, confirms both the Arian Auxentius and the Catholic St. Ambrose for the See of Milan (Valentinian's capital). Ambrose, formerly Roman governor in Milan, takes strong position against Arianism.
375	Valentinian dies, is succeeded by Gratian in West, Valentinian II in Pannonia.
378	Battle of Adrianople: Roman army defeated by Goths, who settle within empire. Valens, last Arian emperor, killed.
380	Edict of Theodosius declares Trinitarianism of Nicene Council to be only true Catholic religion; ends state support for old polytheism.
381	Priscillian becomes ultra-ascetic bishop of Avila. Bishops at Council of Saragossa condemn eight canons of Priscillianism.
382	Emperor Gratian again removes Altar of Victory.
383	The forces of Maximus defeat and murder Gratian.
	Maximus becomes emperor in Britain and Gaul, ruling from Trier.
	Symmachus, pagan urban prefect of Rome, chooses Augustine to be professor of rhetoric in Milan, the capital of Valentinian II.
384	Ambrose helps negotiate compromise in which Theodosius and Valentinian recognize Maximus as emperor in north.
	Symmachus writes to young emperor Valentinian II, requests restoration of Altar of Victory. Thanks to Ambrose, request is denied.
384(?)	Ambrose and Martin intercede with Maximus in Trier to spare life of Priscillian.
385	Priscillian is convicted in a secular court and executed by sword.[5]
386	Empress Justina, Arian widow of Valentinian I (d. 375), is defeated by Ambrose in Affair of the Milan Basilica.

386	August: Augustine, after a visit by Symmachus's friend and protégé Ponticianus, converts to Christianity.
387	Maximus invades Italy; forces Valentinian II to flee from Milan to Theodosius.
387(?)	Augustine's friend Paulinus meets St. Martin, is cured of an eye infection.
388 July:	Theodosius defeats and kills Maximus; meets Ambrose in Milan.
December:	Theodosius learns Christian mob has destroyed synagogue at Calliniacum on the Euphrates; orders synagogue rebuilt at the expense of the bishop; Ambrose persuades Theodosius to retreat from this position.[6]
390	Augustine writes *Confessions*.
April:	Theodosius orders huge massacre at Thessalonica; Ambrose punishes him by denying him communion until Christmas Day.[7]
391	Augustine ordained bishop of Hippo.
392	Paulinus of Nola and wife Therasia decide to sell their properties.
410	Abbey of Lérins founded by St. Honoratus.

As the Catholic Church became gradually absorbed into the wealth, power, and social structure of the Roman Empire, the quest for a better alternative society was not lost but found its home in a new popular monastic movement, notably with St. Anthony (d. 356) in Egypt.

Augustine has recorded in his *Confessions* (8:6) the importance of monastic renunciation in inspiring his own conversion to Christianity in 386 CE. Peter Brown has also documented how, in the same period, the wealthy began to enter the church "in growing numbers, often stepping into leadership roles as bishops and as Christian writers. . . . From then onward, as members of a religion that had been joined by the rich and powerful, Christians could begin to think the unthinkable—to envision the possibility of a totally Christian society."[8]

That was not to be. But in chapter 12 we will see how in northern Europe, monastic communities, no longer in the desert margins of society, began with St. Martin of Tours to exert an authoritative persuasive influence on the culture and education of the *whole* society, above all the illiterate *pagani* (countrymen) of the rural areas.[9]

Is there perhaps an analogy with the enhanced status of Buddhist monasteries after China was reunited in 589 CE by the Sui emperor Wendi? Wendi's son, Yangdi, after constructing a new capital at Luoyang, "established four Places of Enlightenment (*daochang*). . . . Two of these *daochang* were Buddhist monasteries, Huiri and Fayun. [Huiri] was of special, personal importance to Yangdi. . . . It was there, on Yangdi's orders, the monk Zhiguo . . . started a massive project to classify and catalog Buddhist sutras extant at the time."[10]

The yin or Dark Age in Europe began to end with the restoration by Charlemagne (d. 814) of a semblance of central authority. It shifted more clearly around 1000 CE, when the Mediterranean, after major setbacks to the brilliant Abbasid Empire in Baghdad, was reopened to a marked revival of trade and cities, especially in Italy.

It is easy to see the cultural importance of that revival, which was followed by the achievements of St. Thomas, Dante, and Botticelli. I hope to argue here that in this return to urban culture, there was, as always, loss as well as gain.

PIVOTAL SHIFTS, FLUCTUATIONS IN CLIMATE, AND DISEASE

The process of structural innovation after creative disruption is analogous to the tectonic shifts described by earth scientists, where the slow buildup of unreleased pressure between moving plates leads to a violent release and rearrangement effected by earthquakes. Cultural evolution also tends toward the stability afforded by law; but this very stability, resulting in a social order and structure, will come increasingly under pressure as it is slowly distanced from its social origins.

It is becoming common for writers on cultural evolution to speak of tectonic shifts as well. (The term *tectonic* originally meant "pertaining to construction"—as in "architecture"—and thus can allude to the rigidity of the social constructions preceding and following them.) Wherever outmoded structures collapse, such as of the Bronze Age cities (ca. 1200 BCE), the Western Roman Empire in 476 CE, and the Eastern in 1453, it makes sense to speak of tectonic shifts. These are usually local. But where local tectonic shifts can be seen as phases of a more universal change, we can speak of a pivotal shift.

It has been suggested that the systolic rhythm I have described in pivotal cultural shifts—from consolidation to disruption, urban to rural, and eventually back—corresponds to deep periodic disruptions in our biological and physical environment as well. Recently both imperial collapse and the outbreaks of disease contributing to it have been linked to fluctuations in climate. With only limited evidence, a climate shift has been blamed for the fall of the Han Empire:

> Well before the Han dynasty finally ended in 220, effective power had passed to regional warlords, the scene thus being set for the subsequent division of the empire into three separate states. This transitional phase has the hallmarks of being shaped by climatic adversity. Though the data to test this thoroughly are lacking, the preliminary indications point to undue aridity in the Yellow River basin.[11]

Climatologists have argued that two years of extreme famine and disease in 43–42 BCE, caused by darkened skies from a volcanic mega-eruption in Alaska, may have helped to first end Egyptian autonomy and then "end the Roman Republic."[12] Scientists have also alleged that, "beginning in 165 A.D., smallpox helped ruin the Roman Empire, sowing more destruction than foreign armies ever could."[13] The two events were accompanied by the early spread of Christianity as a protest religion, and eventually its radical conversion (by the Edict of Thessalonica in 380) into the state religion of the slowly decaying Roman Empire.

In 536 a similar cataclysmic eruption in Iceland caused rampant crop failure and famine in Europe. This was followed by an outbreak of bubonic plague, "wiping out one-third to one-half of the population of the eastern Roman Empire and hastening its collapse."[14] The scope of the Byzantine Empire was irreversibly reduced during the so-called Byzantine Dark Ages of circa 600–800. Both it and its traditional enemy, the Sassanid Neo-Persian Empire (which fell in 651), were first weakened by plague and then supplanted in North Africa and Central Asia by the energetic new religion of Islam.

We see a similar development in China, where a disastrous famine in 873 depopulated the countryside and led to a series of agrarian revolts. The once illustrious Tang dynasty, in power for three centuries, collapsed in 907. In the resulting chaos (907–979), the prevalent authority of Tang Buddhism was shaken, to be replaced by a revitalized neo-Confucianism into which some Buddhist principles were incorporated.

The next major catastrophe, the so-called Black Death of the mid-1300s, has been seen by some historians "as a sharp turning point, accounting for many subsequent events and trends in Western civilization, even those that occurred many years afterward, such as the Reformation."[15]

With respect to the Dark Age,

> Work by dendro-chronologists and ice-core experts points to an enormous spasm of volcanic activity in the 530s and 540s CE, unlike anything else in the past few thousand years. This violent sequence of eruptions triggered what is now called the "Late Antique Little Ice Age," when much colder temperatures endured for at least 150 years.

> This phase of climate deterioration had decisive effects in Rome's unravelling. It was also intimately linked to a catastrophe of even greater moment: the outbreak of the first pandemic of bubonic plague. . . . However, the decisive factor in Rome's biological history was the arrival of new germs capable of causing pandemic events. The empire was rocked by three such intercontinental disease events. The Antonine plague [165–180 CE] coincided with the end of the optimal climate regime, and was probably the global debut of the smallpox virus.

The empire recovered, but never regained its previous commanding dominance. Then, in the mid-third century, a mysterious affliction of unknown origin called the Plague of Cyprian sent the empire into a tailspin. Though it rebounded, the empire was profoundly altered—with a new kind of emperor, a new kind of money, a new kind of society, and soon a new [official] religion known as Christianity. Most dramatically, in the sixth century a resurgent empire led by Justinian faced a pandemic of bubonic plague, a prelude to the medieval Black Death. The toll was unfathomable; maybe half the population was felled.[16]

As we might expect, such huge natural disasters can occur randomly; the dates we have just reviewed—43 BCE, 536 CE, 873, and 1347—are unrelated and do not form a clear temporal pattern. But when we turn from these four disasters to the consequent social disruptions in their wake, a clearer pattern does emerge. The major periods of chaos, each terminating a phase in our ethical evolution or ethogeny, are regularly separated in their emergence by roughly half a millennium.

Disaster	Political Disruption	New Religion
43–42 BCE famine	Fall of Roman Republic, 17 BCE	Christianity, ca. 40 CE
536–541 famine and plague[17]	Byzantine Dark Ages, 800–900[18]	Islam, 622
873 great famine in China	Fall of Tang dynasty, 907	Neo-Confucianism, ca. 1000
1347–1351 Black Death	End of papal predominance	Protestant Reformation, 1515

The positive outcomes of each of these disruptions—including the religious breakthroughs noted in the right-hand column—constitute part of the continuous evolution of our ethos (our ethogeny) that is the topic of this book. This evolution or unfolding proceeds by its own dialectic of disruption and renewal, in which emergent dissatisfaction with a decaying status quo breeds energy for innovation.

Disasters may contribute to this disruption, just as an autumn gale will help strip dying leaves from an oak tree. But the cause of the leaves' dying is organic to the oak itself, not caused by the storm. (I am making this point against those historians who argue that social and cultural systems are so embedded in their inertia that *only* disasters can change them.)

For example, the historian Walter Scheidel has written that "throughout history, only massive, violent shocks that upended the established order proved powerful enough to flatten disparities in income and wealth."[19] (I shall question this claim later in the conclusion to this book.)

Similarly, disasters do little to affect the tempo of tectonic disruption and change. Before the famine of 23 BCE, the Roman Republic had already been weakened and demoralized by a century of civil wars and plagues, and it disappeared less than a decade later. But Byzantium, though irreparably weakened by the plague of 536, experienced a last period of temporary successes under Justinian (527–565) before suffering major setbacks in the seventh century.[20]

Tectonic shifts under our soil cause major earthquakes to occur with somewhat predictable regularity. The same can be said of the tectonic shifts that have underlain our disruptive, continuous ethical evolution (ethogeny). Under the flow of endless cultural change, a deeper pattern of buildup and release remains roughly the same.

CATASTROPHES AND PROGRESS

From what we might call the Apollonian or yang perspective of historians and social scientists, these calamitous disruptions are often regretted as interruptions or even regressions in the process of cultural evolution.

My intention is to show that in Europe, the disruptive shift to a yin or Dark Age (ca. 500–1000 CE)[21] was not just a necessary stage in ethical evolution; it was, on the ethical level, a positive one. It partly destroyed but also partly enhanced "the legacy of antiquity," preparing Europe for the renewal of ancient culture at a higher level.

This will require a deeper exploration of why I talk of civilizations as yang or yin, two terms that can be traced back to the Axial Shift.[22] For now let us just define *yang* in lay terms as whatever is knowable to "reason" and explicable in language (control of which is associated with the left hemisphere of the brain), that is, the realm of our normal communication and interaction with the external world. The inner world beyond language and comprehension is the realm of yin, a corresponding but darker realm of consciousness that can only be hinted at negatively in language, as in the Daodejing of Laozi (sixth century BCE):

The Dao that can be expressed ("Daoed") is not the true Dao,

or the *pensée* of the mathematician Blaise Pascal (d. 1662):

The heart has its reasons that reason cannot know,

or more recently the equation by Max Weber of modernism with the limiting "disenchantment of the world":

the loss of the overarching meanings, animistic connections, magical expecta-
tions, and spiritual explanations that had characterized the traditional world,
as a result of the ongoing "modern" [i.e., yang] processes of rationalization,
secularization, and bureaucratization.[23]

In the spirit of Pascal and Weber, I shall for now refer to yin as the realm of
enchanted consciousness *not* knowable to reason (the realm, if you will, of
the Dionysian mysteries, which [according to Euripides and Ovid] the ratio-
nalist Pentheus hoped both to investigate and to ban, but which, in a return
of the repressed, destroyed him for his hubris[24]). I shall argue that the realm
of yin had a great shaping influence on cultural evolution through the Third
Pivotal Shift, the Dark Age of 500–1000 CE.

WHY DO WE REMEMBER THIS
PERIOD AS THE DARK AGE?

Let me recapitulate the dialectical evolution of the term "Dark Age," whose
connotations have shifted in step with the rise of modernist rationalization.

> Petrarch was the very first to speak of the Middle Ages [i.e., his own age] as
> a "dark age," one that separated him from the riches and pleasures of classical
> antiquity and that broke the connection between his own age and the civilization
> of the Greeks and the Romans.[25]

Today, however, the term is "now rarely used by historians because of
the value judgment it implies. Though sometimes taken to derive its mean-
ing from the fact that little was then known about the period, the term's
more usual and pejorative sense is of a period of intellectual darkness and
barbarity."[26]

If, however, we are beginning to enter a postmodern, post-secular yang-yin
era, perhaps we can recognize and respect the moon of endarkenment along
with the sun of enlightenment.

Years ago, I wrote an unpublished book-length scholarly study of
Anglo-Latin poetry in the age of Bede and Alcuin (seventh–ninth centuries
CE).[27] Echoing a phrase from the Black Power movement of that time, I
concluded that "dark is beautiful." It is in that spirit, without any antipa-
thy to the positive achievements of enlightenment, that I hope to describe
the achievements of the Dark Age. I offer the thoughts that follow to the
increasing number who speculate that "our entire civilization (the 'modern'
or 'first-world' civilization, for lack of better terms) might go the way of the
classical civilization of antiquity [to] a new dark age."[28]

Recent books, such as James Bridle's *New Dark Age*, have argued that our recent technological achievements present us with an uncontrollable future in which human purposes may no longer prevail or even survive. Others worry that globalization has awakened hopes it has failed to satisfy and contributed to new diseases and other problems it increasingly cannot control. Still others observe that global warming has already contributed to famine-driven unrest, such as the Arab Spring in Tunisia or the Boko Haram in Nigeria.

> The cataclysmic civil war, terror war, and international conflict in Syria are being reclassified as the first climate change war based on the staggering drought that preceded it. That, in fact, has been called "the worst long-term drought and most severe set of crop failures since agricultural civilizations began in the Fertile Crescent many millennia ago."[29]

Prophesies of doom have characterized Western civilization since at least the book of Revelation, and I myself have no idea whether the yang legacy of the Enlightenment is sustainable (as I hope) or not. Also unclear is whether the obvious setbacks to the nineteenth-century belief in progress are a presage to a new Sixth Pivotal Shift; it is too early to tell.

I do however have a hunch: that the modernist age of hard-edged ideologies, including both scientism and fundamentalism, may be yielding to a postmodern replacement of yang or yin certainties by more modest ambiguities. Whether this process leads destructively to cynicism and anomie, or constructively to openness and enlargement of views, is itself uncertain. I believe however that whether the predominant result is destructive (i.e., disruptive) or constructive will be partly up to ourselves.

Either way, I would like to think, a better understanding of ethogenic process, including the past processes of a Dark Age, can contribute to a more fortunate result.

Chapter Nine

Earlier Dark (Yin) Ages, Disruptions, and Mnemohistory

Since beginning this book I have become aware that similar pivotal shifts or moments, *before* the so-called Axial Revolution, have recently been reported by earth scientists and archaeologists. Research into these moments by others reinforces the patterns that I have been describing, particularly with respect to recurring Dark Ages. I shall briefly review three of these alleged shifts, warning the reader in advance that the claims for all three, though impressively documented by both scientific and paleographical data, are still being contested by other researchers using similarly impressive methods.

1. The first alleged shift I shall speak of is the so-called Neolithic Revolution of circa 10,000 BCE, when many human cultures are said to have transferred from a lifestyle of hunting and gathering to one of agriculture and settlement, allowing for a large increase in population.[1] For some time this transition to farming has been recognized as an "early human response to a unique sequence of climatic events."[2]

2. Another alleged shift occurred almost eight millennia later, around 2200 BCE. According to the findings of an important geological congress in 2018,

Agricultural-based societies that developed in several regions after the end of the last Ice Age were impacted severely by the 200-year climatic event ["an abrupt and critical mega-drought"] that resulted in the collapse of civilizations and human migrations in Egypt, Greece, Syria, Palestine, Mesopotamia, the Indus Valley, and the Yangtze River Valley. Evidence of the . . . climatic event has been found on all seven continents.[3]

According to the archaeologist Harvey Weiss, "a global abrupt climate change deflected or weakened the Mediterranean westerlies and the Indian Monsoon and generated synchronous megadrought across the Mediterranean, west Asia, the Indus, and northeast Africa. Dry-farming agriculture domains and their productivity across west Asia were reduced severely, forcing adaptive societal collapses, regional abandonments, habitat tracking, nomadization, and the collapse of the Akkadian Empire."[4]

A consensus among archaeologists had already agreed that "the Empire of Akkad collapsed in 2154 BCE, within 180 years of its founding. The collapse ushered in a Dark Age period of regional decline that lasted until the rise of the Third Dynasty of Ur in 2112 BCE."[5]

(This claim does not note that the oldest known legal code, the Code of Ur-Nammu, and the oldest version of the Gilgamesh epic, both in Sumerian, are dated to approximately 2100 BCE.)

3. A third alleged shift, and the one most relevant to this book, was the sudden and dramatic collapse of Bronze Age culture in the eastern Mediterranean around the years 1300–1200 BCE. According to the classical historian Robert Drews, "within a period of forty to fifty years at the end of the thirteenth and the beginning of the twelfth century almost every significant city in the eastern Mediterranean world was destroyed, many of them never to be occupied again."[6]

Many scholars of classical Greece, focusing on written records, have described as another "Dark Age" the ensuing "period from the demise of Mycenaean civilization to the earliest appearance of alphabetic Greek in the eighth century."[7] For example, Eric Cline, in *1177 B.C.: The Year Civilization Collapsed*, has argued that 1177 BCE "was a pivotal moment [his term] in the history of civilization—a turning point for the ancient world . . . frequently described by scholars as the world's first Dark Age."[8] For Cline, the preceding Bronze Age was a 'Golden Age' of internationalism and globalization," and it was only "centuries later that a new cultural renaissance emerged."[9]

Cline's very readable book includes a fascinating review of recent paleoclimatic research. One seminal article he cites describes periods of cooling events measured by variations in the southern limits of arctic "ice-rafted debris (IRD) events," which "are thought to occur approximately (but not precisely) every 1,500 years."[10]

The article in question looks at evidence from drillings in the North Atlantic ocean bed and concludes, "The ice-rafted debris (IRD) events exhibit a distinct pacing on millennial scales, with peaks at about 1400, 2800, 4200, 5900, 8100, 9400, 10,300, and 11,100 years ago."[11] This translates to 600 CE, 800 BCE, 2200 BCE, 3900 BCE, 6100 BCE, 7400 BCE, 8300 BCE, and 9100 BCE.

These dates briefly fascinated me. The IRD event of 1400 BP (Before Present; i.e. 600 CE) fits with the acute climate downturn of 536 CE I discuss above (attributed to volcanic activity clouding the skies of Eurasia and possibly farther).[12] The consequences of this drastic cooling were first famine and then plague, cited as a cause for the ensuing Byzantine Dark Ages, and the displacement of Christianity in Byzantine Asia and North Africa by Islam.

Moreover, the IRD event of 4200 BP (2200 BCE) corresponds exactly with the date of the "abrupt and critical mega-drought" alleged by the 2018 International Commission on Stratigraphy to have caused "the collapse of civilizations and human migrations in Egypt, Greece, Syria, Palestine, Mesopotamia, the Indus Valley, and the Yangtze River Valley."[13]

However, the whole field of paleoclimatology is rife with disputing articles. The Wikipedia article "Bond Event" (i.e., IRD event) claims that more recent work on petrologic tracers of drift ice in the North Atlantic "has shown that these tracers provide little support for 1,500-year intervals of climate change, and the reported c. $1,500 \pm 500$-year period was a statistical artifact."

The article cited for this claim, by Stephen Obrochta and others, is as elegantly and brilliantly argued as the Bond article it deconstructs.[14] The claim for the "abrupt and critical mega-drought" of 2200 BCE has been similarly disputed, again with equal brilliance.[15]

Fundamental to my "poem in prose" is the notion that the cultural development of mankind has profited from both yang ages of enlightenment and also yin or "Dark" ages of endarkenment. Especially with regard to the latter (the primary focus of my book), I see the data as insufficient for falsifiable demonstration ("scientific proof") but rich for profitable poetic meditation.

I have only recently dipped into the field of paleoclimatology, with its rich data from, for example, stalactites, dendrochronology, and plankton variations in the ocean seabed. But I am already tempted to see the authors of these articles as doing what I have been doing, drawing on rich data to provide poems in prose. I say this approvingly, thinking of A. L. Rowse's maxim that "history is a great deal closer to poetry than is generally realised."[16] I see that maxim also as a warning not to be too credulous about "scientific" findings. Meanwhile, the International Commission on Stratigraphy, which sponsored the notion of the 2200 BCE mega-drought, has frozen discussion until its next meeting in 2028.[17] We may have a clearer picture of pre-axial climate history then. Or we may not: *The dao which can be daoed is not the true dao.*

What does emerge from so much data is that, from the earliest stages of social and cultural development, there have been periodical cultural shifts from expansion (yang urbanization) to disruption and recision (yin rurification) and back.[18] In the cultural transitions from more literate and rational (yang) to less literate and more spiritual (yin), the loss of power and security for those in control is often accompanied by the liberation of new energies emerging from the once dominated.

Around 1000 BCE, for example, the loss of dominant Hittite and Ugaritic cultures was more than compensated for by the emergence of new and less ephemeral cultures—notably Judaism—along with the first alphabets. Eric Cline quotes the conclusion of William Dever that

> perhaps the most important conclusion to be drawn about the "Dark Age" [of ca. 1,000 BCE] . . . is that it was nothing of the sort. Gradually being illuminated by archaeological discovery and research, [this period] emerges rather as the catalyst of a new age—one that would build on the ruins of Canaanite civilization and would bequeath to the modern western world a cultural heritage . . . of which we are still the benefactors.[19]

This ability to see gain out of loss is, I believe, helpful as we begin to consider the transition, 1,500 years later, from ancient Rome to the European Dark Age.

ARCHEOLOGY, PLAGUE, AND THE BIRTH OF JUDAIC MONOTHEISM

In preparation for this, let us look a little more closely at what happened during and after Cline's Golden Age in the fourteenth century BCE. The city-states of Canaan had been dominated by Egypt since their defeat at the Battle of Megiddo in 1479 BCE. From 1479 to 1150 BCE, when the land of Canaan was part of the Egyptian Empire, what was golden for Egypt was oppression for Canaan (a doubleness true of all golden ages except the mythical first one).

> Slaves were demanded as tribute from the rulers of the Canaanite city-states, who presumably rounded them up from the local population or captured them from other towns. The correspondence between Canaanite rulers and the Egyptian Pharaoh discovered at El Amarna (dating to ca. 1360–1335) record the following human tribute sent to or requisitioned by Pharaoh:
>
> - 10 women sent by;ayAbdi-Aštarti of Amurru (EA 64)
> - 46 females and 5 males sent by Milkilu of Gezer (EA 268)
> - [x]prisoners and 8 porters sent by;ayAbdi-Ḫeba of Jerusalem (EA 287)
> - 10 slaves, 21 girls, and [8]0 prisoners sent by;ayAbdi-Ḫeba of Jerusalem (EA 288).[20]
>
> [El Amarna was the new capital briefly established by the outlier Pharaoh Akhenaten (ca. 1350–1335), whose premature installation of the world's first monotheism was soon terminated (and his new capital abandoned), perhaps after twin disasters of foreign invasion and plague.]

A second, apparently larger category of Canaanite slaves consisted of prisoners of war captured and brought to Egypt by military campaigns.

. . . Thutmose III, the founder of the Egyptian Empire, claims to have taken over 7,300 Canaanite prisoners of war, and his son, Amenhotep II, claims to have taken over 89,600 Canaanite captives. In Ramesside times, the capture of Canaanite prisoners was a regular anthem in accounts of military conquests. . . .

> Along with the capture of prisoners of war, there is evidence of the deportation of sizeable Canaanite populations to Egypt. The huge number of captives listed by Amenhotep II has been interpreted as a deliberate policy of mass deportation of subject peoples, aptly described by Donald Redford as "tactics of terror."[21]

Ronald Hendel concludes very plausibly that

> the evidence surveyed here suggests that many of the local settlers in early Israel had memories, direct or indirect, of Egyptian slavery. These memories were linked to no single Pharaoh, but to Pharaoh as such, that is, to the array of Pharaohs whose military campaigns, vassal tributes, mass deportations, and support of the slave trade forced many Canaanites into Egyptian slavery. Not all of these slaves need to have escaped with Moses—or to have escaped at all—to create the bitter memory of Egyptian slavery among the early population of Israel.[22]

He assembles further evidence from El Amarna to make an analogous case for the veridicality of the biblical plagues:

> *Letter from Cyprus* (EA 35)
> Behold, the hand of Nergal [the Mesopotamian god of death and plague] is now in my country; he has slain all the men of my country. . . . The hand of Nergal is in my country and in my own house. There was a young wife of mine that now, my brother, is dead.[23]

Hendel suggests that the Egyptian Manetho's account of a successful leper revolt may be, as Jan Assmann argued,

> a distorted memory of an actual epidemic that swept across the Near East during and after the reign of Akhenaten for at least twenty years in the mid- to late fourteenth century B.C.E. A contemporary Egyptian medical text . . . calls this disease "the Canaanite illness."[24]

Of course, the biblical account would have us believe that the slavery of the Israelites, in Egypt since the time of Joseph and his brothers, had nothing to do with the documented slavery of the Canaanites. But this biblical distinction is unlikely. According to Mark Smith,

Despite the long regnant model that the Canaanites and Israelites were people of fundamentally different culture, archaeological data now casts doubt on this view. The material culture of the region exhibits numerous common points between Israelites and Canaanites in the Iron I period (c. 1200–1000 BC). The record would suggest that the Israelite culture largely overlapped with and derived from Canaanite culture. In short, Israelite culture was largely Canaanite in nature. Given the information available, one cannot maintain a radical cultural separation between Canaanites and Israelites for the Iron I period.[25]

ENHANCING HISTORY WITH MNEMOHISTORY

This finding from archeology is corroborated by recent studies in genetics.[26] Its irreconcilability with the biblical account outlines the gap in knowledge filled by the mnemohistorical research of Jan Assmann:

> Unlike history proper, mnemohistory is concerned not with the past as such, but only with the past as it is remembered. It surveys the story-lines of tradition, the webs of intertextuality, the diachronic continuities and discontinuities of reading the past. Mnemohistory is not the opposite of history, but rather is one of its branches.[27]

Quoting Assmann, Hendel adds (in his book *Remembering Abraham* quoted above),

> The data for mnemohistory are texts, artifacts, and other evidence of cultural discourse about the remembered past, and its object is to discern how such discourses are constituted and how they serve to inform and influence the cultural present. Assmann emphasizes that this kind of study focuses on the ways a culture "shap[es] an identity by reconstructing its past." The habits of cultural life and the multifarious interests of the present exert selective pressures on collective memories of the past, creating a version of the past with present relevance. How the past becomes a meaningful frame for the present is the particular burden of mnemohistory.[28]

Both Assmann and Hendel treat Akhenaten (d. 1334 BCE) as a ruler soon forgotten by history but dimly remembered in Jewish mnemohistory—as a forerunner of Mosaic monotheism.[29] (This would make him, in effect, another cusp pioneer ruler like Cyrus, Alexander, Constantine, Charlemagne, Frederick II, and Napoleon.[30])

Assmann sees Akhenaten as "a figure both of enlightenment and of intolerant despotism, forcing his universalist monotheism onto his people with violence and persecution."[31] He claims that this rigorous distinction "between true and false in religion" marks the beginning of

the history of religious antagonism. . . . The first conflict between two funda-
mentally different and mutually exclusive religions in the recorded history of
humankind occurred in Egypt in the fourteenth century B.C.E. . . . It is this
constructed mental or cultural space that has been inhabited by Europeans for
nearly two millennia.[32]

Assmann concludes that "it is this hatred brought about by Akhenaten's revo-
lution that informs the Judeophobic texts of antiquity," and, before that, the
"anti-Canaanism" of the five Mosaic books of Torah.[33]

I find the explanations of Assmann and Hendel about mnemohistory useful
for rethinking otherness on two levels, both history and ethogeny, and also
yang and yin. What are *opinions and myths* ("the past as it is remembered")
on the level of history, notably the widely shared belief that (for example)
Elijah, Jesus, St. Martin, and St. Aidan all worked miracles, can become *facts*
on the level of ethogeny, facts so important during the Dark Age that they
affected political history as well. We shall see when we discuss Gregory of
Tours and Bede that, as a rule, miracle history is an example of mnemohis-
tory, of events from the margins of literacy, usually reaching literate minders
orally, not observed by them at firsthand.

MNEMOHISTORY AND MYTHOGENESIS

The cultural memories of mnemohistory are the product of mythogenesis, as
described by Richard Slotkin:

> Myth-making is a primary attribute of the human mind and . . . the process of
> mythogenesis in a culture is one of continuous activity rather than dramatic
> stops and starts. True myths are generated on a sub-literary level by the histori-
> cal experience of a people and thus constitute part of that inner reality which the
> work of the artist draws on.[34]

Mnemohistory is the memory of mythogenesis, and is inseparable from it.
Both flourish in subliterary dark ages, in the relative absence of recorded
data that trammel the imagination. Mythogenesis, as opposed to the conscious
mythopoeia of Tolkien and others, is natural, indeed inevitable, as anyone
knows who has watched how memories of the same event will diverge over
the years, grow, and embellish themselves, in separated minds.[35]

Writing this chapter has helped me recover the following suppressed
memory. I had a former student visit me, years later, to tell me that one of
her most important college experiences had been when I was lecturing on
Dante's *Paradiso*, and a white dove flew into the classroom. I replied that I
remembered the event vividly; however, I doubted that my lecture had been

on the *Paradiso*, and, as a birdwatcher, I was certain the bird had just been a common brown California towhee. Undaunted, she replied confidently, "Oh, no! Professor Scott. It was a white dove!"[36]

As a youth, I worked one summer in a lumber camp along with self-identified *acadiens* from New Brunswick, and I heard them discuss among themselves the Martin-style miracles of their local curés: how one had stopped the flow of blood from an axe wound, and another had summoned a rainstorm to deal with a hayrick fire.[37] Acadian culture in those days was unadulteratedly "subliterary" and oral, because first the British and then New Brunswick had denied *acadiens* the right to an education in their own language.

As a result,

L'Acadie n'était pas seulement française, mais acadienne, c'est-à-dire vieille France, France d'avant Louis XIII, France du Poitou et de Touraine. . . . L'Acadie était mémoire autant que continuité, dépositaire autant que permanence; l'Acadie était comète traînant dans sa queue un répertoire de fables et de fabliaux, de croyances et de traditions . . . de légendes et de mythes.

Acadia was not only French, but Acadian, that is to say France of bygone days, France before Louis XIII, France of Poitou and Touraine. . . . Acadia was as much memory as continuity, depository as much as permanency; Acadia was a comet tail dragging in its wake a repertory of fables and fabliaux, of beliefs and traditions . . . of legends and myths.[38]

It is relevant that Dark Age magical thinking could survive orally in North America, well into Weber's era of disenchanted modernity.[39]

Recent surveys have shown that 72 percent of people in the United States and 59 percent of people in the United Kingdom also believe that miracles take place. In explanation, Prof. Nagasawa suggests that belief in miracles has cognitive and developmental origins: "On the face of it, believing in miracles seems to be incompatible with modern life. It seems unlikely, however, that they will disappear any time soon as they have deep cognitive roots in human psychology."[40]

In much of the world belief in miracles is still virtually unchallenged by modern life. In 2002–2005, I encountered it in what I would now call the dominant yin culture of Buddhist northern Thailand. There college-trained medics, at the hospital where I tutored nurses in English, would come out each morning to leave food for the *phi* (village spirits or ghosts), at the traditional feeding post the hospital maintained for this purpose.[41] A venerated monk I met there was believed by most to have miraculous powers, powers that were not just respected and obeyed in the forest by cobras, but venerated by them.

I must confess that I was profoundly impressed, indeed changed, by the spirituality, kindness, and generosity of the people my wife and I knew when we lived in Buddhist northern Thailand. I have written elsewhere, and will repeat here, that we in America and Europe can learn much from them.[42]

Chapter Ten

Benign Cultural Progress in the Third Pivotal Shift: The Dark Age

A pivotal shift in cultural evolution can be seen as a period of widespread cultural change in which there is a violent transition from a moribund ethos and political system to a new one. By this definition, there is a strong case for seeing a pivotal shift at the beginning of the Common Era, when the victories of Roman armies, especially in the eastern Mediterranean, expanded Rome (like Athens before it) from a civic to an imperial polity. And in Rome, as in Athens before it, a so-called golden age of letters ended soon after the limited democracy that had sustained it.

As we have seen, this second expansive shift was paralleled by the consolidation of Chinese unity under the Han dynasty (206 BCE–220 CE) and of Indian unity under the Śātavāhanas from the first century BCE onward. In the case of China at least, the imperial unification by the Qin dynasty in 221 BCE was a cutoff date closing the period of what were remembered as the Five Classics (*Wǔjīng*, 五經).[1] This is close to the second- and first-century BCE date ascribed by many scholars to the closing of the Hebrew Bible canon.[2]

In this transition to empire, the destruction of the Herodian kingdom and the Temple in Jerusalem finalized the emergence of Rabbinic Judaism and also the birth of Christianity—today the largest religion in the world. Major events also occurred in China, with the emergence of cultic Taoism, and in India, with the emergence of Mahayana Buddhism. The new religions can be distinguished collectively from those of the Axial Age. The earlier tended to accept the permanence of a hostile world and to focus on survival in it (Judaism) or escape from it (early Buddhism) through the development of a moral life. The new religions shared a new emphasis on a collective and salvational as well as individual level, with hope for deliverance from an alien present to a more benign future condition.

I want in this chapter to make the case for a Third Pivotal Shift about a half millennium later, again spanning developments from China to western

Europe. These may be summarized briefly as a temporary retrenchment to a less metropolitan-centered civilization. (In the case of Islam, this retrenchment was brief and was followed by an urban "golden age," usually understood to have begun with the reign of Abbasid caliph Harun al-Rashid, 786–809.) In northern Europe in particular, the high civilization associated with Rome's urban dominance was replaced for five centuries by the radically simpler culture of rural monasteries.

In *Plagues and Peoples* (1976), William McNeill attributed the end of both the Han Empire (220 CE) and the Roman Empire (476) to deurbanization from the spread of unfamiliar diseases along the Silk Routes, an ironic consequence of the new silk trade that had marked both Rome's and China's imperial prosperity.[3] But I shall be arguing that this disruption was followed by a number of positive cultural evolutions.

Let me begin with the sweeping away of a corrupted ethos in the Third Pivotal Shift so as to produce lasting cultural change (ethogeny).

THE CLOSURE BY "BARBARIANS" OF THE ROMAN GLADIATORIAL GAMES

The Dark Age is often remembered for the murderous aristocratic violence depicted in the so-called *History of the Franks* by Gregory of Tours (d. 594; see chapter 14). But this violence does not distinguish the start of the Third Pivotal Moment from the start of the Second, which at one point saw no less than four emperors in a single year, 69 CE.

More distinctive, and more indicative of a lasting cultural shift, was the permanent and overdue closing, by the "Vandal barbarians" in the sixth century, of Rome's murderous gladiatorial "games" (*sic*; *ludi*). These games dated back to the militarization of the Roman citizenry after the Second Punic War (218–201 BCE) and continued, often sponsored by Christian families, after Rome's nominal (and top-down) conversion to Christianity. Constantine, the first Christian emperor, officially banned the games in 325, "ostensibly as an offence to God,"[4] but he himself felt obliged by public demand to violate his own interdiction.

It is no accident that the original recruitment of gladiators was from the ranks of defeated enemy soldiers who were now slaves. There was little choice for them. Josephus recounts how those soldiers captured after the Jewish Revolt (66–73 CE) who were not selected for gladiatorial training were instead sent directly to the arena to be executed publicly as *noxii* (public enemies).[5]

Though their origins had suggestions of human sacrifice, the games became an immensely popular source of entertainment, arousing a kind of animal excitation with sexual overtones.[6] Augustine describes how his young friend and student Alypius, who eventually became a bishop and saint, came to detest the "filths of the arena" (circensium sordes) that had once attracted him. Yet when his friends dragged him back to the games and he vowed to sit there with his eyes closed, the temptation was too much for him.

> For when one fell in the fight, a mighty roar from the people beating strongly on him, he opened his eyes, and was struck with a deeper wound in his soul, than the other was in his body. . . . For as soon as he beheld that blood he drank it down with a kind of savageness; nor did he turn away, and drinking up the cup of fury, he was delighted with the guilty contest, and he became drunk with a delight in blood [et hauriebat furias, et nesciebat; et delectabatur scelere certaminis, et cruenta voluptate inebriabatur].[7]

In *Mimesis*, Erich Auerbach saw Alypius's struggle with his own first nature as representative of all those living in a partially but not completely converted era:

> It is not merely a random Alypius whose pride . . . is thus crushed; it is the entire rational individualistic culture of classical antiquity: Plato and Aristotle, the Stoa and Epicurus. A burning lust has swept them away.

And Auerbach draws attention to Augustine's style of narrating Alypius's conflict, eschewing the urbane rhetoric of classical antiquity for the simple style of the Vulgate Bible.

> The tone . . . is at once dramatic and paratactic. . . . A new *sermo humilis* is born, a low style, such as properly would only be applicable to comedy, but which now reaches out far beyond its original domain, and encroaches upon the deepest and highest, the sublime and the eternal.[8]

Auerbach sees the larger drama behind the personal one, the new consciousness of double-mindedness in the psyche that marks the shift from the ancient idea of man as a "rational animal" (a view dominant from Aristotle to Porphyry) to the more complex double vision of man as a creature drawn toward both sin and grace.

The Second and Third Pivotal Shift did not alter our human condition itself so much as our relationship to it.[9] A delight in blood (*cruenta voluptas*) is still with us. Blood sports persist. Bullfights are still held in the old Roman arena at Arles. Cockfighting, a sport also common in ancient Rome, is widespread in southeast Asia (often in rituals with sacrificial overtones) and in at least four countries in Latin America.[10]

Despite overwhelming public opposition and a longstanding ban, fox hunting shows no signs of abating in the UK. The 2018 hunt season alone saw 550 reports of illegal hunting, though these figures only represent known incidents.[11]

Public executions, once viewed by thousands, still officially persist, but only in North Korea, Iran, Saudi Arabia, and Somalia (as well as, until recently, areas held by ISIS in Syria).[12]

It is tempting to believe that, at least in the anglophone West, the satis-faction of such cravings is no longer a licit activity and no longer officially sponsored at public events. The gladiatorial games were intended to familiar-ize Roman male citizens with blood and death, when they were required to serve for ten years in the army. (This function can be compared to the habit by which foxhunters "blood" their dogs or children with the blood of their victims.[13]) But such cravings are now unacceptable, and those who pursue such attractions are now usually regarded as psychopaths if not criminals.

As for gladiatorial games themselves, there is no country today where you can attend one in public. In fact, this has been true since the sixth century; what ended them was the final collapse of Roman slave-based society. The fierce Christian chronicler of Roman iniquities and barbarian virtues Salvian of Marseilles (fl. 440–50) writes that it was the barbarians, not the Christians, who did away with them:

> In these [the Roman games] the greatest pleasure is to have men die, or, what is worse . . . to have them torn to pieces . . . to have men eaten, to the great joy and the delight of the onlookers. . . . There are no shows given now in Mayence . . . nor at Cologne, for they are now controlled by the barbarians. They are not being performed in the most noble city of Trier . . . nor finally in many other cities of Gaul and Spain. What hope have Christians [i.e., Catholics, who, when Trier was recaptured, joined nobles in petitioning for restoration of the games] in the sight of God when these evils only cease to exist . . . when Roman cities themselves have come under the control of the [Arian Vandal] barbarians?[14]

I won't pretend this was a painless transition. According to J. B. Bury, the "torrent of barbarians" invading Gaul first massacred many people in Mayence and "sacked and set fire" to Trier.[15] But after this disastrous but brief disruption, the abolition of the games proved to be permanent.

How deep was the change? In American football, young men, usually but not always with limited career options, are hired to entertain us with such vio-lence that, even if only one player has been killed on the playing field, a great many will eventually die too young and with impaired mental capacity.[16]

BENIGN DEVELOPMENTS IN DARK AGE SOCIETY

Both in the West and in the East there were other positive developments (with lasting influence) from the decline of cities and of central imperial power. In the case of the West, two of these developments have now been widely recognized. The first and most important is the decline of chattel slavery and the evolution toward a less rigidly hierarchical stratification of society. To quote Perry Anderson,

> The slave mode of production was the decisive invention of the Graeco-Roman world, which provided the ultimate basis both for its accomplishments and its eclipse. . . . The solstice of classical urban culture always also witnessed the zenith of slavery; and the decline of one, in Hellenistic Greece or Christian Rome, was likewise invariably marked by the setting of the other.[17]

The second and related change is a consequent burst of technical innovation. The waning of top-down enforcement power saw the decline of remote land ownership relying on forced labor, and this liberation of the agricultural work process also led to fundamental improvements in agriculture, notably the replacement of the wooden scratch plow by the iron heavy plow. This made it easier "to exploit the dense, rich, alluvial bottom lands which, if properly handled, would give the peasant far better crops than he could get from the light soils of the uplands."[18]

The resulting increase in food production made possible population growth, urbanization, and the growth of leisure. It was, in short, an important precursor to the reurbanization beginning around 800–1000 CE, which I characterize as the Fourth Pivotal Shift.

> But the heavy plough, according to [Marc] Bloch, did more than stimulate northern Europe by raising the level of productivity; it played a decisive part in reshaping the peasant society of the north. The manor as a co-operative agricultural community was, in fact, typical not of the Mediterranean lands but only of areas which employed the heavy plough, and there appeared to be a causal connexion between plough and manor.[19]

The historian Lynn White gives other examples, such as the development of the stirrup, which revolutionized the use of the horse in combat, and the development of fulling mills for cloth making. His overall conclusion was that "in technology, at least, the Dark Ages mark a steady and uninterrupted advance over the Roman empire."[20]

Anderson endorses this assessment, even more energetically:

Slave relations of production determined certain insurmountable limits to ancient forces of production, in the classical epoch. Above all, they ultimately tended to paralyze productivity in both agriculture and industry. . . . Nothing is more striking, in any comparative retrospect, than the overall technological stagnation of Antiquity. It is enough to contrast the record of its eight centuries of existence from the rise of Athens to the fall of Rome, with the equivalent span of the feudal mode of production which succeeded it, to perceive the difference between a relatively static and dynamic economy.[21]

The historian Chris Wickham also notes the improvement of peasant conditions in the Dark Age, along with a marked decline in disparity of wealth. He attributes this to the decline of state authority, which meant that taxes

had all but disappeared from the disorganized west by the year 700. [According to Wickham,] "The whole economic basis for political action shifted, from taxation to landowning." The effect was to stimulate agricultural production since peasants were no longer subject to confiscatory taxation by the state. . . . Wickham points out that the European peasantry during the so-called Dark Ages was not only unusually free by the standards of the day, but even dominant. As he puts it: "in general the economy of most of the north is likely to have followed the logic of peasant, not aristocratic choices and needs for a long time. This is supported by the *rarity of large concentrations of wealth* in the early medieval archaeology of the north, with the significant exception of Denmark, until the Viking period."[22]

The historian Walter Scheidel writes that this diminution of wealth disparity occurred through all of western Europe:

In the 5th century CE, a terrifying array of disasters—internal strife, barbarian invasions, climate change—brought down the western half of the empire. The vast fortunes of the super-rich . . . vanished. To make matters worse, 100 years later bubonic plague first entered Europe, a raging pandemic that carried off a large share of its population. The disease killed so many workers that the price of labour soared, while that of land, now abundant and bereft of cultivators, plummeted, leaving the masses better off and landlords poorer.[23]

He argues that, more generally, established states have led repeatedly to wealth disparity, from which the only relief has come from repeated major disruptions (we might say, repeated Dark Ages):

From time to time, it turns out, history has pushed a reset button, driving down inequality in marked, if only temporary fashion. It is only by surveying its full sweep, over thousands of years, that we can discover the dynamics that drove this process. And these dynamics turn out to be very disturbing indeed: every time the gap between rich and poor shrank substantially, it did so because of traumatic, often extremely violent shocks to the established order. Catastrophic plagues, the collapse of states and, more recently, mass-mobilisation war and transformative revolution, are the only forces that ever levelled on a grand scale. No other—and less bloody—mechanisms have even come close. In a time of rising inequality, what does this imply for our own future?[24]

The generative technological, economic, and social developments of the Dark Age are now increasingly acknowledged. I see them as the fruit of a temporary return to a healthier reframing of society on a more local rather than imperial scale (the manor—or monastery—rather than the megacity). For eighteen months I encountered and later praised such smaller-scale living in northern Thailand: "We saw vividly in Thailand what the eco-philosopher E. F. Schumacher learned in Burma (now Myanmar) a half century earlier: Small is beautiful. Less is more. Happiness is found close to the necessities of life, not in needless complexity and meaningless multiplicity of choice."[25]

But one noncyclical improvement is less recognized. I see this Dark Age return to a smaller-scale intimacy as the key to an invaluable development and breakthrough in poetry, toward a style both simpler and also more psychologically satisfying. In a history of enmindment, particularly a poetic one, this yin development is fundamental.

(Also relevant, and far more dominant at that time, was a parallel evolution of liturgical chanting into melodic plainsong, cherished and enhanced in Benedictine monasteries. This in turn was accompanied by the development of staff notation for music, a key role being played by the monk Guido of Arezzo, d. after 1033.)

The evolution in poetry was both a symptom of, and a major contribution to, the dialectical evolution of a new, more yin-oriented mindset and ethos in general. The response, if you will, of the repressed right hemisphere of the brain.

Among the all-time greatest poets of China (indeed, of the world) were Li Bai (701–762), Wang Wei (701–761), and Du Fu (712–770). And all three began as court or bureaucratic poets who, because of major social disruptions, came to write most of their greatest work in and about the countryside, after seeking refuge from the court in simpler communities.

Wang Wei spent his final years as a rural recluse, immersing himself in the Chan (Zen) Buddhist culture that renounced both society and rationality. Of the three, he is thus the most comparable to Western monastery poets of the same era, notably Fortunatus (ca. 530–ca. 600/609) and Alcuin (ca. 735–804), whom we shall discuss shortly.

These three Chinese poets of the Middle Tang era became eminences in the canon of Chinese poetry, and thus of Chinese high culture. Because of recent controversy over the social role of canons and high culture, I should also make clear that they all became critics of Chinese court culture and indeed pioneer spokesmen for a counterculture of power from below. Both Li Bai and Du Fu in particular must be counted among the world's first antiwar poets (against even China's own imperial wars), and both wrote intimately about ordinary people and their sufferings, having suffered themselves.

We shall see also that Alcuin (d. 804), when he left monastic surroundings for the court of Charlemagne, did not hesitate to persuade the king to rescind a law that ordered the killing of pagans who refused baptism (see chapter 14). One cannot imagine Virgil challenging Augustus in this way. The Dark Age, in short, was the first era in which we can confidently talk of poets who were also spokespeople for a less violent counterculture, slowly emerging from below.

THE POST-CATASTROPHIC BREAKTHROUGH OF DARK AGE HIGH CULTURE—CHINA

Let us look first at the culturally far more developed high culture of China in this period, when the decline of central Confucian power facilitated the spread of Mahayana Buddhism, particularly in the era of the Northern Wei Empire (386–535 CE). This is comparable to the post-imperial high monastic culture that followed the largely swordless conversion to Christianity in Ireland and northern England.

I suspect that the common element I shall describe in these two developments can be attributed to a cross-cultural fusion of (1) a primitive tribal community whose culture was primarily oral, with (2) a literate society and culture marked by an unstable polarity of liberty and oppression. And I shall argue that the result was a significant refinement in the notion of a liberty and high culture not based on class dominance.

These liminal developments at the margins of Eurasia occurred during the Dark Age that is said to have occurred in this period, both in China (220–581 CE) and later in Europe (roughly 400–1000 CE). It was the weakening of central Chinese authority, with its class-distinguished Confucianism, that allowed the more tribal Northern Wei Empire to introduce both Buddhism and Taoism at every level of their society. And it was the weakening of central Roman authority that resulted in Christianity, by now a state-enforced religion, reaching Ireland in the fifth century without the corrupting assistance of Roman legions.

In China the decay of court culture was marked by a celebration of its opposite: escape from formality to the simplicity of nature. In the second half of the third century, the Seven Sages of the Bamboo Grove "wished to escape the intrigues, corruption and stifling atmosphere of court life during the tail end of the politically fraught Three Kingdoms period of Chinese history. [They] gathered in a bamboo grove . . . where they enjoyed, and praised in their works, the simple, rustic life . . . contrasted with the life of politics at court."[26]

The greatest poet of the Six Dynasties period, Tao Qian (T'ao Ch'ien, Tao Yuanming; 365–427),[27] followed their example:

> Tao Yuanming spent most of his life in reclusion, living in a small house in the countryside, reading, drinking wine, receiving the occasional guest, and writing poems in which he often reflected on the pleasures and difficulties of life in the countryside, as well as his decision to withdraw from civil service. His simple, direct, and unmannered style was at odds with the norms for literary writing in his time.[28]

Two brief examples will illustrate their natural directness. The first is straightforward:

> Chill and harsh the year draws to its close:
> In my cotton dress I seek sunlight on the porch.
> In the southern orchard all the leaves are gone:
> In the north garden rotting boughs lie heaped.
> I empty my cup and drink it down to the dregs:
> I look towards the kitchen, but no smoke rises.
> Poems and books lie piled beside my chair:
> But the light is going and I shall not have time to read them.
> My life here is not like the Agony [of Confucius] in Ch'ēn,
> But often I have to bear bitter reproaches.
> Let me then remember, to calm my heart's distress,
> That the Sages of old were often in like case.

The second shifts more explicitly from the yang of the public world and Confucianism to a Buddhist/Taoist yin beyond words:

> I built my hut in a zone of human habitation,
> Yet near me there sounds no noise of horse or coach.
> Would you know how that is possible?
> A heart that is distant creates a wilderness round it.
> I pluck chrysanthemums under the eastern hedge,
> Then gaze long at the distant summer hills.
> The mountain air is fresh at the dusk of day:

The flying birds two by two return.
In these things there lies a deep meaning;
Yet when we would express it, words suddenly fail us.

Stephen Owen summarizes the immense importance of Tao Qian to the poets of the High Tang who followed him, poets who from the Song period onward were considered to have been "the apogee of all Chinese poetry." In his words,

Tao Qian answered all their needs. T'ao's simple diction opposed the court poet's artifice and refinement; T'ao's rebellious freedom opposed the court poet's obsequiousness; T'ao's emphasis on writing poetry for purely personal pleasure provided an alternative to the social necessity that motivated the court poem. T'ao Ch'ien was the perfect model of the free and individual poet."[29]

The great Song era poet Su Shi (1037–1101) even preferred the work of Tao Qian to that of Li Bai and Du Fu, generally considered to be the two greatest High Tang masters.[30]

DARK AGE HIGH CULTURE IN IRELAND AND ENGLAND

A remarkably similar liberation from elite formalism to a simpler nature poetry occurred a little later in Dark Age France, Ireland, and Northumbria. Though these areas had no mature poets comparable to Tao Qian, they did produce poems of engaging rustic simplicity in which they broke with the decadent urbanity of a preceding era.

In chapter 12 we shall briefly discuss the poet Fortunatus (ca. 530–ca. 600), a classically trained Italian, who moved first to a court in Merovingian France and then again to a monastery. There, as we shall see, he (rather like Wang Wei) "could concentrate not on grandeur and power but on the objects of everyday life: eggs, violets and meals together."[31]

We see the same monastic simplicity in an Anglo-Latin lyric of the Northumbrian poet Alcuin:

"De Luscinia" (To a Nightingale)

The hand that snatched you from that hedge of broom
Did so from envy of my happiness.
O nightingale, you filled my heart with song
And with sweet music my mind's weariness.
Therefore let all the birds now gather round

From every side at once, and join their voice
To mine lamenting you with grievous sound.

Humble in color, you were in song sublime
Your voice spread widely from that tiny throat,
Singing sweet melody in diverse measure,
Always praising God in every note.
What wonder then if angels, seraphim
Perpetually can sing to their Creator,
When you on earth sing equally to him.[32]

Technically this is an elegy in a tradition going back to the more sophisticated threnodies of Catullus for his beloved's sparrow (Catullus 2) and Ovid for his beloved's parrot (*Amores* 2.6). But Alcuin's intention is quite different: to write not with irony but with sincerity.

We can better see the freshness of Alcuin's poem by contrasting it with a late antique example from Archbishop Eugenius II of Toledo (d. 657). This poem consists of several examples of panegyric *outdoing* as a formal topos, celebrating the victory in song of the nightingale over the cithara, the pipe, the seeds of care, the swan, the garrulous swallow, and the illustrious parrot. It is a late, debased, and almost parodic reductio ad absurdum of the ancients' need in poetry to be *clever*.

Alcuin, in contrast, praises the nightingale not for her heroic invincibility but as a simple example of humility and dedication for himself to follow. The importance of this contentedness in poetry can easily be overlooked in our ethogeny, until we think back to how remote it was from the tone of Latin poetry in the age of Ovid, and how much closer it is to our own expectations from poetry.

Alcuin's Latin style is admittedly immature and transitional. As if Latin were for him a second language in which he felt insecure, he composes much of his poem from fragments of antique poetry. But at this poem's heart is a freshness from a new source: the vernacular verses in the margins of Irish manuscripts. (Nora Chadwick attributes the special quality of this Celtic poetry to "the simplicity and integrity of the [Irish] spiritual elite [who] lived a life purified from material desires in simple communion with nature."[33])

Alcuin's conceit—"you, too, little bird, are a little monk"—is found in one of these Irish marginalia, which also celebrates nature not for its own sake but as emblematic of a benign force behind it:

Ah blackbird, thou art satisfied
Where thy nest is in the bush:
Hermit that clinkest no bell,
Sweet, soft, peaceful is thy note.[34]

The serenity of Tao Qian's lyric to his hut, the fruit of a settled meditative life, is found also in the address of Alcuin to his cell—even though the poem responds to a much more serious loss than of a nightingale:

O my cell, beloved habitation,
Prosper forever, O sweet cell of mine.
Trees with their murmuring limbs surround you
Forever heavy with their flowers and leaves.
Your fields will bloom with salutary herbs
The doctor's hand seeks out for skillful cure.

Rivers with flowering banks surround you too
Where a fisherman rejoicing casts his nets.
Your cloister has the smell of apple blossom,
Easter lilies mixed with scarlet roses,
While every type of bird recites its matins
Praising its creator orally.
Here once the master's gentle voice recited,
Transmitting books of wisdom by his mouth.
In you at proper times the praise of God
Sounded from peaceful voices, peaceful minds.
I weep you now, my cell, with tearful muse,
And with groaning heart lament your fate.
Suddenly you have fled the poets' songs
And an unknown crew now occupy their place.
Now neither Flaccus nor Homerus holds you,
No students sing their songs within your walls.
All temporal beauty turns with just such speed
And all things change in their appointed times.
Nothing endures, nothing is eternal:
The shadowy night obscures the sacred day,
Frigid winter blasts the pretty flowers,
A sadder wind disturbs the quiet sea.
Where golden youth once coursed a rapid stag
A tired old man now hangs upon his stick.
Why do we love you, world so fugitive?
You flee from us, on all sides fall away.

Then fleer, flee. Let us love Christ instead,
Our hearts be resolute in love of God.
Let Him defend his servants in the field
And snatch our hearts above to Paradise.
When with all our hearts we praise and love,
Who is our pious glory, life, hope, health.[35]

In the background of this poem is the Viking destruction of the seminal Northumbrian abbey Lindisfarne in 793. Initially, as we shall see in chapter 14, Alcuin's belief that monastic education was God's work was severely shaken: "Never before has such terror appeared in Britain as we have now suffered from a pagan race."[36] Later, in a long poem, "On the Destruction of the Monastery of Lindisfarne," he compared the abbey's fall to the destruction of Jerusalem and Rome; yet even so, he closed with hope in the continuing mission of Christian minders.[37]

In this short poem, the *contemptus mundi* at the poem's center ("Why do we love you, world so fugitive? / You flee from us") is subordinated to the confident affirmation of survival at the outset ("Prosper forever. . . . Your fields will bloom with salutary herbs"), answered by a renewal of faith: "Then fleer, flee. Let us love Christ instead, / Our hearts be resolute in love of God."

In chapters 7 and 12, I discuss how St. Martin's model of monastic *sancta simplicitas*, emulating that of the apostles, gave rise to a welcome Dark Age poetics that celebrated rustic simplicity, exactly what pagan Roman grammarians had once condemned. These two poems exemplify it, as do the poems of Tao Qian.

TAO QIAN, ALCUIN, AND THE HISTORY
OF LEISURE AND FREEDOM

Especially in the case of Tao Qian, it is easy to underestimate the importance of this heightened return to simplicity. Even the great critic Stephen Owen misses it when he calls Tao Qian a "georgic poet."[38] Georgic poetry, whether in the Chinese Book of Odes or Hesiod's *Works and Days*, celebrates the activity of cultivation as a functional participation in the processes of nature. Tao Qian's poems are on an altogether different plane: a celebration of leisure and liberty. Nature becomes an entity in itself, contemplated rather than acted upon by the poet.

As Zhong Rong recognized in the fifth century, "such lines of his as 'With happy face I pour the spring-brewed wine' and 'The sun sets, no clouds are in the sky' are pure and refined in the beauty of their air. These are far from being merely the words of a farmer. He is the father of recluse poetry past and present."[39]

Let me quote just one more poem by Tao Qian to illustrate his point.

> "Return to the Field"

> When I was young, I was out of tune with the herd:
> My only love was for the hills and mountains.

Unwitting I fell into the Web of the World's dust
And was not free until my thirtieth year.
The migrant bird longs for the old wood:
The fish in the tank thinks of its native pool.
I had rescued from wildness a patch of the Southern Moor
And, still rustic, I returned to field and garden.
My ground covers no more than ten acres:
My thatched cottage has eight or nine rooms.
Elms and willows cluster by the eaves:
Peach trees and plum trees grow before the hall.
Hazy, hazy the distant hamlets of men.
Steady the smoke of the half-deserted village,
A dog barks somewhere in the deep lanes,
A cock crows at the top of the mulberry tree.
At gate and courtyard—no murmur of the World's dust:
In the empty rooms—leisure and deep stillness.
Long I lived checked by the bars of a cage:
Now I have turned again to Nature and Freedom.[40]

This elevation beyond social constraints in his poetry is recognized also by a recent contemporary critic:

Tao [Qian] has a holy status in the history of Chinese literature and is accredited "the poet of poets" because he was naturally inclined toward Nature and would find himself chanting Nature since Nature was part of his life. While living to the rhythm of Nature, he was bestowed with maximum freedom, thus becoming a fundamentally beautiful, though simple, epitome of poetic dwelling on the earth. His complex of the *tianyuan* ["Fields and Gardens," which "refers to the country of rustic charm, Arcadian simplicity, and contentment"], "returning to life's essentials," and "aspiration to the Peach-blossom Springs" [the Chinese equivalent of Arcadia] have become spiritual symbols of traditional agricultural China and been built into the collective unconscious of the Chinese.[41]

At least in the West, both leisure (*otium*) and freedom could not, in the age of antiquity, be enjoyed in this innocent, uncontaminated way. As we saw, both were the product of a severely stratified social system dependent on slavery. To repeat yet again what I quoted from Perry Anderson at the outset of this chapter,

The solstice of classical urban culture always also witnessed the zenith of slavery; and the decline of one, in Hellenistic Greece or Christian Rome, was likewise invariably marked by the setting of the other.[42]

I believe that the flowering of monastic culture in the wake of the deurbaniza-tion of antiquity was an indispensable stage for the liberation of high culture from slavery, in other words, in moving society toward a relatively more classless culture as the product of a free-floating artistic intelligentsia.[43] (Tao Qian and Alcuin, from this perspective, are closer to us than to their antique predecessors.)

But to support this claim will require a closer examination of the Dark Age, focusing on changes in the nature of violence, oppression, freedom, leisure, and finally love. What we will be examining will in short be nothing less than another stage in the history of cultural evolution, or what I defined at the out-set as our ethogeny, the demonstrable evolution of humanity's second nature as Burke saw it, "shaped by our cultural environment."[44]

Chapter Eleven

Secular and Spiritual Power

THE SEPARATION OF POWERS
AND THEIR DISPERSION

In the last two chapters we have been looking at the Dark Age evolution away from the yang of imperial order and domination toward a gentler yin *communitas*, particularly at the tribal edges of the written world. One major feature of the Third Cultural Shift is the evidence we see for this evolution in both China and the West following the breakup of the Han Empire after 220 CE and the Roman Empire in 476.

As this chapter will focus on the West, let us begin with a cursory review of developments in China that paralleled those in Europe. These include, according to Chinese legal historian Zhao Dingxin,

1. major rebellions in the final days of empire (the Chinese Yellow Turban Rebellion in 184 CE, the same year as the revolt of the Bagaudae in Gaul and Spain and the Circumcellions in Numidia), attributed to the stress of increasing taxation and in some cases linked to dissident religions;[1]
2. the breakup of central power and its replacement by competing regional centers of power;
3. a decline in trade and currency;
4. a serious decline in population (in China, from the sixty million of the Eastern Han dynasty [220 CE] to about fifteen million by the end of the Western Jin dynasty in [420]);[2]
5. with a resultant deurbanization;
6. barbarian incursions from the north;

7. the decline of official civic religion and the rise of unofficial religions (Daoism and Mahayana Buddhism in China, Christianity in the West); and
8. the cultivation along tribal lines of local deities or saints.

As we saw in chapter 8, another similarity, not noted by Zhao, was a period of intense missionary monastic activity, especially among liminal tribal populations, from northern China to Ireland.

But by listing all these similarities, our attention is drawn to a dramatic difference between Dark Age developments in the Far East, where there were religious persecutions, and northern Europe, where in comparison there were few (mostly martyrdoms by pagans of missionary monks like St. Boniface and his followers). The fourth and fifth centuries were an era of intense religious persecutions in Persia (under the new Sassanian dynasty), in the Eastern Roman Empire (where Bishop Athanasius "sentenced Arians to prison, floggings, and torture," and armed bands of Christian monks systematically destroyed Jewish synagogues and killed Jews),[3] and in North Africa. But until the church started mounting crusades (in 1095 CE) after the Fourth Pivotal Shift, there were few major persecutions in northwestern Europe.[4]

Unlike Persia and Byzantium, secular power in China and northwestern Europe broke up, while religion remained strong. But in China, foreign rulers like the Northern Wei, while initially favoring Buddhism to preserve the unity of their tribal (Tuoba) cadres, also relied on Confucian elites to govern their Han majorities. Soon the Confucians gained the upper hand, and Buddhists now found themselves persecuted.

In 446 Emperor Taiwudi, in response to a local tribal revolt, ordered "the total destruction of Buddhist statues and scriptures, [and] that Buddhist monks should be buried alive."[5] Other persecutions would follow. Though Confucianism and Buddhism would somewhat interact and modify each other, a tendency to regard Buddhism as alien persisted, down to the massacre in 1853 of thousands of Buddhist monks by the Taiping army protesting Manchu rule.

In China, three post-Axial religions—Confucianism, Taoism, and Buddhism—would continue to contest each other. But in northwestern Europe, monastic Christianity as propagated by Saints Martin and Patrick had essentially no violent opposition, except from illiterate pagans. When minor differences arose, these could be peacefully resolved (like a conflict between the Roman and Irish calculations of Easter at the 664 Synod of Whitby). The result, as we shall see, was an unstable equilibrium between religious and secular (and also monastic and episcopal) power.

In short, the yin disruption of yang order was shorter-lived and less consequential in China than in the West. The yin experience of the Third Pivotal Shift in the West would be longer lasting and lead to more lasting and profound consequences. A key consequence was the settled but uneasy division of political power between church (eventually the papacy) and state.

THE DARK AGE CONTRIBUTION TO THE RULE OF LAW: LIMITS TO SECULAR POWER

Nowhere do we see this more clearly than in the Dark Age's contribution to the West's slow evolution from a rule of power toward a rule of law. An initial step in this direction had been the consolidation of a Mediterranean-wide Pax Romana in the first two centuries of the Common Era.

Romans celebrated their freedom under law as the crowning achievement of their civilization. With the course of time, however, the institutional legislation of the republic was increasingly overridden by unilateral imperial edicts. As noted by Perry Anderson, "the political distance travelled from Cicero's *legum servi sumus ut liberi esse possimus* ('We obey laws in order to be free') to Ulpian's *quod principi placuit legis habet vicem* ('The ruler's will has force of law') speaks for itself."[6]

But the concentration of enforcement power in the person of the emperor hastened the decentralization of this secular power, which was challenged by the increasing acceptance and legitimacy of the church, especially in the West. St. Ambrose (d. 397), a former praetor who became bishop of the imperial capital of Milan, demonstrated this when he excommunicated the emperor Theodosius for having ordered the massacre of seven thousand people in Thessalonica (ca. 390) in response to the murder there of a German officer in the imperial army.[7] The emperor was forced to do penance for his action, an event of lasting significance in the history of canon law and beyond.

(As in his earlier rebuke of Emperor Maximus for the murder of Priscillian [ca. 385, see chapter 12], Ambrose's motives were ecclesiastical rather than humanitarian. In 388, after mobs urged by a bishop burned a Syrian synagogue, Theodosius ordered the synagogue to be rebuilt with the bishop's own funds. Ambrose persuaded him to rescind the order, saying, "Do not pray for this people [the Jews], nor show mercy to them."[8])

In ordering Theodosius to repent, Ambrose cited Nathan's rebuke of King David for murder (2 Sam 12:9); and the examples of both Nathan and Ambrose were subsequently codified into medieval canon law by Gratian (d. ca. 1150).[9] Already before this codification, Pope Zachary in 751 had the last of the Frankish Merovingian kings, Childeric III, deposed and tonsured, enabling the Carolingian Pepin of Herstal to replace him.[10] The legal basis for the dynastic transition was in short supplied by the papacy.

The stage was set for the so-called Carolingian Renaissance, a brief period of cultural revival due to fruitful collaboration between clerics like Alcuin (d. 804) and the secular Carolingian court (see chapter 14). The liberal arts were revived, schools multiplied, and trade was encouraged, resulting in urban growth—all harbingers on the cusp of the Fourth Pivotal Shift that would soon follow.

Zachary acted at the behest of Pepin, but when Pope Gregory VII successfully ordered the humiliating penance of Emperor Henry IV at Canossa in 1077, he exerted his own untrammeled papal power. In 1170, after knights supporting King Henry II murdered Archbishop Thomas à Becket of Canterbury, they were excommunicated by the pope; they then submitted as ordered by him to fourteen years of service in the Holy Lands. Four years later, Henry humbled himself by doing public penance at Becket's tomb.

The Western equilibrium was not stable. Pope Innocent IV (d. 1254) was so politically and militarily powerful that he attempted to subjugate the Holy Roman emperor Frederick II. The conflict severely weakened both papacy and empire, neither of which ever recovered. After an interregnum of sixty-seven years (1245–1312), the empire was reconstituted north of the Alps, while the papacy, under French domination, was moved to Avignon, also for sixty-seven years (1309–1376).

The weakening of the two central powers in Europe both reflected and advanced the power of cities and the middle class. It also released the forces that led to the Reformation and Renaissance—the Fifth Pivotal Shift. The military energies that had been mustered in crusades against Islam gave way to brutal conflicts inside Europe, but (as we shall see) the principle of divided power survived and ultimately prospered.

But the medieval system of divided power in the West (perhaps comparable to the balance in China between the forces of *wu* [the military] and *wen* [the mandarinate]) did not occur in Constantinople, where church forces were more divided. There, when the archbishop, St. John Chrysostom (d. 407), became involved in a conflict with the emperor Arcadius, it was the emperor who forbade St. John to take communion with him, after which "the emperor sent him into exile."[11]

Byzantium became a cockpit of ecclesiastical power struggles, as a result of which large elements of the church, notably the Monophysites of Syria and the Levant, were first excommunicated and then vigorously persecuted by the emperor, with the result that many of them became early converts to Islam.[12] To this day, notably in Russia, the Orthodox Church has never played a balancing political role comparable to that of Rome.

DIVIDED POWER AS PREVAILABLE: THE EXAMPLE OF MAGNA CARTA

At the risk of oversimplifying, I would say that in the West a united church restrained a divided and challenged political power,[13] creating a separation of enforcement powers. In the East a united empire restrained a divided and challenged church, eliminating such separation. I think it useful to consider the consequences of these events in terms of what was and what was not prevailable, and to distinguish furthermore between something prevailing as a political institution and as an inspiring cultural principle.

The prevailability of institutions is too ephemeral to assess. At the zenith of the Third Pivotal Shift about 500, the Roman Empire in the West had ceased to exist but was surviving in the East. By the time of the Fourth Pivotal Shift five centuries later, a new Holy Roman Empire had been recreated in the West, and in 1204 the Fourth Crusade from the West would plunder Constantinople and temporarily dissolve its Asian empire into a "Frankocracy" of competing Crusader states. By 1500 both the Roman Church and the flourishing cities of Italy had seen (and passed) the zenith of their influence, while now it was the Orthodox Empire in Constantinople that had ceased to exist.

What can we say of today, when the Christian West, now dominated by America, is being challenged by the so-called "Third Rome" of Moscow, now the main seat of the surviving Orthodox Church? It is clear that the challenge of Soviet communism, as exemplified by Khrushchev's UN boast, "We will bury you," did not succeed. But what of Russia's challenge under Putin to America in Europe, a contest that could determine the future preeminent power of the world? I think that, to adapt what Zhou Enlai once said about the consequences of the French Revolution, it is too early to say.

There is a difference when we come to compare the inspiring cultural principle of divided power, as it prevailed in Rome, with that of unitary power, the legacy of Byzantium. Here, if only on paper, divided power has prevailed. Implemented in the American Constitution of 1788, it is now incorporated as a principle in the constitutions of nations everywhere in the world, including those of Russia and China.[14]

It was once customary to trace the origins of divided and separated powers, as in the U.S. Constitution's subordination of the president to the rule of law, to the Magna Carta negotiated between Henry's son King John and his barons at Runnymede in 1215. But the political standoff that produced Magna Carta was part of a larger conflict between church and state: John's struggle with Pope Innocent III over who should appoint the archbishop of Canterbury. As a result of this struggle, Innocent had excommunicated John in 1209. The sanction against John was only lifted when John recognized the pope's candidate, Stephen Langton, as archbishop.

The pope's challenge to John's power is recognized as a major factor in the crisis that produced Magna Carta in 1215. Even more importantly, it put Stephen Langton in a leadership position to intervene in the struggle between the king and his barons, to secure the king's vow to observe certain rights, and to obtain the king's signature to Magna Carta.[15]

MAGNA CARTA'S IMPORTANCE
AS A CULTURAL MYTH

As a *political* attempt to restore peace, the Magna Carta of 1215 was a fiasco. Less than three months later, both sides repudiated it, marking the outbreak of a major civil war. Successive renegotiations of the Great Charter in 1225 and 1297 did lead to a limited and waning application of its principles in the later Middle Ages. But Tudor historians "viewed King John in a positive light as a hero struggling against the papacy" and showed "little sympathy for the Great Charter or the rebel barons."[16] For the same reasons, the oppressed Catholic minority now praised the charter.

With Stuart monarchs arguing for the divine right of kings, Magna Carta, increasingly mythologized, was utilized in opposition by both legal theorists like Sir Edward Coke and radical Levelers like John Lilburne. Then Magna Carta, with its talk of "the freemen of England," was used by Whigs to legitimate the so-called Glorious Revolution of 1688—an act of mythopoeia mocked as "a setback for the course of English historiography."[17]

It was in this context that Magna Carta was utilized in drafting the charters of the colonies of Virginia and Massachusetts.[18] And in turn the revolutionaries of 1776 believed they were fighting to defend liberties that had been guaranteed by Magna Carta.

Recently a prominent civil rights lawyer has characterized the charter as an agreement between a "feudal king" and "thuggish barons." The Whigs, too, were mostly oligarchs intervening to replace royal privileges with their own.[19] And the growth of corporate power has forced awareness that the American Constitution, though a guide to the world in establishing the rule of law, was also largely a product of oligarchs. The flip side of its efficiency in curbing the powers of the state is its corresponding weakness in curbing the wealth and powers of the 1 percent. Since 1886, corporations have even assumed the equal protection rights designed by the Fourteenth Amendment for the American people. But America is still struggling to resolve whether it will be predominantly a democracy or an oligarchy.

It is as a *cultural* myth that Magna Carta has been important, embodying the principle usually referred to as "the rule of law," but which I prefer to think of as an equilibrium between divided powers. A search for "Magna Carta + Donald Trump" in 2019 yielded over a half million hits, most of them like this one from the *Chicago Tribune*: "We Americans are the political heirs of the Earl of Warren [*sic*; Warrenne] and his fellow barons who demanded a ransom from King John, eight centuries ago."[20]

As cultural myth, Magna Carta preserves something precious established in the Dark Age, the idea that, as St. Isidore of Seville (d. 636) wrote in his *Sententiae*, "it is just that the prince should obey his own laws" (iustum est principem legibus obtemperare suis),[21] a response to Ulpian's "Quod principi placuit legis habet vicem" (The ruler's will has force of law). Isidore's principle is now embedded in an emerging global ethos, having survived the disruptive waning of any clerical power to enforce it.

THE CÁIN ADAMNÁIN (LAW OF ADOMNÁN)

The last chapter dealt with the theme of the Dark Age as a yin period of rest and reformation of our yang society. This chapter has focused on secular matters of enforcement power and law, yang public arrangements with diminishing concern for the yin. But I would like to close the chapter with a yin episode—little more than an anecdote, perhaps—about an Irish monastic input to the history of law, one that in the short run was about as effective as Magna Carta but in the long run more forward-looking.

In 697, a synod of Martinian clerics and chieftains at Birr in Ireland adopted the Cáin Adamnáin (Law of Adamnán), also known as the Lex Innocentium (Law of Innocents), the so-called Geneva Conventions of the ancient Irish. This supplied rules for the protection of women and noncombatants in time of war.[22] According to one account, the law was prompted when Adamnán (the ninth abbot of Iona after its founder St. Columba) had a dream vision in which his mother rebuked him for not protecting the women and children of Ireland.

From a medieval Gaelic manuscript comes this version, in which the angel speaks in clerical Latin:

> On Pentecost eve a holy angel of the Lord came to him, and again at Pentecost after a year, and seized a staff, and struck his side, and said to him: "Go forth from Ireland, and make a law in it that women be not in any manner killed by men, through slaughter or any other death, either by poison, or in water, or in fire, or by any beast, or in a pit or by dogs, but that they shall die in their lawful bed. Thou shalt establish a law in Ireland and Britain for the sake of the mother

of each one, because a mother has borne each one, and for the sake of Mary, mother of Jesus Christ, through whom all are. Mary besought her son on behalf of Adamnan about this law.[23]

If a woman committed murder or other major crimes, she was to be set adrift in a boat with a paddle and a container of gruel. In this way God would determine her outcome; she would not be killed by a human. The code was to be enforced in both Ireland and in Britain and thus is an event in the evolution of international (though not canon) law.

In both versions we sense the overarching providential presence that we shall also sense in the Irish epic *Táin Bó Cualinge*, or *Cattle Raid of Cooley* (see chapter 12). We also see this law being attributed to a yin *inspiration*, of a kind that can be traced from the Old Testament prophets to Dante, Blake, Wordsworth, and Czeslaw Milosz. The detail that the angel spoke in clerical Latin reminds us why, in seventh-century Ireland and Scotland, the church was listened to. It commanded the precious asset of literacy, which laymen at all levels of society, despite their illiteracy, could see the value of and respected.

Just as importantly, the emergence of the Cáin Adamnáin proves the possibility of a cultural development from freer and purer motives than the Magna Carta, which was the product of little more than an ugly and basely motivated power struggle. I think of it as illustrating what I mean by ethogeny or cultural change as opposed to merely political change.

From a purely legal or yang perspective, the Cáin Adamnáin can be compared to the Peace of God (Pax Dei; first proclaimed in 989) and Truce of God (Treuga Dei; first proclaimed in 1027). The first two sought to protect the powerless and the third to limit the days of the week on which wars could be fought. All three have been cited as pioneer examples of efforts to create a movement fostering peace, or at least limited war. All three largely failed to meet these goals in their own times, yet in retrospect they can be seen as part of a long-term expansion from below.

Both Ireland and Scotland in particular continued to be ungovernable areas of violent tribal conflict, in the midst of which Martinian monasticism had established a strong and enduring presence. It makes sense that the Cáin Adamnáin, this premature contribution to the emergence of nonviolence, should proceed from these regions during the Third Pivotal Moment of the Dark Age. In the same way, the nonviolent spokesman Mahatma Gandhi (1869–1948) emerged from the colonial violence of South Africa and India, and his Muslim counterpart and follower Abdul Ghaffar Khan (1890–1988) from the strife-torn Pashtun border.

The Pax Dei and Treuga Dei, in contrast, arose in areas of western France where decades earlier Charlemagne had briefly established order, an achievement soon lost but still remembered. They were movements of the Fourth Pivotal Shift, where nostalgia for a lost order united a larger segment of society.

Their efforts were not fruitless. The American historian Frederick S. Paxton has argued that the French people, faced with a "king unable and the nobility unwilling to act," and "imbued with a 'national spirit' peculiarly creative in the fight against political and social ills, turned to spiritual sanctions as the only available means to limit violence."[24]

BELATED POSTSCRIPT

The preceding paragraphs, under the provisional title "Secular and Spiritual Power," were originally the first historical chapter of this book. Reviewing them four years later, I realize that after four years of writing, I have acquired a deeper view of contrasting powers over millennia: namely, between an original power from above (enforcement) and a slowly augmenting power from below (empowerment).

The divided powers of emperor and papacy in medieval Europe represent only a small part of this spectrum. To have described them as "secular" and "spiritual" was, I now see, misleading: the contest that gave rise to Magna Carta was, as I see it, a contest between two conflicting nodes of enforcement. And the division of power between them was, like the American Constitution, only a stage in an evolving dispersion of power from above, in response to slowly growing pressures (i.e., power) from below (e.g., the American Revolution, the mid-twentieth-century civil rights movement, Solidarity in Poland, the recent anti-lockdown protests in China).

It is a symptom of our post-Enlightenment episteme that in it the word *spiritual*, according to the *OED*, has two different and occasionally opposing meanings, either "I.1.a. Relating to or concerned with the human spirit or soul," or "4. Of or relating to religion, the church, or the clergy; religious, ecclesiastical." Religions, like cultures, have histories, and successful religions acquire secular power, at which point their spirituality (in the first sense) is challenged. Even Buddhism, originally nonviolent, has recently produced murderous regimes in Sri Lanka, Myanmar, and (briefly) Cambodia.

And whatever the outcome of that challenge, we can see a deeper spirit, or what I will call (to avoid confusion) *pneuma*, which refines religions along with their cultures in the direction of greater nonviolence and community. In a short time perspective, the opposite very often appears to be true, that, as Yeats wrote in 1919,

> The best lack all conviction, while the worst
> Are full of passionate intensity.

But in the long view, we see the forces of decency survive and increase, unlike the forces of mindless violence that Yeats feared.

An important example of *pneuma* reshaping religion is the development of religious tolerance. Originally Buddhism, Judaism, Catholicism, and Islam all encoded in their scriptures the notion that their particular path was the unique path to nirvana, enlightenment, or salvation. But all these religions have evolved away from, and in some cases have rejected, this simplistic and self-righteous view. Today most major states and major religions are showing increasing responsiveness to power from below. The result is a hopeful trend toward a softening of their power.

Another way to put this is that the communitarianism of small-scale or so-called primitive societies (in which enforcement is minimized) is being approached, very slowly, in the global ethosphere. I will give an example of the former that I read of from the slash-and-burn hill tribes of northern Thailand: faced with an incorrigibly antisocial individual, they would respond, if persuasion failed, by simply moving to a new settlement and leaving the culprit behind. That is clearly not possible on a global scale. But to become less coercive and more compassionate is not only possible; in the long term it is I believe what is happening.

Here is the difference noted above between the Cáin Adamnáin of the Third Pivotal Moment and the Treuga Dei of the Fourth. The latter was a step toward the system of international law currently in place in our post-Enlightenment episteme. But the Treuga Dei, like international law today, relied on an enforcement power, in the Treuga's case, the enforcement power of the church.

In the more primitive and ineffectual case of the Cáin Adamnáin, by contrast, Abbot Adamnán had little or no enforcement power; his early effort to curb violence, inspired by a dream, depended on his and his allies' ability to persuade the warring Irish chiefs. In this sense it was utopian. But for this very reason it, being "idealistic" and "visionary," may someday, like Thomas More's *Utopia*, be recognized as a valuable precursor to a new, post-secular era.

Chapter Twelve

St. Martin and the Diminution of Social Violence

Earlier I distinguished between (1) our biological nature, given to us at birth and which evolves very slowly in what we might call geological time; (2) our culturally molded second nature, which has evolved in the course of recent human history along with culture itself; and (3) our third nature or moreness, the power beyond our culturally defined second nature by which we can contribute to ethogeny or cultural change.

In chapter 10 I argued that the Dark Age was not at all an age of stagnation, as some still argue, but of limited but vital cultural evolution. With the decay of outmoded and repressive imperial social systems, it saw a renewal of creative development in social organization, technology, and even the high culture we are at present conditioned to associate with urban civilization.

In this chapter I want to make an even bolder claim: that the renewal of cultural evolution in the West following the release from antique culture was accompanied by a concurrent evolution in human capacity for what (for want of a better word) we normally call civility, but which I prefer to think of as whole-mindedness, and in particular whole-minded love. One reason for this was that the cultural leaders of this era were not kings or even bishops but saints, and among these saints were some with wholehearted commitment to their moreness, which empowered them to change not just themselves but the world.

The official abolition in 380 of paganism in the Roman Empire was an important but minor phase in this evolution. A more important factor was what we shall look at in this chapter: the grassroots conversion of country folk (*pagani*; from which we get our word *pagans*), and later barbarians, by whole-minded missionary monks in the tradition of St. Martin and St. Patrick. (But the parallel evolution in this era among non-Christians suggests that the spread of Christianity was a symptom of a wider pivotal shift.)

URBAN CHRISTIAN VIOLENCE AND
THE MONASTIC REACTION

Though our dictionaries have inherited the practice of defining *civility* as refinement and *barbarism* as cruelty, we cannot use these terms to distinguish between ancient Roman citizens and their enemies. A panegyric written to praise the Roman emperor Maximinianus Herculius (ca. 250–319 CE) celebrates the fact that under his command "all of the Chaebones and all of the Eruli were hacked to pieces."[1]

No such slaughter accompanied the celebrated sack of Rome by the "barbarian" Visigoth Alaric in 410. Indeed, Peter Brown makes the "sack" (his quotation marks) sound like a normal Roman act of pillage:

> Alaric did not act against Rome out of barbaric bloodlust. He had no wish to destroy Rome as the symbolic center of the Roman empire. He was like any other Roman general in a time of civil war. He headed an army that needed bonuses. He would raise the money that he needed through ransoms and through the systematic pillage of great cities. . . . Far from being a bloodbath, the Visigothic sack of Rome was a chillingly well-conducted act of spoliation. The gilded statues of the Forum vanished. Huge loads of cash along with gold and silver plate left the city when the Visigoths marched out again only three days later.[2]

(Brown does not mention the three days of rape that occurred, according to both Gibbon and Bury, and which obsessed St. Augustine in book 1 of *The City of God* [1.5, 16, 19, 28; henceforth *Civ. Dei*].[3])

The official conversion of the empire to Christianity produced no instant increase in public civility. A case in point was the spate of rioting in Alexandria which climaxed with the murder in 415 of the Neoplatonic philosopher and teacher Hypatia. Only a few years before, under the Christian patriarch Theophilus, Christians as well as Platonists had attended Hypatia's classes. But Theophilus died in 412 without naming a successor. His nephew Cyril defeated a competitor for the title, but only after three days of street fighting.

> Cyril then began to settle scores. As soon as he took power he punished the Novatianists (a Christian sect that had supported [Cyril's opponent]) by ordering the confiscation of their church property. Then, in 414, he . . . ordered his supporters to seize the synagogues in the city and drive the Jews from their homes.[4]

This persecution aroused the ire of Orestes, the imperial prefect of Egypt, and led to more fighting in the streets between supporters of Orestes and Cyril. Orestes turned for support to prominent members of the civic elite, including Hypatia. It appears that in response, Christians, instigated by Cyril, began to circulate rumors that Hypatia was a magician. Believing these rumors, "a man named Peter assembled a mob to find Hypatia. When they did so, they brought her to the Caesareum and dragged her through the streets till she died. His crowd then burned her body at the Cinarron, a place outside the city." This treatment was the well-established way of dealing with the bodies of "particularly abhorrent criminals."[5]

The murder of Hypatia has to be considered in the context of recurring violence in both rural and urban Egypt, notably after the so-called Bucolic War in 172–173 CE. This was a widespread revolt in rural Egypt against excessive taxation; it took years to suppress, severely damaged the Egyptian economy, and marked the beginning of a serious economic decline. Though slavery was not as widespread an institution in Egypt as elsewhere, the disparity in income and wealth was just as great and put increasing stress on the fabric of society in the empire's declining years.

One consequence of this violence, income disparity, and decay was an increase of sectarianism in the cities, including the severe sect of Novatianists mentioned above. But another was the monasticism of the Desert Fathers like St. Anthony (d. 356), a radical return to a simpler Christianity, remote from and untainted by secular power rather than assimilated to it.

A particular goal of these monks was to overcome "the 'demon' of anger. However provocative the circumstances, a monk must never respond aggressively to any attack. One abbot ruled that there was no excuse for violent speech, even if your brother 'plucks out your right eye and cuts off your right hand.' A monk must not even look angry or make an impatient gesture . . . Evagrius of Pontus (d. 399), one of the most influential monastic teachers, drew on Paul's doctrine of kenosis [emptying] and instructed monks to empty their minds of the rage, avarice, pride, and vainglory that tore the soul apart and made them close their hearts to others."[6]

The monastic movement in the Eastern Empire spread "rapidly, demonstrating a widespread hunger for an alternative to a Christianity that was increasingly tainted by imperial associations. By the end of the fifth century, tens of thousands of monks were living beside the Nile and in the deserts of Syria, Egypt, Mesopotamia, and Armenia."[7] The same period saw an energetic increase in missionary monastic activity, from the Far East (where monastic missionaries brought Mahayana Buddhism from Central Asia to China) to Gaul and Ireland.

But Christian monasticism in the West was in one respect markedly different from monasticism in the East. The two dominant figures in it, St. Martin and St. Augustine, were both inspired by the example of St. Anthony, but they focused the social energy of monasticism in a new direction, not to escape from the inhabited world but to *convert* it.

TWO EXEMPLARS OF A DEEPER CONVERSION: ST. MARTIN AND ST. AUGUSTINE

Clearly the nominal conversion of a society to Christianity did little by itself to diminish violence. An important role was played in the ensuing years by two contrasting movements in Christianity, each inspired by an exemplar of "third nature" or moreness. The first was the spread of the popular missionary monasticism launched by St. Martin of Tours (d. 397). The second was the great enhancement of Christian thought and literature exemplified by St. Augustine (354–430).

These two movements had little to do with each other, and their occasional overlaps were often antithetical. It is reported that St. Martin (who worked in the countryside) abandoned his career as a soldier after his conversion, saying, "I am a soldier of Christ: it is not lawful for me to fight."[8] St. Augustine (who worked in cities) argued in contrast that "to wage war at God's bidding is in no way contrary to the commandment, 'Thou shalt not kill'" (*Civ. Dei* 1.21).

I wish to focus on these two quite different figures partly because their differences are illuminating, and partly because their divergent influences together are major figures in the rapid cultural evolution (or ethogeny) of the later Dark Age. The two men, in their different ways, strengthened the possibility of that commitment central to both cultural development and this book: *to love with all your heart and all your soul and all your might* (or mind, or moreness; Matt. 22:37, cf. Deut. 6:5).

It is harder to demonstrate this with St. Martin and his successors, such as Irish monks like St. Columbanus (d. 615) and St. Aidan (d. 651). Like Jesus, all of these men worked among illiterates and left few records of themselves (Martin in fact left nothing); we remember them for what they accomplished (and their posthumous reputations), not for what little they wrote.

More importantly, what we now read in the *Catholic Encyclopedia* of missionary monks like St. Martin, or some of his Celtic successors, Patrick (d. ca. 461) among the Irish, Ninian (d. ca. 431) among the Picts, and Columba (d. 597) among the Scots, is dubiously documented, derived from Lives (vitae) that in some cases were written long after the death of their subjects.

These vitae, like the *Vita S. Martini* of Sulpicius, are less interested in their subjects' success as proselytizers than in their *virtutes*, which can refer to their *miracles*, to their *power to enact miracles*, or in some cases to *God's divine power in the world* to which these saints, through their humility and asceticism, had access.[9] (Thus, what most of the vitae write about is of little interest to contemporary historians.)

Let us note again the dramatic dialectical reversal in meaning here of the word *virtus*. Originally signifying the strength and prowess of a man (*vir*), as in the *arete* of Homer's *Iliad*, by the time of St. Martin it had come to mean a power acquired, it was believed, by humility and self-abasement and by neglecting one's own strength in order to partake of God's.

HOW MUCH CAN WE REALLY KNOW OF ST. MARTIN?

Sulpicius Severus (d. ca. 425), the principal chronicler of St. Martin (d. 397), allegedly met the saint "several times at his monastery."[10] Yet his detailed accounts of Martin's miracles have come under especially critical review. Over a century ago, a French scholar, Etienne-Charles Babut, observed that, for over a half-century until the 460s (when Bishop Perpetuus of Tours elevated the tomb and relics of St. Martin into a pilgrimage center), there was almost no corroborating mention of St. Martin by other Gaulish authors.[11]

It is particularly significant that contemporary authors in Gaul with a sympathetic monastic bias, notably John Cassian (d. 434) and Salvian (d. ca. 470), do not ever refer to St. Martin.[12] Babut put forward the radical proposition that St. Martin might have been largely a creation of Sulpicius, whose *Vita S. Martini* was largely concocted from earlier sources such as the *Vita S. Antoni* by St. Athanasius (d. 373).

Babut's claim that Sulpicius "created" St. Martin has since been modified, notably by those who propose that Sulpicius was transmitting an oral tradition.[13] For the public awareness of St. Martin was far too devoted and widespread to be traced to a single source.[14] Clare Stancliffe suggests that, after Martin was succeeded as bishop by his critic Brice, "those Marmoutier monks who remained most faithful to the tradition of Martin" may have congregated at Sulpicius's country estate of Primuliacum and shared their reminiscences of Martin there.[15] They in turn would have transmitted oral reports of Martin's *virtutes* from lay followers of St. Martin. These may have included folkloric elements, which became increasingly frequent, and increasingly fictional, as hagiographic literature developed in the later Middle Ages.[16] Sulpicius's account, in other words, is grounded in mythogenesis and mnemohistory.

SULPICIUS'S ANTIPATHY TO THE
WEALTH OF THE CHURCH

Over a century ago, it was estimated that "in France, including Alsace and Lorraine, there are at the present time three thousand six hundred and seventyfive churches dedicated to St. Martin, and four hundred and twentyfive villages or hamlets are named after him."[17] A search for St. Martin on Google Maps reveals that the bulk of these are concentrated in a crescent reaching from Ireland through northern France to northern Germany—areas converted, as we shall see, by missionary Celtic and Northumbrian monks in the Martinian or persuasive tradition.

Gregory of Tours (d. 594) reported in his *History of the Franks* (where Martin is mentioned over one hundred times) that Martin's *virtutes* (extending even to dust from his tomb) were prayed to by believers and feared by the wicked. According to Gregory, they could affect history:

> When King Clothar [d. 561] levied a tax on church property, all the bishops consented except one. When Injuriosus of Tours [d. 546] manfully refused . . . the king was alarmed and being afraid of the power of the blessed Martin he sent after him . . . praying for pardon and admitting the wrongfulness of what he had done. (Gregory of Tours, *Historia Francorum* 4.2)

Martin's historical influence cannot be doubted. There is still a consensus, "however, that Sulpicius had a strong tendency to exaggerate as well as a good deal of malice toward the contemporary clergy."[18]

Sulpicius was indeed a priest with a strong antipathy to the growing wealth of the episcopate. His contemporary Jerome, also an exponent of church poverty and asceticism, had contemplated writing a history of the church "from the coming of the Savior to . . . the dregs our time—[how] the Church . . . waxed in persecution . . . and, after the coming of Christian emperors, became greater indeed in power and riches but meaner in virtues."[19]

Walter Goffart observes that "the *Chronicle* of Sulpicius Severus went some way toward carrying [Jerome's program] out and, as a result, almost failed to come down to us" (it was preserved in a single manuscript from the eleventh century).[20]

It is also quite likely that, as was reported within a century, Sulpicius "in his old age was temporarily deceived by the Pelagian heretics,"[21] some of whom opposed corrupt ecclesiastical wealth as vigorously as himself. (In the next chapter we shall see that the radical claim of one Pelagian tract, "Get rid of the rich and you will find no poor," was strenuously attacked by St. Augustine.)

An example of Sulpicius's "malice" (reinforced later by Gregory of Tours) was his report that Martin's successor as bishop of Tours, Brice (Brictio; d. 444),

> who had possessed nothing before he entered the clerical office, having, in fact, been brought up in the monastery by Martin himself, was now keeping horses and purchasing slaves. For at that time he was accused by many of not only

having bought boys belonging to barbarous nations, but girls also of a comely appearance (Sulpicius Severus, *Dialogues* 3.15).[22]

All of Sulpicius's writings about Martin are indeed "a standing indictment of the pomp and grandeur with which many of the Gaulish bishops in the fourth and fifth centuries lived. Riding a horse, for example, was a mark of social standing."[23]

In his *Vita S. Martini*, Sulpicius wrote that Martin was only persuaded to leave his hermitage by a townsman of Tours, on the pretext "that his wife was ill." He and other townsmen then rushed Martin to Tours, demanding that he be made bishop. There was however opposition to Martin's asceticism from some of the other bishops, who were "impiously" offering resistance, "asserting forsooth that Martin's person was contemptible, that he was unworthy of the episcopate, that he was a man despicable in countenance, that his clothing was mean, and his hair disgusting" (Sulpicius Severus, *Vita S. Martini* 9).

Martin's asceticism emulated that of Eastern monks in Egypt, and when founding his first community at Ligugé in 361—often cited as "the first monastery in the West"—he followed an Egyptian model. But it was indeed anomalous in western Europe, where he was a forerunner by a generation or two of what would become standard monastic practice.[24] Even Jerome (d. 420), the church doctor who did most to promote the ideal of asceticism, was more at home in an environment of what Peter Brown calls "learned *otium*"; Megan Williams comments that "his attraction seems to have been to the ascetic idea rather than the ascetic life."[25]

Yet what must have seemed idiosyncratic to the Gaulish bishops was in fact a symptom of a profound cultural revolution taking place at the highest levels of society: a transvaluation of economic wealth, from its being seen as a source of security to its being rejected instead as a threat to it. Christ of course had said that "If thou wilt be perfect, go and sell that thou hast, and give to the poor" (Matt. 19:21). That had resonated well with the poor of the earth; the rich did not take this caution seriously until the second half of the fourth century.

In *Through the Eye of a Needle*, Peter Brown describes the "unmistakable—even shocking—'markers'" of the "unimaginably wide horizon opened up to humanity by the Christian message[:] . . . outreach to the poor . . . a sharp elevation of forms of total sexual renunciation—of virginity, of monastic withdrawal, and even, in certain circles, of clerical celibacy."[26]

Brown's magisterial book focuses on four prominent culture shapers of the fourth century: Saints Ambrose (d. 397), Jerome (d. 420), Augustine (d. 430), and Paulinus of Nola (d. 431). All four were what Malcolm Gladwell, in *The Tipping Point*, would call "connectors" in the lead-up to the Third Pivotal Shift, mediating the links between the vast majority of otherwise weakly connected individuals. (Ambrose, Augustine, and Jerome are remembered as three of the four doctors of the Roman Catholic Church, along with Pope Gregory I [d. 604].)

Of these four, all but St. Ambrose became monks. And even Ambrose, after he was both baptized and made bishop of Milan in the same week, immediately adopted an ascetic lifestyle and apportioned his money to the poor, donating all of his land and making only provision for his sister Marcellina (who had become a nun).[27]

Ambrose and Paulinus were born into Rome's ruling class and were wealthy, in contrast to Augustine and Jerome who came from middling families in outlying districts of Africa and Dalmatia. But all four accepted that, to join the thriving new community of Christians, they could not just, like Bill Gates today, be generous to the poor; they should imitate Christ's counsel "to sell that thou hast" (Matt. 19:21). In this they followed the example not just of the Gospel but of Martin's monastery at Marmoutier, where (according to Sulpicius) many "were considered [habebantur] of noble rank," yet "no one possessed anything of his own; everything was put into the common stock."[28]

Then, like today, many nominal Christians could not understand such an extreme renunciation of the world. The poets Ausonius (d. ca. 393) and Paulinus of Nola (d. 431), both born into patrician Christian families, had been friends until Paulinus decided to be baptized, dispose of his wealth, and become a monk. Thereafter, Ausonius, "totally unable to understand his friend's attitude, . . . can only believe that he is crazed."[29]

This was also the response of the late Latin poet Rutilius Namatianus (fl. fifth century), who though probably pagan was not unfriendly to the Christianity practiced by ordinary people. But in his poem describing his trip through the Mediterranean in the year 416 is a hostile denunciation of monks on the island of Capraria (now Capraia), between Elba and Corsica:

> What madness [*rabies*] of a brain diseased so fond
> As, fearing evil, to refuse all good?[30]

Peter Brown describes how in that one generation between Ausonius and his friend Paulinus of Nola, who as we shall see was one of Augustine's very few friends who knew both Sulpicius and Martin, the desire of the wealthy to display their splendor—their "sheer *éclat*" that both overawed and delighted—abated.[31] Paulinus and his wife Therasia were one of the richest couples in the West, but in 392 they joined a few other wealthy Romans in giving all of their wealth to the church.

There were practical reasons for doing so, not mentioned by Brown in this context. At the Battle of Adrianople (378), the Goths handed the Roman army its first major defeat in a century. More than this, they destroyed that army's core and were able to settle within the limits of the empire. (In this context, revolts of armed peasants, or Bacaudae, which had been largely suppressed after the Roman imperial crisis of the third century, reappeared and were a menace to wealthy estates, especially in Gaul.) Wealth's changing status in this period should impress on us the extent to which wealth, as much as political authority or paper currency, is less an absolute than a function of social acceptance, an acceptance that disparities of wealth risk calling into question and even terminating.

The Goths' impunity soon led to their "unparalleled spoliations" of the wealthy in northern Italy, followed by Alaric's sack of Rome in 410. But in that sack, while the homes of the wealthy were burned, the churches escaped unharmed—a softening of the usual practice of warfare which was triumphantly emphasized by St. Augustine in book 1 of *The City of God*.[32]

With the disruption of a secure urban order, wealth now made one not secure but a target. The responses to this challenge ranged from the superficial to the profound. The commonest response of the rich was merely to abandon an imperial role, seek refuge in an ecclesiastical one, and live much as before. For example, Sidonius Apollinaris (d. ca. 485), son-in-law of Emperor Avitus, was an urban prefect and Roman senator before becoming bishop of Clermont (where he was succeeded by his son and grandson).

The effect of this was to increase the wealth, and in due course the power, of the church. Conversely, since churches had been granted tax immunity by Constantine, the wealth and power of the state were diminished, more and more radically so as emperors like Theodosius felt compelled to increase taxes on the lay community.

Of the four doctors of the Catholic Church, the three who lived in this cusp era—St. Ambrose (d. 397), St. Jerome (d. 420), and St. Augustine (d. 430)—surrendered their property; all but Ambrose, moreover, did so by becoming monks (like Paulinus of Nola). The fourth doctor, Pope Gregory I (d. 604), also first became a monk, marking the decisive papal acceptance of the once marginalized and derided values of monasticism.

All these men, when surrendering their wealth, surrendered their lifestyle and became ascetic, but to varying degrees. All attached great importance to celibacy as a means of redirecting sexual energy toward God. The wealthy (Ambrose and Paulinus) gave generously to the poor, thus enlarging the social fabric; but to do so they maintained control of their wealth, to this purpose, after renouncing it.

Paulinus (like Pope Gregory after him) restricted his diet, to the point of affecting his health, eating "beans pounded with millet, in order that I might learn more quickly to lay aside the refined choosiness of a senator."[33] Paulinus would later be remembered as St. Paulinus of Nola, befriended and admired by Saints Jerome, Ambrose, and Augustine (*Civ. Dei* 1.10), and "whose

closest friend and correspondent in the years immediately following his con-
version was none other than Sulpicius Severus."[34] A letter of Paulinus (18.3)
confirms that Martin miraculously cured Paulinus of an eye ailment.

This authoritative corroboration of a miracle in the *Vita S. Martini* (ca.
19) makes Paulinus's cure the only one of Martin's alleged miracles to be
accepted by modern historians like Peter Brown.[35] The more dramatic exam-
ples that once made Martin celebrated, such as a snake turning away when
ordered by Martin to do so (Sulpicius, *Dialogues* 3.9), are no longer in favor.

In his *Dialogues*, Sulpicius Severus offered a credible explanation for the
Gaulish silence about Martin. He had another speaker, Gallus, claim that St.
Martin's posthumous reputation extended to Ethiopia and India, yet was held
in disregard by the Gallican clergy.

> All the more wretched on this account is this country of ours [Gaul], which
> has not been found worthy to be acquainted with so great a man, although he
> was in its immediate vicinity. However, I will not include the people at large
> in this censure: *only the clerics, only the priests know nothing of him; and not
> without reason* were they, in their ill-will, disinclined to know him, inasmuch
> as, had they become acquainted with his virtues they must have recognized their
> own vices.[36]

Babut gave some credibility to this localized "conspiration de silence" in
Gaul, noting that the first corroboration of Martin's existence is found far off,
in the *Ecclesiastical History* (443–44 CE) of Sozomenus (d. ca. 450), writing
in Palestine.

The Gallic silence was broken in the 460s, after the tomb of St. Martin was
elevated into a pilgrimage center by Bishop Perpetuus of Tours, making Tours
become the wealthy "religious metropolis" of Gaul. However, the antipathy
of Gallic bishops before then is noted by Peter Brown in his definitive study
of Third Moment Christian ambivalence about earthly wealth, *Through the
Eye of a Needle*:

> Martin . . . was elected bishop of Tours against the wishes of the provincial
> bishops and their distinctly mediocre urban clergy. Rather, Martin enjoyed the
> support of a network of substantial landowners. . . . The monasticism that made
> Martin a hero to the villa-owning aristocracy of Gaul was long resented and
> resisted by the more middling clergy of many Gallic cities.[37]

Written history will inevitably reflect the bias of an author's episteme, and
what does not get reported can also be significant. I will repeat the observa-
tion of Brown's magisterial *Through the Eye of a Needle*, that

the creation of a rural Christianity in Spain, Gaul, and Italy remains the dark side of the moon in the study of the churches in this period. Yet it is one of the great changes of the age.[38]

On the level of ethogeny, however, of the noosphere, or of Popper's "World 3," the *Vita St. Martini* by Sulpicius becomes one of the predominant forces during these great changes of Western and particularly Celtic monasticism. Babut calls it the most read, loved, and imitated of saints' vitae, with hundreds of manuscript copies from all ages.[39] It is contained for example in the ninth-century *Book of Armagh*, along with miraculous legends of St. Patrick, another legendary innovator who is alleged to have met St. Martin on a visit to Gaul.

The facts concerning St. Martin remain obscure. It is clear though that, as we shall see, the *Life of St. Martin* inspired and inaugurated a new and powerful tradition of ascetic missionary monks, first Celtic (Patrick, Columba, Columbanus) and later Northumbrian (Willibrord). In contrast to the papally ordered monastic mission of St. Augustine of Canterbury (d. 604) to King Æthelberht of Kent, the Celtic missionaries were self-motivated and sometimes took great risks. Though often well born, they tended to be (like St. Martin) ill at ease in high society.

We shall continue to talk of the influence of St. Martin, as it was remembered at the time, and as it is remembered still by Catholic sources. Especially after his tomb became a pilgrimage center, that influence extended to high society and culture as well, as witnessed by the voluminous prose writings of Gregory of Tours (d. 594; see below) and the poetry of Venantius Fortunatus (d. ca. 600).

Fortunatus, an Italian by birth, was deeply impressed by the *simplicitas* of Martin's life and legacy, which inspired in him a new rustic poetics. We do not see this in his *Life of St. Martin*, a panegyric written in classical hexameters with occasional epic flourishes,[40] but in his brief friendship poems which are written to nuns, St. Radegund and Agnes. He knew these two royal women as a sister and the abbess in a monastic community founded by Radegund in Poitiers, where Fortunatus himself served in some form of lay capacity.

Brian McGuire has observed that "the simplicity and directness of his poetry to Radegund and Agnes would have been impossible had they lived at court." But in a monastery, where Radegund and Agnes were officially a sister and a mother (Fortunatus himself served in the abbey as a lay official), "Fortunatus could concentrate not on grandeur and power but on the objects of everyday life: eggs, violets and meals together."[41]

Apparently his "passionate friendship" with Agnes gave rise to gossip if not scandal, to which Fortunatus responded in a poem:

Mother to me in honor, sister sweetly loved, whom I esteem with devotion, faith, heart, and soul, with heavenly affection, and not with any bodily sin; I love, not in the flesh, but what the spirit yearns for. . . . Alas, I bewail my danger, the fear lest a whisper with malicious words block my feelings.[42]

ST. MARTIN AND ST. AUGUSTINE

St. Martin's tradition of rural evangelism can be contrasted with the urban, literate, often upper-class Christianity associated with St. Augustine, whose *Confessions* are a signal event (sometimes described as the first true auto-biography) in the evolution of the Western literary canon, and indeed of Western consciousness. His approach in that work to the impossible ideal of whole-minded loving provides a benchmark by which we can measure the progress in the centuries that followed.

These two men represent two different aspects of Christianity, the bottom-up and the top-down, the prayer meeting and the university, that to this day are far from reconciled. In a more general way, they represent the two basic aspects of society, the country and the city, the yin and the yang, that today, in most parts of the world, are sadly lacking balance and mutual understanding.

St. Augustine, it is true, attributed his conversion in part to his amazement at the wonderful example of St. Anthony in the desert, "almost in our own times" (*Confessions* 8.6). Yet Augustine's excited surprise on first learning of St. Anthony draws attention to the complete absence in his voluminous writings of any reference to his contemporary St. Martin, not only the pioneer Western monk in the Eastern style but by then also a bishop.

My urban, college-educated friends know about St. Augustine but little or nothing about St. Martin. I suspect the reverse may be true for many in the church as a whole. Martinmas is still celebrated in the Catholic calendar; there is no equivalent feast for St. Augustine. In my global gazetteer, there are eight entries for St. Martin and only two for St. Augustine (both of them in North America). And it is possible that those who pray the St. Martin of Tours Novena (now available as an app on the internet) know more about St. Martin than about St. Augustine.

Both men were converts to Christianity who came from the margins of the empire: St. Martin (who was "not an aristocrat") from Sabaria in Pannonia (now Hungary), and St. Augustine from Thagaste in Numidia (now Algeria). St. Martin, "the first western monk to become a bishop,"[43] is remembered for his persuasive missionary work among "the country people, the *pagani*, whom he moved out [from the city] to evangelise."[44] He and his Irish and

Northumbrian successors had much to do with the expansion of Christianity north of the Alps.

On the other hand, the North African regions proselytized by St. Augustine were soon lost to the Arian Vandals and ultimately to Islam. For St. Augustine was an intellectual, not an evangelist; his most successful conversion was of his own spirit, as recorded in the *Confessions*, which has become a model for other great elite conversions since.

MARTIN'S VIEW OF THE CHURCH'S EARTHLY POWER, AND AUGUSTINE'S

The two men had radically different attitudes toward earthly power. When an ascetic lower-class bishop, Priscillian, was convicted of heresy by his fellow bishops, Martin appealed to the emperor Maximus twice, first to spare the life of Priscillian and a second time not to persecute his surviving followers. On the first count he was unsuccessful: Priscillian was tortured and killed in 385. The second time, Martin successfully persuaded the emperor to relent, but only at the price, which he later regretted, of taking communion with the vengeful bishops.

Sulpicius writes that thereafter,

> when it happened that he cured some of the possessed more slowly and with less grace than usual, he at once confessed to us with tears that he felt a diminution of his power on account of the evil of that communion in which he had taken part for a moment through necessity, and not with a cordial spirit. He lived sixteen years after this, but never again did he attend a synod, and he kept carefully aloof from all assemblies of bishops.[45]

In the next chapter we shall have cause to celebrate St. Augustine's generative masterpiece *The City of God*, where he argued that the true home for humanity is not the "earthly city" (civitas terrena)—marked by "love of self" (amor sui) and "dominated by the lust for domination" (dominandi libido dominatur)—but the city of God (civitas Dei), united by fellowship in the "love of God [amor Dei] carried as far as the contempt of self."[46] But Augustine also recognized that the church, as presently incarnated, was a *corpus permixtum* (Augustine, *De Doctrina Christiana* 3.32) and relied on a coercive earthly power which he, when he became bishop of Hippo, was prepared to use.

In contrast to St. Martin, St. Augustine endorsed a coercive approach to heretics. At one point he had been opposed to persecuting them, but his losing struggles as bishop with the Donatists in Africa led him to change his mind. In a letter of 417 to the Roman governor Bonifacius, he wrote that there is

> a persecution of unrighteousness, which the impious inflict upon the Church of Christ; and there is a righteous persecution, which the Church of Christ inflicts upon the impious. . . . She persecutes in the spirit of love, they in the spirit of wrath; she that she may correct, they that they may overthrow: she that she may recall from error, they that they may drive headlong into error.[47]

And whereas Martin sought to rescue heretics from the secular jurisdiction of the emperor, Augustine considered it appropriate for the church to hand heretics over to the emperor's authorities so that the church would not be involved in their physical torture.

[Interpolation: After writing this book I now see how applicable Augustine's judgment about the earthly city is today to our culture, which has become so "coerced by coercive power" (*dominandi libido*) that it is now controversial, as well as difficult, to be inspired, as in Martin's era, by spiritual (i.e., pneumatic) power. (Dorothy Day of *The Catholic Worker*, a recent imitator of St. Martin, is now being considered for sainthood, but for much of her life she was, like Martin, at odds with the Catholic hierarchy, as well as under surveillance by the FBI.)

Not just our mindset but our language has diminished by this coercive cultural shrinking. The word *virtutes*, encapsulating the excitement of an era preparing for the apocalypse, no longer means the miraculous extra-rational powers energizing history, as reportedly exercised by Martin and other saints. Today it just means "virtues."

Recognizing this forces us to reconsider the process by which the Enlightenment divided our culture from its religious matrix and to see this process, which originally functioned as a progressive liberation, as risking a vital deprivation, indeed in some respects a regression to a pagan era.

But these brief paragraphs about modern despiritualization should not blind us to the recent defeats of coercive power by spiritual power I referred to in the introduction, such as that of Gandhi's satyagraha (truth power) movement in South Africa and India, the Solidarity movement in Poland, or the civil rights movement of the 1960s in America.[48]

[End of interpolation.]

THE SUCCESS OF ST. MARTIN'S PERSUASIVE
TRADITION IN NORTHERN EUROPE

The persuasive missionary tradition of itinerant monastics, following Martin, blossomed in Ireland, where at first, as far as we know, whole tribes rather than individuals were converted, and whole communities with their children lived at first in something resembling a common life.[49] And Irish monks in turn continued this missionary work in other lands. An Irish tradition developed of voluntary *peregrinatio pro Christo*, in which individuals permanently left their homes and committed themselves to a yin life of perilous "white martyrdom."[50]

Outstanding examples of this Irish tradition were St. Columba (d. 597), who around 563 established the abbey of Iona in Scotland, St. Columbanus (d. 615) in the outlying regions of Merovingian Burgundy and Lombard Italy, and St. Aidan (d. 651), who from Iona established around 634 the abbey of Lindisfarne in Anglian Northumbria.

Bede (d. 735) depicts Aidan's proselytizing as purely persuasive, free from any coercion:

> He neither sought nor loved any thing of this world, but delighted in distributing immediately among the poor whatsoever was given him by the kings or rich men of the world. He was wont to traverse both town and country on foot, never on horseback, unless compelled by some urgent necessity; and wherever in his way he saw any, either rich or poor, he invited them, if infidels, to embrace the mystery of the faith or if they were believers, to strengthen them in the faith, and to stir them up by words and actions to alms and good works.[51]

Bede writes that it was the recently converted king of Northumbria, Oswald, "being desirous that all his nation should receive the Christian faith," who had arranged for Aidan to come from Iona (*Hist. Eccl.* 3.3). But in his account Aidan was as uncomfortable in the company of secular authority as Martin before him: "If it happened, which was but seldom, that he was invited to eat with the king, he went with one or two clerks, and having taken a small repast, made haste to be gone with them, either to read or write" (*Hist. Eccl.* 3.5).

Ecclesiastical authority (with its precious asset of literacy) and royal authority reinforced each other,[52] and Bede, an Angle possibly of noble or even royal birth,[53] is as we shall see no foe of royalty. But his *History* abounds with peripatetic monks who voluntarily risked and on occasion endured painful martyrdoms,[54] for no other motive than the excitement (or moreness) prevalent in that era, of participating in the spread into new areas of a literate and civilizing religion.

In the next century, Irish-trained Northumbrian monks like St. Willibrord (d. 739) continued this missionary work. In close alliance with the Frankish court under Pepin of Herstal and Charles Martel, evangelization and subjugation proceeded together into Frisia and other parts of Germany, providing a softer restructuring of German tribes than would have occurred by simple conquest.[55]

This softer transition was a factor in the gradual substitution of serfdom for slavery.[56] No single event can be cited to illustrate this slow process. However, "the historical synthesis which finally occurred was, of course, feudalism. . . . The catastrophic collision of two dissolving modes of production—primitive and ancient—eventually produced the feudal order which spread through mediaeval Europe. . . . Serfdom itself probably descends both from the classical statute of the *colonus* and from the slow degradation of free Germanic peasants by quasi-coercive 'commendation' to clan warriors."[57]

The transition was neither continuous nor painless. Chris Wickham writes that, as "a general development of the ninth and tenth centuries in the West, . . . peasants were slowly and steadily excluded from the public sphere, and, in more general terms, ever more clearly subjected to aristocrats and churches, the great private landowners."[58]

The monastic missionaries' success in conversion was matched by their role in preserving their distillate of ancient Latin literature. Thomas Cahill exaggerates, but his proud claim has merit:

> "The weight of the Irish influence on the continent," admits James Westfall Thompson, "is incalculable." . . . More than half of all our [Catholic] biblical commentaries between 650 and 850 were written by Irishmen. Before the end of the eighth century, the exiles had reached Modra in Moravia . . . and there are traces of the [Irish] White Martyrs as far as Kiev. . . . Monastic manuscript art had traveled from the workshops of Syria and Egypt by way of Ireland and Britain and, at last, to the continent of Europe.[59]

But with the acceptance of Gregorian reforms by Charlemagne, the centuries-old practice of itinerant monasticism was gradually replaced by that of coenobial living according to the Benedictine rule. Instead of shaping the future, monasticism was adjusted to survival within the existing status quo.

The stage was set for the Fourth Pivotal Shift: the revival of cities, trade, and central authority in the second millennium. But we cannot leave the monastic missionaries of northern Europe without recognizing that this was an era of monastic missionaries elsewhere as well. The seventh-century Tang dynasty in China saw the arrival of Nestorian missionary monks from Syria.[60] In the same century, the so-called Thirteen Assyrian Fathers arrived from Mesopotamia to strengthen Christianity in Georgia.[61] The work of the

Irish in eighth-century Moravia, when interrupted by a Slavic ruler seeking independence from the Franks, was taken up instead by the Thessalonican brothers Saints Cyril and Methodius.

CULTURAL REJUVENATION AT THE FRONTIER

What sustained the extraordinary morale of the itinerant monks in northern Europe, living alone or in small numbers among often hostile heathens? The misnamed Gelasian Sacramentary, said to be the sacramentary used by Willibrord's successor St. Boniface (d. 754) in his missionary work, contains a series of *formulae* recognizing both the role of itinerant monastics and also the *unanimitas* of the common life.[62]

A ready seed ground for such *unanimitas* was the tribal frontier, such as what Cahill describes as "chilly, citiless Ireland" in the fifth century, when "men worked in close cooperation by day and slept side by side by night. Even the king was one's intimate—and the Irish word *ri* suggests an intimacy that could never be imagined of *rex*."[63]

The intimacy of the Irish, even among foes in battle, is well illustrated by the *Táin Bó Cualinge* (often translated as *The Cattle Raid of Cooley*), the major Irish oral epic, dated in part (on linguistic evidence) to the eighth century. It is often compared to the *Iliad* but in my view is simultaneously far more primitive (mythical creatures take part in the heroic combats) and also far more culturally developed. It deals with violence, but not with naked violence. Though the action concerns the theft of a bull in pre-Christian Ireland, the perspective of the poem is much larger than the events it describes, larger in a way that to me can only suggest the author's exposure to the culture of an unconflicted Christianity.

For example, when the Morrígan, a phantom queen, fights the hero Cú Chulainn three times, in the form of an eel, a wolf, and a heifer, Cú Chulainn wounds her in each combat. But in the end she returns to him in the form of an old woman and offers him three drinks of milk. With each drink Cú Chulainn blesses her, and the blessings heal her wounds.[64] Blessings occur repeatedly in the *Táin*, and their efficacy suggests an invisible benign presence underlying the narrative, such as we do not look for in the *Iliad* but do see as empowering the *virtutes* of St. Martin.

Later the action depends on a series of single combats. But the enemies whom Cú Chulainn fights share bonds with him in a manner wholly absent from the *Iliad*. One enemy is his foster father Fergus, and Cú Chulainn negotiates an agreement with him that he will yield in this combat, provided that Fergus will yield in their next.

In the last of these combats, the enemy is Cú Chulainn's foster brother Ferdia. The friendship between the two combatants is compared by Cahill to that between Achilles and Patroclus, but of course Achilles and Patroclus were Greek allies, not opponents. Eventually Cú Chulainn will kill Ferdia, but first he attempts to persuade him not to fight:

> "When we were with Scáthach and Uathach and Aife we always set out together to the battles and battlefields, to the strife and the struggle and the forests and deserts and dark mysteries."

He spoke further:

> "Fast friends, forest companions,
> we made one bed and slept one sleep
> in foreign lands after the fray
> Scáthach's pupils, two together,
> we'd set forth to comb the forest."[65]

In the *Iliad*, even the gods are in conflict, and this explains the bitterness of the mortal fight at Troy. In the *Táin*, on the other hand, the theft and the combats are overshadowed by glimmerings of a larger humanity in a larger moral universe.

This faith, in which "the meek will inherit the earth" (Psalm 37:11, Matt. 5:5), arose in the ethos of those not in power, such as the "meek and lowly" Jesus (Matt. 11:28). Thanks to the vibrant energy of Martinian monastic Christianity, it came to shape the ethos of a nascent Irish ruling class.

THE IRISH SUCCESS COMPARED TO THE ECLIPSE OF CATHOLICISM IN NUMIDIA

Swordless monastics were brilliantly successful among the unlettered tribes of northern Europe. By contrast, Augustine's efforts to eradicate the heresies of Donatism and Pelagianism in North Africa, with the help of state power, are an instructive disaster. Even before his death in 430, the Vandals, who were Arians rather than Catholics, were on the point of ousting Rome from Numidia.

> Within a decade, Catholic bishops were exiled as "heretics." The Vandals even used the former anti-Donatist laws that had imposed exile after 411. Vandal rulers applied the laws unchanged to the Catholic clergy. By a strange (and not wholly undeserved) irony of fate, many of the friends of Augustine (notably Possidius of Calama, his biographer) ended their lives as exiles in Italy. They

had been driven from their cities by the same laws against heresy that they had petitioned for, thirty years before, in order to drive out their Donatist rivals.[66]

The effective displacement of North African Christianity by Islam in the seventh and eight centuries stands in marked contrast to the survival of Christianity in Egypt and Syria. Very few parts of the world have seen the virtual extirpation of Christianity once it has been well established. Augustine's homeland of Numidia is one of them.

I do not wish to suggest that we should blame this failure on Augustine. In contrast to Ireland and northern Europe, North Africa had been subjected to centuries of ruthless imperial exploitation and taxation. A resulting spirit of violent rebelliousness continued, both in Numidia and in the Middle East, even after the Muslim takeover. To this day, these regions continue to be plagued by cruel alternatives: civil conflict or else tyranny.

Augustine's political efforts to save a Catholic Numidia were probably doomed, like Dante's hopes in the thirteenth century for a revived Holy Roman Empire, or Milton's efforts in the seventeenth century to preserve the English Commonwealth. These failures illustrate the principle that major social and political changes must be preceded by appropriate cultural change.

But like Dante and Milton, Augustine was successful on a noetic level and contributed to the refinement and advancement of western European culture. I hope to show this in the next chapter.

Chapter Thirteen

Augustine as Prophet of the Third Pivotal Shift

St. Augustine, the man from the ancient world we know more intimately than any other, is also an enigma to us. As a young man, was he a seeker, zealously looking for the peace that comes from loving God? Or was he, as Peter Brown refers to him at one point, an ambitious "provincial professor 'on the make'"?[1] As he described himself in his mental crisis leading up to his conversion, he was an exemplar of human doubleness: in his own Ovidian words, "My inner self was a house divided against itself" (*Confessions* 8.8.1). Like other monks to this day, he knew what it was to be torn by his own need to love: to love sex (as a "seething cauldron of lust"; *Confessions* 3.1), or to love God.

What kind of lover was he? Peter Brown notes that although Augustine cherished his friendships and writes about them,

> one figure is notably absent—Augustine's concubine. . . . This woman lived with Augustine until 385, when he dismissed her on becoming betrothed to a young heiress. Concubinage of this kind was a traditional feature of Roman life. Even the Catholic church was prepared to recognize it.[2]

Concubinage with one's social equal, however, was not recognized. The Lex Julia on Adultery introduced by Augustus in 23 BCE left "only prostitutes, procuresses, slaves and peregrines [noncitizens] . . . as possible concubines."[3]

Augustine was ambitious, and he also had a powerful libido he could not control. He confessed to God that even "within the walls of your church" he would "relish the thought of lust, and gratify it too" (*Confessions* 3.3; Brown takes this to mean he would go there "to find a girl-friend"[4]). Even Augustine's saintly mother, Monica, was also ambitious for her son and did not think he should restrict his passions "to the bound of married love. This was because she was afraid the bonds of marriage [in provincial Africa] might be a hindrance to my hopes for . . . my success" (*Confessions* 2.3).

Conversion and baptism were still taken seriously in the fourth century, in the spirit of Jesus's call for a complete change of heart ("For whosoever will save his life shall lose it: and whosoever will lose his life for my sake shall find it"; Matt. 16:25). The expectation of the early church had been that baptism should be followed by a renunciation of sin; a single lapse from this commitment would be followed by eternal damnation. The second-century *Shepherd of Hermas* slightly mitigated this doom: in a vision, a man who had entertained lustful thoughts for his dead wife was told that there was a second chance to repent and receive God's grace—but only once.

Augustine was tormented because choosing God would mean renouncing lust. The agony of his conversion under a fig tree begins with a reference to the "fetters of lust" (vinculo desiderii concubitus; *Confessions* 8.6.1) holding him back. It ends when, as commanded by the voice of a child ("Take, read"; tolle, lege), he picks up the Epistles of St. Paul and reads Romans 13.13–14: "Not in reveling and drunkenness, not in lust and wantonness. . . . Rather, arm yourself with the Lord Jesus Christ; spend no more thought on nature and nature's appetites" (*Confessions* 8.12.29). He decides to follow not only Jesus but also St. Anthony: being baptized a Christian means for him that he will also become celibate, and soon a monk.

LEARNING TO THINK WITH *ALL YOUR MIND*

From now on Augustine was able to love God according to his adopted precept: that "God is to be loved, with all your heart and all your soul and all your mind."[5] The doubleness and self-division that we saw earlier in classical Latin love poetry, and in Augustine himself, was now overcome: beginning in his first postconversion book, his *Soliloquies*, he wrote love poems to God in the wholehearted devoted style of a modern love poet, not as an urbane classical one:

> At last I love Thee alone, Thee alone follow, Thee alone seek, Thee alone am I ready to serve: for Thou alone, by right, art ruler; under Thy rule do I wish to be. Command, I pray, and order what Thou wilt, but heal and open my ears that I may hear Thy commands, heal and open my eyes that I may see Thy nod; cast all unsoundness from me that I may recognize Thee! Tell me whither to direct my gaze that I may look upon Thee, and I hope that I shall do all things which Thou commandest! (*Soliloquies* 5)

A more famous example is in his *Confessions*:

I have learnt to love you late [Sero te amavi], Beauty at once so ancient and so new! I have learnt to love you late! . . . The beautiful things of this world kept me far from you and yet, if they had not been in you, they would have had no being at all. You called me; you cried aloud to me; you broke my barrier of deafness. You shone upon me; your radiance enveloped me; you put my blindness to flight. You shed your fragrance about me; I drew breath and now I gasp for your sweet odour. I tasted you, and now I hunger and thirst for you. You touched me, and I am inflamed with love of your peace. (*Confessions* 10.27)[6]

Augustine's breakthrough to a unified yin-yang mind is only the first of the ways that I consider him, like Virgil before him, to have been a pathfinder, or prophet, for the great pivotal shift that was already beginning in his lifetime.

Much more was at stake than just the future of love poetry. After his conversion, Augustine entered into a new way of yin-yang empathic thinking, with more of his entire being than just the yang intellect with which he had studied the Neoplatonists:

The books of the Platonists . . . do not contain the expression of this kind of godliness—the tears of confession, thy sacrifice, a troubled spirit, a broken and a contrite heart, the salvation of thy people, the espoused City, the earnest of the Holy Spirit, the cup of our redemption. (*Confessions* 7.21)

It was from the Apostle Paul, Augustine wrote, that

I learned to rejoice with trembling . . . and found that whatsoever truth I had read there [in the Law and the Prophets] was declared here with the recommendation of Your grace. . . . For it is one thing, from the mountain's wooded summit to see the land of peace,[7] and not to find the way there . . . and another to keep to the way that leads there. (*Confessions* 7.21)

Thus, by "Your grace only, through Jesus Christ our Lord" (*Confessions* 7.21), Augustine stepped beyond Platonic reasoning into what was for him a new path. Simple people had been tracing this path for over three centuries. But, as Augustine quotes Jesus, these things are hidden "from the wise and prudent, and . . . revealed unto babes" (Matt. 11:25; quoted in *Confessions* 7.21). What in St. Paul's time had been the refuge of the oppressed and dispossessed would now for over a millennium become the mindset of those in power.

In this way, partly by discerning the curve of the future and partly by influencing that curve, Augustine became a prophet as well as a symptom of the cultural shift beginning in his lifetime.[8] I believe this strongly, despite all I wrote in the last chapter (and will return to in this) about Augustine's futile efforts, using the power of the sword, to preserve Rome's doomed authority in his native North Africa.

More pertinently, I am quite aware that there is also a strong rhetorical streak in everything that Augustine wrote and that his tropes are not necessarily original. For example, when he declares, "Now I hunger and thirst for you," he is of course echoing the Sermon on the Mount: "Blessed are they which do hunger and thirst after righteousness: for they shall be filled" (Matt. 5:6). Pierre Courcelle has demonstrated that the description of Augustine's actual conversion contains "'*de fiction littéraire et de symbolisme.*' As for the fig tree under which Augustine cast himself in the agony of mind that immediately preceded his sudden yielding to Christ, . . . it recalled the fig tree under which, according to the Gospel of Saint John (I.48), Nathanael sat, a tree which is constantly interpreted by Augustine as symbolizing the mortal shade of sin that spreads over the human race."[9]

Despite his intention to lead a new life in Christ as a monk, Augustine still retained traces of his earlier training as a Roman citizen and a Roman rhetor. His notions of "authenticity" and "authority" were not ours: he measured the truth of a statement by how it coincided with divine revelation in scripture, not with mere factual details.

But I have no hesitation in saying that Augustine felt and wrote about love not with a traditional pagan sensibility like Ovid's but with a more unified religious sensibility in which his first and second natures reinforced each other. We see signs of this from before his conversion. Augustine tells us in his *Confessions* that he wept in his studies over the death of Dido, which came about from loving Aeneas, all the while not crying over his own death, "which happens from not loving you, God, the light of my heart and the bread of the internal mouth of my soul and the virtue marrying together my mind and the breast of my thoughts" (*Confessions* 1.13).

Augustine spontaneously responded then as readers have ever since, against the classical view voiced by his contemporary Servius (early fifth century), namely, that Virgil's treatment of the Dido story was "virtually in the comic style—no wonder, as it deals with love" (paene comicus stilus est; nec mirum, ubi de amore tractatur).[10]

AUGUSTINE AND *THE CITY OF GOD*

Augustine's sensibility and language of love is not the only way in which he prefigured the pivotal cultural shift that was beginning to emerge in his lifetime. Augustine saw his finding of peace through renunciation and turning (conversion) to God not as a personal matter but as the fulfillment of a deeper drive innate in all humans, and hence also in all societies.

This drive underlies the pattern of his two most innovative and enduring works. The first is his *Confessions* (397–400 CE), often described as the first

Western or modern autobiography.[11] As Augustine memorably writes in his opening paragraph, "You have made us for yourself, O Lord, and our heart is restless until it rests in you" (Fecisti nos ad te, Domine, et inquietum est cor nostrum donec requiescat in te; *Confessions* 1.1). (A very free translation might be, "We do not become fully ourselves until we venture into our third nature or moreness.")

That same quest underlies Augustine's vision of cultural development in human history, as described in Augustine's other great masterpiece, *The City of God* (*Civ. Dei*; 413–25 CE). This was written after the sack of Rome in 410 by Alaric the Goth; but it would be wrong to read it as just a polemical defense of Christianity against the pagan charge that Rome's conversion to Christianity was responsible for its fall.

His book, indeed, is a defense of Christianity. But his core argument can also be stated in enduring secular terms: that our true ultimate destiny is not a corrupt city united by violence and the lust to dominate from above (*libido dominandi*) but a community of those associating freely from below out of love. I see in this a lasting, innovative insight: that significant human history is not the visible chaos of endless political conflict, but on a deeper level, deeper even than the noetic level, the history of cultural evolution, or what I call ethogeny.

Czeslaw Milosz, independently, raised the same possibility of a deeper pattern in history when he asked,

> Is there any immanent force located in *le devenir*, in what is in the state of becoming, a force that pulls mankind up toward perfection? Is there any cooperation between man and a universe that is subject to constant change?[12]

This question arose out of his earlier sentiment, well justified in my opinion, that he considered his writing of poetry "a kind of higher politics, an unpolitical politics."[13] But for Milosz, who frequently spoke of a Manichean streak in himself, this immanent force is not omnipotent, and so he immediately distinguished his question about an immanent force from "the providentialist philosophy propagated by Bossuet."[14]

Peter Brown similarly distinguished between *The City of God* and the *Histories against the Pagans* (*Historiae Adversus Paganos*) of Augustine's disciple Orosius (d. ca. 418), a providentialist precursor of Bossuet. Brown pointed out that "Augustine shared neither Orosius' interest in palliating the barbarian invasions, nor his basic assumptions about the providential role of the Roman Empire."[15]

Augustine himself is usually called a providentialist by today's professional historians, rigorously trained to limit their conclusions to what can be proven from empirical data. Well over a century ago, according to Max

Nordau, "Robert Flint . . . enter[ed] a wise caution against the view of St. Augustine, Orosius, Bossuet, and their disciples, whose 'assertion of the existence, power, and wisdom of the First Providential Cause . . . is not supported by adequate proof.'"[16] But Augustine's view of history, although undeniably providential, was also dialectical and arguably tragic in a way that the Panglossian optimism of Orosius and Bossuet was not.

Augustine's account of history overall records the conflict of two different kinds of society. One, exemplified by Rome, is an "earthly city, a city which aims at domination, which holds nations in enslavement, but is itself dominated by that very lust of domination" (*Civ. Dei* 1.1). The second, "incomparably more glorious than Rome, is that heavenly city in which for victory you have truth; for dignity, holiness; for peace, felicity; for life, eternity" (*Civ. Dei* 2.29).

But Augustine, as Brown points out, hoped to persuade educated pagans, many of them now refugees from Alaric in Africa. His strategy to win them over was to rely on the authorities that had shaped them, like himself, in school. Two of these Augustine relies on in particular. One is Virgil's *Aeneid*; the other, the republican historian Sallust (d. ca. 35 BCE), who like Virgil and Augustine had been born outside Rome but who in 52 BCE had served in the declining republic as a tribune of the plebs.

Constrained by the violent and divisive politics of that era, Sallust turned for protection to Julius Caesar, just as Virgil had turned to Caesar's adopted son Octavian/Augustus. But underlying his various histories was a strong sense that many Americans will understand: that Rome, which had become a republic out of love of liberty, had lapsed into a city of repression, corrupted by wealth and power:

> But when our country had grown great through toil and the practice of justice, when great kings had been vanquished in war, savage tribes and mighty peoples subdued by force of arms . . . then Fortune began to grow cruel and to bring confusion into all our affairs. Those who had found it easy to bear hardship and dangers, anxiety and adversity, found leisure and wealth, desirable under other circumstances, a burden and a curse. Hence the lust for money first, then for power [Igitur primo pecuniae, deinde imperi cupido], grew upon them; these were, I may say, the root of all evils.[17] For avarice destroyed honour, integrity, and all other noble qualities; taught in their place insolence, cruelty, to neglect the gods, to set a price on everything. (Sallust, *Bellum Catilinae* 10.1–3)

Quoting Sallust's depictions of violent power's dialectical instability, sinking from freedom into oppression, St. Augustine too speaks of Rome's "moral deterioration" (*Civ. Dei*, 2.18):

After this, when [Roman] fears were gradually diminished—not because the wars ceased, but because they were not so furious—that period in which things were ordered with justice and moderation drew to an end, and there followed that state of matters which Sallust thus briefly sketches: "Then began the patricians to oppress the people as slaves, to condemn them to death or scourging, as the kings had done, to drive them from their holdings, and to tyrannize over those who had no property to lose."[18]

"In early times it was the love of liberty that led to great achievements," Augustine repeated; "later it was the love of domination" (*Civ. Dei* 5.12). This picture of a Rome lapsing into a "libido dominandi," a term Augustine acknowledged taking from Sallust,[19] was reinforced by a number of telling quotations from the *Aeneid*. One of these was the ambiguous prophecy in *Aeneid* 6 that we have already discussed:

> Remember, Roman: your empire will rule nations
> And these will be your arts:—to impose the custom of peace,
> To spare the downfallen and bring down the proud.

> > (*Aeneid* 6:851–53, quoted in *Civ. Dei* 5.12)

Ignoring any possible echo of Isaiah in this passage, Augustine commented, justifiably:

The Romans practiced these "arts" with the more skill when they were less given to . . . the lust to accumulate wealth—that corrupter of morality—by robbing their less fortunate fellows." (*Civ. Dei* 5.12)

The effects of this disastrous decline were reversed, according to Augustine, by the coming of Jesus. And the evidence he uses to persuade educated pagans of this is nothing other than Virgil's fourth eclogue:

The most renowned of poets also spoke of him, in a poetical manner certainly, for Christ is represented by an imaginary portrait of another person, but with complete truth, if the person is referred to as Christ. This is what Virgil says:

> With you for guide, whatever trace remains
> Of our past crimes, shall all be done away;
> The world shall then be freed from endless fear.[20]

Thus Augustine saw in history an alternate peaceful city, building in nonviolent antithesis to the violent earthly one:

In one city love for God rules, in the other city love for the self. But God's city cannot be identified with the Christian church that exists here and now, according to Augustine; rather, this concrete church is instead a mixed body (*corpus permixtum*)[21] that consists of both the city of God and the earthly city. It is only possible to distinguish between the cities eschatologically, and the church's journey through history is therefore a pilgrimage until it reaches the peace of the heavenly city at the end of the ages.[22]

In other words, there is an analogy between the pilgrimage of the individual in time and the pilgrimage of the church. Just as Augustine was able, through his conversion, to order his own spirit in a *caritas ordinata*, so the church is tending toward a condition of "ordered consensus" (ordinata . . . consensio), "ordered obedience" (ordinata oboedientia), and "ordered harmony" (ordinata concordia; literally, "hearts all in accord").[23] In like manner, just as Augustine's own "mind is largely fixed on the heavenly city" (Augustine, *Epistles* 155.17), so "the eternal City of God . . . has its chief regard fixed on that which is Eternal."[24]

In the book's last chapter, Augustine viewed history as a process in which, with the passage of time, the human will is evolving toward a greater ability to acknowledge and find rest in God. He summarized this process with the hexameric doctrine (central to Jewish Kabbalism) that the history of mankind can be seen consisting of six millennial ages, corresponding to the six days of creation. This will be followed by the seventh millennium, when God's intention is fulfilled at last,

> that man should first receive a free will by which he was able not to sin [posse non peccare], and at last a free will by which he was not able to sin [non posse peccare]—the former being adapted to the acquiring of merit, the latter to the enjoying of the reward. . . . There shall be accomplished the words of the psalm, Be still, and know that I am God (Psalm 46:11). . . . For we shall ourselves be the seventh day, when we shall be filled and replenished with God's blessing and sanctification. There shall we be still, and know that He is God. (*Civ. Dei* 22.30)

Knowing that I risk the disapproval of some theologians, I shall dare to say that Augustine has preserved and transmitted the magnanimous vision of early Christianity, that through history there not only can be but will be a great change, indeed redemption.[25]

That is my vision of ethogeny: as a cultural evolution toward a nonviolent global community living peacefully in nonselfish moreness as a process.

AUGUSTINE, WOMEN, AND NEOPLATONISM

It is no accident that when Augustine, following the example of his mentor Ambrose, speaks of "ordered consensus" (ordinata . . . consensio) and "ordered harmony" (ordinata concordia), he is echoing the "caritas ordinata" of the Vulgate Song of Songs:

> Ambrose often adapts the erotic imagery of the Song to describe the individual's ascent to God. His use of eros symbolism in speaking about the ascent of the soul to the divine and the union of the soul with God borrows also from certain Platonic and Neoplatonic themes with which Augustine was also conversant. Augustine, after all, received his Neoplatonic apprenticeship in philosophy in Milan some time after learning from Ambrose how biblical texts could be interpreted allegorically (*Confessions* 6.4.5–6).[26]

The idea that intellectual love leads to a vision of God was one shared with the Neoplatonist pagans that Augustine was hoping to convert, just as it had been a feature of Augustine's own Neoplatonism in the period just before and after his own conversion. It can be traced back to Diotima's account of the ascent to heavenly beauty in the *Symposium*; and like Plato he tends to treat this intellectual love as if it were preeminently male. Quoting St. Paul, "It was not Adam, but Eve, who was seduced" (1 Tim. 2:14), Augustine commented that Eve was "the inferior of the human pair" (*Civ. Dei* 14.12). This reflected his "thesis (deriving from [the Jewish Platonist] Philo) that Eve somehow lacked intellectual vision or 'represented' the senses."[27]

We see here, as we saw earlier with Plato as well, how powerful shapers of culture worked from within tradition in order to advance it. The idea that women could represent a higher form of yin mind, not a lower one, would have to wait for the Fourth Pivotal Shift and Dante's privileging of Beatrice's understanding above that of Virgil.

I wrote in *Poetry and Terror* that "our cultural ontogeny recapitulates our cultural ethogeny."[28] I ventured this thought intuitively, having no specific example in mind. But it now seems to me that Augustine brilliantly illustrates this principle. Having assimilated Platonism, Roman history, the Bible, biblical exegesis, and Plotinus (d. 270 CE), Augustine, with his conversion, carried "the best that has been thought and said" into a successful new phase of cultural history.

That cultural "best" still included an unsophisticated stereotyping of genders, even though Plotinus had already included a number of women among his philosophy students. In the background of Augustine's stereotyping, consider what he has to tell us about his own parents. According to the account in his *Confessions*, Augustine's father, Patricius, was a lower-level administrator with a violent temper, irreverent and unfaithful, but willing to sacrifice for the sake of his son's good education. His African mother, St. Monica (whose name suggests that she may have been a Berber), identified herself as a Catholic but was relatively uneducated, with a naive piety that led her (until corrected by Ambrose) to leave offerings of food and wine at the oratories of local saints (*Confessions* 6.2).[29]

The most exalted moment in the *Confessions* occurs when Augustine is in Ostia with his mother, who was already close to death:

> My mother and I were alone, leaning from a window which overlooked the garden in the courtyard of the house where we were staying. . . . Our conversation led us to the conclusion that no bodily pleasure, however great it might be and whatever earthly light might shed lustre upon it, was worthy of comparison, or even of mention, beside the happiness of the life of the saints. As the flame of love burned stronger in us and raised us higher towards the eternal God, our thoughts ranged over the whole compass of material things in their various degrees, up to the heavens themselves, from which the sun and the moon and the stars shine down upon the earth. Higher still we climbed, thinking and speaking all the while in wonder at all that you have made. At length we came to our own souls and passed beyond them to that place of everlasting plenty, where you feed Israel for ever with the food of truth. (*Confessions* 9.10)

Patricius might seem to typify the violent earthly state, Monica the heavenly one. But the intellectual edifice of Augustine's magnum opus was designed for an educated audience of men like Patricius, not naive women like Monica. The African church Monica had wished to baptize Augustine into was "exceptionally narrow and conservative," and the African Manichees to whom Augustine first turned presented themselves as radical reformers with a clearer vision of Christ's wisdom and the divinity of the soul.[30]

Then in Milan Augustine was exposed to the Neoplatonic ideas of Plotinus. In contrast to rigorous Manichean dualism, Plotinus taught that "the One, the highest level of being," was a source "from which emanates (literally, flows out), or radiates, all else that there is."[31]

By this path Augustine was readied for conversion, and by this path Augustine reached out to fellow intellectuals who were still pagan.

AUGUSTINE, JEWS, AND THE END OF THE WORLD

The interaction between Neoplatonic and Jewish thought (a continuous tradition from Philo to Kabbalists like Isaac the Blind [d. ca. 1235]) opened Augustine's mind in *The City of God* to including Jews in God's capacious design for history. According to its rubric, book 18 of *The City of God* expounded Augustine's "Doctrine of Witness, that Jews received prophecy predicting Jesus, and that Jews are dispersed among the nations to provide independent testimony of the Hebrew Scriptures."

In his stinging indictment of Christian anti-Semitism, James Carroll treats Augustine more favorably than he does some contemporaries—notably St. John Chrysostom (d. 407), whose attacks on the Jews were followed by a mob's destruction of the main synagogue in Antioch. Carroll contrasts Augustine's counsel from scripture, "Do not slay them" (Psalm 59:11; quoted in *Civ. Dei* 18.46), with John Chrysostom's, "Slay them before me" (Luke 19:27). And he also quotes the grateful acknowledgment from Moses Mendelssohn (d. 1786) that but for Augustine's "lovely brainwave, we would have been exterminated long ago."[32]

This represents only one side of Augustine's position on the Jews. In his polemical writings against the Manichees and Donatists, Augustine often repeated Christian slurs *contra Iudaeos*. Even though he was not directly targeting Jews themselves, some of this rhetoric was later converted into law, particularly in Visigothic Spain. "In the two centuries that stand between Augustine (d. 430) and Sisebut (d. 621), the Jews' legal status had altered more drastically than it had in the full sweep of the seven centuries that stand between Alexander the Great and Augustine. In this sense, Christian rhetoric *contra Iudaeos* [including Augustine's] had real effects."[33]

This legal consequence was never intended by Augustine. "As we now know from his recently discovered letters, in radical contradistinction to his former spiritual guide Ambrose, Augustine insisted that the law should protect Jews as well as Christians."[34]

AUGUSTINE AND THE MONK-BISHOP EXPERIMENT

Reflecting a Jewish notion in the Talmud, Augustine converted the millenarianism of early Christianity into the hexameral doctrine that the world was now in its sixth and final age, with the seventh being eternal rest (the sabbatical millennium) after the Final Judgment.[35]

For such a purified church in its final stages, it seemed clear to Augustine and his contemporaries that a monastery—where "all goods are common to all [sunt illis omnia communia] and there is among them but one mind, one heart directed to God [est illis anima una et cor unum in Deum]" (Augustine, *Enarratio in Psalmum* 83.4)—should provide leadership. The monastery, in other words, represented a return to the ideal recorded in Acts of the primitive church.[36]

Augustine, following St. Martin, was a leader in developing a brief but generative Western tradition of monk-bishops.[37] He had come in 391 to the African port city of Hippo, where he established a monastery in the garden enclosure of the main church. A year later, Augustine, still a monk, was ordained a presbyter. In 396, on becoming bishop, he drew on members of the monastery to join him in the administrative duties. Eventually ten members of the monastery left to become bishops of African dioceses.

In creating the novelty of a monastery at an urban focus of power, rather than at a remote distance from it, Augustine had a precedent in St. Martin. In 371, on becoming bishop of Tours, Martin had established a monastery across the Loire River at Marmoutier. According to Sulpicius Severus, "Martin and some of the monks who followed him built cells of wood" and lived together. After the loss of a child, Paulinus of Nola followed a track similar to Martin's and Augustine's. He and his wife disposed of their great wealth and withdrew from the world, but not from their home in Nola. Then in 383 Paulinus became a priest, and in 410 bishop of Nola.

The island monastery of Lérins in Provence became a virtual seedbed for a generation of Gallic monk-bishops. One was Hilary of Arles (d. 449), who left Lérins to become bishop of Arles in 429. "Following the example of Augustine . . . he is said to have organized his cathedral clergy into a 'congregation,' devoting a great part of their time to social exercises of asceticism."[38]

In the short run, it appeared that the practice of appointing monk-bishops was short-lived. The Augustinian goal of preparing the church for the Seventh Age proved at odds in Gaul with the task of maintaining church harmony in the Sixth. Responding to complaints from lesser clergy that they were being passed over for promotion, Pope Celestine I in Rome wrote a long letter to the bishops of Provence condemning this "new brotherhood of wanderers and outsiders . . . who did not grow up in the [local] church, but came from another religious setting."[39]

The last Gallo-Roman monk-bishop I know of was Caesarius of Arles (d. 542), who after some years at Lérins was consecrated bishop in 502. Less than a century later, the Rule of St. Benedict, endorsed by Pope Gregory I (a former monk, d. 604), standardized the rules in Mediterranean regions for an ongoing monastic practice that was distanced from the ongoing secular world.[40] But soon after the monk-bishop tradition started dying in Gaul it began to flourish with great vigor in the northern areas of Celtic proselytism, where priests were few, abbots served also as bishops, and cities were almost nonexistent (see chapter 14).

The waning away in Gallo-Roman regions of the monk-bishop tradition in the fifth and sixth centuries paralleled the radical decline of the size and cultural importance of cities. But the underlying idea of *The City of God*, that the highest culture was far more important than the fate of any earthly city, found its embodiment in the key feature of the Third Pivotal Shift, namely that, for almost half a millennium, high culture was preserved, refined, and augmented in rural monasteries, not in cities.

For a millennium, the Augustinian philosophy of history shaped views of culture the way that the heliocentric model of the universe shaped views of nature. In a sense it is still with us. I know of no subsequent historiosopher whose views, like those of Vico, Marx, or Toynbee, cannot be traced in part to *The City of God*.[41]

POSTSCRIPT: AUGUSTINE, THE ROMAN
DEEP STATE,[42] AND ETHOGENY

Was Augustine's decision to convert the result of completely spiritual motivations? Or was it also driven by a provincial ambition to join the surviving elements of the ruling class, both Catholic and secular, in a deep strategy for the preservation of elite Roman social culture?

It was thanks to a series of wealthy patrons that Augustine had advanced from his home town of Thagaste to school at Madaura, then Carthage, Rome, and finally the imperial capital, Milan. For this last appointment, as professor of rhetoric, he was selected by the urban prefect, Q. Aurelius Symmachus, a wealthy pagan.

Jennifer Ebbeler gives an oversimplified account of how the Manichee Augustine could be of use to the pagan Symmachus in the latter's contest with his Catholic relative Bishop Ambrose. She writes that Peter Brown

> infers that "in the summer of 384, Symmachus had every reason to welcome a non-Catholic in so important a post."[43] Brown is here alluding to the infamous "Battle of the Altar" waged between Symmachus and Ambrose over the restoration of the Altar of Victory to the Roman curia. He and others conclude that Symmachus's appointment of Augustine was a form of revenge for the emperor Valentinian's support of Ambrose's strident polemic against the Altar of Victory as a symbol of traditional Roman religion.[44]

But if indeed Symmachus recruited Augustine as an ally against Ambrose (Brown's account is less clear-cut), his decision was a major mistake. For it was by coming to Milan that Augustine met Ambrose, who, following Augustine's conversion, would guide him in the next phase of his new life as a Christian.

In the summer of 386, retiring from his teaching post, Augustine joined his friend Alypius in the circle of another senior Milan professor, Verecundus. There the two were visited by Ponticianus, who Brown notes was "yet another successful protégé of Symmachus."[45] Ponticianus, an African Christian "who held a high position in the Emperor's household" (praeclare in palatio militans)[46] and who earlier had probably been an *agens in rebus* (secret agent),[47] told Augustine how two other *agentes in rebus* had discovered a *Life of Anthony* and had been instantly converted.[48] Augustine records how "all the time Ponticianus was speaking, my conscience gnawed away at me" (*Confessions* 8.7). The next event recorded is his own conversion.

Ponticianus was not the only *agens in rebus* to affect Augustine's career. Another *agens*, possibly Augustine's future biographer Possidius, "prompted Augustine [after his return as a Catholic to Africa] to leave Thagaste for Hippo."[49] Yet another *agens*, Evodius, was baptized and then with Possidius joined Augustine at his newly founded monastery in Hippo.[50]

The *agentes in rebus*, translated by Brown as "secret police" or "special agents," were a late and "equally sinister" reorganization of the detested *frumentarii* who had served as spies for the imperial court:

> The *frumentarii* quickly earned the hatred of society. In the 3rd century, association with the heads of the service could produce severe repercussions. In 217, Macrinus appointed Marcus Oclatinus Adventus, the former head of the *frumentarii* and the prefect of the Praetorian Guard to the Senate. With one decision, Macrinus alienated most of the Roman establishment and made his own political destruction inevitable—so much were the *frumentarii* resented. Diocletian [d. 316] terminated the *frumentarii* because of their abuses and loathsome reputation. The emperor's decision netted him great popularity, but a short time later the equally sinister and far better organized *agentes in rebus* were created as a replacement.[51]

Why would agents with this reputation convert to Christianity and then play a repeated role in Augustine's own career? Without evidence, I will speculate that what motivated them may have been their service for the imperial bureaucracy.[52]

For in 380, just six years before Augustine's conversion, the emperor Theodosius, together with his co-emperors Gratian and Valentinian II, had issued the so-called Edict of Thessalonica. This declared Trinitarian Christianity, pronounced by the Nicene Council of 325 CE, to be the only legitimate imperial religion and the only one entitled to call itself Catholic. And in 382 the emperor Gratian (d. 383), who since 379 had been seeking his spiritual guidance from Ambrose, removed the pagan Altar of Victory from the Roman Senate House.

Underlying these decisions was the emerging consensus, vigorously promoted by Ambrose, that the Catholic Church, rather than the state or its old religion, was the best way to preserve and rejuvenate the decaying Roman *res publica*. Such concerns had underlain Constantine's decisions to first tolerate Christianity and then enforce Catholic conformity on it by the Council of Nicaea (which was convened in 324 by the messengers of the *agentes in rebus*).[53]

Since that time, the imperial power itself had fragmented. Competing emperors of different faiths (Catholic, Arian, and pagan) fought among themselves and sometimes brought in barbarians as their allies. (For example, Alaric the Arian Visigoth had served as a Roman general under Theodosius, before resigning when he was refused the reward he expected.)

But the Roman establishment also had a practical interest in Africa, where many fourth-century Roman noble families had originated,[54] and where most of their wealthiest estates were located. (Both Paulinus of Nola and Symmachus had estates in Africa, where Symmachus served briefly as proconsul.) These families could not help but feel threatened by the Donatists, a quintessentially anti-Roman sect (cf. Donatus Magnus's remark, "What has the emperor to do with the church?" which had helped inspire a major revolt against Rome in 372 CE.) "Donatus wished to gain all Africa, wrote Augustine . . . and it seems that he very nearly succeeded."[55]

After as well as before his conversion, Augustine's life shows signs of being guided by outside forces. This is particularly true of the odd way in which Augustine, on his return to Africa, was guided from his small native town of Thagaste, his first choice of domicile, to Hippo Regius, where he would eventually become bishop:

> Consider the *agens in rebus* episode in the *Vita* [*Augustini* by Possidius]. When Augustine returned to Africa from Italy, he lived in his hometown of Thagaste, but soon felt compelled to go to Hippo Regius because he had received report of an *agens in rebus* [possibly, Hermanowicz argues, Augustine's future fellow monk Possidius] who, on the verge of adopting an ascetic life, sought Augustine's company and reassured him that he would give up the world gladly if only he could hear salutary words from Augustine's lips. Augustine arrived at Hippo and spent his time with the officer; every day Augustine was told a decision was imminent, but it never came.[56]

Hippo was an ancient port town, important enough to be chosen by the Vandals as their first capital after their invasion of Numidia. Donatists were the dominant faction in Hippo, with their own bishop. When in 396 Augustine became the Catholic bishop there, "he found that his own party was in a minority."[57]

Augustine's path to the bishopric had been accelerated by the unusual high-level decision to have him preach, when he was still a presbyter and not yet even a priest, at the important Synod of Hippo in 393.[58] Augustine's polemics helped lead to the outlawing of Donatism at the Council of Carthage in 411.

AUGUSTINE AND PELAGIUS

Augustine then turned to a new target: the teachings of the British monk Pelagius (d. ca. 420) and his disciples. Once again, he did not do so on his own initiative:

> Augustine was drawn into a direct criticism of Pelagius when he was asked to reply to the latter's *De Natura*, in which Pelagius had written that it was possible for a man to be sinless. Augustine responded that "the logical conclusion of his arguments is to put righteousness and salvation outside Christ and His Church . . . if human nature can assure itself of eternal life unaided, then faith in Christ is needless." This critique of *De Natura* was later included with the evidence against Pelagius sent from Africa to Pope Innocent in Rome.[59]

One of the Pelagian disciples' tracts, "On Riches" (De Divitiis), was perhaps the most radical political attack on wealth we find in late antiquity. Its slogan, "Tolle divitem et pauperem non invenies" (Get rid of the rich and you will find no poor), would be at home in a Facebook post about wealth disparity today.[60] The tract's contents were reported to Augustine as saying,

> A rich man who remains in his riches will not enter the Kingdom of God unless he sells all that he has; nor will those be of any use to him [in securing salvation] even if he uses them to fulfill the commandments [that is, by giving alms].[61]

In the words of Peter Brown, "because of their radical nature, Augustine was determined to take a stand against Pelagian ideas on wealth."[62]

It is easy to envision earthly reasons for Augustine's and the African Catholic bishops' denunciation of Pelagius. Without support from almsgiving, the Catholic Church in Africa would be severely weakened in what Brown calls its "determined war of wealth" against Donatists and other rival Christian sects.[63]

> They . . . would have favored growth in Church membership among the upper class and therefore would want to avoid making severe demands on conduct that might have deterred that growth. Augustine specifically opposed Pelagian demands for rich Christians to give up their wealth in a letter to Hilarius.[64]

Thanks to Augustine, a second Council of Carthage in 418 denounced eight specific Pelagian doctrines (without specifically addressing the sensitive issue of wealth).[65] But at first it appeared that this attack on Pelagius, which Brown characterizes as a "witch-hunt,"[66] might be overruled in Rome. Following an initial failure to condemn him by Pope Innocent I (d. 417), Pelagius was specifically acquitted by a synod of Italian bishops under

Pope Zosimus (d. 418).[67] Zosimus then wrote a letter to the African bishops, reproving Pelagius's accusers.

Undeterred, Augustine and his allies appealed successfully to the secular authority of the imperial court: a general, Valerius, who was a trusted servant of the Emperor Honorius. (Augustine wrote directly to Valerius, while Alypius promised the latter's cavalry "eighty Numidian stallions, fattened on the estates of the church."[68]) With "a second and harsher rescript, issued by the emperor on 9 June, 419 . . . Augustine's triumph was complete."[69]

However, Augustine's attacks on Pelagius, even if some can be dismissed as polemical, were not merely self-serving; they were deeply rooted in his views on humanity's frailty and need for salvation through the church. Paul Tillich describes the controversy between the two men as a debate that has been repeated several times in the history of the church: "The question is whether the moral imperative is dependent on the divine grace for its actualization, or whether divine grace is dependent on the fulfilment of the moral imperative."[70]

I once used to call myself a semi-Pelagian because of my ongoing dislike of the theological doctrine of original sin (a doctrine dating back to Tertullian, d. ca. 220 CE, and consolidated in Roman theology by St. Augustine). But writing this book has opened my eyes to the importance of grace as understood by Augustine. The Pelagian view, that grace is "helpful but not necessary,"[71] that one can earn salvation by moral uprightness, now strikes me as inadequate. In secular terms, it fails to appreciate adequately our need for moreness, supported by a circumambient outside environment, to do more than just act in accordance with our existing ethos. We all have the capacity to be impelled beyond this, to question the alleged self-sufficiency of present humanity and instead respond to an inchoate something by which we are, so to speak, hoisted up from above or within.

I do not mean at all by this that one must be a Christian to be saved, but that, from a post-secular perspective, devotion to moreness (our yin-inspired third nature, grace) should be distinguished from mere moral uprightness (our yang-motivated second nature, works). Even a committed atheist who feels impelled to take dangerous risks for the sake of human betterment is, as I see it, the recipient of this kind of grace.

This said, I still conclude from all this that Augustine, like Virgil before him, became influential in part from his usefulness to elites at a higher level. I make this point to establish a distinction between his services as a man to the status quo, and the scope and influence of his writings. The latter cannot be reduced to the status of propaganda for a ruling class. Just as Virgil's epic of empire contained within it an anti-violent sentiment that Augustine used *against* empire, so Augustine's *City of God* indicted domination and oppression in a way that made his book prophetic of still further changes to come.

This difference illustrates the dialectical interplay I referred to earlier between social (cultural) and mental (noetic) development. The latter is not socially determined but contains an element of freedom. This is what distinguishes the dialectic of Darwinian nature (the survival of the fittest) from ethogeny, the evolution of our cultural world. In words that Czeslaw Milosz quoted from the Viconian historiosopher Tadeusz Brzozowski, "Whoever is a creator and inventor of value, whoever conceives of the future not as a stream carrying strengthless human puppets but as a task, connects everything with value."[72]

I have tried to show that noetic pathfinders like Augustine, along with Plato and the others I have discussed, both gathered value from their heritage and projected the result into a new future—a future that was partly due to the failings of the status quo and partly due to the vision of the pathfinders themselves.

I believe that our own age, after the development and decay of the Enlightenment values of the eighteenth century, is now, like Augustine's Rome, in need of such a pathfinder. Augustine is still relevant for that task; his judgment of a corrupt society—"Justice being taken away, what are kingdoms but great robberies?" (Remota itaque iustitia quid sunt regna nisi magna latrocinia?)—should be inscribed on the lintels of our courthouses today.[73]

As Czeslaw Milosz told a Harvard audience four decades ago, "some basic confidence is needed, a sense of open space ahead of the individual and the human species." And as he said a little later, in the quote from Simone Weil that I never understood until writing this book, "from where will a renewal come to us, to us who have spoiled and devastated the whole earthly globe? Only from the past, if we love it."[74]

Chapter Fourteen

Bede, Alcuin, and the
Waning of the Dark Age

AN AGE OF MARKED CLOSURES AND BEGINNINGS

If I were to write a second volume, it would open the Fourth Pivotal Shift with the cusp era of Charlemagne (d. 814 CE), the restorer of the first tentative central authority in western Europe, and Alcuin (d. 804), the master of his Palace School, whom I view as one of the major progenitors of the reurbanized educational culture that still shapes us (as well as an innovator of our current tradition of poetry, clearly different in intention and achievement from the classical poetry of antiquity).[1]

If written, my second volume would discuss the Carolingian era as an age of *beginnings*, or more accurately recommencements: of central power, of international trade,[2] of universities, and of urban culture—and also of a new tradition of yang scholastic philosophy, and of a yin poetry that, like the Song of Songs and Virgil at his best, reaches, like modern poets in various degrees, through affective metaphors and associations, toward the realm of the unsayable.

As a transition from this volume, the present chapter will consider the same material more from the perspective of *closures*: above all the shift from a domestic rural economy based largely on production from chattel slavery and serfdom, toward an urban economy relying instead on capital from trafficking in foreign slaves from abroad. Among the subtle disruptions of this period, we shall look at the secularization of the papacy and monasteries in the steely embrace of the Carolingians, as a result of which the Augustinian distinction between the earthly and the heavenly city became still more eroded if not erased.

But first we shall consider the writings of three major chroniclers of the Third Pivotal Moment—Gregory of Tours (d. 594), Pope Gregory (d. 604), and Bede (d. 734)—to show that in all three minders, their concern in history was less justice and the yang political state than the yin *virtutes* or miraculous powers of saints.

GREGORY OF TOURS' FAITH IN THE EFFICACY OF SAINTLY *VIRTUTES* (POWERS)

The Dark Age can be defined as an era when the yin of myth dominated human behavior more than the yang of positive fact. The internecine feuds between venal Merovingian rulers are of less relevance to what endures of importance from that era of French history than the growing importance of St. Martin's tomb in the sixth century as a pilgrimage center. This was responsible for the increasing importance of Tours as an economic and cultural center of Merovingian France.

This shift of emphasis can be seen in the writings of the late Gallo-Roman minder St. Gregory of Tours (d. 594). All of his works, including his four books on the miracles of St. Martin, his other hagiographies, and above all his *Ten Books of Histories* (really, "Stories"; *Decem Libri Historiarum*; misleadingly remembered today as *The History of the Franks*), were written to demonstrate the *virtute*s ("powers"; i.e., miracles) of sanctity and their victories over sinners—in St. Gregory's own words, to "fire others with that enthusiasm by which the saints deservedly climbed to heaven."[3]

Gregory's moralistic purpose in his so-called *History* is made clear in his preface to book 2:

> I do not think that we shall be condemned thoughtlessly if we tell of the happy lives of the blessed [virtutes sanctorum] together with the deaths of the wretched [excidia miserorum], since it is not the skill of the writer but the succession of times that has furnished the arrangement.[4]

Commenting on this passage, the contemporary historian Walter Goffart observes that "a history that proceeds by juxtaposing the *virtutes sanctorum* to the *excidia miserorum* has no place for heroism in any but a religious setting."[5] If Gregory chooses to record the defeat of Attila the Hun by the Roman general Flavius Aetius (d. 454), it is in order to observe, "Theodore, king of the Goths, was slain in the battle. Now let no one doubt that the army of Huns was put to flight by the intercession [by prayer] of the bishop mentioned above [Anianus of Orleans]" (*History*, 2.7). Goffart comments,

Gregory's closest approximation of a Roman hero is Theodosius I: his weapons were vigils and prayers rather than the sword. Aëtius, whose name surely retained luster in Gregory's Gaul, is neatly disposed of: Bishop Anianus of Orléans calls him out of Arles to deal with the Huns; the bishop's prayers win the battle.[6]

In the era of modernity and postmodernity, Gregory's *Histories* have frequently been misunderstood. According to Goffart, this is true even of the seminal book *Mimesis* by the great Erich Auerbach, who "believed that what 'Gregory relates is his own and his only world.' This seems not to be the case. An ordinary, normal world, which the author and his audience inhabit, is sketchily evoked, as we shall see. But the animation of the *Histories*, monopolizing Gregory's attention and narrative skill, belongs to a realm of extremes and excesses."[7]

To highlight how far Auerbach's reading of the *Histories* is from Gregory's intention, let me quote further from *Mimesis*:

> What he [Gregory] relates is his own and his only world. He has no other, and he lives in it. [Reading the *History*] we can almost smell the atmosphere of the first century of Frankish rule in Gaul. There is a progressive and terrible brutalization. The point is not simply that unqualified force comes to the fire in every local district . . . but also that intrigue and policy have . . . become wholly primitive and coarse. . . . This brutal life becomes a sensible object; to [Gregory], it presents itself as devoid of order and difficult to order, but tangible, earthy, alive.[8]

Auerbach's claim that Gregory depicts a brutalized, anarchic Gaul is of course not baseless. But neither does it describe the Gaul as portrayed by Gregory, a Gaul securely under God where saints are rewarded and villains punished. For example, Gregory's point in writing about Sicharius and Chramnesindus (Auerbach's topic) was in order to show that the former ("a fickle, drunken, murderous person") deserved his wretched fate of murder, and that the latter merited the subsequent protection he received from the royal household.[9]

This providential close to the story was omitted by Auerbach as of no interest; he was instead intent on tracing (in his words) "basic motifs in the history of the representation of reality."[10] Other authors today are similarly uninterested in the miracles and other *virtutes sanctorum*, which Gregory considered to be the point of his narrative, and the saving grace of brutal history.

This is true of even Peter Brown's superb *Through the Eye of a Needle*, cited so many times by me in this prose poem. To illustrate the decline of the Gallo-Roman aristocracy, Brown wrote of the poet-bishop Sidonius Apollinaris (d. 488; the son-in-law of emperor Avitus) that Gregory "remembered him as a pathetic figure. Two priests 'took away from him all power over the estates of the church and reduced him to a pittance, with great ignominy.'"[11]

But Gregory categorically did not remember Sidonius as a "pathetic figure." He remembered him as a powerful and inspiring saint:

> The holy Sidonius was so eloquent that he generally improvised what he wished to say without any hesitation and in the clearest manner. And it happened one day that he went by invitation to a fête at the church of the monastery which we have mentioned before, and when his book, by which he had been wont to celebrate the holy services, was maliciously taken away, he went through the whole service of the fête improvising with such readiness that he was admired by all, and it was believed by the bystanders that it was not a man who had spoken there but an angel. . . . Being a man of wonderful holiness and, as we have said, one of the first of the senators, he often carried silver dishes away from home, unknown to his wife, and gave them to poor people.[12]

Gregory narrated the crime of the two priests in a separate story in order to stress how it resulted in their suffering terrible punishments after someone in a dream had seen the holy Sidonius in a place of judgment.[13]

That both Auerbach and Brown, two of our greatest recent scholars, distorted Gregory's narration in this way is symptomatic of a widespread problem today in remembering the Dark Age. In general, the dark side of Gregory's world is fastened upon as "real," while the compensating miracles are ignored. The explicit belief that sanctity can have miraculous impact in a fallen world survives, as I have noted in chapter 12, but in oral rather than in literate environments.

Less overtly, however, the Dark Age faith in the temporal efficacy of goodness is also now encoded in everyone's cultural DNA. At least until the First World War, the idea that ours is a providential world in which virtue rewards and vice punishes was a notion far more deeply accepted at every level of our culture than it was in the days of the elite audiences of Plato, the Hellenistic philosophers, and Marcus Aurelius, or for that matter in the days of the first Christian communities, whose hope of reward lay principally in an anticipated afterlife.

Walter Goffart is able to see that something positive, even if difficult to define, gathered and asserted itself in the sleep of the European Dark Age. He concludes that Gregory (like Bede after him) did not, as Christopher Dawson once wrote,

> conceive of himself as the spokesman of a "Church [that] remained as the representative of the old tradition of culture." On the contrary, he spoke for something new, different, and assertive. He forces us to confront the possibility that

[what Gibbon called] the "triumph of superstition" has a positive face, whose existence and worth in the history of thought deserves acknowledgment even, perhaps especially, outside a confessional context. For the future of European intellectual development did not hinge only on successive "renaissances" of the classical tradition. Something other than a profitless detour in the history of thought was involved in such non-Hellenic improbabilities as an omnipotent and incarnate God, creation out of nothing, and daily miracles.[14]

POPE GREGORY'S PESSIMISM AS TO THE QUESTION OF HISTORIC PROGRESS

Gregory of Tours' confidence in the secular efficacy of saintly miracles reflected the steady Christian conversion of Gaul around him, irrespective of the recurring feuds and betrayals of the decadent ruling Merovingian families. One symptom of this confidence is his diminished interest in the question of a Second Coming, once considered (even by Augustine) to be imminent. Goffart notes that Gregory's "consistent tendency was to deprecate apocalyptic thinking by vulgarizing it and, in this way, to raise a barrier between human fears and God's well-guarded secret."[15]

This disinterest in the Apocalypse distinguishes him from his contemporary Pope Gregory I (d. 604), the first monk to become pope. Pope Gregory wrote his *Dialogues* (a compendium of miracles by Italian saints, above all St. Benedict) when his native Italy, once largely Christianized, was being ravaged after 568 by the Lombards, a newly arrived and largely pagan Germanic tribe who had not, like their Gothic predecessors, been partially Romanized.

In a memorable passage at the end of book 3 of his *Dialogues* (ca. 592), Gregory considered that the Lombard devastation was proof that the world's end was "present and already come":

Straight after likewise the barbarous and cruel nation of the Lombards, drawn as a sword out of a sheath, left their own country, and invaded ours: by reason whereof the people, which before for the huge multitude were like to thick corn-fields, remain now withered and overthrown: for cities be wasted, towns and villages spoiled, churches burnt, monasteries of men and women destroyed, farms left desolate, and the country remaineth solitary and void of men to till the ground, and destitute of all inhabitants: beasts possessing those places, where before great plenty of men did dwell. And how it goeth in other parts of the world I know not, but here in this place where we live, the world doth not foretell any end, but rather sheweth that which is present and already come. Wherefore so much the more zealously ought we to seek after eternal things, by how much we find all temporal so quickly to be fled and gone. Surely this world were to be contemned, although it did flatter us, and with pleasant

prosperity contented our mind: but now, seeing it is fraught with so many mis-
eries and divers afflictions, and that our sorrows and crosses do daily increase
and be doubled, what doth it else but cry unto us that we should not love it?[16]

Gregory, in short, had lost the Augustinian vision of a world as a
still-developing process of spiritual evolution. With diminished hope for gen-
eral improvement, Gregory focused on rectifying the practices of the church.

But like both Augustine and Gregory of Tours, Pope Gregory was confi-
dent that the fate of the world was not in the hands of the broken states of
their time. It was in the hands of the saints, a view shared a century later by
the historian Bede.

BEDE'S IDYLL OF AN ENGLAND SCHOOLED
IN CHRISTIAN HUMILITY

How different from Pope Gregory's pessimism was the mood in the Celtic and
English north! There Christianity was spread quickly and relatively easily by
missionary monks in the Martinian tradition, bringing with them literacy and
other cultural advantages. The excitement of participating in this rapid and
successful cultural change was transmitted in Bede's *Ecclesiastical History*.

Though Bede's story is dotted with plagues, eclipses, ominous comets, and
unnecessary wars, it is overall an account of a significant and rapid cultural
development over less than two centuries: the conversion and progressive
unification of the formerly pagan Anglo-Saxon peoples in Britain.

Critical comparison of Bede's *History* with its sources reveals it to be
highly idealized, almost indeed a poem in prose.

> A large part of the modern appeal of Bede's work comes from its perceptible
> and unusual dramatic unity. What palliates its episodicity is . . . a compact,
> unfolding, and unusual story: . . . First the emissaries of Gregory the Great, then
> the Irish brought to the English the priceless seed of God's word, which they
> prudently tended into vigorous growth. . . . As a fragment of the larger tale of
> the Almighty's salvific purpose, nothing so poetic and pleasing had ever been
> written in any language, or would be.[17]

At the heart of Bede's pleasant account was the melding of Roman
orthodoxy with Celtic sanctity, above all at the Synod of Whitby (664 CE),
when the bulk of the Irish-trained clergy accepted the Roman calculation of
Easter.[18] Here Bede saw merit on both sides: "Despite his own, strict views
in favor of the 'Roman' Easter [pushed for by the 'lordly Wilfrid'], he never
disguised his respect for the sanctity of the monks of Iona."[19]

Bede praised in particular the Irish-trained monks such as the monk-bishops Aidan (d. 651) and Chad (d. 672), both of whom would, as Bede wrote of Chad, "travel about, not on horseback, but after the manner of the Apostles, on foot, to preach the Gospel in towns, the open country, cottages, villages, and castles" (*Hist. Eccl.* 4.3).[20] The result was an era in Northumbria when priests and clerks, trained at Lindisfarne, "went to the villages for no other reason than to preach, baptize, visit the sick, and, in a word, to take care of souls; and they were so purified from all taint of avarice, that none of them received lands and possessions for building monasteries, unless they were compelled to do so by the temporal authorities" (*Hist. Eccl.* 3.26).

Bede tells anecdotes of both Aidan and Chad to highlight their Martinian renunciation of horses (in contrast to the worldly Brice criticized by Sulpicius). Archbishop Theodore from Rome (and originally Tarsus in Asia) wished Chad to ride on horseback when the situation demanded, "and when Chad strongly resisted . . . Theodore himself did lift him on horseback with his own hands, knowing him to be indeed a holy man" (*Hist. Eccl.* 4.3).

Likewise, King Oswin gave Aidan a "very fair horse" (equum optimum) for crossing streams or other necessities; but soon Aidan met a beggar asking for help, and (in a Martinian response) gave him the "royally saddled" horse. The king, learning of this, was upset at giving a beggar a royal horse when there were cheaper ones available. Aidan replied immediately, "What are you saying? Is that son of a mare dearer in your sight than that son of God?" The two men then went in to dinner, but soon the king, taking off his sword, came over and knelt before Aidan, "beseeching to be reconciled to him" (*Hist. Eccl.* 3.14). Bede's anecdote illustrates how the ascetic humility and self-depreciation praised polemically by the alleged Pelagian heretic Sulpicius, and feared by the Gaulish bishops of that time, became through his own *History* a unifying ideal for church and lay people alike.

Bede's ideal of *humilitas* is somewhat different from Sulpicius's: Martin was indifferent to high culture, whereas Aidan was a teacher:

His life was so far removed from the slackness [segnitia] of our time, that all they which walked with him, were they professed into religion or were they laymen, must needs study; that is, bestow their time either in reading Scripture or in learning the Psalter. (*Hist. Eccl.* 3.5)

But the story of Aidan and the royally accoutered horse is told as an example of *humilitas*—the remarkable humility here less that of Aidan (who is amply praised elsewhere) than of King Oswin (*Hist. Eccl.* 3.14).

Bede's *Ecclesiastical History* illustrates ethogeny: secular matters such as battles, or dynastic shifts and intermarriages, are only narrated insofar as they pertain to the rapid spread of Christian culture. But one should not be misled by the title: Bede's subject is the conversion of an entire society and area, not just the fortunes of the Angles and the church.[21] Thus for example he spends much time on the *virtutes*—meaning not just virtues but miracles—of his model King Oswald, "beloved of God," who, when at Heavenfield fighting King Cadwallon of the Britons, prayed first to a cross and thus won victory. Thereafter, people would cut splinters from the cross and soak them in water, which could quickly cure both men and beasts (*Hist. Eccl.* 3.1–2). Later, after Oswald was slain in another battle, the site of his death became a place where people would go for cures; the place itself cured a horse (*Hist. Eccl.* 3.9).

The *History* closes with a hopeful acknowledgment of the Saracens' defeat at Tours (732): "The Saracens, like a very sore plague, wasted France with pitiful destruction, and themselves not long after were justly punished in the same country for their unbelief." But this news was offset by troubles back in Northumbria, leaving Bede open-minded as to what the future might bring.[22]

Bede has written an idyll of an England where, despite setbacks, church and state, Aidan and Oswald, could work selflessly together to change human society. Like Sulpicius and Pope Gregory the Great, Bede closes with a nostalgic sense that in the slackness (or what Jerome called the "dregs") of the present, something of this ideal has been lost.

Bede's *History* became a foundational document in the evolution of British identity, and not just for the English. Scottish Presbyterians pointed to the argument at the Synod of Whitby attributed by Bede to Colman, the Irish abbot of Lindisfarne, that the Celtic calculation of Easter followed that of the Eastern churches proselytized by St. John the Evangelist (*Hist. Eccl.* 3.25). From this the historian George Buchanan (d. 1583) derived the notion that the original missionaries to Scotland "were non-Petrine, Johannine Christians from Asia Minor [rather than Rome]."[23]

Bede's idyll did not last long. Writing less than a century later, Alcuin wrote of an England that had become disrupted and demoralized—ready for a cultural shift. But we cannot leave Bede's *Ecclesiastical History* without referring to a point so obvious that it is rarely acknowledged. Bede's *History*, recognized as a landmark in the evolution of English identity, was nonetheless written in Latin (though it acknowledged the importance of the vernacular in the verse of the illiterate poet Caedmon). It could hardly have been otherwise: to be literate in that era was to be literate in Latin.

But the corrupted Latin of Gregory of Tours's *History of the Franks* represented the contemporary evolution of late Latin into French.[24] Bede's Latin, learned at a monastic school, was part of an Anglo-Latin culture quite alien to the Anglo-Saxon language and culture of the Northumbrian court. This was a split that reflected Augustine's transfer of allegiance from the earthly city to the City of God.

In a moment we shall see how this split was expanded by the educational reforms of Alcuin (d. 804). But we should notice how the split survived in Britain: the great English Renaissance minders like More, Milton, Hobbes, and even Locke all wrote in Latin. This was partly so that their writing could be read on a continent now split into many vernaculars. But it was also partly (and perhaps principally, in the case of More) to prevent their works from being misinterpreted by the less educated.

The shadow of this split extends to the present day. It justifies our thinking of Bede's culture as in one sense countercultural, in the spirit of Isaiah's criticizing the Judaic establishment or Virgil's warning against the dangers of militaristic empire. In another sense, Latinity itself now became established as the dominant culture from which the emergent vernacular countercultures would eventually rebel.

THE "DONATION OF PEPIN": THE CHURCH BECOMES A TEMPORAL POWER

Meanwhile, the power vacuum on the continent was slowly filled by the future Carolingian dynasty of Charlemagne, who as mayors of the Palace (a restraining influence originally imposed on the kings by restive magnates) gained control over their nominal rulers. They did so with the approval of the popes in Rome, who now looked north for secular support after their links to the Eastern Empire had been effectively broken.

As the French historian Henri Pirenne wrote, for four centuries, following the collapse of Rome, "in the midst of the prevailing decadence only one moral force held its own: the Church, and for the Church the Empire still existed."[25] But communications with the Byzantine emperor became more difficult with the Lombard irruption into Italy in 568, after which the imperial presence was gravely weakened and the churches of Rome and Constantinople divided more and more frequently on doctrinal issues—such as the Monophysite controversy (640–681), the Iconoclastic controversy (726–787), and whether or not the word *filioque* ("and with the son") belonged in the Nicene Creed (causing the East–West Schism of 1054).

In 751, Pope Zachary (significantly, the last Greek pope) endorsed the decision of Pepin the Short to proclaim himself king of the Franks. This was as significant an act for the papacy as it was for the Pepinid family, whom we remember as Carolingians. Over the next half century, Pepin and his son Charles (soon to be Charlemagne) strengthened the papacy against the Lombards, as the Greek emperors had failed to do. But in defending the church, they also changed it.

In the same year, the Lombards overran the Exarchate of Ravenna, the last vestige of the Roman Empire in northern Italy. When the Lombard king proceeded to demand the submission of Rome to Lombard taxation, a new pope, Stephen II, crossed the Alps and appealed for relief in person to Pepin. In response, Frankish armies entered Italy in 755 and 756 and decisively defeated the Lombards. In the resulting treaty, the Lombards, at Pepin's insistence, ceded the territory of the Ravenna Exarchate to the pope.

This so-called Donation of Pepin made the pope, for the first time, a significant temporal ruler, and thus part of Augustine's earthly city.[26] Charlemagne in 774 decisively defeated the Lombards, expanded the bequest to the pope, and declared himself the Lombard king. Soon a forged (and probably Frankish) decretal, the so-called Donation of Constantine, made the claim that the whole of the Western Empire had been given by Constantine to the papacy. A half century later, Dante would fiercely denounce this immersion of the church in temporal affairs.

CHARLEMAGNE, CHRISTENDOM, AND SLAVERY

Leopold von Ranke (d. 1886), the father of recent methodological history, gives a German perspective on the redirection of this era:

> One of the most important epochs in the history of the world, the commencement of the eighth century, when on the one side Mohammedanism threatened to overspread Italy and Gaul, and on the other the ancient idolatry of Saxony and Friesland once more forced its way across the Rhine. . . . The compound of military and sacerdotal government which forms the basis of all civilization from that moment arose into being. From that moment conquest and conversion went hand in hand.[27]

As I understand it, when Pepin of Herstal (d. 714) subdued the Frisians, he eliminated pagan authority, leaving the ground open for Northumbrian monks like Willibrord (d. 739) to conduct voluntary perilous conversion missions in the Martinian style. But his great-grandson Charles's campaign against the Saxons, in response to their destruction of a Frisian church, was accompanied in contrast by forced conversion.[28] This included the Verden Massacre of 4,500 pagan Saxon prisoners in 772 and a subsequent law: "If any one of the race of the Saxons . . . shall have scorned to come to baptism and shall have wished to remain a pagan, let him be punished by death."[29] As I indicate below, the sword, once the persecutor of the cross, had indeed become its enforcer.

The text of this law was soon modified on the advice of Alcuin, representing the Martinian monastic spirit that "faith is a free act of the will, not a forced act. We must appeal to the conscience, not compel it by violence. You can force people to be baptized, but you cannot force them to believe."[30]

After a second sustained campaign against the Avars, in what became the newly created Ostmark (Austria), Alcuin's emphasis on voluntary baptism and tithing had a humanizing effect that would endure.

> Alcuin ingeniously drew upon his own monastic background and experiences to forge a new ideology based on mercy, humility, obedience, and an inner change of heart. Alcuin did not merely graft an important new influence onto the cultural renewal of the Carolingian era but effectively reinvigorated and relegitimized missionary efforts for a long time to come as well.[31]

Thereafter beheading ceased, but there was still a downside to Charlemagne's incursions east. The fate of those who remained pagan was now increasingly to be exported to the prosperous Abbasid caliphate: a commerce first of German pagans, but then increasingly of Slavs (as the word "slave" reminds us).[32]

One of these Slavic slaves (a Greek Orthodox Christian), after being manumitted in Constantinople, was later venerated a saint in the Byzantine Church. From his vita we hear of the ugly conflict that erupted, after the death of Byzantine St. Methodius in 885, over whether the recently converted region of greater Moravia would worship by the Roman or the Byzantine rite. Frankish troops "in the service of the Slavonic ruler descended on the two hundred disciples in the cathedral school" of St. Methodius and sold some of the younger men, including priests and deacons, who were then resold as slaves in Venice (despite a nominal ban there on the slave trade).[33] Slaves were also traded directly for gold and silver with the caliphates in Baghdad and Seville, facilitating a revival of a moribund cash economy.[34]

ALCUIN AND THE INCIPIENT REURBANIZATION OF EUROPE

The revival of trade and money fostered the gradual reurbanization of Europe in the Fourth Pivotal Shift (ca. 1000 CE). The benefits were cultural as well as economic: Alcuin moved from the church of York to become master of the new Palace School of Charlemagne at Aachen, where he developed it into the central stimulus of the Carolingian Renaissance. Soon the cosmological speculations of John Scotus Eriugena (d. ca. 877) at this school would signal (for yang thinkers like Charles Freeman) the incipient revival of intellectual philosophy as it is understood in the twenty-first century. Alcuin brought to the continent the Northumbrian project of restoring church Latin to classical standards. Roger Wright has argued that before his reforms, "late Latin" had been indistinguishable from "early Romance," but after them on the continent, "Latin became . . . a foreign language for everybody."[35]

This separation of clerical Latin and its speakers from the vernaculars of both rulers and people was compensated for by another of Alcuin's radical reforms: Charlemagne's Capitulary of 787. This established, along with the Palace School, an expanded network of schools, to recruit and train Latin speakers (i.e., future clergy) from *every* level of society: the germ of a modern society, subordinate to an urban capital, but with the goal of education for all who desired it.[36]

But this incipient yang revival was accompanied by a decline of the pacific yin ethos of *humilitas* of the Dark Age rural monasteries. The persuasive power of Martinian monks was being superseded even as coercive state power was recovering. This was due in part to Viking raids, which predictably grew more frequent as monasteries, once ascetic, grew wealthier. In particular, the destruction of Lindisfarne by Viking raiders in 793 severely shook Alcuin's faith that missionary monasticism was God's work, divinely protected. As he wrote to King Æthelred of Northumbria,

> Lo, it is nearly 350 years that we and our fathers have inhabited this most lovely land, and never before has such terror appeared in Britain as we have now suffered from a pagan race, nor was it thought that such an inroad from the sea could be made. Behold, the church of St. Cuthbert spattered with the blood of the priests of God, despoiled of all its ornaments; a place more venerable than all in Britain is given as a prey to pagan peoples.[37]

But Alcuin also complained of the corruption of contemporary English princes:

> They were tyrants, not rulers; for they plundered their people shamelessly. The whole land was a prey to intestine strife; rival claimants to the throne murdered and pillaged, regardless of their subjects.[38]

The king to whom Alcuin wrote, Æthelred, merited Alcuin's condemnation; from his accession to his murder in 796, his reign was marked by continuous internecine violence.

THE DARKER LEGACY OF THE
THIRD PIVOTAL MOMENT

In the slavery-supported reurbanization of Europe under the cusp ruler Charlemagne, we see the oppression of slavery shifting from domestic to external oppression. This marks the beginning of darker coercive aspects in the Fourth Pivotal Moment, many of which are still with us.

Of these, one of the most serious was the institution of spiritual Crusades. These began as defensive Carolingian victories against invading Muslim armies, first at Toulouse in 721 and then definitively at Tours in 732. But the age of the Crusades (1095–1481) did not so much end as segue into the following age of weaponized international exploration and exploitation overseas, initially in the name of the cross.

American leaders of this century have described their own overseas invasions as "crusades," while many others, at home and abroad, have denounced them as war crimes. One eventual consequence of this cultural xenophobia was the revival of chattel slavery as an underpinning of the economy—now in remote colonies rather than in the homeland. Today, chattel slavery has been almost ubiquitously abolished; however, by most accounts, a majority of people still live in conditions of poverty, and a significant percentage in extreme poverty.

Another consequence, more immediate, was the revival of lethal anti-Semitism and persecution of Jews. This occurred in Muslim Spain with the Berber pillage of Córdoba in 1013 and the massacre of Jews in Granada in 1066, as the liberal culture of al-Andalus began to collapse under the combined pressure of Christian armies from the north and militant Islamic sects from Africa.

Lethal attacks on Jews followed soon after in Christian Europe, also attributable to Christian-Muslim antagonism. Armies in the Middle Ages lived "off the land," and if necessary off of cities.[39] The undisciplined ragtag army of the First Crusade, on arriving at Speyer, Worms, and Mainz (1096 CE), proceeded without provocation to rob and murder Jews in these cities, a shameful revival of a tradition that led to the bureaucratic genocide of the Holocaust almost a millennium later.

I may seem in these paragraphs to have veered from chronicling our cultural development or ethogeny, the stated topic of this book, into matters of economic and political development. But as I see it I have not. We cannot achieve a mind creatively at peace with itself until we achieve a supporting ethos or culture that is creatively at peace with the world. I believe, like Xu Jilin, that the path toward that better ethos is not through cultural amnesia but by recuperating the radical cultural aspirations of our past.[40]

If one takes a long view of history, one has to see and admit that, although the abolition of chattel slavery in America in 1865 was an important event in the painfully slow emancipation of the oppressed, slavery, though far better disguised than before, is still with us. And this slavery, of both blacks and whites, continues, as in Athens and Rome, to be the underpinning of our urban culture as we now know it. In keeping with the pattern that emerged during the Third Pivotal Moment and the later European empires, much of that enslavement is now lodged abroad through great power exploitation of the Third World.[41]

As to whether or not we have made progress toward the ideals of our *tianxia*, the evidence I have presented so far does not compel a confident decision either way. It is safe to say that, thanks to great technical progress in communications, we are closer to the possibility of a peaceful global community than before. But at the same time, great technical advances in modes of warfare have increased the chances of a massive global disruption—the end of an era, in effect, and the opening of an opportunity for a new pivotal shift.

Part of me will continue to hope that our future will be largely peaceful rather than violently disruptive. I continue to believe that although suffering (*dukkha*) is inevitable, war, mass indiscriminate lethal violence by humans against humans, is not. If we take the long view of cultural development, I believe that power from below has been gaining increasing power to restrict, and modify, power from above. I shall try to justify this belief in my next chapter.

Above all, I believe that healthy human beings are at home in hope and alienated when we lose it.

THE THIRD MOMENT'S BRIGHTER LEGACY: THE INFLUENCE OF NONCOERCIVE ON COERCIVE POWER

There is relatively little written evidence to demonstrate a positive cultural evolution in the Dark Age. Perhaps, however, it can be illustrated by citing two anecdotal instances of the improved moral influence of clergy like Alcuin on coercive power. We have seen that St. Martin failed in his humanitarian appeal to an emperor to spare bloodshed, while Alcuin, after four centuries of Dark Age cultural evolution, was strikingly successful.

It just so happens that each pivotal shift since the first was accompanied by memorable interactions between leaders of noncoercive and of coercive power. Let us compare these and later incidents in hopes of establishing a longer perspective on them.

Ca. 380 Ambrose intercedes with Emperor Theodosius, and St. Martin with Maximus.

Ca. 785 Alcuin intercedes with Charlemagne after the Massacre of Verden.

Ca. 1500 Many cultural leaders advise those with coercive power (e.g., Sir Thomas More with Henry VIII), but with mixed results.

1939 Einstein and other scientists persuade Roosevelt to authorize research into the possibility of a bomb from uranium.

As we saw, Ambrose successfully persuaded Theodosius to rescind an order he had issued; whereas St. Martin, having elicited a promise from Maximus not to shed Priscillian's blood, watched him renege on his promise. The two responses between them illustrate the gap in that era between coercive and noncoercive power. Ambrose prevailed over Theodosius in a matter of political power. Martin made a purely humanitarian appeal, which Maximus only partly responded to. Coercive power in the fourth century was rarely responsive to purely humanitarian appeals.

But in 785, after four centuries of Dark Age cultural evolution, the situation had changed dramatically. After Charlemagne ordered the execution of 4,500 rebellious Saxons in the Verden Massacre, Alcuin was able to persuade him to adopt a more lenient policy.[42] Alcuin's authority derived from his literacy, necessary for the reestablishment of a functioning legal state. Charlemagne, in contrast, was semi-illiterate; even his biographer Einhard (d. 840) "admitted that the king had only limited ability to read and write."[43] At this time, according to Chris Wickham, "the importance of intellectuals for the political practice of the ninth-century West was as great as or greater than it would ever be again in the Middle Ages."[44]

Has there been comparable influence since then? In the Renascence or Fifth Pivotal Shift, thanks to the invention of the printing press and the breakup of the Catholic Church dominance over learning, minders played a wide new spectrum of roles in relation to top-down power.

At one extreme was the Alcuin-like Bartolomé de las Casas (d. 1566), Europe's first whistle-blower, who exposed Spanish atrocities in the New World and later campaigned successfully at the royal court for humane legal reforms to the Spanish slave labor system there (including involuntary baptism).[45]

Mid-spectrum was the poet and former monk Martin Luther (d. 1546). His success at generating bottom-up reform gave him a leadership power, which he used to preach nonviolence against the German Peasants' Revolt of 1524–25. This allied him with the Electors of Saxony.[46]

At the top-down extreme was Machiavelli's *The Prince* (*Il principe*; written in 1513 but first published in 1532). Its clearest influence was on the dowager queen of France, Catherine de Medici (d. 1589), "who got the credit of having introduced the book into France, and . . . 'Italianized' French life and politics."[47] Catherine was the chief royal power during the reigns of her three immature sons, and thus both she and the book are commonly blamed for the deaths of thousands of Huguenots in the St. Bartholomew's Day massacre of 1572.

Machiavelli wrote other works more in the spirit of cultural humanists. But *Il Principe*, which explicitly sought to free political issues from considerations of values, is today remembered as one of the main founders of modern political science, a revolutionary landmark in the development of a realist, materialist social science, with particular relevance to international relations as practiced today.[48] From the perspective of this book, it can be seen as successful because it served the purposes of those possessing coercive power, rather than challenging that power.

Turning now to our present century, one can cite, as an influence comparable to Alcuin's successful appeal to Charlemagne, Einstein's famous letter of 1939 to President Roosevelt, warning that German scientists might win the race to build an atomic bomb. Roosevelt eventually replied that he had set up a committee consisting of civilian and military representatives to study uranium, a decision that bore fruit in the Manhattan Project and the atomic bomb. Alcuin diminished violence, whereas Einstein (albeit for the best of reasons) merely enhanced it.

One can glean hope from the fact that scientists today, dealing with increasingly unhinged and unethical coercive powers, are slowly responding with a noncoercive collective authority comparable to that enjoyed in the Dark Age by the church. But the larger story of Einstein and the bomb illustrates how unable scientists were at first to exercise their potential noncoercive power. Einstein himself was not permitted to work on the Manhattan Project; the army and Vannevar Bush (the engineer entrusted to develop the project) denied him a work clearance on the grounds that his pacifist leanings and celebrity status made him a security risk. Robert Oppenheimer, who headed the Los Alamos Laboratory and is remembered as the father of the atomic bomb, had his clearance revoked after he opposed the development of the hydrogen bomb.

In 1944, Joseph Rotblat resigned from the Manhattan Project after it became clear that the bomb was now being developed for offensive rather than defensive purposes.[49] He returned to a teaching post in Liverpool, where in 1957 he organized and then became secretary-general of the influential, privately funded Pugwash Conferences on Science and World Affairs. These brought together scholars and public figures from both East and West to seek solutions to global security threats. Initially the British government thought them little more than communist front gatherings. But the presence of high-level scientists from both the United States and the Soviet Union, notably Andrei Sakharov, enabled Pugwash to lay the groundwork for the Partial Test Ban Treaty of 1963, the Nonproliferation Treaty of 1968, the Anti-Ballistic Missile Treaty of 1972, the Biological Weapons Convention of 1972, and the Chemical Weapons Convention of 1993. For this achievement, Rotblat and Pugwash were jointly awarded the Nobel Peace Prize in 1995.

The great danger presented by governmental nuclear strategies of mutually assured destruction created an international consensus of concerned nuclear scientists that ultimately forced a significant change in the global international arms chase. Governments proved incapable of initiating sane initiatives, but luckily the same governments proved capable of responding to saner policies from leaders of noncoercive power.

We think of these leaders, for want of a better word, as "intellectuals." But in fact the greatest of them, Einstein, Rotblat, and Sakharov, shared a cultural dimension that gave them more than intellectual authority, in my view very akin to the more than intellectual authority enjoyed with Charlemagne by Alcuin, the greatest poet of his generation.

Of the three, Sakharov, despite being held under house arrest for six years, was the thinker whose

> opinion was heard at the very top of the Soviet power pyramid, his proposals formed global policy, and not only in the field of . . . nuclear weapons. . . . [His] brochure "Reflections . . . " of 1968, which was launched by Samizdat [and] confiscated by KGB . . . , was . . . carefully studied by the then leader of the USSR, Leonid Brezhnev and, according to his instructions, by other members of the Politburo. [His proposals] significantly influenced the international policy of the USSR . . . the ABM Treaty . . . the policy of "détente," the "Helsinki Act" of 1975 with its human rights "third basket."[50]

The opening of socialist societies under the Helsinki Accords led to the appearance almost immediately of mass popular movements like Solidarity in Poland, which contributed to the ultimate fall of the Soviet Union.

As to what I mean by a spiritual dimension shared with Einstein, I will offer one quote from Sakharov that exemplifies the post-secular mindset of this book: "I am unable to imagine the universe and human life without some guiding principle, without a source of spiritual 'warmth' that is nonmaterial and not bound by physical laws."[51]

Einstein made a similar distinction, between "knowledge of what is" and "the goal of our human aspirations." The latter "exist in a healthy society as powerful traditions . . . [which] come into being not through demonstration but through revelation, through the medium of powerful personalities. One must not attempt to justify them, but rather to sense their nature simply and clearly. The highest principles for our aspirations and judgments are given to us in the Jewish-Christian religious tradition."[52]

My hope is to see noncoercive persuasion, reinforced by the impetus of our cultural evolution, regain the political standing it was beginning to acquire through the four centuries of the Dark Age, and that in time this will inspire the further growth of a noncoercive global public opinion to restrain and increasingly guide our increasingly fallible regional governments.

Chapter Fifteen

End of the Poem in Prose

Like history itself, this poem in prose ends inconclusively, looking beyond its end. So end Genesis, the Pentateuch, the Jewish bible. As they close, Virgil's and Dante's otherworldly visions of peace are both brought down more prosaically by their anticlimactic endings. All I conclude about our future is that in our culture lies our hope.

In this I am echoing Czeslaw Milosz, who drew on the work of Erich Heller, Dostoevsky, and Blake to attack the "vulgarized scientific *Weltanschauung* propagated by the schools."[1]

This weakening of the consensual values in our culture was once defended as an increase in personal freedom. But more recently that weakening has emerged as a threat to personal freedom rather than an enhancement of it. In the last century, visionaries like Richard Rorty or Martin Luther King could still dream of America as a land stumbling erratically toward greater peace, freedom, and equality. That dream, losing its cultural roots, is weaker today.[2]

I would like to question the widespread belief in determinism that one finds in today's social sciences—understandably, because that assumption of determinism facilitates the methods, often quantitative, that one encounters there. In particular, we find the belief that we are constrained by determinism with respect to two dominant social problems that have shaped this book. The first is the major problem of increasing disparity of wealth. The second, related problem is the ongoing pursuit in many parts of the world of modern high-tech warfare.

The assumption of determinism is so normal today that it is easy to overlook it. With respect to the problem of disparate wealth, I will repeat a quotation from an excellent historian, Walter Scheidel, whom I cite on four other occasions in this book: "Throughout history, *only* massive, violent shocks that upended the established order proved powerful enough to flatten disparities in income and wealth."[3]

And with respect to the problem of war, the experienced political scientist Graham Allison summarized, as what he called the "Thucydides trap," the message he drew from his reading of Thucydides's *History of the Peloponnesian War*: "It was the rise of Athens, and the fear that this inspired in Sparta, that made war *inevitable.*" This gloomy message led him to conclude that, in Washington's deliberations about China policy, "declarations about 'rebalancing' or revitalizing 'engage and hedge,' or presidential hopefuls' calls for more 'muscular' or 'robust' variants of the same, amount to little more than aspirin treating cancer."[4]

In other words, Allison's presumption that such wars are inevitable led him to the kind of conservative practical conclusions that are common among leaders today, and that Barbara Tuchman, in her classic book *The March of Folly*, characterized as the disastrous "wooden-headedness" of leaders on the eve of World War I: "assessing a situation in terms of preconceived fixed notions while ignoring or rejecting any contrary signs."[5]

But both of these assumptions can be and have been challenged, particularly Scheidel's. Thomas Piketty, a leading figure in the field of wealth disparity, has written,

> Sweden used to be a very unequal country until the beginning of the 20th century. And then, following a very large social mobilization by trade unions and the Social Democratic party, Sweden became one of the most equal countries in history. You could say the U.S., after the Great Depression, also turned to a very progressive tax system and reduced its inequality enormously.[6]

The assumption that wars are inevitable, in contrast, is far less often questioned. But I believe that if one is conscious of cultural evolution (ethogeny), it becomes hard not to question it, even using the evidence that Allison used to support his claim.

ARE MAJOR WARS INEVITABLE? ETHOGENY SUGGESTS NOT

Allison defended his claim of a "Thucydides trap" by generalizing from the example of Sparta's challenge to Athens:

> In fact, in 12 of 16 cases over the last 500 years in which there was a rapid shift in the relative power of a rising nation that threatened to displace a ruling state, the result was war.

His argument was widely noticed, to the extent that it even drew a response from President Xi Jinping in China, after President Trump promised to be "tough on China" and warned that "a complete decoupling from China" was an option.[7] Xi's response in one speech was that "the growing trend toward a multipolar world will not change,"[8] and in another that the "Thucydides trap . . . can be avoided . . . as long as we maintain communication and treat each other with sincerity."[9]

But a closer look at Allison's four exceptions to his rule suggests, at least to a poet who believes in the power of cultural evolution (ethogeny), a counterargument: that in the last century, forces opposed to war have gained a strength they never had before. Allison's four exceptions to the "Thucydides trap" were without exception recent: the tensions between the United Kingdom and the United States (early twentieth century), the USSR and Japan (1970s–1980s), the USSR and the United States (1940s–1980s), and the UK (along with France) and Germany (1990s–present).

Three of these four crises occurred in the last century, and two of them in the last half century. In other words, Allison's own evidence can be taken as evidence that the status of war in society is not a fixed or determined state of affairs but part of an evolving process. I believe moreover that wars today are not just less likely to break out; they are also more likely to be terminated by public opinion before they escalate to full-fledged disruption.

This discussion of Allison's "Thucydides trap" is relevant here on the political level as relevant to the case that the world today is experiencing change due to emerging persuasive power and nonviolence. But its greater relevance is on the meta- or cultural level. Allison is not just a representative practitioner of political science; he is an outstanding one. A cofounder of the Trilateral Commission, he has twice been awarded the Pentagon's Distinguished Public Service Medal. Three of his books have been best sellers, and one of them was selected by the *New York Times* as one of the "100 most notable books of 2004."

PEOPLE POWER AS A SYMPTOM OF CULTURAL EVOLUTION

We have seen "people power," a new socio-cultural-political concept but one long in gestation, emerge as a significant factor, perhaps a determining one, in the close to the biggest recent crisis of all: the long Cold War face-off between the United States and the Soviet Union.

I am referring to two of the recent and unprecedented successes of non-violent civil resistance movements. One was the role of the U.S. antiwar movement in helping to terminate the Vietnam War—a war that under Nixon risked becoming nuclear.[10] I believe this is the first time ever that organized dissent in the streets helped to terminate a major war. (As we have seen, the nuclear arms race of the United States and the USSR was also mitigated in part by proposals that were generated by these nations' scientists at Pugwash meetings.)

The second event, even more amazing, was the ultimate success of the Polish Solidarity movement in securing the withdrawal of the Soviet army (then the world's largest) from Polish territory. Central to this success was the intense Catholicism of the Polish people, skillfully roused and restrained by an intellectually mobilized coalition of spiritual and lay leaders.[11]

In short, Allison's list overlooked the rather conspicuous counterevidence that wars may have recently become less inevitable because of increasingly successful popular resistance to them. This resistance can be traced to the writings of the American intellectual Henry David Thoreau (though Ralph Waldo Emerson and the theologian William Ellery Channing have also been cited).[12]

Thoreau of course was an outlier in his generation. But a century later, after major antiwar poems from two world wars, the nonviolent resistance lyrics of Bob Dylan and others captured the hearts of a generation and became a factor in changing military history. This committed yearning for peace drew strength from its much deeper sources in our ethogeny than the hard-nosed countercurrent of Machiavelli and Hobbes can muster.

Dylan himself said of his song "Blowin' in the Wind" that it was a "spiritual. I took it off a song called 'No More Auction Block.'" And according to Alan Lomax, the song "No More Auction Block/We Shall Overcome," was sung by former slaves who fled to Nova Scotia after Britain abolished slavery in 1833.[13]

But this quest for peace and freedom is resonant with voices from every stage in the evolution of Western culture. I have cited the seminal example of Virgil's fourth eclogue, verses 16–17—"He will be deified, be seen by gods / And rule a world his father pacified"—which in turn was consonant with Isaiah 9:6: "For unto us a child is born . . . and his name shall be called . . . the everlasting Father, the Prince of Peace."

I see a maturation (ethogenetically speaking) of these messianic aspirations in the inspiring spiritual that in the 1960s antiwar movement we must have sung hundreds of times, often before and during mass arrests:

> We shall overcome, we shall overcome,
> We shall overcome some day.
> Deep in my heart, I do believe,
> We shall overcome some day.[14]

Dreams, visions, beliefs, and aspirations, associated with our right hemisphere, cannot be precisely delineated or quantified. And thus they tend to be ignored by left-hemisphere deterministic social science, to the latter's detriment. But they do affect cultural history, especially in a Dark Age when the social conditions for urban rationality are relatively deficient. (Hence the immense cultural influence of the nonviolent St. Martin, doomed to be underreported by fact-based historians.)

The influence of dreams can be permanent. In the background of "We Shall Overcome" we can also see St. Augustine's consoling vision of history aging slowly toward an era of Sabbatical peace (see chapter 13). And perhaps we should even mention the premature aspiration to limit warfare in the seventh-century Law of Adamnán, said to have been inspired by an abbot's dream (see chapter 11).

The Enlightenment itself in its early stages was a product of right-hemisphere vision as well as left-hemisphere calculation. Newton, in his Scholium or comment on his *Principia Mathematica*, linked his demonstrations of gravity in the universe, theologically, to a radical anti-trinitarian theology, going back behind the Nicene Creed to the God of the Old Testament. In his words, "The most beautiful System of the Sun, Planets, and Comets, could only proceed from the counsel and dominion of an intelligent and powerful being.[15]

The secular reading of Newton, excluding God and angering Blake, would come later.

The "clockwork universe" aspect of the Newtonian world view, for example, is not to be found in the *Principia*; it was added by Laplace late in the eighteenth century, after the success of the theory of gravity in accounting for complex deviations from Keplerian motion became fully evident.[16]

That is the meaning of "Enmindment" in this book's title: that we should restore the impoverished secular mindset of left-hemisphere Enlightenment, that which is widespread today, toward an enlarged synergy of both hemispheres, like that which guided Newton.

BALANCING OUR DREAMS AND OUR ANALYSIS: THE ROLE MODELS OF ELLSBERG AND MILOSZ

To reprise what I said in the introduction, enmindment is the meaningful integration, or at least equilibration, of secular enlightenment (yang) with spiritual enlightenment (yin). Just to say this reminds me of my close friend Daniel Ellsberg, who used to say, in effect, "Contemplating my latest analysis [yang] of our perilous political situation, I then pray with all my heart [yin] that my analysis is wrong." Clearly the synergy of both hemispheres contributed to his alienation and commitment to change the world.

A similar dialectical synergy marked both the poetry and the practice of Czeslaw Milosz. In 1947 Milosz published in Warsaw a long poem, passed by the censors of postwar Poland's first coalition government, that predicted a centuries-long future for Poland under Russian domination. Its gloomy prospect was summed up by the poem's conclusion:

> Let us go in peace, simple people,
> Before us awaits
>   —"the Heart of Darkness."[17]

Yet, even though engulfed in the oppressive avalanche of twentieth-century history, everyone still has the challenge, and the opportunity, to mitigate it.

> You float on this social fact
> Like a nut in a Nile cataract.
>
> But you are not so helpless,
> And even if you are but a stone in a field,
> The avalanche must alter its course
> By the stones over which it flows.
> And, as someone used to say,
> You can thus influence [wpłyń] the avalanche,
> Ease [łagodź] its savagery and cruelty,
> For this, one will need bravery[18]

A little later in the same poem, Milosz pointed, as I am here, to a healing equilibration of our own mind (yang) and heart (yin) together:

> Salvation [ocalenie] is only in you.
> Perhaps it is simply a healthy mind
> And a balanced heart [serca równowaga].[19]

This is a simple formula, but one that may take years to fully absorb and exemplify. In the case of both Ellsberg and Milosz, immersion in a disruptive war helped shake them from their previous lives of accommodation, as did powerful love for the women who later became their wives. Milosz's separation from his earlier life was finalized by the loss of all his possessions, even those he was carrying on him, as he escaped on a road away from devastated Warsaw.[20]

In this post-secular time passionate divisions, sometimes between retro and generative spiritualities, threaten more and greater wars. So let each of us, mindful of our own internal yin-yang doubleness, resolve to balance the urgent need to preserve the best of the precious world we now enjoy, against the urgent need to make it better.

Hopefully, this may contribute to a less fervid politics, and a healthier, friendlier culture.

CONCLUDING UNSCIENTIFIC POSTSCRIPT

Over the years, an intention has emerged from writing this unintentional book. It is to endorse the simple idea that our real but imperfect progress in cultural development (our ethogeny) has been and will be achieved by revising and improving upon all of our past cultural achievements, the spiritual or yin as well as the secular or yang.

More specifically, I hope the world will come to see, as I have come to see, that both enlightenment and endarkenment, expansion and recision, yang and yin, are healthy phases in the slow but steady pulse of human cultural development.

This will involve developing a greater appreciation than is common today for the cultural achievements of the Dark Age (and its yin predecessors), both for dropping remnants of the previous classical urbanization that had become distasteful (like gladiatorial games) and for its own cultural achievements (like the diminution of chattel slavery) that are admittedly hard to pinpoint. In discussing the latter, my purpose has not been to turn my readers into medievalists, but to strengthen within them that awareness in them of that "spiritual 'warmth' that is nonmaterial" referred to by Sakharov.[21]

I hope further that in this dialectical process we see the slow evolution of hard, violent power into soft, persuasive power. Admittedly by selection, I have sketched a pattern through the millennia whereby those who mind and who care, moved by their inner moreness, have responded to and strengthened a *nisus* or tendency in human affairs toward nonviolent change. The hope articulated in the Paternoster, "Thy kingdom come," eventually inspired the liberation movements of the 1960s in the American South and of the 1980s in Poland. We can see here an example of the very slow mitigation of coercive violence from above by the growing concordance from below of the disempowered.

As this consensus gathers social acceptance, this mitigation becomes political. But minds must be changed before institutions can be, and that task is cultural. John Adams observed that the American Revolution was not the Revolutionary War: "It was in the minds of the people . . . in the course of fifteen years, before a drop of blood was shed at Lexington."[22] Almost two centuries later, the Solidarity leader Adam Michnik made a similar comment: "Poland's peaceful transformation . . . was preceded by an almost two-decade effort to build institutions of civil [as opposed to political] society."[23]

The process described in this book can perhaps be summed up in a mantra: "The way of moreness is the empowerment of mind." We are becoming aware that, underlying the vagaries of political struggle, our true human history does not lie in the accidents and divisions of political conflict but in the relative coherence of our dialogical cultural development, our ethogeny.

May this book be a small contribution to that awareness.

Appendix

A Personal Note after
Finishing This Book

Writing this book has helped me to see more clearly that I, like all of us, have been far more shaped in my thinking than I realized by living in an era of cold war—a war against Russia first, but now extended to cool but slowly escalating engagements against both China and Islam.

This shaping began for me when I read for a B. Phil. degree in politics at Oxford between 1950 and 1952. I became profoundly alienated by being expected to read and endorse *The Open Society and Its Enemies* (1945) by Karl Popper, a sustained attack on the historicist thinking of Plato, Hegel, and Marx. This book, in my eyes at least, amounted to no less than an attempt to dismiss cultural historicist thinking itself, along with the role of disruption in social change.[1]

Though the book was widely praised at the time, by authors as diverse as Gilbert Ryle, Bertrand Russell, and Sidney Hook, I considered the attacks on Plato, and especially Hegel, to be little better than cheap propaganda. As I was unaware of Hook's praise of the book, I did not know he had already conceded that Popper's treatment of Hegel was "downright abusive" and "demonstrably false."[2]

Today it is quite widely recognized that the book's arguments are seriously flawed, even that its methods (to quote Walter Kaufman) "are unfortunately similar to those of totalitarian 'scholars'—and . . . spreading in the free world, too."[3] But it is still widely praised, as one of the Modern Library Board's one hundred best nonfiction books of the twentieth century. And it still underlies the aggressive ideological liberalism that has remained the cultural underpinning of a U.S. foreign policy while a cool war against China begins again to heat up.[4]

More importantly, I must confess that in my distaste for Popper, I overreacted and became for two or three years what you might call a Hegelian true believer. My abreaction to Oxford may also help explain my surprising decision, as an un-self-questioning agnostic, to spend a week with a French-Canadian friend, during an Oxford spring break, at a Catholic monastery, La Pierre Qui Vire, in France.[5]

I now look back on Popper's book, and on contemporary books such as *The Captive Mind* by Czeslaw Milosz, as understandable rhetoric from the episteme of the early cultural Cold War in western Europe; and I now identify more clearly with the anti-Soviet cause. In particular, I have always since believed wholeheartedly in an open society, though not as an end in itself but as an opportunity for something more peaceful and just.

More specifically, I have come to concede some merit to Popper's one-sided but defensible and widely shared critique of Plato, as summarized by Gilbert Ryle's approving comment (in a review of Popper's book) that Plato was "Socrates' Judas."[6] And I can see that my own response to Popper, both then and since, is also one-sided, as reflected in this book's inadequate treatment of Socrates, Aristotle, and even Plato's *Republic*. But, perhaps, to engage with the dialectic of cultural history, one has to be somewhat one-sided.

So I will conclude this digression by agreeing with Kaufman's critique of Popper. By ceasing to think about the arc of our cultural development, I see a risk that our current thinking, especially about freedom, risks failing to move forward in needed ways beyond certain eighteenth-century Enlightenment attitudes.

(Among those moving beyond reductive scientism, I have been happy to discover Karl Popper himself, with his idea of a "World 3"—the products of thought—interacting with "World 1"—the world of physical objects and events—through the mediation of "World 2"—the world of individual mental processes. Popper's World 3 exhibits similarities with the evolutionary noosphere of Teilhard de Chardin, which I identify with in chapter 1.[7] The historic evolutions of Popper's World 3 and Teilhard's noosphere approximate to my notion of ethogeny.)

What we Westerners tend to lack today is not just a more insightful appreciation of the heritage that has made us what we are, but also the ability, where needed, to deeply criticize that heritage (its millennia of latent or active xenophobic anti-Semitism, for example). To move beyond cold war, our great need is not just to liberate ourselves from our history but also to see, and hopefully guide, history's own persistent momentum toward this liberation. One way to see this book, in short, is as my belated and one-sided response to Karl Popper.

After further reflection, I have come to believe that Popper was not just an idiosyncratic outlier. On the contrary, he was indeed representative of the mindset into which I was being initiated. Defined by its opposition to both fascism and communism, that postwar mindset, still englobing us, had become complacently biased on the cultural level against *any* magnanimous ambitions for major social change on the political level. I now see that bias reflected, for example, in the works of my teacher Isaiah Berlin, another true minder along with Popper, as a failure to sustain the creative momentum of the Enlightenment at its original creative best.

My teaching years were bookended by two Popper-friendly works: Daniel Bell's *The End of Ideology* (1960) and Francis Fukuyama's *The End of History* (1992). But I saw that insane complacency as partly responsible for the needless bloodshed of the Vietnam War, quickly followed by the 1965 U.S.-assisted massacre in Indonesia, my horror at which inspired my poetic trilogy *Seculum*.[8]

Knowing that in this enmindment book I was out of my depth, I decided from the outset to write "a poem in prose" and allowed myself, as in my poetry, to be guided in my explorations by my intuitions. I was hoping that this history of enmindment would develop as a prose analogue to my trilogy *Seculum*, comprising the books *Coming to Jakarta: A Poem about Terror*, *Listening to the Candle: A Poem on Impulse*, and *Minding the Darkness: A Poem for the Year 2000*. Those three prepositions—*about, on,* and *for*—reflected a Hegelian process from the discursive (yang) back to the impulsive (yin), followed by an attempt at synthesis (yang and yin are prominent in the third volume, and echoed in its title).

By the third volume, I was explicitly trying to reconcile these yang and yin elements in myself and in my culture. Not until I was composing chapter 2 of this book did I realize that I was explicitly returning to that same forgotten ambivalence between yang "golden ages" of enlightenment and yin dark ages of endarkenment (we have seen that there were more than one). Already in *Candle* I had written that that poem "meditates at the margins of language and consciousness, for 'endarkenment' as well as 'enlightenment.'"[9] And already in *Darkness*, after the great Berkeley firestorm of 1991, I had written

> I believe in enmindment
> the translation of light
> into awareness of the dark[10]

Later, in *Deep Politics and the Death of JFK* (1993), I wrote,

> In my poetry I take issue with the Enlightenment contempt for poetry and religion; I propose that, in the spirit of Dante or the *Tao Te Ching*, we should move instead toward a deeper Enmindment that respects the truths of darkness, as well as those of light.[11]

I naively assumed that I was alone in my use of the two terms "endarkenment" and "enmindment." But the New Age theologian Matthew Fox has since "called for more 'endarkenment' as a corrective to our too intense involvement with 'enlightenment.'"[12] By the year 2007 the *Guardian* could refer, disparagingly but prophetically, to the current "age of endarkenment."[13] And in 2010 the term received a lengthier and more balanced examination in *Psychology Today*.[14]

The *Oxford English Dictionary* recognizes the verbs *endarken* and *enmind* (along with *enlight*, citing all three as obsolete), but it does not the two corresponding nouns.[15] If there is merit to this book's treatment of the present—as evidenced in our present's misremembering of its past—then perhaps someday both nouns will soon be there too.

Today there is an ugly drama in our media of a global political retrogression toward outmoded styles of violent autocracy. It is not at all clear whether this political regression will be a short-term interruption of history, like so many before it, or a long-term and generative redirection of it. But behind the ugly headlines in the media we can perceive a cultural shift, difficult to summarize in headlines, that guarantees there will be generative ethogenical change.

Will that change contribute to the continuing long-term mitigation of political violence? The answer to that question will depend in large part on the responses of states and similar established institutions, and to the initiatives of poets and other dedicated minders, more and more of them in the streets.

Four Poems

PRESENCE

For Robert and Rebecca Tracy

i

In the corner of a field not ploughed
        where small trees were beginning to grow
    a well-worn horseshoe

In the flattened area
        next to the mossy grinding rock
    a pierced bone bead

and yes, in that chipping ground
        up behind Yosemite
    in the High Sierra

imperfect arrowheads
        amid the blaze
    of glinting obsidian flakes

We who can appreciate
        the works of say Hölderlin
    or the *Nimrod* of Elgar

the great enterprise to hunt down
        in art the ineffable
    should not forget that

at unexpected moments
        one can still feel and hear
    even in an abandoned field

269

what I can only call
        the presence
    albeit transitory

of something else

ii

Albeit transitory!
        the shoe nailed to the lintel
    of the old shed that by now

must have collapsed
        the bead strung on a necklace
    by a young woman

who lost it long before she died
        the arrowheads
    as I had given my word

left where they were

iii

Just as cosmic space
        is knowable
    by those specks of light

at great distance from each other
        that we see again
    when not in cities

so the long stretch of life
        reveals its curvature
    by those widely separated

moments when we are
        brushed
    by this awareness

of an Other
that we do not know

MORENESS

This is a biosphere
of moreness

Just as the cardinal flower
    has a throat that fits
    the length of the hummingbird bill

so an electron is precisely
    the interactions in its field
    and we who at first

care only for ourselves
    only become human
    from interactions with others

I think this is why Moshe
    taught us to love God   Deut. 6:5
    with all of our heart

and all of our soul
    and all of our *meod*   מְאֹד
    which when I meditate

I am quite sure means
    what I sense just then merging
    with the world around me

and which I can only describe
as moreness

ii

I need to be clear about this
    Meod in dictionaries is defined   מְאֹד
    as *force* or *muchness* or *abundance*

But what I mean
    is not that force of id
    which troubled me for decades

as a Buddhist I used to think
    escape from that self
    was into non-being

but now I am content to pass
        into the space of moreness
    that way less than electric field

where I stood beside Maylie
        cooking in the bunkhouse
    after picking apricots all day

and where I first saw
        my four-pound daughter Cassie
    cupped in a nurse's hand

and where I shared with a friend
        a low smoky sunrise
    from a mountain top in Tennessee

what I still feel when Ronna
        asleep in bed
    stirs when I think of rising

and drapes her arm across me

                       iii

Our need as humans—
to be more than we are

People have to get it
the universe is not as Newton

is said to have imagined
a timeless clockwork

it has a history
and like ourselves

and our thin sliver of ethogeny
is getting somewhere

DEEP MOVEMENTS

Earth! You seem so solid
      when I plant my feet squarely
   to pick up the newspaper

but this morning because there is sun
      I am reminded
   that it rises now

not over the Boder-Billings' driveway
      but two houses further south
   in Susan Blew's redwoods

earth's slanted axis saving us
      from eternal rainless summer
   a cyclical movement

too slow for most of us
      ever to discern
   like the erratic cycle through time

of rising and collapsing empires
      behind which one deeper shift
   appears not to be cyclical—

the entropic spread
      of the drifting cosmos
   after the big bang

or the violent disruption
      of decaying cultures
   to make space for new ones

like the end of the Bronze Age
      the collapse of Babylon and Mycenae
   with those quarreling rapist gods

remembered in Homer
      along with Linear B
   restricted to palace sites

clearing a permanent space
      for the spread of monotheism
   and demotic alphabets

as with the collapse of Rome
    a further clearing
    when the torrent of invading Vandals

after sacking Mainz and Trier
    put a final end
    to that practice (which could only

have been developed and refined
    by a slave-owning city)
    of watching for entertainment

gladiators be killed

MYTHOGENESIS

The OED defines
both mythopoeia and mythogenesis
as the same: *the creation of myths*

This is to tell the OED
the two are not the same
but different aspects of creation

For mythopoeia think Tolkien
or the example of Salome
who according to Matthew
danced at Herod's court
instructed by her mother
and was rewarded with what she desired
John the Baptist's head   Matt. 14:8

From this Wilde's drama
had Salome kiss the head
Huysmans described her
as *the Beast of the Apocalypse*
and Strauss added
from another source
the Dance of the Seven Veils

this was conscious myth-making
which we expect from art
in a secular era

but in mythogenesis
the mind does not make something up
something occurs to it
or maybe just happens in it
in response perhaps
to the purposive needs of DNA

as in the case
of my artless
former student

who told me her most memorable
moment at university

had been when I was lecturing
on Dante's *Paradiso*
and a white dove
flew into the classroom
remembering the event
I replied to her
it was not the *Paradiso*
and I was certain the bird had been
a brown California towhee

undaunted she replied
in total confidence
Oh no Professor Scott
it was a white dove

like peasants recalling
the miracles of St. Martin
for Sulpicius Severus

may this help us
be more understanding of
if not sympathetic to

the dawn of a Dark Age

Notes

NOTE ABOUT THE COVER IMAGE

1. From 1204 to 1261, after the Fourth Crusade conquered and looted Constantinople, it served as a Roman Catholic cathedral.

2. See chapter 8. The costly construction of St. Peter's Basilica in Rome from 1503 to 1513 coincided with the Reformation it helped provoke, a comparable downturn in the predominant power of the Roman Catholic Church.

3. The new mosaic of the Virgin and Child was accompanied by a polemical inscription, now partially destroyed: "The images which the imposters [i.e., the Iconoclasts] had cast down here pious emperors have again set up."

INTRODUCTION

1. As is implicit in the original and etymological meaning of "revolution," a "turning around."

2. *Collins Dictionary*. Cf. Allyson Chiu, "Do Dreams Mean Anything? Why Do I Feel Like I'm Falling? Or Wake Up Paralyzed? We Asked Experts," *Washington Post*, November 4, 2021: "Dreams are a type of *mentation*, or mental activity, that occurs when people are asleep and generally consists of vivid, hallucinatory visual content that is often bizarre or has irregular narratives." Cf. also Dale Purves et al., *Neuroscience* (Sunderland, MA: Sinauer Associates, 2001), https://www.ncbi.nlm.nih .gov/books/NBK10964/#:~:text=The%20ability%20to%20forget%20unimportant ,the%20normal%20erasure%20of%20information: "The ability to forget unimportant information may be as critical for normal mentation as retaining information that is significant."

3. Czeslaw Milosz, *The Witness of Poetry* (Cambridge, MA: Harvard University Press, 1983), 109.

4. *Collaborative International Dictionary of English*.

5. E.g., Simone Weil, *Venice Saved* (London: Bloomsbury Academic, 2019): "Yes, we are dreaming. Men of action and enterprise are dreamers; they prefer dream to reality. But they use arms to make others dream their dreams." Here and elsewhere

Weil links dreaming to what I call our human "moreness": our need to be more than we are. "Moreness," like "Minding," was an early title for this book.

6. The *Oxford English Dictionary* dates the current use of the noun "intellectual" "from the late 19th cent. often with mildly disparaging connotations of elitism and probably influenced by the use at that time of French *intellectuel* to denote any of the culturally minded supporters of Alfred Dreyfus." For early use of "intelligentsia," it cites the *Times* (London), October 16, 1886: "Another wonderful resource of Russian writers . . . is the denunciation of the Bulgarian 'Intelligentsia,' which means all the intelligent classes of the country, with their corrupting ideas from Western Europe, as being responsible for the misdirected and anti-Russian temper of 'the people.'"

7. Colin Loader, "Free Floating: The Intelligentsia in the Work of Alfred Weber and Karl Mannheim," *German Studies Review* 20, no. 2 (1997): 223.

8. Loader, "Free Floating," 225.

9. In both books, I follow and cite the view of Iain McGilchrist that "the left hemisphere tends to deal more with pieces of information in isolation, and the right hemisphere with the entity as a whole, the so-called *Gestalt*." Iain McGilchrist, *The Master and His Emissary: The Divided Brain and the Making of the Western World* (New Haven, CT: Yale University Press, 1919], 4.

10. C. S. Lewis, *The Pilgrim's Regress* (Grand Rapids, MI: Eerdmans, 1943), 202, emphasis added.

11. Tania Lombrozo, "The Truth about the Left Brain/Right Brain Relationship," NPR, December 2, 2013, www.npr.org/sections/13.7/2013/12/02/248089436/the -truth-about-the-left-brain-right-brain-relationship. Cf. Harry K. S. Chung, Jacklyn C. Y. Leung, Vienne M. Y. Wong, and Janet H. Hsiao, "When Is the Right Hemisphere Holistic and When Is It Not? The Case of Chinese Character Recognition," *Cognition* 178 (September 2018): 50–56, https://pubmed.ncbi.nlm.nih.gov/29775858/#:~: text=Holistic%20processing%20(HP)%20has%20long,LVF)%2FRH%20processing %20advantages: "Holistic processing (HP) has long been considered a characteristic of right hemisphere (RH) processing. Indeed, holistic face processing is typically associated with left visual field (LVF)/RH processing advantages."

12. Peter Dale Scott, *Ecstatic Pessimist: Czeslaw Milosz, Poet of Catastrophe and Hope* (Lanham, MD: Rowman & Littlefield, 2023), 227–29.

13. T. S. Eliot, *Notes towards the Definition of Culture* (New York: Harcourt Brace, 1949), 26. Philip Larkin's "Aubade," by this definition, was deficient in culture.

14. Eliot, *Notes towards the Definition of Culture*, 85.

15. George Orwell, "Culture and Classes," *Observer*, November 28, 1948, 4.

16. Eliot, *Notes towards the Definition of Culture*, 32, emphasis in original.

17. Milosz, *The Witness of Poetry*, 14; discussion in Scott, *Ecstatic Pessimist*, 217–19.

18. Eliot, *Notes towards the Definition of Culture*, 28. Culture is grounded in the prevailing human need for a God, as someone either to express thanks to, or alternatively to pray to.

19. Jason Crawford lists thirteen, beginning with Bernard Stiegler's *The Re-Enchantment of the World*, Gordon Graham's *The Re-enchantment of the World*, Silvia Federici's *Re-enchanting the World*, and Joshua Landy and Michael Saler's *The*

Re-Enchantment of the World; Crawford, "The Trouble with Re-Enchantment," *Los Angeles Review of Books*, September 7, 2020, https://lareviewofbooks.org/article/the -trouble-with-re-enchantment). Crawford's list does not include the prototype book by Morris Berman, *The Reenchantment of the World* (Ithaca, NY: Cornell University Press, 1981), which announced an "end of the Newtonian age."

20. W. A. Meeks, *The First Urban Christians: The Social World of the Apostle Paul* (New Haven, CT: Yale University Press, 2003), 73.

21. The term *post-truth* was named Oxford Dictionaries' "Word of the Year" in 2016, after the term's proliferation in the 2016 U.S. presidential election and the Brexit referendum in the United Kingdom.

22. Jürgen Habermas, "Notes on Post-Secular Society," *New Perspectives Quarterly* 25, no. 4 (2008): 17–29, https://www.resetdoc.org/story/a-post-secular-society -what-does-that-mean.

23. Charles Taylor, *A Secular Age* (Cambridge, MA: Belknap, 2007), 22: "Western modernity, including its secularity, is the fruit of new inventions, newly constructed self-understandings and related practices, and can't be explained in terms of perennial features of human life."

24. Czeslaw Milosz, "If There Is No God," in *Second Space* (New York: Ecco, 2004), 5.

25. Milosz, *The Witness of Poetry*, 109.

26. Peter Dale Scott, *Ecstatic Pessimist: Czeslaw Milosz, Poet of Catastrophe and Hope (*Lanham, MD: Rowman & Littlefield, 2023), 7–8, 33.

27. Czeslaw Milosz, *The Witness of Poetry* (Cambridge, MA: Harvard University Press, 1983), 69; Octavio Paz, *Children of the Mire: Modern Poetry from Romanticism to the Avant-garde*(Cambridge, Mass., Harvard University Press, 1974), 1. Cf. Michael Palmer, *Active Boundaries: Selected Essays and Talks* (New York: New Directions, 2008), 106, etc. RRR

28. Czeslaw Milosz, *The Captive Mind* (New York: Vintage, 1990), v.

29. *Ecstatic Pessimist*, 7–8, 33.

30. Czeslaw Milosz, *The Land of Ulro* (New York: Farrar, Straus & Giroux, 1985), 94

31. Milosz, *The Land of Ulro*, 94.

32. Milosz, *The Land of Ulro*, 275.

33. Martin Luther King, "Speech to the Fourth Continental Convention of the AFL-CIO, 1961": "I'm convinced that we shall overcome because the arc of the universe is long but it bends toward justice."

34. Soviet-style oppression of religion in Russia has subsided but is still active against foreign missionaries, in particular against Jehovah's Witnesses. There have also been oppressive campaigns against Muslims in Chechnya and Dagestan, though religious issues there are only part of the story.

35. From the *Oxford English Dictionary* (henceforward *OED*): "Episteme, *n*. Scientific knowledge, a system of understanding; *spec.* "(Foucault's term for) the body of ideas which shape the perception of knowledge in a particular period." This book could be summarized, one-sidedly, as a survey of shifts in epistemes since antiquity.

36. Not all cultural development exhibits this pattern. Societies and their cultures can sicken when their conditions of life become too adverse, as in the case of the Norse Greenlanders in the fifteenth century, once thought to have died out because they could not adapt to the loss of sustenance from the so-called Little Ice Age. A more complex recent consensus is that these colonies in Greenland were "doomed by 'fatal Norse conservatism in the face of fluctuating resources'"; Eli Kintisch, "Why Did Greenland's Vikings Disappear?," *Science*, November 10, 2016, https://www.sciencemag.org/news/2016/11/why-did-greenland-s-vikings-disappear.

37. *Oxford English Dictionary*, s.v., emphasis added.

38. Cf. Peter Dale Scott with Freeman Ng, *Poetry and Terror: Politics and Poetics in "Coming to Jakarta"* (Lanham, MD: Lexington Books, 2018), 185.

39. "Man, in his moral nature, becomes, in his progress through life, a creature of prejudice, a creature of opinions, a creature of habits, and of sentiments growing out of them. These form our second nature, as inhabitants of the country and members of the society in which Providence has placed us." Edmund Burke, *Edmund Burke: Selected Writings and Speeches*, ed. Peter Stanlis (New York: Doubleday, Anchor, 1963), 494.

40. The nonspecific term *moreness* includes more familiar notions, such as metta (loving-kindness), compassion, and selfless love.

41. Robert Faggen, "The Art of Poetry No. 70," *Paris Review*, Winter 1994, emphasis in original, https://www.theparisreview.org/interviews/1721/czeslaw-milosz-the-art-of-poetry-no-70-czeslaw-milosz.

42. Xu Jilin, "The New Tianxia: Rebuilding China's Internal and External Order," trans. Mark McConaghy, Tang Xiaobing, and David Ownby, Reading the China Dream, https://www.readingthechinadream.com/xu-jilin-the-new-tianxia.html.

43. In truth, there can be no exact translation. Western values, unlike Chinese (or Jewish) mores, are more sharply divided between those that are enforced by public law and those (including religious values) that are regarded as private. It is helpful here to look at the ongoing discussion of John Rawls's concept of an "overlapping consensus" as a secular basis for human rights, and the post-secular expansion of it to give "religious believers their fair share in the collective task of determining the future moral trajectory of Western societies"; Ulrike Spohn, "A Difference in Kind? Jürgen Habermas and Charles Taylor on Post-secularism," *European Legacy* 20, no. 2 (2015): 120. This entire volume, like my comments here, can be read as a prolegomenon to that post-secular perspective.

44. The so-called Qing golden age, like the so-called golden ages of Greece, Rome, Spain, etc., was, as this book will argue, a period in which the dominant classes flourished, but very much at the expense of those they enslaved. See, e.g., chapter 7.

45. Xu Jilin, "The New Tianxia."

46. See Zhao Tingyang, *All under Heaven: The Tianxia System for a Possible World Order* (Berkeley: University of California Press, 2021), where the prospect of *tianxia* is compared to the Kantian dream of universal peace. For the ethogeny or cultural evolution of the term, see Wang Ban, ed., *Chinese Visions of World Order: Tianxia, Culture, and World Politics* (Durham, NC: Duke University Press, 2017).

47. A "mindset" (dated by the *OED* to 1909) is hopefully not truly "set"; it is, or should be, in process as its spirit develops.

48. *OED*, emphasis added.

49. *OED*.

50. In the sense defined in the *OED* as "the state, condition, or character of a town or city; urban life."

51. See chapter 10.

52. Xu Jilin, "The New Tianxia." As translated, Xu's statement is problematic. Early Judaism showed concern for the whole of humanity, but its concern was not universal.

53. Bei Dao, *Forms of Distance*, trans. David Hinton (New York: New Directions, 1993), 53. For another example, see Ha Jin, "Ways," in *Between Silences: A Voice from China*, by Ha Jin (Chicago: University of Chicago Press, 1990), 63.

54. "One of the striking things about Martin Luther's vision of the Christian life is its utter simplicity. Against the background of medieval piety, with its myriad holy orders, its penances, and its pilgrimages, Luther presented a Christianity for everyone." Carl R. Trueman, "Keep It Simple Stupid: Martin Luther on the Christian Life," Crossway, October 29, 2014, https://www.crossway.org/articles/keep-it-simple-stupid-martin-luther-on-the-christian-life.

55. Wang Yangming would later criticize those who "waste their time competing with one another writing flowery compositions in order to win acclaim in their age, and . . . no longer comprehend conduct that honors what is fundamental, esteems what is real, reverts to simplicity, and returns to purity." Justin Tiwald and Bryan W. Van Norden, eds., *Readings in Later Chinese Philosophy* (Indianapolis: Hackett, 2014), 275.

56. Possibly by mass starvation if major steps are not taken swiftly to moderate climate change. See, for example, World Food Program, "Act Now on Climate Crisis or Millions More Will Be Pushed into Hunger and Famine," November 18, 2021, https://www.wfp.org/stories/act-now-climate-crisis-or-millions-more-will-be-pushed-hunger-and-famine. Cf. chapter 9.

57. Martin Luther King, "The Significant Contributions of Jeremiah to Religious Thought" (student essay, Crozer Theological Seminary, 1948), https://kinginstitute.stanford.edu/king-papers/documents/significant-contributions-jeremiah-religious-thought.

58. One can see a parallel distinction in Hannah Arendt's contrast between power and violence. Arendt, *On Violence* (New York, Harcourt, Brace & World, 1970), 35–36.

59. "Inequality has been written into the DNA of civilization ever since humans first settled down to farm the land. Throughout history, only massive, violent shocks that upended the established order proved powerful enough to flatten disparities in income and wealth. They appeared in four different guises: mass-mobilization warfare, violent and transformative revolutions, state collapse, and catastrophic epidemics. Hundreds of millions perished in their wake, and by the time these crises had passed, the gap between rich and poor had shrunk." Walter Scheidel, "The Only Thing, Historically, That's Curbed Inequality: Catastrophe," *The Atlantic*, February

21, 2017, https://www.theatlantic.com/business/archive/2017/02/scheidel-great
-leveler-inequality-violence/517164. Cf. Walter Scheidel, *The Great Leveler: Violence and the History of Inequality from the Stone Age to the Twenty-First Century* (Princeton, NJ: Princeton University Press, 2017).

60. In the course of time, I came to chant on awakening the first two of these, starting with the Tisarana. I felt this was a practice that reinforced the yin context of my yang thinking. As the content of the words became more and more familiar, I tried to meld the meaning of my words with the yin-minded act of chanting itself.

61. Emile Durkheim, as translated in Robert N. Bellah, *Religion in Human Evolution: From the Paleolithic to the Axial Age* (Cambridge, MA: Belknap, 2011), 1, emphasis added.

62. Cf. Isa. 1:17, 55:6–9, Jer. 7:5–7; Amos 5:114–15; Mic. 6:8; Zech. 6:4–7:14. In the last decade, social scientists have mounted a series of attacks on Jaspers's notion of an "axial age," accusing him of cherry-picking details from a too restricted number of cultures. I have read only one such study: Laura Spinney, "When Did Societies Become Modern? 'Big History' Dashes Popular Idea of Axial Age," *Nature*, December 9, 2019, https://www.nature.com/articles/d41586-019-03785-w. After finishing a draft of this book, I see the *Nature* article as a misguided attempt to analyze a yin (unmeasurable) notion using yang (quantifiable) techniques. See next section.

63. Only recently did I discover that writers on organizational theory have also used yin and yang to characterize the notion that "potential paradoxical values coexist in any culture and they give rise to, exist within, reinforce, and complement each other to shape the holistic, dynamic, and dialectical nature of culture"; Tony Fang, "Yin Yang: A New Perspective on Culture," *Management and Organization Review* 8, no. 1 (2012): 25–50, https://onlinelibrary.wiley.com/doi/full/10.1111/j.1740-8784 .2011.00221.x. Cf. Peter Ping Li, "Toward a Geocentric Framework of Trust: An Application to Organizational Trust," *Management and Organization Review* 4, no. 3 (2008): 413–39, https://www.researchgate.net/publication/228215800_Toward_a _Geocentric_Framework_of_Trust_An_Application_to_Organizational_Trust: "The tenet of 'holistic duality' posits that a phenomenon or entity cannot be complete unless it has two opposite elements."

64. See chapter 7.

65. Stephen Greenblatt, *The Swerve: How the World Became Modern* (New York: Norton, 2011), 94.

66. Charles Freeman, *The Closing of the Western Mind: The Rise of Faith and the Fall of Reason* (New York: Knopf, 2003), 202–3, xix.

67. Freeman, *The Closing of the Western Mind*, 215. Cf. Peter Brown, *Power and Persuasion in Late Antiquity: Towards a Christian Empire* (Madison: University of Wisconsin Press, 1992), 16–17.

68. Sulpicius actually wrote that Martin, "jealously maintaining his own poverty," refused Valentinian's many offers of gifts, "as he did on all similar occasions." Sulpicius Severus, *Dialogues* 2.5, https://www.newadvent.org/fathers/35032.htm.

69. Freeman, *The Closing of the Western Mind*, 245; citing Philip Rousseau, *Ascetics, Authority, and the Church in the Age of Jerome and Cassian* (Oxford: Oxford

University Press, 1978), 152. Rousseau's work relies in turn on the *Life of St. Martin* by Sulpicius Severus (chapter 24).

70. "Martin was not popular amongst aristocratic bishops." Marilyn Dunn, *The Emergence of Monasticism: From the Desert Fathers to the Early Middle Ages* (Oxford: Blackwell, 2000), 63.

71. I would have liked to call the Christianity attributed to Martin "primitive" or "apostolic" Christianity, but these epithets are claimed by all elements of the Catholic Church, the lofty as well as the lowly. Bede, for example, chooses to tell us that as soon as the top-down papal mission of Bishop Augustine of Canterbury and his monks arrived in Kent, "they began to follow the apostolical life of the primitive church." Bede, *Ecclesiastical History of the English Church*, 1.26.

72. Cf. Michel Foucault's distinction between "deductive" and violent sovereign power and its gradual partial replacement by a more life-oriented "biopower." Foucault, *History of Sexuality*, trans. Robert Hurley, vol. 1 (New York: Pantheon), 1978), 137.

73. Peter Brown, *Through the Eye of a Needle: Wealth, the Fall of Rome, and the Making of Christianity in the West, 350–550 AD* (Princeton, NJ: Princeton University Press, 2014).

74. Brown, *Through the Eye of a Needle*, xxiii, emphasis added.

75. Two chapters each are devoted to Ambrose and Paulinus, one to Jerome, and no less than six to Augustine.

76. Augustine, *City of God*, 1:10: "Thus our Paulinus, bishop of Nola, who voluntarily abandoned vast wealth and became quite poor, though abundantly rich in holiness, when the barbarians sacked Nola, and took him prisoner, used silently to pray, as he afterwards told me, 'O Lord, let me not be troubled for gold and silver, for where all my treasure is You know.'" Cf. Augustine, Letter 27.2.

77. Brown, *Through the Eye of a Needle*, 51, 215, 217. The third repeats a quote in the vita from Martin that Paulinus "is someone to imitate." The second records only that Paulinus "had met Martin and even been cured of an infection of the eye by him." This cure, perhaps the very least miraculous of the feats for which Martin was venerated in his lifetime, is often the only one recorded by modern historians because it is the only one reported from not one but two contemporary sources.

Brown's historicist methods scant Martin even more strikingly in his companion volume, *The Rise of Western Christendom: Triumph and Diversity, A.D. 200–1000* (Malden, MA: Blackwell, 2003). Here Martin, while alive, though clearly very relevant, merits mention on only two pages; his tomb at Tours (a pilgrimage site after 460) merits eight.

78. Brown, *Through the Eye of a Needle*, 510.

79. I shall use the much-abused term *myth* in the first sense recognized by the *OED*: "A traditional story, typically involving supernatural beings or forces, which embodies and provides an explanation, aetiology, or justification for something such as the early history of a society, a religious belief or ritual, or a natural phenomenon."

80. J. B. Bury, "The Science of History," in *Selected Essays of J. B. Bury*, ed. Harold Temperley (Cambridge: Cambridge University Press, 1939), 4. Bury's polemical statement, almost immediately contested, targeted nationalist historians like Leopold

von Ranke for privileging so-called golden ages, and philosophers of history like Hegel who contorted bodies of evidence onto a Procrustean bed of theory.

81. Geoffrey Barraclough, *History in a Changing World* (Oxford: Blackwell, 1955).

82. A. L. Rowse, *The Use of History* (New York: Macmillan, 1945), 55. In this spirit, I have written this book as a poem in prose. (It may be relevant that *poema* in Greek and *factum* in Latin both mean the same thing: "something made.")

83. E. H. Carr, *What Is History?* (New York: Vintage, 1961), 23.

84. Prov. 5:15, 19–20.

85. Karl Marx, *The Eighteenth Brumaire of Louis Bonaparte*, trans. Eden Paul and Cedar Paul (London: Allen & Unwin, 1926), 23.

86. Martin Luther King, "Speech to the Fourth Continental Convention of the AFL-CIO," 1961: "I'm convinced that we shall overcome because the arc of the universe is long but it bends toward justice." King was quoting from the abolitionist Unitarian preacher Theodore Parker (d. 1860), controversial in his own day. As we shall see in chapter 12, this providentialist view of metahistory is traceable to St. Augustine.

87. Simone Weil, quoted in Czeslaw Milosz, *The Witness of Poetry* (Cambridge, MA: Harvard University Press, 1983), 114.

88. I will refer to "the Enlightenment" despite the historian J. G. A. Pocock's useful warning that "there is no single or unifiable phenomenon describable as 'the Enlightenment,' but it is the definite article rather than the noun which is to be avoided." Pocock, "Historiography and Enlightenment: A View of Their History," *Modern Intellectual History*, April 2008, 83–84.

89. Jennifer Pitts, *A Turn to Empire: The Rise of Imperial Liberalism in Britain and France* (Princeton, NJ: Princeton University Press, 2005), 1. Pitts kindly does not mention that Mill's *On Liberty* was written in 1867, when Parliament was seriously considering outlawing the opium traffic, and that it can only too easily be read as an impassioned last-ditch defense of the East India Company's lucrative opium trade.

90. Pitts, *A Turn to Empire*, 139–40; citing *Collected Works of John Stuart Mill* (Toronto: University of Toronto Press, 1963–1991), 10:123, 120; 18:272:

> Mill resisted racial or biological determinism, and he emphasized that national characters were mutable over time, even in unexpected directions. Still, he tended to describe national characters through a series of dichotomies—advanced-backward, active-passive, industrious-sensuous, sober-excitable—and to assign the more flattering labels predominantly to the English and Germans, and the latter to the Irish, French, southern Europeans, and "Orientals" (with characters deteriorating as one moved south and east). . . . Mill . . . settled for classifications that enabled him to group "the native states of India" with "savage life" in which "there is little or no law," "no commerce, no manufactures, no agriculture, or next to none." He declared in *On Liberty*, "The greater part of the world has, properly speaking, no history, because the despotism of Custom is complete. This is the case over the whole East."

91. Karl Marx, "The Future Results of British Rule in India," *New York Daily Tribune*, August 8, 1853, https://marxists.architexturez.net/archive/marx/works/1853/07/22.htm.

92. For Guinea-Bissau, see Rachel Maddow, *Blowout: Corrupted Democracy, Rogue State Russia, and the Richest, Most Destructive Industry on Earth* (New York: Random House, 2019). If I should get to write my second volume, it might get to look more closely at that mindset, and in particular how secular neoliberalism, in the name of "development," has invaded the cultural space of believing nations and dialectically spawned monsters, like al-Qaeda and ISIS.

93. Peter Dale Scott, "Talks at the Yenan Forum," in *Crossing Borders* (New York: New Directions, 1995), 61.

CHAPTER ONE

1. Peter Dale Scott, "Confession," in *Mosaic Orpheus* (Montreal: McGill-Queen's University Press, 2009), 39, https://www.flashpointmag.com/mosaicof.htm.

2. Thomas Merton, "Monastic Experience and East-West Dialogue" (notes for a paper to have been delivered at Calcutta, October 1968), in *The Asian Journal of Thomas Merton*, ed. Naomi Burton and James Laughlin (New York: New Directions, 1973), 313.

3. Jürgen Habermas, "Notes on a Post-secular Society," *Sign and Sight*, June 18, 2008, https://www.signandsight.com/features/1714.html.

4. *The Intimate Merton: His Life from His Journals*, ed. Patrick Hart and Jonathan Montaldo (San Francisco: HarperSanFrancisco, 1999), 116.

5. Robert N. Bellah, *Religion in Human Evolution: From the Paleolithic to the Axial Age* (Cambridge, MA: Belknap, 2011), 1. Cf. Emile Durkheim, *Les formes élémentaires de la vie religieuse, le système totémique en Australie* (Paris: F. Alcan, 1912). Bellah's inclusion of "beliefs" in his translation has been challenged by Gavin Flood, *Religion and the Philosophy of Life* (Oxford: Oxford University Press, 2019), 19.

6. Karl Jaspers, *The Origin and Goal of History* (London: Routledge and K. Paul, 1953), 7. Jaspers's book has since been faulted for reflecting "the traditional fiction of three totally unrelated peoples and traditions [Greek, Indian, Chinese] as 'cultural islands' that had absolutely no contact of any kind with each other until much later times"; Christopher I. Beckwith, *Greek Buddha: Pyrrho's Encounter with Early Buddhism in Central Asia* (Princeton, NJ: Princeton University Press, 2015], ix. Beckwith adds in a footnote, however, "that Jaspers's book is nevertheless very insightful and is still worth reading today."

7. Bellah, *Religion in Human Evolution*, 266.

8. Bellah, *Religion in Human Evolution*, 312.

9. Bellah, *Religion in Human Evolution*, 271; quoting S. N. Eisenstadt, introduction to *The Origins and Diversity of the Axial Age*, ed. Eisenstadt (Albany: State University of New York Press, 1986), 1.

10. In the Deuteronomic Sh'ma, significantly, the recitation is an act of unequivocal commitment to divine authority rather than to any other. The violent tribulations of the last century, akin to the cultural disruptions of the Axial Age, have created situations where this separation of spiritual from temporal authority again became a

priority. One such situation was in the 1960s and 1970s, when America, a predomi-
nantly Christian country, was waging an aggressive war against Buddhist Vietnam.
At this time, a number of peace-loving North Americans, including Gary Snyder and
myself, began for the first time to practice Buddhism. Though I may not have been
mindful of it then, it is hard now not to see this act as a significant expression of
diminished faith in the aggressive authority of a dominant and increasingly militant
Western civilization.

11. And on prophets over priests. The succeeding pivotal shifts retain this hierarchy.

12. Bellah, *Religion in Human Evolution*, 269.

13. "Research . . . has concluded that Deuteronomy probably began to be composed
in the seventh century BC albeit using older material, and that it did not reach its final
form until after the exile (i.e., late sixth to early fifth century BC)." James D. G. Dunn
and John W. Rogerson, eds., *Eerdmans Commentary on the Bible* (Grand Rapids,
MI: Eerdmans, 2003), 153.

14. Sally Mallam, "Judaism," Human Journey, https://humanjourney.us/ideas-that
-shaped-our-modern-world-section/axial-age-religions-judaism.

15. Cf. Isa. 1:11. Normally in this book I quote from the King James Version,
for reasons I explain in chapter 6. Here, however, I have relied on clearer and more
admonitory translations used in the Yom Kippur service of atonement and asking
forgiveness.

16. Bellah, *Religion in Human Evolution*, 266.

17. Bruno Snell, *The Discovery of the Mind: In Greek Philosophy and Literature*
(New York: Dover, 1982). For example, Achilles in book 1, on orders from Athena,
curbs his anger at Agamemnon (*Iliad* 1:188–221).

18. Julian Jaynes gives other examples in the *Iliad* of this possession from
below: "It is not Ajax who is zealous to fight but his *thumos* (13:73); nor is it Aeneas
who rejoices but his *thumos* (13:494; see also 14:156)"; Jaynes, *The Origin of Con-
sciousness in the Breakdown of the Bicameral Mind* (Boston: Houghton Mifflin,
1976), 262. The main thesis of Jaynes's controversial book is that the response of
Iliadic heroes to divine voices reflects the actual hallucinatory condition of warriors
in that preconscious era, akin to the plea of insane murderers today that they killed
because a voice told them to. See chapter 3.

19. Cf. discussion in Peter Dale Scott with Freeman Ng, *Poetry and Terror: Politics
and Poetics in "Coming to Jakarta"* (Lanham, MD: Lexington Books, 2018), 147.

20. Someone else's account of cultural development might emphasize another
feature. For example, Erich Auerbach, in his classic survey *Mimesis*, focused on
developments in realism, "the representation of reality." But I will continue to think
that poets with large ideas play a special role in cultural development, that thus there
is a modicum of truth, at a higher level, in Percy Bysshe Shelley's clumsily overstated
claim that "poets are the unacknowledged legislators of the world." (Defending this
claim in *A Defence of Poetry* [1821, 1840], Shelley wrote that poetry "awakens and
enlarges the mind itself by rendering it the receptacle of a thousand unapprehended
combinations of thought," while "ethical science arranges the elements which poetry
has created," leading to increased civility.)

21. An example is the development of compassion for Aeneas's discarded lover, the Carthaginian queen Dido, as we see in *The Tragedy of Dido* by Christopher Marlowe (d. 1593). Dido's story was treated lightly by the fifth-century grammarian Servius, commenting on the *Aeneid*: "It's all about schemes and subtleties, so that it is virtually in the comic style—no wonder, as it deals with love" (paene comicus stilus est; nec mirum, ubi de amore tractatur). Why comic? Perhaps also because of Aeneas's happy escape for the more serious business of a war that would lead to the founding of Rome? For Dante, of course, Christian love, as personified in Beatrice, the pilgrim Dante's ultimate guide, was precisely what Virgil could not comprehend.

22. My notion of *ethogeny* owes much to both Hegel's and especially Eliot's thoughts on the history of mind. But where Eliot's notion of that history was of a permanent order, unchanged by additions, my notion is of a generative process, with an open future. Cf. Robert Crawford, *Young Eliot: From St. Louis to The Waste Land* (New York: Farrar, Straus and Giroux, 2015), 331-32.

23. Talmud, Shabbat 31a; quoted in Warren Zev Harvey, "Love: The Beginning and the End of Torah," *Tradition: A Journal of Orthodox Thought* 15, no. 4 (1976), https://traditiononline.org/love-the-beginning-and-the-end-of-torah. Similarly, Rabbi Akiva (ca. 50–135 CE) stated that "love thy neighbor as thyself" is "the great rule in the Torah" (*Sifra, Kedoshim* 4:12; *Yer. Nedarim* 9:4; *Gen. Rabbah* 24:7; cf. *Avot de-Rabbi Natan*, version B, 26).

24. Snell, *The Discovery of the Mind*.

25. https://biblehub.com/hebrew/3966.htm.

26. This was fortunate because by then I had written a poem using this translation.

27. "Man, in his moral nature, becomes, in his progress through life, a creature of prejudice, a creature of opinions, a creature of habits, and of sentiments growing out of them. These form our second nature, as inhabitants of the country and members of the society in which Providence has placed us." Edmund Burke, *Edmund Burke: Selected Writings and Speeches*, ed. Peter J. Stanlis (New York: Doubleday, Anchor, 1963), 494.

28. Scott, *Poetry and Terror*, 184.

29. Sigmund Freud, *New Introductory Lectures on Psychoanalysis*, trans. James Strachey (London: Penguin, 1973), 112.

30. Freud, *New Introductory Lectures*, 95–96.

31. Czeslaw Milosz, *The Witness of Poetry* (Cambridge, MA: Harvard University Press, 1983), 37; Czeslaw Milosz, *The Captive Mind* (New York: Vintage International, 1990), 237.

32. Cf. Cassandra Sheppard, "The Neuroscience of Singing," December 11, 2016, https://uplift.love/the-neuroscience-of-singing: "The neuroscience of singing shows that when we sing our neurotransmitters connect in new and different ways. It fires up the right temporal lobe of our brain, releasing endorphins that make us smarter, healthier, happier and more creative. When we sing with other people this effect is amplified. . . . Singing in groups triggers the communal release of serotonin and oxytocin, the bonding hormone, and even synchronises our heart beats." Even chanting alone, I feel altered by binding myself to ancient texts.

33. "The noosphere has grown in step with the organization of the human mass in relation to itself as it populates the Earth. As humanity organizes itself in more complex social networks, the higher the noosphere will grow in awareness. . . . The densest collection of complex information we know of thus far is the human being, and human activity gives rise to even greater complexity. Teilhard states that this reflective consciousness is 'the specific effect of organized complexity,' and that it follows that some sort of intensification of human consciousness is the next step of human evolution" ("The Noosphere [Part I]: Teilhard de Chardin's Vision," https://teilhard .com/2013/08/13/the-noosphere-part-i-teilhard-de-chardins-vision.) See P. Teilhard de Chardin, *The Phenomenon of Man* (London: Collins, 1959). For the biosphere, see Alan Marshall, *The Unity of Nature* (London: Imperial College Press, 2002).

34. Karl W. Deutsch, "Medieval Unity and the Economic Conditions for an International Civilization," *Canadian Journal of Economics and Political Science* 10, no. 1 (1944): 18.

35. Jay Ruud, "Dante and the Jews," in *Jews in Medieval Christendom: Slay Them Not*, ed. Kristine T. Utterback, 147–62 (Leiden: Brill, 2013); Catherine S. Cox, *The Judaic Other in Dante, the Gawain Poet, and Chaucer* (Gainesville: University Press of Florida, 2005).

36. "Innocent III. (Lothario Conti)," *Jewish Encyclopedia* (1906 edition): "He wrote, also, to the Count of Nevers, whom he threatened with excommunication if he continued to protect the Jews (*Epistolæ* x. 120, ed. Baluz., II., p. 123): 'The Jews, like the fratricide Cain, are doomed to wander through the earth as fugitives and vagabonds, and their faces must be covered with shame. They are under no circumstances to be protected by Christian princes; but are, on the contrary, to be condemned to serfdom.'"

CHAPTER TWO

1. An exception: the words in the Italian Bible (Ma liberaci dal male [from the evil]), in contrast, were translated by a humanistic Camaldolese monk (d. 1481).

2. Before the King James Version of 1611, Matthew 6:13 in the Tyndale Bible (1525), like that of Wycliffe (1384) before it, was almost identical: "leede vs not into temptacion: but delyvre vs ffrom yvell." Wycliffe's English Bible, by its mere existence, was such a threat to clerical authority that one could be executed for merely possessing it. His resource was not the Greek but the Latin Vulgate (sed libera nos a malo); Latin does not use a definite article. In contrast, William Tyndale, who was executed in 1536 for heresy, was part of the scholarly Renaissance. Thus he was able to use Erasmus's publication in 1516 of the Greek scriptures, which contained in Matthew 6:13 the phrase "apo tou ponerou, ἀπὸ τοῦ πονηροῦ." I cannot explain why in Tyndale's translation the word "the" was omitted.

3. See Thomas Merton, *Raids on the Unspeakable* (New York: New Directions, 1966); *Conjectures of a Guilty Bystander* (Garden City, NY: Doubleday, 1966). Also Czeslaw Milosz, *Essay on Poetry* (New York: Ecco, 1991).

4. It is now thought that the alleged Sibylline prophecies summarized by Virgil—

> Now comes the last age of the Sibyl's song;
> The great order of ages begins anew.   5
> Now Justice returns, Saturn's Age returns;
> Now a new generation descends from the lofty sky.
> With a new breed of men sent down from heaven. (*Eclogues*
> 4.4–12)—

may have been texts from Hellenized Jews of about the second century BCE, perhaps in Alexandria.

5. Young's Literal Translation has "Thy will come to pass, as in heaven also on the earth."

6. Alfred North Whitehead, *Science and the Modern World* (Cambridge: Cambridge University Press, 1926, 1953), 64.

7. Alfred North Whitehead, *Process and Reality: An Essay in Cosmology* (New York: Free Press, 1929, 1979), 42.

8. Compare also Jesus's first preaching, "Repent: for the kingdom of heaven is at hand" (Matt. 4:17).

9. "Ancient Jewish History: Hellenism," Jewish Virtual Library, https://www.jewishvirtuallibrary.org/hellenism-2.

10. In my ignorance, I can only wonder whether the Mahayanan emphasis on bodhisattvas and healing the world developed in response to Buddhism's loss of status with the collapse of the famous Buddhist king Aśoka's Mauryan Empire in 185 BCE.

11. Josephus, *Antiquities* 15.18.1, 5.

12. Revelation 6:9: "And when he had opened the fifth seal, I saw under the altar the souls of them that were slain for the word of God, and for the testimony which they held."

13. Judaism, in contrast, never encouraged martyrdom. But it does honor the *Aseret hāRūgēi Malk̲ūt̲*, "The Ten Royal Martyrs," who were martyred by the Roman Empire in the period after the destruction of the Second Temple. They are remembered at Yom Kippur.

14. *Passio Sanctarum Perpetuae et Felicitatis* 9; Thomas J. Heffernan, *The Passion of Perpetua and Felicity* (Oxford: Oxford University Press, 2012).

15. Richard Brown, "Analects of Confucius Book 3: I Follow the Zhou!," https://brownbeat.medium.com/analects-of-confucius-book-3-i-follow-the-zhou-d7cc7c9699ab.

16. Robert N. Bellah, *Religion in Human Evolution: From the Paleolithic to the Axial Age* (Cambridge, MA: Belknap, 2011), 399.

17. However, recent scholars such as Michael Nylan and Martin Kern have suggested that Sima Qian's horror stories about the Qin emperor, including the claim that scholars were buried alive, was Han dynasty propaganda designed to slander the Qin dynasty they overthrew. Cf. John King Fairbank and Merle Goldman, *China: A New History* (Cambridge, MA: Belknap, 1998), 62.

18. A. C. Graham, *Disputers of the Tao: Philosophical Argument in Ancient China* (La Salle, IL: Open Court, 1989), 372.

19. Hung Shih-Ti, "The Struggle between 'Emphasizing the Present While Slighting the Past' [Qin] and 'Using the Past to Criticize the Present,'" *Chinese Studies in History* 8, nos. 1–2 (1975): 116–31.

20. Bellah, *Religion in Human Evolution*, 477.

21. For *wen* and *wu*, cf. Yuan-kang Wang, *Harmony and War: Confucian Culture and Chinese Power Politics* (New York: Columbia University Press, 2011), 14; John K. Fairbank, "Varieties of the Chinese Military Experience," in *Chinese Ways in Warfare*, ed. Frank A. Kierman Jr. and John K. Fairbank (Cambridge, MA: Harvard University Press, 1974), 7–9. *Wu* (force, the military) created the first Chinese state, and attempted to extinguish *wen* (civility, Confucianism), but *wen* Confucianism prevailed for a while. This book will consider this ongoing dialectic in the light of the end of the western Roman empire, and of the American political "system."

22. John King Fairbank and Merle Goldman, *China: A New History* (Cambridge, MA: Belknap, 1998), 62.

23. Livia Kohn, *Daoism Handbook* (Leiden: Brill, 2000), 264–66.

24. After a successful rebellion in 184 CE against the Han Empire, the Shanshi Dao movement created a fully independent theocratic state, Zhang Han, in the Hanzhong valley of Sichuan. Kohn, *Daoism Handbook*, 140.

25. Andrew Ollett, *Language of the Snakes: Prakrit, Sanskrit, and the Language Order of Premodern India* (Berkeley: University of California Press, 2017), 12.

26. Kanai Lal Hazra, *Pāli Language and Literature: A Systematic Survey and Historical Study* (New Delhi: D. K. Printworld, 1994), 5.

27. Franklin Edgerton, "The Prakrit Underlying Buddhistic Hybrid Sanskrit," *Bulletin of the School of Oriental Studies* 8, nos. 2–3 (1936): 501–16, 502.

CHAPTER THREE

1. Simon M. McCrea, "Intuition, Insight, and the Right Hemisphere: Emergence of Higher Sociocognitive Functions," *Psychological Research and Behavior Management* 3 (March 2010): 1–39, https://www.ncbi.nlm.nih.gov/pmc/articles/PMC3218761.

2. Kate Horowitz, "Are Left-Handed People Really More Creative?," Mental Floss, August 1, 2019, https://www.mentalfloss.com/article/84560/are-lefties-really-more-creative.

3. Even, as the Chinese noted, the yang of southern flora on the sunny north slopes of canyons, and the yin of northern flora on the shaded south slopes. This can be seen in Big Sur country.

4. Cf. Bruno Snell, *The Discovery of the Mind: In Greek Philosophy and Literature* (New York: Dover, 1982), 31: "Homer's man does not yet regard himself as the source of his decisions . . . he feels his course is shaped by the gods."

5. In saying this, I am questioning Bruno Snell's assertion (*Discovery*, 22) that the Olympian gods in the *Iliad* "constitute a well-ordered and meaningful world." Zeus and Hera in the *Iliad* are capable of the long view, but not a "well-ordered and meaningful one."

6. Julian Jaynes, *The Origin of Consciousness in the Breakdown of the Bicameral Mind* (Boston: Houghton Mifflin, 1976), 72. Later, in response to criticisms of his book, Jaynes defined consciousness as "introspectable mind-space," distinguishing it from cognition.

7. Jaynes, *The Origin of Consciousness*, 365, 366.

8. Jaynes, *The Origin of Consciousness*, 86.

9. Julie Kane, "Poetry as Right-Hemispheric Language," *Journal of Consciousness Studies* 11, nos. 5–6 (2004): 21–59, https://psyartjournal.com/article/show/kane-poetry_as_right_hemispheric_language.

10. I will give here just two examples from the article: (1) "Indeed, one could assert that the degree of right-hemispheric involvement in language is what differentiates 'poetic' or 'literary' from 'referential' or 'technical' speech and texts," and (2) "Ornstein et al. (1979) found that subjects reading technical text produced stronger electroencephalogram (EEG) signals from their left than from their right hemispheres, indicative of greater brain activity in the former region, while the effect was reversed for subjects reading stories that were high in imagery." Kane, "Poetry as Right-Hemispheric Language."

11. Dr. Friedrich Sommer, email message to author, November 10, 2010, my emphasis. In a subsequent email, Dr. Sommer added, "Reassessing the recent literature, the evidence for his theory is thin in the book, and still being investigated. An anatomical study by the Almut Schuez lab in 2014 finds evidence for a significant difference of fibre calibers (fibre thickness inversely relates to speed) in one of three brains."

12. Robert Miller, *Axonal Conduction Time and Human Cerebral Laterality* (Boca Raton, FL: CRC Press, 1996).

13. "Robert Miller and OCTSPAN," https://www.robertmiller-octspan.co.nz. Miller was ultimately honored for a lifetime of research into schizophrenia, a condition studied also by Jaynes, who reported sympathetically that it is characterized by "increased right hemisphere activity"; Jaynes, *The Origin of Consciousness*, 429.

14. Peter Dale Scott, *Coming to Jakarta: A Poem about Terror* (New York: New Directions, 1989), 9–24, 76; cf. Peter Dale Scott with Freeman Ng, *Poetry and Terror: Politics and Poetics in "Coming to Jakarta"* (Lanham, MD: Lexington Books, 2018), 5–9, 75–76, 183–87; Peter Dale Scott, *Listening to the Candle: A Poem on Impulse* (New York: New Directions, 1992), I.ii, 6–7.

15. Robert Alter, *The Book of Psalms: A Translation with Commentary* (New York: Norton, 2007), xx.

16. Jared Diamond, "Disunity Is Strength," *Prospect Magazine*, July 20, 1997; summarizing Jared Diamond, *Guns, Germs, and Steel: The Fates of Human Societies* (New York: Norton, 1997).

17. Constance A. Cook and John S. Major, *Defining Chu: Image and Reality in Ancient China* (Manoa: University of Hawaii Press, 2004), book description.

18. Cf. "Song of Songs," The Bible Project, https://thebibleproject.com/explore/song-of-songs/: "The Song of Songs is a collection of ancient Israelite love poems that celebrates the beauty and power of God's gift of love and sexual desire."

19. Anne Carson, *Decreation: Poetry, Essays, Opera* (New York: Knopf, 2006), 57.

20. This verse alone should be enough to rebut the fashionable deconstructive claim that "the Song of Solomon is nothing, really, but a poem about extravagant lovemaking, male and female oral sex." "The Sultry Song of Solomon," OMG: Center for Theological Conversation, October 17, 2012, http://omgcenter.com/2012/10/17/the-sultry-song-of-solomon.

21. The King James Version reads, "My beloved put in his hand by the hole of the door, and my bowels were moved for him."

22. Ariel Bloch and Chana Bloch, *The Song of Songs: A New Translation* (New York: Random House, 1995), 7.

23. Consider Jesus's first preaching, "Repent: for the kingdom of heaven is at hand" (Matt. 4:17).

24. Rabbi Shefa Gold, "Elulian Mysteries," https://www.rabbishefagold.com/library/workshops/. See chapter 6.

25. Margaret Starbird, *The Woman with the Alabaster Jar: Mary Magdalen and the Holy Grail* (Rochester, VT: Bear & Company, 1993).

26. Philo, *Hypothetica* 11:1–4.

27. Some now consider that John the Baptist may have been an Essene. See R. Jared Staudt, "John the Baptist and the Essenes," https://sjvlaydivision.org/john-the-baptist-essenes.

28. This is closely echoed in the socialist maxim "From each according to his ability, to each according to his needs," used by Louis Blanc in his book, *L'Organisation du travail* (1839). Karl Marx popularized it in his *Critique of the Gotha Program* (1875).

29. For the tradition of two Messiahs, see John Joseph Collins, *The Apocalyptic Imagination: An Introduction to Jewish Apocalyptic Literature* (Grand Rapids, MI: Eerdmans, 1998), 161ss.

30. E.g., the *Florilegium* from Qumran, https://www.livius.org/articles/religion/messiah/messiah-2-military-leader/#4QFlorilegium.

31. "Who Were the Essenes? What Social Archaeology Tells Us about the Essenes of Qumran," Biblical Archaeological Society, May 7, 2023, https://www.biblicalarchaeology.org/daily/biblical-sites-places/biblical-archaeology-sites/who-were-the-essenes/. Cf. Jean Duhaime, *The War Texts: 1QM and Related Manuscripts* (London: T & T Clark International, 2004).

32. Compare this with Enoch 1:9, translated from the Ethiopic (found also in Qumran scroll 4Q204): "And behold! He cometh with ten thousands of His Saints To execute judgment upon all, And to destroy all the ungodly: And to convict all flesh Of all the works of their ungodliness which they have ungodly committed, And of all the hard things which ungodly sinners have spoken against Him."

33. 2 Esdras 10:41-44, "41, The woman who appeared to you a little while ago, whom you saw mourning and whom you began to console (42. you do not now see the form of a woman, but there appeared to you a city being built). 43. and who told you about the misfortune of her son—this is the interpretation: 44. The woman whom you saw is Zion, which you now behold as a city being built."

34. Stephen R. Bokenkamp, "Time after Time: Taoist Apocalyptic History and the Founding of the T'ang Dynasty," *Asia Major* 7, no. 1 (1994): 59–88. The Taipingjing

dealt "with the relationship between man and heaven, man's sins against heaven and the resulting punishment, the approaching apocalypse, and heaven's promise of salvation"; Barbara Hendrischke, *The Scripture on Great Peace: The Taiping Jing and the Beginnings of Daoism* (Berkeley: University of California Press, 2007), 3.

35. Scott, *Poetry and Terror*, 184–86.

CHAPTER FOUR

1. The next verse tells Jews not to "sow thy field with two kinds of seed" (Lev. 19:19).

2. David in turn tells Solomon, "I am distressed for thee, my brother Jonathan: very pleasant hast thou been unto me: thy love to me was wonderful, passing the love of women" (2 Sam. 1:26).

3. Hegel's dialectic of *Herr* and *Knecht* is almost universally, and misleadingly, translated as "the master-*slave* dialectic." But *Knecht* unambiguously means "servant," not "slave," and the difference is significant.

4. Georg Wilhelm Friedrich Hegel, *Vorlesungen über die Philosophie der Geschichte* (Leipzig: Reclam, 1971), 875.

5. These simplistic stereotypes are now discredited. But scientists have offered a more sophisticated differentiation between male and female brains: "New research on the neural connections within the human brain suggests sex-based differences that many have suspected for centuries: women seem to be wired more for socialization and memory while men appear geared toward perception and coordinated action. The female brain appears to have increased connection between neurons in the right and left hemispheres of the brain, and males seem to have increased neural communication within hemispheres from frontal to rear portions of the organ. Bob Grant, "Male and Female Brains Wired Differently," *The Scientist*, December 4, 2013, https://www.the-scientist.com/the-nutshell/male-and-female-brains-wired-differently-38304.

6. E.g., Reyn Guyer, *Right Brain Red: 7 Ideas for Creative Success* (Austin, TX: River Grove Books, 2016); Dorothy Lehmkuhl, *Organizing for the Creative Person: Right-Brain Styles for Conquering Clutter, Mastering Time, and Reaching Your Goals* (New York: Potter/Ten Speed/Harmony/Rodale, 2011).

7. Michael S. Gazzaniga, "The Split Brain Revisited," *Scientific American*, July 1998.

8. E.g., the prize-winning book by Iain McGilchrist, *The Master and His Emissary: The Divided Brain and the Making of the Western World* (New Haven, CT: Yale University Press, 2019).

9. Robert Linssen, *Living Zen* (New York: Grove Press, 1988), 207; citing Sylvain Lévi, *Le Bouddhisme et les Grecs*, *Revue de l'histoire des religions* 23 (1891). In addition, "during the Classical Age because many Scythians then lived in Athens, where a number of them even served as the city's police force"; Christopher I. Beckwith, *Greek Buddha: Pyrrho's Encounter with Early Buddhism in Central Asia* (Princeton, NJ: Princeton University Press, 2015), 5.

10. Ian Morris, "The Greater Athenian State," in *The Dynamics of Ancient Empires: State Power from Assyria to Byzantium*, ed. Ian Morris and Walter Scheidel (Oxford: Oxford University Press, 2008), 115.

11. Two decades earlier, a lost play on the Persian War by Phrynichus was considered to be anti-Athenian in tenor. Future performances were banned and the author fined.

12. For example, it was retranslated and produced in New York in 2003 on the occasion of George W. Bush's invasion of Iraq.

13. For the first reading, Wikipedia cites, for example, Charles Segal, *Euripides and the Poetics of Sorrow: Art, Gender and Commemoration in Alcestis, Hippolytus and Hecuba* (Durham, NC: Duke University Press, 1993), 165; for the second, e.g., Thomas Harrison, *The Emptiness of Asia: Aeschylus' "Persians" and the History of the Fifth Century* (London: Gerald Duckworth, 2000).

14. Casey Dué, "Identifying with the Enemy: Love, Loss, and Longing in the *Persians* of Aeschylus," in *The Captive Woman's Lament in Greek Tragedy* (Austin: University of Texas Press, 2006), Harvard Center for Hellenic Studies, https://archive.org/details/captivewomanslam0000duec.

15. "Herodotus: On the Customs of the Persians," *Ancient History Encyclopedia*, https://www.ancient.eu/article/149/herodotus-on-the-customs-of-the-persians.

16. Stuart Lawrence, *Moral Awareness in Greek Tragedy* (Oxford: Oxford University Press, 2013), 199.

17. As we shall see, "the first philosopher in the West to give perfectly explicit expression to cosmopolitanism was the Socratically inspired Cynic Diogenes in the fourth century BCE. It is said that "when he was asked where he came from, he replied, 'I am a citizen of the world [kosmopolitês]'" (Diogenes Laertius VI 63)." "Cosmopolitanism," Stanford Encyclopedia of Philosophy, https://plato.stanford.edu/entries/cosmopolitanism/#GreeRomaCosm.

18. "The Sophists." Stanford Encyclopedia of Philosophy, https://plato.stanford.edu/entries/sophists/.

19. Roger Scruton, "The Return of the Sophist," Society for Philosophy in Practice, 2011, http://www.practical-philosophy.org.uk.

20. Bernard Knox, *The Oldest Dead White European Males and Other Reflections on the Classics* (New York: Norton, 1993), 96–97.

21. According to Diogenes Laertius and Cicero, the agnosticism of Protagoras led to his expulsion from Athens and the burning of his books. But there is no contemporary corroboration for these two late reports, which Burnet doubts. John Burnet, *Greek Philosophy: From Thales to Plato* (London: Macmillan, 1981).

22. "Human Nature: Justice versus Power; Noam Chomsky debates with Michel Foucault," 1971, https://chomsky.info/1971xxxx.

23. Ian Johnson, "The Flowers Blooming in the Dark," *New York Review of Books*, March 26, 2020, 47; quoting Xu Jilin, *Rethinking China's Rise: A Liberal Critique*, ed. David Ownby (Cambridge: Cambridge University Press, 2018).

24. A few lines later, Socrates comments, "People do say they [the former statesmen] have made the city great [megalen, μεγάλην]; but that it is with the swelling

of an imposthume [abscess], due to those men of the former time, this they do not perceive" (518e).

Karl Jaspers, the philosopher to whom we owe the notion of the Axial Moment (*Achsenzeit*), associated Plato with it; Karl Jaspers, *The Origin and Goal of History* (London: Routledge & K. Paul, 1953). For me the Greek participants in the Axial Moment or First Pivotal Shift would be Thales (d. 547 BCE) and Pythagoras (d. ca. 495 BCE), matched by the unknown founders of the Orphic and Eleusinian Mysteries. Euripides and Plato, for their features noted here, are for me cusp figures clearly associated with the lead-up to the Second Pivotal Shift.

25. Discussion in Lowell Edmunds, "The Practical Irony of the Historical Socrates," *Phoenix* 58, nos. 3/4 (2004): 193–207.

26. Xu, *Rethinking China's Rise*, 12: "China should develop modern civilization, following world trends and at the same time employing her own cultural traditions to make her own contributions to the development of universal civilization."

27. And can we see it in his endorsement of the contrast of Hesiod (f. ca. 700 BCE) between the first race of the Golden Age ("Noble, averters of evil"; Hesiod, *Works and Days*, 122ff, quoted in Plato, *Cratylus* 398a) and the "iron race" of today. In this way, Plato gives both a timeless notion of the better alterity which in chapter 1 I identified with the *sacred*, and also a historic one. But he modernizes Hesiod's notion of a "hero" (ἥρως) by deriving the term etymologically from either "love" (ἔρως) or "able to ask questions" (ἐρωτᾶν); thus, "the heroes turn out to be orators and askers of questions" (*Cratylus*, 398c–d).

28. When I wrote this section, I was not yet aware of Harold Haarman's book, *Plato's Philosophy Reaching Beyond the Limits of Reason* (Hildesheim: Georg Olms Verlag, 2017), whose title epitomizes the yin feature of Plato I talk about here.

29. The "Heavenly Aphrodite" is the same name given by Herodotus (*Histories* 1.105) and others to the Phoenician goddess Ishtar, known to the Greeks as Astarte.

30. Friedrich Hölderlin, *Sämtliche Werke und Briefe*, ed. Michael Knaupp (Darmstadt: Wiss Buchg, 1998), 1:196, my translation.

31. Peter Dale Scott, *Ecstatic Pessimist: Czeslaw Milosz, Poet of Catastrophe and Hope* (Lanham, MD: Rowman & Littlefield, 2023), 135; quoting from Czeslaw Milosz, *Provinces* (Hopewell, NJ: Ecco, 1991), 121; Czeslaw Milosz, "The Boundaries of Art," in *Legends of Modernity: Essays from an Occupied Poland, 1942–43* (New York: Farrar, Straus & Giroux, 2005), 130–31.

32. Scott, *Ecstatic Pessimist*, 133–36, 161–62, 167–69.

33. As has the name of his school, the Academy, established just outside Athens in a grove dedicated to Hecademus. The *OED* lists "epicurean" without a capital *E*, but only in its derivative sense of "gluttonous."

34. Alfred North Whitehead, *Process and Reality* (New York: Free Press, 1978), 39.

35. André Goddu, *Copernicus and the Aristotelian Tradition: Education, Reading, and Philosophy in Copernicus's Path to Heliocentrism* (Leiden: Brill, 2010), 279.

36. Goddu, *Copernicus*, 261a. More recently, Whitehead's "repudiation of fundamental materialism . . . echoes loudly in the work of recent theorists such as Robert Griffiths, Roman Omnès, Wojciech Żurek, and Murray Gell-Mann, among several others, whose own repudiation of fundamental materialism and 'quantum-classical'

dualism is the most recent attempt to solve a philosophical problem of χωρισμός [chorismos, separation] introduced by Plato—the supposed chasm separating what is [the realm of ideas] from what appears to be." Michael Epperson, *Quantum Mechanics and the Philosophy of Alfred North Whitehead* (New York: Fordham University Press, 2004), xiv.

37. Another arrives with the drunken Alcibiades.

38. Pausanias's speech also reflects the custom (of which we shall say more in chapter 7) that permitted free love to freeborn men but not to freeborn women: "But the love of young boys should be forbidden by law, because their future is uncertain; they may turn out good or bad, either in body or soul, and much noble enthusiasm may be thrown away upon them; in this matter the good are a law to themselves, and the coarser sort of lovers ought to be restrained by force; as we restrain or attempt to restrain them from fixing their affections on women of free birth" (*Symposium* 181d–182a).

39. Christine Downing, *Myths and Mysteries of Same-Sex Love* (New York: Continuum, 1989), 243.

40. In the passage "no man is such a craven that Love's own influence cannot inspire him with a valor that makes him equal to the bravest born (oudeis houto kakos hontina ouk an autos ho Eros entheon poieseie pros areten, hoste homoion einai to aristo phusei, οὐδεὶς οὕτω κακὸς ὄντινα οὐκ ἂν αὐτὸς ὁ Ἔρως ἔνθεον ποιήσειε πρὸς ἀρετήν, ὥστε ὅμοιον εἶναι τῷ ἀρίστῳ φύσει; 179a), Eros the god is cognate with "hero," and "valor" or virtue (*arete*) with the war god Ares.

CHAPTER FIVE

1. Alexandrian trade with China was probably indirect, through Persia; Jan V. D Crabben, "Hellenic Trade Routes, 300 BCE," Ancient History Encyclopedia, https://www.ancient.eu/image/67/hellenic-trade-routes-300-bce. But the known civilized world had expanded to reach from the Atlantic to the Pacific.

2. After about 125 BCE they were joined by Ctesiphon, the winter capital of the Parthians and later Sasanians. By about 600 CE, before its capture by Muslims in 637 CE, Alexandria grew to an estimated population of five hundred thousand, making it the second-largest city in the world at that time.

3. An Edict of Aśoka, engraved in stone, reads:

The conquest by Dharma has been won here, on the borders, and even six hundred yojanas [four thousand miles] away, where the Greek king Antiochos ["Antiyoga," of Syria] rules, and beyond there where the four kings named Ptolemy ["Turamaya," of Egypt], Antigonos ["Antikini," of Macedonia], Magas ["Maki," of Cyrenaica] and Alexander ["Alikasudara," of Epirus].

4. See Jerry H. Bentley, *Old World Encounters: Cross-Cultural Contacts and Exchanges in Pre-Modern Times* (Oxford: Oxford University Press, 1993).

5. Richard H. Popkin, "David Hume: His Pyrrhonism and His Critique of Pyrrhonism," *Philosophical Quarterly* 1, no. 5 (1951): 385–407; William B. Huntley, "David Hume and Charles Darwin," *Journal of the History of Ideas* 33, no. 3 (1972): 457–70.

6. "The Lurianic Kabbalah," The New Kabbalah, http://www.newkabbalah.com/plato.html.

7. The Midrash of Philo, 2:24, https://www.sefaria.org/The_Midrash_of_Philo.2.24?lang=bi; Adam Afterman, "From Philo to Plotinus: The Emergence of Mystical Union," *Journal of Religion* 93, no. 2 (2003): 178: "Both [Bernard] McGinn and [Moshe] Idel have noted the importance of mystical union in Philo's thought and its possible influence on the articulated discussions of unio mystica in Plotinus and consequently on the entire Western mystical tradition. . . . Philo's interpretation of the biblical commandment to 'cleave' to God as mystical union is a fascinating moment when 'theistic union' was born out of a synthesis of Platonism and Philo's Judaism."

8. Ian Johnson, "The Flowers Blooming in the Dark," *New York Review of Books*, March 26, 2020, 47; quoting Xu Jilin, *Rethinking China's Rise: A Liberal Critique*, ed. David Ownby (Cambridge: Cambridge University Press, 2018). Compare the restrictive meaning in Merriam-Webster of *ethos*, discussed in the introduction to this book (pp. 9–15).

9. Werner Jaeger, *Paideia: The Ideals of Greek Culture*, trans. Gilbert Highet, 3 vols. (New York: Oxford University Press, 1945), 2:70. To illustrate his claim, Jaeger cites the response of the philosopher Stilpo (d. ca. 280 BCE) when offered compensation for his losses after the sack of his city Megara: "No one carried off my paideia."

10. Georg Wilhelm Friedrich Hegel, *Introduction to the Philosophy of History*, trans. J. R. Sibree (New York: American Home Library, 1902), 16:56.

11. Thomas S. Engeman, "Nietzsche's View of Socrates," *Journal of the History of Philosophy* 15, no. 1 (1977): 118–19; quoting from Werner Dannhauser, *Nietzsche's View of Socrates* (Ithaca, NY: Cornell University Press, 1974), 212–13.

12. Rogerio Miranda de Almeida, *Nietzsche and Paradox*, trans. Mark S. Roberts (Albany: State University of New York Press, 2006), 17.

13. Werner Dannhauser, *Nietzsche's View of Socrates* (Ithaca, NY: Cornell University Press, 1974), 66. Cf. Lewis Call, "Nietzsche as Critic and Captive of Enlightenment" (PhD diss., University of California, Irvine, 2005), http://rousseaustudies.free.fr/articleNietzscheCritic.html: "Again we see Socrates here as the turning point, the break between worthwhile pure science and the more questionable modern science that was to come. We also see a kind of scientist very different from the decadent, modern 'man of science' Nietzsche so enthusiastically excoriates."

14. James Romm, "What Did India Learn from the Greeks?," reviewing Richard Stoneman, *The Greek Experience of India: From Alexander to the Indo-Greeks* (Princeton, NJ: Princeton University Press, 2019), *New York Review of Books*, April 9, 2020. See also Adrian Kuzminski, *Pyrrhonism: How the Ancient Greeks Reinvented Buddhism* (Lanham, MD: Lexington Books, 2008).

15. Christopher I. Beckwith, *Greek Buddha: Pyrrho's Encounter with Early Buddhism in Central Asia* (Princeton, NJ: Princeton University Press, 2015); cited in

Richard Stoneman, *The Greek Experience of India: From Alexander to the Indo-Greeks* (Princeton, NJ: Princeton University Press, 2019), 347–48.

16. On very little evidence, Beckwith argues that Laozi ("The Old Master") is actually a Chinese representation of the Buddha.

17. Stoneman, *The Greek Experience of India*, 354.

18. Joan B. Burton, *Theocritus's Urban Mimes: Mobility, Gender, and Patronage* (Berkeley: University of California Press, 1995), 41, http://ark.cdlib.org/ark:/13030/ft4p3006f9.

19. Diogenes Laertius, *Lives of the Eminent Philosophers*, 6.63. If this late record is correct, Diogenes the Cynic would appear to have made the first known use of this term.

20. Malcolm Schofield, *The Stoic Idea of the City* (Chicago: University of Chicago Press, 1999).

21. Joshua J. Mark, "Zeno of Citium," Ancient History Encyclopedia, https://www.ancient.eu/Zeno_of_Citium.

22. Earlier, in the *Protagoras* (337c7–d3), Plato quotes the sophist Hippias as saying to a group of Athenians and foreigners, "Gentlemen present . . . I regard you all as kinsmen, familiars, and fellow-citizens—by nature and not by convention; for like is by nature akin to like, while convention, which is a tyrant over human beings, forces many things contrary to nature."

23. David M. Engel, "Women's Role in the Home and the State: Stoic Theory Reconsidered," *Harvard Studies in Classical Philology* 101 (2003): 268. Plato in book 5 of the *Republic* had Socrates suggest that the best women should participate as guardians and philosopher rulers of the ideal polis. But the proposal was presented in a fantastical context that others in the dialogue (or since) could not take seriously. For discussion, see Mary Townsend, *The Woman Question in Plato's "Republic"* (Lanham, MD: Lexington Books, 2017).

24. Epicurus, *The Art of Happiness*, trans. George K. Strodach (New York: Penguin, 2012), 36, 56–58.

25. Epicurus, *The Art of Happiness*, 39.

26. Stephen Toulmin, *Cosmopolis: The Hidden Agenda of Modernity* (New York: Free Press, 1990) [Zeno]; Stephen Greenblatt, *The Swerve: How the World Became Modern* (New York: Norton, 2011) [Epicurus].

CHAPTER SIX

1. Joan B. Burton, *Theocritus's Urban Mimes: Mobility, Gender, and Patronage* (Berkeley: University of California Press, 1995), 41.

2. "Greek served as the lingua franca in Egypt after the conquest by Alexander the Great in 332 BCE, when it replaced Aramaic, the administrative language of Persian Egypt. It was the vernacular of the ruling elite and of the many immigrants and veterans who had come in the wake of the establishment of Macedonian rule." Jacco Dielemann and Ian S. Moyer, "Egyptian Literature," in *A Companion to Hellenistic Literature*, ed. James Clauss and Martine Cuypers (Oxford: Blackwell, 2014), 432.

3. Aramaic would have been the normal street language of Jews. But the treasury of records found in the *genizah* of a Cairo synagogue show secular use of Hebrew in bankers' accounts, merchants' lists, and children's jottings.

4. There were synagogues in all five divisions.

5. Christelle Fischer-Bovet, "Counting the Greeks in Egypt Immigration in the First Century of Ptolemaic Rule" (version 1.0, Princeton/Stanford Working Papers in Classics, October 2007), 3, 22; citing D. W. Rathbone, "Villages, Land and Population in Graeco-Roman Egypt," *Cambridge Classical Journal*, 1990, 103–46; J. G. Manning, *Land and Power in Ptolemaic Egypt: The Structure of Land Tenure* (Cambridge: Cambridge University Press, 2003). I slightly discount Fischer-Bovet's careful calculations because she does not consider the fact that, as is normal with military occupations, there was considerable intermarriage between Greek troops and the native Egyptians.

6. As late as the 1940s, Alexandria still had large numbers of both Greeks and Jews—with twelve synagogues and at least forty thousand Jews.

7. "Most Demotic literary manuscripts date to the Ptolemaic or Roman period, but that should not necessarily lead to the conclusion that Demotic literature only bloomed late." Jacco Dielemann and Ian S. Moyer, "Egyptian Literature," in *A Companion to Hellenistic Literature*, ed. James J. Clauss and Martine Cuypers (Chichester: Blackwell, 2014), 433.

8. Cf. Reza Aslan, *Zealot: The Life and Times of Jesus of Nazareth* (New York: Random House, 2013), 34: "If that claim is true, then as an artisan and day laborer, Jesus would have belonged to the lowest class of peasants in first-century Palestine, just above the indigent, the beggar, and the slave. The Romans used the term *tekton* for any uneducated or illiterate person, and Jesus was very likely both."

9. Bezalel Bar-Kochva, *Pseudo-Hecataeus, On the Jews: Legitimizing the Jewish Diaspora* (Berkeley: University of California Press, 1996), 72.

10. There is no corroboration for the story in 3 Maccabees that Ptolemy IV Philopator (222–205 BCE) rounded up all the Jews in Egypt to be trampled to death by drunken elephants.

11. Philo, *Legatio ad Cajum* 36; Josephus, *Antiquities* 15.2.2, 23.12.

12. H. I. Bell, "Anti-Semitism in Alexandria," *Journal of Roman Studies* 31 (1941): 2.

13. Simon Schama, *The Story of the Jews: Finding the Words* (London: Bodley Head, 2013), 4.

14. Schama, *The Story of the Jews*, 91. Egyptian synagogue dedication stones, routinely thanking Ptolemies II or III, are the oldest synagogue fragments found anywhere in the world. Like the word *synagogue* itself, they are in Greek.

15. A. Fr. Gfrörer, *Byzantinische Geschichten* (Graz: Vereins-Bucher., 1872–1877), 1, 308, also 2, 111–18.

16. Mireille Hadas-Lebel, *Philo of Alexandria: A Thinker in the Jewish Diaspora* (Boston: Brill, 2012), 36. Babylonian Jews were also very numerous and wealthy and every year sent large amounts of silver and gold to the Temple in Jerusalem.

17. They also constitute two of the five books of the megillah read at special festivals, compared to only one (the book of Esther) from the contemporary Babylonian tradition.

18. Burton, *Theocritus's Urban Mimes*, 41.

19. Christine Mitchell Havelock, *The Aphrodite of Knidos and Her Successors: A Historical Review of the Female Nude in Greek Art* (Ann Arbor: University of Michigan Press, 1995), 127. Cf. Theocritus, *Idylls* 15.106–11 (the dirge's address to Aphrodite): "Anointed by thee, according to the word [muthos] of men, our queen the daughter of Berenice was made immortal."

20. Both were called *philadelphoi*, i.e., sibling lovers.

21. James Henry Breasted, *A History of the Ancient Egyptians* (New York: Scribner, 1923), 217.

22. Eleni Vassilika, *Greek and Roman Art* (Cambridge: Cambridge University Press, 1998), 74. Arsinoë's influence has given rise to nuanced discussion. Havelock identifies a half-naked statue, draped at the waist, as "a cult statue erected in Egypt during the reign of Arsinoe II" (*The Aphrodite of Knidos*, 88), but concludes that "even though Arsinoe was credited with a close relationship to Aphrodite, as far as we know she was never represented as Aphrodite—especially as a nude Aphrodite—in statuary"(128).

23. J. F. Carspecken, "Apollonius Rhodius and the Homeric Epic," *Yale Classical Studies* 13 (1952): 101. Jason is "chosen leader because his superior declines the honour, subordinate to his comrades, except once, in every trial of strength, skill or courage, a great warrior only with the help of magical charms, jealous of honour but incapable of asserting it, passive in the face of crisis, timid and confused before trouble, tearful at insult, easily despondent, gracefully treacherous in his dealings with the love-sick Medea."

24. Thalia Papadopoulou, "The Presentation of the Inner Self: Euripides' Medea 1021–55 and Apollonius Rhodius' Argonautica 3, 772–801," *Mnemosyne* 50, no. 6 (1997): 642n: "It is important to note that Apollonius has been given the credit for commencing with Arg. 3, 772–801 the tradition of the stylized *interior monologue*; see R. Scholes-R-Kellogg, *The Nature of Narrative* (New York, 1966), 177–82 and 285."

25. Sarah B. Pomeroy, *Women in Hellenistic Egypt: From Alexander to Cleopatra* (New York: Schocken Books, 1984), 78: "In the Classical period, in tragedy, romantic love was viewed as anti-social. The love of Phaedra for Hippolytus, of Medea for Jason, of Heracles for Iole, and of Haemon for Antigone, for example, conflicted with obligations toward kin and state. And finally destroyed entire families and cities. In the milieu of the Alexandrian poets, in contrast, there were fewer attachments to kin group and state. Romantic liaisons between individuals flourished in their stead."

26. We see a little of the same gap in time between present and past, author and voice, in Ecclesiastes 12:8–10, a roughly contemporary but much more Hellenistic work in the *prosopa* or mask of a "king of Jerusalem" (Eccl. 1:1), and in Mishnaic Hebrew, showing Greek and Aramaic influence and Persian loan words. To these stylistic similarities to the Sing of Songs, we should add also the Teacher's repeated celebration of enjoyment (e.g., Eccl. 5:18–19, 8:15), which has been compared to the teachings of Epicurus (d. 269 BCE).

27. Bruno Snell, *The Discovery of the Mind: In Greek Philosophy and Literature* (New York: Dover, 1982), 266.

28. Gianni Barbiero, *Song of Songs: A Close Reading*, trans. Michael Tait (Boston: Brill, 2011), 60.

29. Stephen Mitchell, on Ariel Bloch and Chana Bloch, *The Song of Songs: A New Translation* (New York: Random House, 1995), back cover.

30. Bloch and Bloch, *The Song of Songs*, 3.

31. Cheryl Exum, *Song of Songs* (Louisville, KY: Westminster John Knox Press, 2005), 73. Theodore's commentary did not survive and is known only from attacks on it. But the theory that the Song was an epithalamium celebrating Solomon's marriage survived through the seventeenth century; cf. Adam Clarke (d. 1832), "Introduction to the Canticles, or Song of Solomon," https://www.studylight.org/commentaries/eng/acc/song-of-solomon.html: "The Song most certainly celebrates a marriage; whether between Solomon and the daughter of Pharaoh, or between him and some Jewish princess, has not been fully agreed on among critics and commentators."

32. Bloch and Bloch, *The Song of Songs*, 30. Cf. Robert Alter, *Strong as Death Is Love* (New York: Norton, 2015), 1.

33. Bloch and Bloch, *The Song of Songs*, 3, 31. Full disclosure: I am thanked by the Blochs for my comments on their manuscript translation and generally admire their final product, but I lost an argument with them over verse 3:7, where the Blochs, to ward off an allegorical reading, insert a line ("Oh the splendors of King Solomon!") that, as they admit, "has no equivalent in the Hebrew text" (Bloch and Bloch, *The Song of Songs*, 71, 161).

34. Bloch and Bloch, *The Song of Songs*, 32.

35. Bloch and Bloch, *The Song of Songs*, 30.

36. Augustine, *City of God*, 17:20, emphasis added.

37. Tania Lombrozo, "The Truth about the Left Brain/Right Brain Relationship," NPR, December 2, 2013, emphasis added, https://www.npr.org/sections/13.7/2013/12/02/248089436/the-truth-about-the-left-brain-right-brain-relationship.

38. Cf. Gerson Cohen, "The Song of Songs and the Jewish Religious Mentality," in *Studies in the Variety of Rabbinic Cultures* (Philadelphia: Jewish Publication Society, 1991), 13: "While the Song of Songs may contain very ancient strata, the work as we have it now cannot have been completed before the Macedonian conquest of the Near East and rise of the Hellenistic culture."

39. William G. Seiple, "Theocritean Parallels to the Song of Songs," *American Journal of Semitic Languages and Literatures* 19, no. 2 (1903), 108–15; Bloch and Bloch, *The Song of Songs*, 25n.

40. Theocritus, *Idylls* 10.27–30: "Darling Bombyca, everyone else calls you a Syrian [i.e., a slave], sunburnt, and scrawny; to me you are honey-brown" (tactfully echoed in Virgil's *Eclogues* 10.38–39: "You're dark, Amyntas? So are dark violets and hyacinths"). If relevant, this reminiscence of Theocritus in the Song would contrast the class consciousness of the Theocritan *Idylls* with the liberating sense of equality between the two lovers, whatever their background (2:16; "My beloved is mine, and I am his"). Cf. Barbiero, *Song of Songs: A Close Reading*, 59–60. For a survey of beautiful black lovers in ancient literature, see Frank M. Snowden, *Before*

Color Prejudice: The Ancient View of Blacks (Cambridge, MA: Harvard University Press, 1983), 77.

41. E.g., Morris Jastrow's interpretation of the Song as "a collection of secular love songs." Morris Jastrow Jr., *The Song of Songs: Being a Collection of Love Lyrics of Ancient Palestine* (Philadelphia: J. B. Lippincott 1921), 6.

42. Cf. Gianni Barbiero, *Song of Songs: A Close Reading*, 60: "The city-nature contrast is a recurrent *motiv* in the Song."

43. Charles Segal, *Poetry and Myth in Ancient Pastoral: Essays on Theocritus and Virgil* (Princeton, NJ: Princeton University Press, 1981), 8.

44. Fox suggests (p. 79) that, in Egyptian as well as Greek love songs, a woman may be compared to a horse. On the other hand, I find unpersuasive his comparison of the "love-wolf" in Egyptian poetry to the foxes of 2:14. Michael Fox, *The Song of Songs and the Ancient Egyptian Love Songs* (Madison: University of Wisconsin Press, 1985), 78, 114.

45. See Marcia Falk, "The Wasf," in *A Feminist Companion to the Song of Songs*, ed. Athalya Brenner, 225–33 (London: Bloomsbury, 1993).

46. Chester Beatty I manuscript, ca. 1100 BCE; in Fox, *The Song of Songs and the Ancient Egyptian Love Songs*, 52.

47. Edmund S. Meltzer, "In Search of Sinuhe: 'What's in a Name?'" (paper presented at the Fifty-Eighth Annual Meeting of the American Research Center in Egypt, Toledo, Ohio, April 20, 2007), https://web.archive.org/web/20111007013806/http://www.ceae.unlugar.com/meltzer.htm.

48. Robert Graves, ed., *The Song of Songs* (New York: Clarkson Potter, 1973), 16.

49. Bloch and Bloch, *The Song of Songs*, 29.

50. Phyllis Trimble, "Depatriarchalizing in Biblical Interpretation," *Journal of the American Academy of Religion* 41, no. 1 (1973): 30–48, 45; quoted by Falk, "The Wasf," 232.

51. Chester Beatty I manuscript, ca. 1100 BCE; in Fox, *The Song of Songs and the Ancient Egyptian Love Songs*, 67–68, 74.

52. For the last line, Robert Alter suggests, "I am in a swoon of love. The literal sense of the Hebrew is 'lovesick.' But that sounds too pathetic, or adolescent, in English." Alter, *Strong as Death Is Love*, 15.

53. Alter translates 5:10 as "I am a wall / and my breasts are like towers. / Then I was in his eyes / like a town that finds peace." In a footnote he explains that "the Hebrew merely has "like one [feminine] who finds peace." Alter, *Strong as Death Is Love*.

54. She first says, "My beloved is mine and I am his" (dodi li v'ani dodi; 2:16), and later reverses the order: "I am my beloved's and he is mine" (ani li-dodi v'dodi li; 6:3). "Li" does not simply imply possession; as the Blochs note elsewhere, "it may mean something like 'dedicated to,' or in some way 'associated with.'" Bloch and Bloch, *The Song of Songs*, 137.

55. For the divergence in translation, see Bloch and Bloch, *The Song of Songs*, 150.

56. Augustine, *De Doctrina Christiana* 1.3–40; Irene O'Daly, *John of Salisbury and the Medieval Roman Renaissance* (Manchester: Manchester University Press,

2018); Dante, *Paradiso* 19:139–48; Paola Nasti, "The Wise Poet: Solomon in Dante's Heaven of the Sun," *Reading Medieval Studies* 27 (2001): 103–38.

57. "Perhaps no other work in the scriptures captured the allegorical imagination of early Christian thinkers as the Song of Songs." F. B. A. Asiedu, "The Song of Songs and the Ascent of the Soul: Ambrose, Augustine, and the Language of Mysticism," *Vigiliae Christianae* 55, no. 3 (2001): 299.

58. W. W. Fields, "Early and Medieval Jewish Interpretation of the Song of Songs," *Grace Theological Journal*, Fall 1980, 226.

59. Cf. Song 7:12 (KJV): "Let us get up early to the vineyards; let us see if the vine flourish, whether the tender grape appear, and the pomegranates bud forth: there will I give thee my loves." The Blochs have "Come, my beloved, let us go into the fields and lie all night among the flowering henna."

60. And one of those crimes was the murder of Naboth by King Ahab in order to expropriate his vineyard: "Naboth the Jezreelite had a vineyard [kerem hayah li-Naboth], which was in Jezreel, hard by the palace of Ahab king of Samaria" (1 Kings 21:1).

61. The first of these verses is echoed again later in Lekha Dodi, a Renaissance mystical hymn—"Come, Bride" (echoing Song 7:12, "Lecha dodi"), the core of the Kabbalat Shabbat service—that was also inspired by Isaiah, the Talmud, and the Song of Songs.

62. The Blochs translate this line as "Again, O Shulamite, dance again, that we may watch you dancing." But in a very long and defensive endnote they tacitly acknowledge that the word "dancing" is their addition. The analogous verse from the Song of Deborah that they use for justification ("Awake, awake, O Deborah! Awake, awake, strike up the chant!" ['uri, 'uri, deborah, 'uri, 'uri, dabberi shir]; Judges 5:12) is quoted almost verbatim in the mystical Lekha Dodi: "'uri, 'uri, shir dabberi" (6:3).

63. The command "Shuvah" is repeated in Jeremiah 3:7, this time with sexual overtones; see Jeremiah 7–8 (KJV):

[7] And I said after she had done all these things, Turn thou unto me. But she returned not. And her treacherous sister Judah saw it.

[8] And I saw, when for all the causes whereby backsliding Israel committed adultery I had put her away, and given her a bill of divorce; yet her treacherous sister Judah feared not, but went and played the harlot also.

64. Midrash Tanchuma, Bamidbar 11, Sefaria, https://www.sefaria.org/Midrash_Tanchuma%2C_Bamidbar.12.1?lang=bi&with=all&lang2=en.

65. The original Hebrew of this verse

שׁוּבִי שׁוּבִי הַשּׁוּלַמִּית, שׁוּבִי שׁוּבִי וְנֶחֱזֶה-בָּךְ
Shuvi, shuvi, ha-Shulammit
Shuvi, shuvi, ve-nehezeh bach

is reasonably translated in the King James Version as "Return, return, O Shulamite; return, return, that we may look upon thee." The only excuse for the Blochs' imposition of "dancing" here is from the impenetrable second half of the verse—

> Mah tehezu be-Shulammit
> Ki-meholat ha-mahanayim—

which the Blochs take to mean, literally, "Do again, do again . . . and we will watch you . . . as the dance of the two camps"; Bloch and Bloch, *The Song of Songs*, 196, 198, 199. Changing "ha-mahanayim" to "bi-mahanayim," they translate the second half of the verse as "Why do you gaze at the Shulamite / as she whirls / down the rows of dancers?"

But the Jewish scholars of the Septuagint translated "Ki-meholat ha-mahanayim" as "ἡ ἐρχομένη ὡς χοροὶ τῶν παρεμβολῶν," usually rendered in English as "She comes as bands of armies." (The word χοροὶ, originally "dances," later came also to mean "troops.") Hence the King James Version: "As it were the company of two armies."

66. An even more extreme postmodern demystification of this passage is found in Athalya Brenner, "Come Back, Come Back the Shulammite," (Song of Songs 7.1–10): A Parody of the *Wasf* Genre," in Brenner, *A Feminist Companion to the Song of Songs*, 234–59.

67. At verse 3:7, they admit, "We have introduced a first line . . . that has no equivalent in the Hebrew text." Bloch and Bloch, *The Song of Songs*, 161.

68. Ulrike Spohn, "A Difference in Kind? Jürgen Habermas and Charles Taylor on Post-secularism," *The European Legacy* 20, no. 2, (2015): 127; citing Charles Taylor, *A Secular Age* (Cambridge, MA: Belknap, 2007), 22: "Western modernity, including its secularity, is the fruit of new inventions, newly constructed self-understandings and related practices, and can't be explained in terms of perennial features of human life."

69. Fox, *The Song of Songs and the Ancient Egyptian Love Songs*, 176, 177.

70. Bloch and Bloch, *The Song of Songs*, 221.

71. Rashi, commentary on Song 8:14, https://www.chabad.org/library/bible_cdo/aid/16452/showrashi/true/jewish/Chapter-8.htm.

72. Daniel Lord Smail, *On Deep History and the Brain* (Berkeley: University of California Press, 2007), 11, emphasis added.

73. These are emphasized by Geula Twersky, who sees the Song as "a song of riddles," carefully concealing "the hidden treasures of the Temple." Geula Twersky, *Song of Riddles: Deciphering the Song of Songs* (Jerusalem: Gefen, 2018), xvi.

74. "O that thou wert as my brother, that sucked the breasts of my mother! when I should find thee without [bahutz], I would kiss thee; yea, I should not be despised." One can detect here an echo of the "strange woman" or temptress in Proverbs 7:

> Now is she without [bahutz], now in the streets, and lieth in wait at every corner.
> So she caught him, and kissed him, and with an impudent face said unto him . . .
> "Come, let us take our fill of love until the morning: let us solace ourselves with loves."

75. E.g., the paradox of God's discourses with the younger and the older Abraham, discussed in chapter 3.

76. According to the Jerusalem Center for Public Affairs, the first discernible traces of historical anti-Semitism anywhere can be found in the writings of the Egyptian historian Manetho, who wrote no later than the reign of Ptolemy III. It is widely accepted that the world's first-known anti-Jewish pogrom occurred in Alexandria in 38 CE.

CHAPTER SEVEN

1. Roger Scruton, in *Loisir et liberté en Amérique du nord* [Leisure and liberty in North America], by Pierre Lagayette (Paris: PUPS, Presses de l'Université Paris–Sorbonne, 2008), 11.

2. *Liberal* in this sense is defined in the *OED* as "suitable for a person of noble birth."

3. Benjamin Constant, *The Liberty of Ancients Compared with That of Moderns* (1816), in *The Political Writings of Benjamin Constant*, ed. Biancamaria Fontana, 309–28 (Cambridge: Cambridge University Press, 1988), https://archive.is/20120805184450/http://www.uark.edu/depts/comminfo/cambridge/ancients.html.

4. Aristotle, *Nicomachean Ethics* 1177b, 26–32.

5. This rephrases a passage in a 1936 article by Einstein in the *Journal of the Franklin Institute*: "The eternal mystery of the world is its comprehensibility. . . . The fact that it is comprehensible is a miracle."

6. See below, "Moreness," in appendix, "Four Poems."

7. Leah Kronenberg, "Epicurean Pastoral: Daphnis as an Allegory for Lucretius in Vergil's Eclogues," *Vergilius* 62 (2016): 25–56. Cf. Lucretius, *De Rerum Natura* 1.17–19, 29–33:

> O not to see that nature for herself
> Barks after nothing, save that pain keep off,
> Disjoined from the body, and that mind enjoy
> Delightsome feeling, far from care and fear! . . .
> Yet still to lounge with friends in the soft grass
> Beside a river of water, underneath
> A big tree's boughs, and merrily to refresh
> Our frames, with no vast outlay—most of all
> If the weather is laughing and the times of the year
> Besprinkle the green of the grass around with flowers.

8. Orlando Patterson, *Freedom in the Making of Western Culture* (New York: Basic Books, 1991).

9. Perry Anderson, *Passages from Antiquity to Feudalism* (London: Verso, 1978), 21, 22. Orlando Patterson also argues that the concept of freedom "was generated from the experience of slavery"; Patterson, *Freedom in the Making of Western Culture*, xiii.

10. The lightness of *Idyll* 11 is enhanced by its framing: the Cyclops's anguish is a topic of conversation between two who are not involved. In Virgil's imitation in *Eclogue* 2 (Corydon's lament at the end—"Love burns me still; what limit does love know?"), there is no such distancing.

11. Paulinus Pella, *Eucharisticus*, trans. H. G. Evelyn White, in *Ausonius II*, Loeb Classical Library (Cambridge, MA: Harvard University Press, 1949), 319. In most MSS, the author is named "Sanctus Paulinus."

12. Czeslaw Milosz, *The Witness of Poetry* (Cambridge, MA: Harvard University Press, 1983), 63; commenting on Erich Auerbach, *Mimesis* (Princeton, NJ: Princeton University Press, 1953), 154.

13. Alison R. Sharrock, "Ovid," in *A Companion to Roman Love Elegy*, ed. Barbara K. Gold (Malden, MA: Wiley-Blackwell, 2012), 74–75.

14. David Wray, "Catullus the Roman Love Elegist?," in Gold, *A Companion to Roman Love Elegy*, 27; citing Pierre Hadot, *What Is Ancient Philosophy?* (Cambridge, MA: Belknap, 2002).

15. Edwin S. Ramage, "Urbanitas: Cicero and Quintilian, a Contrast in Attitudes," *American Journal of Philology* 84, no. 4 (October 1963): 390, 394.

16. "Discourse concerning the Original and Progress of Satire," trans. John Dryden, in Juvenal, *The Satires of Decimus Junius Juvenalis* (London: Printed for Jacob Tonson, 1693), xxxii.

17. "Non ego sum stultus, ut ante fui" (I am not now the fool I was!; *Amores* 3.11a.32).

18. Carlo Caruso and Andrew Laird, eds., *Italy and the Classical Tradition: Language, Thought and Poetry, 1300–1600* (London: Duckworth, 2009), 145.

19. Herbert H. Yeames, "The Tragedy of Dido. Part I," *Classical Journal* 8, no. 4 (1913): 139–50, 142; cf. p. 139: "For us moderns—so great is the change in point of view that the centuries have wrought—the scandal of the Dido episode has been quite transferred from Virgil's heroine to his hero."

20. Bruno Snell, *The Discovery of the Mind: In Greek Philosophy and Literature* (New York: Dover, 1982), 281, 301. Snell's dream of Virgil's Arcadia as a "spiritual landscape" is methodically demolished in a line-by-line yang analysis by Richard Jenkyns in "Virgil and Arcadia," *Journal of Roman Studies* 79 (1989): 26–39. Jenkyns is right in saying that the Virgilian references to Arcadia do not add up rationally and that, like the *Aeneid*, they include references to both this world and a pastoral alterity. But given Virgil's doubleness in this respect, I believe that Jenkyns's cold realism does not do justice to either Virgil's or Snell's dream. Jenkyns, in short, exemplifies the contemporary yang analytical episteme.

21. Latin-English dictionaries suggest for *facetum*, "clever, adept, witty, humorous." The derivative word in English would seriously underestimate the seriousness under Virgil's imaginative play.

22. Following Servius, Donatus cites as an example *Eclogues* 3.90–91: "Let him who doesn't hate Bavius love your songs, Maevius; and let him also yoke foxes and milk he-goats."

23. Mary M. Alberi, "The Patristic and Anglo-Latin Origins of Alcuin's Concept of Urbanity," *Journal of Medieval Latin* 3, no. 1 (1993): 96.

24. In *Epistola* 53.9, Jerome argues that no one should be offended by the "simplicity and almost baseness of the Sacred Scriptures" (in scripturis sanctis simplicitate et quasi vilitate verborum). A caveat, however. "In real life Jerome adheres to the *sancta simplicitas*; in literature he avoids the *verbosa rusticitas*. His style, though intended to be plain, is anything but simplistic"; Michael von Albrecht, *A History of Roman Literature: From Livius Andronicus to Boethius; With Special Regard to Its Influence on World Literature* (Leiden: Brill, 1997), 1651. Jerome is a cusp figure: trained in urbanity, he aspires to but cannot achieve simplicity. A half millennium later, Alcuin, another cusp figure but born into rusticity, will aim at but not achieve urbanity.

25. Alberi, "Patristic and Anglo-Latin Origins," 95; citing Pierre Riché, *Education and Culture in the Barbarian West*, trans. Jon J. Contreni (Columbia: University of South Carolina Press, 1976), 145–57, e.g., "We do not know the precise impetus for Gregory's conversion. . . . Once his decision was made, however, the lifestyle he chose required that he . . . deny himself every allusion to classical culture" (146).

26. Riché, *Education and Culture in the Barbarian West*, 154; citing Etienne Gilson, *La philosophie au Moyen Age* (Paris: Payot, 144), 224.

27. "In *Epistola* 139, Alcuin praises Paulinus of Aquileia's emended text of the Nicene Creed for its 'scholastic urbanity.' In another letter on the liturgy, *Epistola* 143, Alcuin commends Charlemagne for his pleasure in 'whatever is seasoned with the salt of urbanity.'" Alberi, "Patristic and Anglo-Latin Origins," 95.

28. Dante himself has been praised in modern times both for his *parola ornata*, by the neoclassicist critic Ernst Robert Curtius, and for his *dir soave e piana*, by the antithetical critic Erich Auerbach. See Peter Dale Scott, *Coming to Jakarta: A Poem about Terror* (New York: New Directions, 1989), 89; cf. Peter Dale Scott with Freeman Ng, *Poetry and Terror: Politics and Poetics in "Coming to Jakarta"* (Lanham, MD: Lexington Books, 2018), 94: "There's been a certain amount of forest-city and now female-male contrast in this poem . . . a kind of archetypal playing here of the two versions of power, bottom-up or top-down . . . that are at work in society."

29. Tertullian, *Apologeticus pro Christianis* 17.6; *Patrologia Latina* 1:377.

30. Cf. Thomas K. Hubbard, *The Pipes of Pan: Intertextuality and Literary Filiation in the Pastoral Tradition from Theocritus to Milton* (Ann Arbor: University of Michigan Press, 1998), 46: "The first half of the book has often been seen as a positive construction of a pastoral vision, whilst the second half dramatizes progressive alienation from that vision, as each poem of the first half is taken up and responded to in reverse order."

31. "Aspice, aratra iugo referunt suspensa iuvenci," itself a delicately equilibrated image.

32. Cf. the Song of Songs: "Arise [kumi] my love, my fair one, and come away" (2:13).

33. My translation; adapted in Paul Alpers, *The Singer of the Eclogues: A Study of Virgilian Pastoral* (Berkeley: University of California Press, 1979).

34. Morton Smith, quoted in John J. Collins, *Seers, Sibyls, and Sages in Hellenistic-Roman Judaism* (Leiden: Brill, 1997), 192.

35. Wikipedia, s.v. "Gaius Asinius Pollio," citing Velleius Paterculus, *Roman History* 2.86.

36. John Miller, *Apollo, Augustus, and the Poets* (Cambridge: Cambridge University Press, 2009), 193, 254–55.

37. Ronald Syme, *The Roman Revolution* (Oxford: Oxford University Press, 1939), 202; Dio Cassius, *History of Rome* 47.18.1–3.

38. Plutarch (d. 127 CE) paints a similar picture of Julius Caesar ("Kind Daphnis") as a dictator who crucified his captives on occasion and in his Gallic campaign "took by storm more than eight hundred cities [and] slew [diephtheiren, διέφθειρεν] one million [men] in hand-to-hand fighting." Plutarch, *Parallel Lives* 48.2.6, 48.15.4.

39. St. Augustine, *Epistolae ad Romanos Inchoata Expositio* 1.3; Migne, *Patrologia Latina* 35.2089; citing Virgil, *Eclogues* 4.4.

40. To *Eclogues* 4.24, "The serpent, too, shall perish [occent et serpens]," one can also compare Isaiah 27:1: "In that day the lord will punish Leviathan the fleeing serpent." Similarly, a line in Virgil's *Georgics*, "the crooked pruning-hooks are forged into stiff swords" (1.508), is a reversal of the image in Isaiah 2:4: "And they shall beat their swords into plowshares, and their spears into pruninghooks: nation shall not lift up sword against nation, neither shall they learn war any more." Cf. Joel 4:10: "Beat your hoes into swords, and your pruning-hooks into spears."

41. Josephus, *Antiquities* 14:388–89. It is possible that Isaiah was imitated in the "new songs" (nova carmina) of Pollio, cited by a shepherd at *Eclogues* 3.86. For a general overview, see Thomas Fletcher Royds, *Virgil and Isaiah: A Study of the Pollio with Translations, Notes, and Appendices* (Oxford: Blackwell, 1918).

42. Benjamin Kedar, "Traces of Jewish Traditions," in The *Literature of the Jewish People in the Period of the Second Temple and the Talmud*, ed. Michael E. Stone (Philadelphia: Fortress Press, 2006), 308: "Since all indications point to the fact that the OL [Vetus Latina] is not the product of a single effort, the question arises whether strands of pristine translations, or at least early interpretative traditions can be detected in it. . . . Indeed, a number of scholars are inclined to believe that the OL has at its base pre-Christian translations made from the Hebrew. The proofs they adduce are, however, far from conclusive."

43. The same passage shares with the eclogue a prophecy not found in Isaiah—that voyaging by sea shall cease to be perilous:

> And all pathways of the plain
> And rough hills and high mountains and wild waves
> Of the deep shall be easy in those days
> For crossing and for sailing; for all peace
> On the land of the good shall come. (*Sibylline Oracle* 3.966–70)

44. I have been unable to access *Antimonarchic Discourses in Antiquity*, ed. Henning Börm with Wolfgang Havener (Stuttgart: Franz Steiner Verlag, 2015).

45. Cf. Snell, *The Discovery of the Mind*, 294–95: "The dream of the golden age is as old as man's thinking. . . . But never before Virgil, either in Greek or Roman literature, had this Utopia been so closely interwoven with historical reality as in the *Aeneid*, or indeed earlier in the *Eclogues*."

46. Edward Gibbon, *The History of the Decline and Fall of the Roman Empire* (New York: Modern Library, 1946), 1:61. I hope it is obvious that I do not endorse this view.

47. Matthew Arnold, "On the Modern Element in Literature," http://ahistoryofthepresentananthology.blogspot.com/2015/01/on-modern-element-in-literature-by.html.

48. E.g., Isaiah 2:7: "The arrogance of man will be brought low, and human pride humbled"; Isaiah 29:19–20: "19 The meek also shall increase their joy in the Lord. . . . 20 For the terrible one is brought to nought."

49. When Anchises calls his son "Roman," the epithet marks that Aeneas, like Odysseus in Homer's *Odyssey*, has been changed and is now a man of the future. He is no longer the Trojan who momentarily betrayed his destiny through love of Dido; instead, Anchises's words have "fired his mind with love of the fame to come" (incenditque animum famae venientis amore; *Aeneid* 6:889).These two loves—one sexual, one sublimated—correspond to the two loves of Diotima in the *Symposium*. They correspond also to the two conflicting forces in the *Aeneid*, of "impious Furor" (impius furor), restrained by the closing of the Gates of War in the first prophecy, and the *pietas* held out to Aeneas as a model in the second (*Aeneid* 6:878, 883).Virgil is of course a realist as well as a visionary, and at the close of the epic, Aeneas, like Achilles in the Iliad, does *not* spare his downfallen victim.

50. Milosz, *The Witness of Poetry*, 109.

51. Seamus Heaney, trans., *Aeneid Book VI* (New York: Farrar, Straus & Giroux, 2016), 95. Cf. p. ix: "Anchises' vision [makes] this part of the poem something of a test for reader and translator alike," but also something that "had to be gone through with."

52. W. R. Johnson, *Darkness Visible: A Study of Vergil's Aeneid* (Berkeley: University of California Press, 1976), 108.

53. Seamus Heaney, commencement address at Colgate University, May 1994, in Seamus Heaney Papers, May 22, 1994 (Manuscript, Archives, and Rare Book Library, Emory University, MSS 960, Subseries 1.1, Box 18); quoted in Michael Richard Parker, "Past Master: Czeslaw Milosz and His Impact on the Poetry of Seamus Heaney," *Textual Practice* 27, no. 5 (2013): 844.

54. Seamus Heaney, "Station Island," in *Opened Ground: Selected Poems, 1966–1996* (New York: Farrar, Straus & Giroux, 1998), 235–37.

55. Danny Morrison, "Seamus Heaney Disputed," January 31, 2009, https://www.dannymorrison.com/seamus-heaney-disputed.

56. Heaney, "Station Island," 226, 245.

57. Czeslaw Milosz, *New and Collected Poems, 1931–2001* (New York: Ecco, 2001), 77.

58. Czeslaw Milosz, *Native Realm: A Search for Self-Definition* (New York: Farrar, Straus & Giroux, 1968), 247. Cf. Milosz, "A Semi-Private Letter about Poetry," in *To Begin Where I Am: Selected Essays* (New York: Farrar, Straus & Giroux, 2001), 350–51: "When I wrote in the introduction to *Rescue* that I accepted the salvational goal of poetry, that was exactly what I had in mind, and I still believe that poetry can either save or destroy nations."

59. Milosz, *A Treatise on Poetry* (New York: Ecco, 2001), 59, 60. Commenting on the line, "For contemplation fades without resistance," Milosz explained that this was "a polemic with the T. S. Eliot of *The Four Quartets*. By renouncing the world for the sake of 'the still point,' of perfect stillness outside time, we may deprive contemplation of its intensity" (Milosz, *A Treatise on Poetry*, 123).

60. Milosz, *A Treatise on Poetry*, 118.

61. Peter Dale Scott, *Czeslaw Milosz, Poet of Catastrophe and Hope* (Lanham, MD: Rowman & Littlefield, 2023), 232–35.

62. Milosz, *The Witness of Poetry*, 69.

63. In like manner, Ovid will boast, in the closing lines of the *Metamorphoses* (15.878–79), that "throughout all the ages I shall live in fame." Dante closes the *Vita Nuova* by promising to say of Beatrice things that had never been said of any woman (*d'alcuna*) before. All three poets contrast the transient world they write about (even the golden age was part of a cyclical pattern) with the transcendence through time of the poet's art and reputation.

64. Jeremy B. Lefkowitz, "Grand Allusions: Vergil in Phaedrus," *American Journal of Philology* 137, no. 3 (2016), 487, 488, https://www.jstor.org/stable/26360883. But Phaedrus emphasizes his following in Virgil's footsteps in order to reach an un-Virgilian conclusion: "that his inventiveness and sophistication would ultimately do nothing to improve his position on the margins of Roman literary culture"; Lefkowitz, "Grand Allusions," 487.

65. Lefkowitz, "Grand Allusions," 487.

66. Kathleen McCarthy, *I, the Poet: First-Person Form in Horace, Catullus, and Propertius* (Ithaca, NY: Cornell University Press, 2019), 3.

67. Milosz, *The Witness of Poetry*, 109.

68. Snell, *The Discovery of the Mind*, 292.

69. Snell, *The Discovery of the Mind*, 299.

70. Snell, *The Discovery of the Mind*, 299, 300, 307.

71. E.g., D. A. Little, "The Death of Turnus and the Pessimism of the 'Aeneid,'" *Journal of the Australasian Universities Language and Literature Association* 33, no. 1 (1970): 67–76.[1]. *Aeneid* 7:312, 315, 321, 325–26.

72. *Aeneid* 7:312, 315, 321, 325–26.

73. *Argonautica* 1:462ss, 3:556ss, 1169; George W, Mooney, *Commentary on Apollonius: Argonautica*, http://www.perseus.tufts.edu/hopper/text?doc=Perseus%3Atext%3A1999.04.0068%3Atext%3Dintro; cf. Hermann Fränkel, "Das Argonautenepos des Apollonios," *Museum Helveticum* 14, no. 1 (1957): 1–19.

74. Cf. Brooks Otis, *Virgil, a Study in Civilized Poetry* (Oxford: Clarendon Press, 1964), 337.

75. Matthew 19:21; Peter Brown, *Through the Eye of a Needle: Wealth, the Fall of Rome, and the Making of Christianity in the West, 350–550 AD* (Princeton, NJ: Princeton University Press, 2012). See chapters 8, 12.

76. Milosz, *The Witness of Poetry*, 14.

77. Maxine Chernoff and Paul Hoover, trans., *Selected Poems of Friedrich Hölderlin* (Richmond, CA: Omnidawn, 2008), 131.

78. Peter Dale Scott, "Czeslaw Milosz and Solidarity; or, Poetry and the Liberation of a People," *Brick* 78 (Winter 2006): 67–74; Peter Dale Scott, *Ecstatic Pessimist: Czeslaw Milosz, Poet of Catastrophe and Hope* (Lanham, MD: Rowman & Littlefield, 2023), 17–26.

CHAPTER EIGHT

1. Steele Brand, "The Diseases That Kill Republics: Insights from Ancient Rome's Epidemics," Front Porch Republic, May 9, 2020, https://www.frontporchrepublic.com/2020/05/the-diseases-that-kill-republics-insights-from-ancient-romes-epidemics.

2. Karen Armstrong, "A New Axial Age," Adishakti.org, http://www.adishakti.org/_/a_new_axial_age_by_karen_armstrong.htm.

3. Arians were Christians who followed the creed of the Egyptian presbyter Arius (d. 336), that Jesus Christ was begotten of God the Father but was not coeternal with him.

4. Peter Brown, *Augustine of Hippo: A Biography* (Berkeley: University of California Press, 1969), 81–82; citing F. Homes Dudden, *The Life and Times of St. Ambrose* (Oxford: Clarendon Press, 1935), 1, 270–93. Cf. 2 Corinthians 12:10: "Therefore I take pleasure in infirmities, in reproaches, in necessities, in persecutions, in distresses for Christ's sake: for when I am weak, then am I strong."

5. "Priscillian's execution is seen as the first example of secular justice intervening in an ecclesiastical matter (see Gaudemet 1958:233–34). It clearly illustrates both the tension and the ideological union between the church and imperial authority at the end of the Low Empire, or in other words, the way in which 'the sword of justice' placed itself at the church's service." Ana Maria C. M. Jorge, "The Lusitanian Episcopate in the 4th Century: Priscillian of Ávila and the Tensions between Bishops," *Dicionário da história religiosa de Portugal*, dir. C. A. M. Azevedo (Lisbon: Círculo de leitores), 4:63–67.

6. Ambrose, Epistle 41; Paulus Diaconus, *Life of St. Ambrose* 22–23. Cf. chapter 11.

7. "Ambrose, the Bishop of Milan, withdrew in horror from the emperor's court. He denounced Theodosius' wickedness and banned him from receiving communion until he had repented. The emperor sought absolution and was readmitted to communion on Christmas day 390, after an eight-month penance." John Curran, "From Jovian to Theodosius," in *The Cambridge Ancient History*, vol. 13, *The Late Empire, AD 337–425*, ed. Averil Cameron and Peter Garnsey (Cambridge: Cambridge University Press, 2008), 108.

8. Peter Brown, *Through the Eye of a Needle: Wealth, the Fall of Rome, and the Making of Christianity in the West, 350–550 AD* (Princeton, NJ: Princeton University Press, 2014), 527–36.

9. St. Augustine is generally silent about St. Martin and does not mention him in his *Confessions*. Yet it is curious that Augustine, when expressing surprise at the contemporary primitive Christianity of St. Anthony in Egypt, does not cite the much closer example of St. Martin in Gaul.

10. Victor Cunrui Xiong, *Emperor Yang of the Sui Dynasty: His Life, Times, and Legacy* (Albany: State University of New York Press, 2006), 160.

11. Neville Brown, *History and Climate Change: A Eurocentric Perspective* (London: Routledge, 2001), 88.

12. Paul Voosen, "Alaskan Megaeruption May Have Helped End the Roman Republic," *Science*, June 22, 2020, https://www.sciencemag.org/news/2020/06/alaskan-mega-eruption-may-have-helped-end-roman-republic. Cf. Joseph R. McConnell et al., "Alaska's Okmok Volcano in 43 BCE and Effects on the Late Roman Republic and Ptolemaic Kingdom," *Proceedings of the National Academy of Sciences of the United States of America* 117, no. 27 (2020): 15443–49, https://www.pnas.org/content/117/27/15443: "Egypt's own capacity to defend against Rome was diminished by the famine, disease, land abandonment, and reduced state income that followed the Okmok II eruption."

13. Michael Specter, "How Anthony Fauci Became America's Doctor," *New Yorker*, April 10, 2020, https://www.newyorker.com/magazine/2020/04/20/how-anthony-fauci-became-americas-doctor.

14. Ann Gibbons, "Why 536 Was 'the Worst Year to Be Alive,'" *Science*, November 15, 2018, https://www.sciencemag.org/news/2018/11/why-536-was-worst-year-be-alive.

15. Samuel Kline Cohn, *Plague and Its Consequences: Oxford Bibliographies Online Research Guide* (Oxford: Oxford University Press, 2010), 3.

16. Kyle Harper, "How Climate Change and Plague Helped Bring Down the Roman Empire," *Smithsonian*, December 19, 2017, https://www.smithsonianmag.com/science-nature/how-climate-change-and-disease-helped-fall-rome-180967591: "Genetic evidence suggests that the strain of *Yersinia pestis* that generated the plague of Justinian originated somewhere near western China. It first appeared on the southern shores of the Mediterranean and, in all likelihood, was smuggled in along the southern, seaborne trading networks that carried silk and spices to Roman consumers." Cf. Kyle Harper, *The Fate of Rome: Climate, Disease, and the End of an Empire* (Princeton, NJ: Princeton University Press, 2017).

17. Timothy P. Newfield, "The Climate Downturn of 536–50," in *The Palgrave Handbook of Climate History*, ed. Sam White, Christian Pfister, and Franz Mauelshagen (London: Palgrave Macmillan, 2018), 459, 468–69 (famine); Gibbons, "Why 536 Was 'the Worst Year to Be Alive'" (plague).

18. Michael J. Decker, *The Byzantine Dark Ages* (London: Bloomsbury Academic, 2016).

19. Walter Scheidel, "The Only Thing, Historically, That's Curbed Inequality: Catastrophe," *The Atlantic*, February 21, 2017, https://www.theatlantic.com/business/archive/2017/02/scheidel-great-leveler-inequality-violence/517164.

20. For example, Justininian decisively terminated Ostrogothic dominance of Italy in 554 CE.

21. It is more customary to refer to this period as the "Dark Ages." But in the next chapter I shall discuss earlier "Dark Ages," principally the one that followed the collapse of Bronze Age cities and empires about 1200 BCE. So I shall use "Dark Age" for the most recent half millennium to distinguish it from "Dark Ages" in the plural.

22. For a discussion of yang and yin, see Wing-Tsit Chan, *A Source Book in Chinese Philosophy* (Princeton, NJ: Princeton University Press, 1963), 244–50.

23. Michael Saler, "Modernity and Enchantment: A Historiographic Review," *American Historical Review* 111, no. 3 (2006): 692–716, https://academic.oup.com/ahr/article/111/3/692/13735; citing Max Weber, "Science as a Vocation," in *From Max Weber: Essays in Sociology*, ed. H. H. Gerth and C. Wright Mills, 129–56 (New York: Routledge, 1946).

24. Euripides, *The Bacchae*; Ovid, *Metamorphoses* 3.692–733.

25. Bard Thompson, *Humanists and Reformers: A History of the Renaissance and Reformation* (Grand Rapids, MI: Eerdmans, 1996), 13.

26. *Encyclopaedia Britannica*, s.v. "Migration Period."

27. Peter Dale Scott, "Dark-Age Pastoral: The Poetry of Aldhelm, Bede, and Alcuin," forthcoming.

28. Matt Samberg, "The Coming Dark Age," *Medium*, March 17, 2019, https://medium.com/@mattsamberg/the-coming-dark-age-50d801dd696a.

29. Michael T. Klare, "Why the Paris Climate Summit Will Be a Peace Conference: Averting a World of Failed States and Resource Wars," TomDispatch, November 3, 2015, https://www.tomdispatch.com/blog/176063/tomgram%3A_michael_klare,_are_resource_wars_our_future; citing Joshua Holland, "Syria May Be the First Climate-Change Conflict, but It Won't Be the Last," *Nation*, October 27, 2015, https://www.thenation.com/article/syria-may-be-the-first-climate-change-conflict-but-it-wont-be-the-last.

CHAPTER NINE

1. Jean-Pierre Bocquet-Appel, "When the World's Population Took Off: The Springboard of the Neolithic Demographic Transition," *Science* 333, no. 6042 (July 29, 2011), 333.

2. Mihael Budja, "Archaeology and Rapid Climate Changes: From the Collapse Concept to a Panarchy Interpretative Model," *Documenta Praehistorica* 42 (2015): 171; quoting Herbert Edgar Wright et al., *Global Climates since the Last Glacial Maximum* (Minneapolis: University of Minnesota Press, 1993), 466.

3. "Collapse of Civilizations Worldwide Defines Youngest Unit of the Geologic Time Scale," International Commission on Stratigraphy, July 15, 2018, https://web.archive.org/web/20180715004024/https://stratigraphy.org/index.php/ics-news-and-meetings/119-collapse-of-civilizations-worldwide-defines-youngest-unit-of-the-geologic-time-scale.

4. Harvey Weiss, "Megadrought and the Akkadian Collapse," in *Megadrought and Collapse: From Early Agriculture to Angkor* (Oxford: Oxford University Press, 2017).

5. "The Akkadian Empire," Lumen Learning, https://courses.lumenlearning.com/suny-hccc-worldcivilization/chapter/the-akkadian-empire/#:~:text=The%20Empire%20of%20Akkad%20collapsed,of%20Ur%20in%202112%20BCE.

6. Robert Drews, *The End of the Bronze Age: Changes in Warfare and the Catastrophe ca. 1200 B.C.* (Princeton, NJ: Princeton University Press, 1993), 4.

7. Benjamin W. Fortson IV, *Indo-European Language and Culture: An Introduction* (Malden, MA: Wiley-Blackwell, 2010), 249.

8. Eric Cline, *1177 B.C.: The Year Civilization Collapsed* (Princeton, NJ: Princeton University Press, 2021), xv–xvi: "I strongly suspect that future historians will see the year 2020 as another pivotal moment."

9. Cline, *1177 B.C.*, 40, xvi.

10. Cline, *1177 B.C.*, 163; citing Gerard Bond, William Showers, Maziet Cheseby, Rusty Lotti, Peter Almasi, Peter deMenocal, Paul Priore, Heidi Cullen, Irka Hajdas, and Georges Bonani, "A Pervasive Millennial-Scale Cycle in North Atlantic Holocene and Glacial Climates," *Science* 278, no. 5341 (1997): 1257–66, https://science.sciencemag.org/content/278/5341/1257.full.

11. Bond et al., "A Pervasive Millennial-Scale Cycle."

12. Timothy P. Newfield, "The Climate Downturn of 536–50," in *The Palgrave Handbook of Climate History*, ed. Sam White, Christian Pfister, and Franz Mauelshagen, 447–94 (London: Palgrave Macmillan, 2018).

13. International Commission on Stratigraphy, "Collapse of Civilizations Worldwide." The neat match of dates here is no coincidence: the IRD event dating was part of the evidence considered by the commission.

14. Stephen P. Obrochta, Hiroko Miyahara, Yusuke Yokoyama, and Thomas J. Crowley, "A Re-examination of Evidence for the North Atlantic '1500-Year Cycle' at Site 609," *Quaternary Science Reviews* 55, no. 8 (2012): 23–33.

15. Paul Voosen, "Massive Drought or Myth? Scientists Spar over an Ancient Climate Event behind our New Geological Age," *Science*, August 8, 2018, https://www.sciencemag.org/news/2018/08/massive-drought-or-myth-scientists-spar-over-ancient-climate-event-behind-our-new.

16. A. L. Rowse, *The Use of History* (New York: Macmillan, 1945), 55.

17. Voosen, "Massive Drought or Myth?"

18. Mihael Budja has used Colin Renfrew's terms "anastrophe" and "catastrophe" to describe these recurring rhythms of expansion and recision. See Colin Renfrew and Kenneth L. Cooke, *Transformations: Mathematical Approaches to Culture Change* (New York: Academic Press, 1979), 481–94; Budja, "Archaeology and Rapid Climate Changes," 175. But Renfrew's adaptation of the rhetorical term "anastrophe" is clumsy, and the connotations of "catastrophe" I find wholly inappropriate. Perhaps *diastole* (expansion) and *systole* (contraction) might be more appropriate terms—except that the active energy of the heart is in the contraction; the heart's expansion is a relaxation.

19. Cline, *1177 B.C.*, 185; quoting W. G. Dever, "The Late Bronze–Early Iron I Horizon in Syria-Palestine: Egyptians, Canaanites, 'Sea Peoples,' and Proto-Israelites," in *The Crisis Years: The 12th Century B.C. from beyond the Danube to the Tigris*, ed. W. A. Ward and M. S. Joukowsky (Dubuque, IA: Kendall/Hunt, 1992), 108.

20. Ronald Hendel, *Remembering Abraham: Culture, Memory, and History in the Hebrew Bible* (Oxford: Oxford University Press, 2005), 60. (EA refers to the numbering system of the El Amarna tablets.)

21. Hendel, *Remembering Abraham*, 62.

22. Hendel, *Remembering Abraham*, 63.

23. Hendel, *Remembering Abraham*, 65; citing El Amarna tablet E 35. Cf. Exodus 9:3, "Behold, the hand of the Lord is upon thy cattle"; J. J. M. Roberts, "The Hand of Yahweh," in *The Bible and the Ancient Near East: Collected Essays* (Winona Lake, IN: Eisenbrauns, 2002), 95–101.

24. Hendel, *Remembering Abraham*, 64. Unfortunately, the authenticity of surviving fragments from Manetho that we have, and even the historical existence of their author, have both been challenged.

25. Mark S. Smith, *The Early History of God: Yahweh and Other Deities of Ancient Israel* (Grand Rapids, MI: Eerdmans, 2002), 6–7. Many of the biblical references to Canaanites—"by far the most common ethnic term in the Hebrew Bible" (William G. Dever, *Who Were the Early Israelites and Where Did They Come From?* [Grand Rapids, MI: Eerdmans, 2006], 219)—seem problematically political and hostile, often out of tone with their context. Noah's odd curse on his grandson Canaan for the sin of his father Ham (Gen. 9:20–27) is just one example. (Note that the now discarded term "Hamite" referred to "North African peoples, including the ancient Egyptians and Berbers." Canaanites, in this pseudo-system, were clearly Semites.)

26. A. Nebel, D. Filon, D. A. Weiss, M. Weale, M. Faerman, A. Oppenheim, and M. G. Thomas, "High-Resolution Y Chromosome Haplotypes of Israeli and Palestinian Arabs Reveal Geographic Substructure and Substantial Overlap with Haplotypes of Jews," *Human Genetics* 107, no. 6 (2000): 630–41, https://pubmed.ncbi.nlm .nih.gov/11153918. Cf. Andrew Lawler, "DNA from the Bible's Canaanites Lives on in Modern Arabs and Jews," *National Geographic*, May 28, 2020, https://www .nationalgeographic.com/history/article/dna-from-biblical-canaanites-lives-modern -arabs-jews.

27. Jan Assmann, *Moses the Egyptian: The Memory of Egypt in Western Monotheism* (Cambridge, MA: Harvard University Press, 1997), 8–9.

28. Hendel, *Remembering Abraham*, 58–59; quoting Assmann, *Moses the Egyptian*, 14.

30. A half millennium before Akhenaten, Hammurabi (ca. 1792–1750 BCE) was another cusp pioneer ruler. His Akkadian Code, even if short-lived, is a major milestone in the history of law. And a half millennium later, the Assyrian king Sennacherib (705–681 BCE) has recently been assessed as standing out for having "attempted to create . . . a stable imperial structure [even if ephemeral] immune from traditional problems." Julian Reade, "Studies in Assyrian Geography. Part I: Sennacherib and the Waters of Nineveh," *Revue d'Assyriologie et d'Archéologie Orientale* 72 (1978): 47–72.

31. Assmann, *Moses the Egyptian*, 167.

32. Assmann, *Moses the Egyptian*, 2, 24. We should not forget that religious antagonism also marks the history of India and China.

33. Assmann, *Moses the Egyptian*, 167. In a more recent book, he also addresses the "biblical anti-Canaanism" of the Jewish bible. Jan Assmann, *The Invention of Religion: Faith and Covenant in the Book of Exodus* (Princeton, NJ: Princeton University Press, 2020), 87.

34. Richard Slotkin, *Regeneration through Violence: The Mythology of the American Frontier, 1600–1860* (Princeton, NJ: Princeton University Press, 2000), 4.

35. It is perhaps symptomatic of our era that the *OED* does not distinguish between myth-*making* (left brain) and myth-*experiencing* (right brain) and defines both as "The creation of myths."

36. See below, "Mythogenesis," in appendix, "Four Poems."

37. Sulpicius writes that in response to a request from "an ex-Governor named Auspicius" in Sens, Martin's prayers freed Sens from hailstorms until Martin's death twenty years later; Sulpicius Severus, *Dialogues* 3.7; in F. R. Hoare, ed. and trans., *The Western Fathers, Being the Lives of Martin of Tours, Ambrosius, Augustine of Hippo, Honoratus of Arles, and Germanus of Auxerre* (New York: Harper and Row, 1965), 129. Gregory of Tours records that an attack on King Chlothar by his royal brother and nephew, Childebert and Theodebert, was deterred by a sudden hailstorm sent by St. Martin (*Historia Francorum* 3.28). Bede's *Ecclesiastical History* (3.15) claims that St. Aidan was able to foresee a storm that would threaten the boat bringing a bride for King Oswy of Northumbria, and then supplied an oil that was able to calm it. Chris Wickham considers this "weather magic" of the saints to be a "survival of 'pagan' practices"; Chris Wickham, *The Inheritance of Rome: A History of Europe from 400 to 1000* (New York: Penguin 2009), 170–71.

38. Jean-Luc Desalvo, "France and the French in the Collective Memory of the Acadians," in *Memory, Empire, and Postcolonialism: Legacies of French Colonialism*, ed. Alec G. Hargreaves (Lanham, MD: Lexington Books, 2005), 74, quoting Antonine Maillet, *Les Confessions de Jeanne de Valois* (Montreal: Leméac, 1992).

39. But it may well be a coincidence that the *acadiens'* ancestors came chiefly from Touraine and Poitou, in the area proselytized by St. Martin of Tours.

40. Yujin Nagasawa, "Miracles: A Very Short Introduction," OUPBlog, October 6, 2017, https://blog.oup.com/2017/10/why-people-believe-miracles. Cf. Yujin Nagasawa, *Miracles: A Very Short Introduction* (Oxford: Oxford University Press, 2017). For a more yin perspective, see Daniel Maria Klimek, *Medjugorje and the Supernatural: Science, Mysticism, and Extraordinary Religious Experience* (Oxford: Oxford University Press, 2018), which "proposes a holistic hermeneutical model for understanding supernatural experiences."

41. One time an intern left the ghosts an open bottle of Pepsi, enhanced by a helpful straw.

42. Peter Dale Scott, *The Road to 9/11: Wealth, Empire, and the Future of America* (Berkeley: University of California Press, 2007), xii–xiv: "Happiness is found close to the necessities of life, not in needless complexity and meaningless multiplicity of choice." See chapter 10.

CHAPTER TEN

1. These texts were not canonized as "Five Classics" until the Western Han dynasty (206 BCE–9 CE), when Confucianism became the main cultural and political discourse.

2. Philip R. Davies in Lee Martin McDonald and James A. Sanders, eds., *The Canon Debate: On the Origins and Formation of the Bible* (Peabody, MA: Hendrickson Publishers, 2002), 50: "With many other scholars, I conclude that the fixing of a canonical list was almost certainly the achievement of the Hasmonean dynasty."

3. William H. McNeill, *Plagues and Peoples* (Garden City, NY: Anchor Press, 1976), 119. For example, the so-called Antonine Plague of 165–180 CE, carried by Roman soldiers from a war against Parthia in Asia, is said to have caused up to five million deaths, as much as one-third of the population in some areas.

4. Michael Carter, "Archiereis and Asiarchs: A Gladiatorial Perspective," *Greek, Roman and Byzantine Studies* 44, no. 1 (2004): 43.

5. Josephus, *The Jewish War* 6.418, 7:37–40.

6. Ovid describes the gladiatorial arena as suitable for sexual seduction. Alison Futrell, *The Roman Games: A Sourcebook* (Oxford: Blackwell, 2006), 105.

7. Augustine, *Confessions* 6:7–8.

8. Erich Auerbach, *Mimesis* (Princeton, NJ: Princeton University Press, 1953), 60–63.

9. I will record one memorable personal experience. Some years ago, researching the background of the racist Norwegian mass killer Anders Breivik, I linked, despite intervening warnings from Google, to one of the neofascist websites that inspired him. It was headed by what appeared to be a photograph—actual or Photoshopped—of a very attractive young woman, naked, speared on a long steel rod as if for grilling like a kebab. As in the case of Alypius, the sight provoked a profound hormonal surge in me; but in my case it was a sickening surge of revulsion, not of attraction. I left the site instantly and ceased my research of such websites.

10. Cf. Clifford Geertz, "Deep Play: Notes on the Balinese Cockfight," in *The Interpretation of Cultures: Selected Essays* (New York: Basic Books, 1973), 419–49.

11. "No Wonder Fox Hunting Is Still Prevalent—The Ban Is Designed to Fail British Wildlife," The Conversation, January 30, 2019, http://theconversation.com/no-wonder-fox-hunting-is-still-prevalent-the-ban-is-designed-to-fail-british-wildlife-110454.

12. The last U.S. execution in a public area, an event viewed by twenty thousand, was in 1936. Frances Larson, "Very Short Book Excerpt: The Allure of Execution," *The Atlantic*, November 2014; cited in Frances Larson, *Severed: A History of Heads Lost and Heads Found* (New York: Liveright, 2014), 27.

13. Cf. Peter Dale Scott, *Coming to Jakarta: A Poem about Terror* (New York: New Directions, 1989), 34; Peter Dale Scott with Freeman Ng, *Poetry and Terror: Politics and Poetics in "Coming to Jakarta"* (Lanham, MD: Lexington Books, 2018), 33.

14. Salvian, *De gubernatione Dei* 6.6.15.

15. "Wallia and the Visigothic Settlement in Gaul," Novo Scriptorium, December 10, 2020, https://novoscriptorium.com/2020/12/10/wallia-and-the-visigothic-settlement-in-gaul, summarizing J. B. Bury, *The Invasion of Europe by the Barbarians* (New York: Russell & Russell, 1963).

16. In 1971 Chuck Hughes of the Detroit Lions collapsed after making a catch for a first down and died soon after in hospital. The game continued. *Detroit Free Press*, October 23, 2021.

17. Perry Anderson, *Passages from Antiquity to Feudalism* (London: Verso, 1978), 21, 22. Orlando Patterson also argues that the concept of freedom "was generated from the experience of slavery"; Patterson, *Freedom in the Making of Western Culture* (New York: Basic Books, 1991), xiii.

18. Lynn White Jr., *Medieval Technology and Social Change* (London: Oxford University Press, 1962), 43.

19. White, *Medieval Technology and Social Change*, 44.

20. Lynn White Jr., *Technology and Invention in the Middle Ages* (Cambridge, MA: Mediaeval Academy of America, 1940), 15. For most Westerners, the "Dark Ages" refers to the period after the fall of Rome. But as this book will discuss earlier Dark Ages, notably after the collapse of Bronze Age cities, I shall refer to the most recent one as the "Dark Age."

21. Anderson, *Passages from Antiquity to Feudalism*, 25, 26; citing M. I. Finley, "Technical Innovation and Economic Progress in the Ancient World," *Economic History Review* 18, no. 1 (1955): 29–45; F. W. Walbank, *The Awful Revolution* (Toronto: University of Toronto Press, 1969), 40–41, 46–47, 108–10.

22. Daniel Lazare, "Review of Chris Wickham's 'Medieval Europe,'" History News Network, George Washington University, March 29, 2018, emphasis added, https://historynewsnetwork.org/article/168636.

23. Walter Scheidel, "The Bloodstained Leveller," *Aeon*, June 19, 2017, https://aeon.co/essays/are-plagues-and-wars-the-only-ways-to-reduce-inequality. Cf. Walter Scheidel, *Escape from Rome: The Failure of Empire and the Road to Prosperity* (Princeton, NJ: Princeton University Press, 2019). I take issue with Scheidel's deterministic pessimism in chapter 15, p. 258.

24. Scheidel, "The Bloodstained Leveller." Cf. Walter Scheidel, *The Great Leveler: Violence and the History of Inequality from the Stone Age to the Twenty-First Century* (Princeton, NJ: Princeton University Press, 2018).

25. Peter Dale Scott, *The Road to 9/11: Wealth, Empire, and the Future of America* (Berkeley: University of California Press, 2007), xiii. I suspect that the deep inspiration for my Schumacherian rhetoric was my happy experience in childhood of an equilibrium, between city life in winter and carefree summers of pumping water, heaving blocks of river ice from the icehouse into our icebox, and splitting firewood for the stove.

26. Wikipedia, s.v. "Six Dynasties Poetry."

27. "It is thought that with the demise of the Eastern Jin dynasty in 420, that he began to refer to himself as 'Qian,' meaning 'hiding,' as a signification of his final withdrawal into the quiet life in the country and his decision to avoid any further participation in the political scene." Wikipedia, s.v. "Tao Yuanming," citing H. C. Chang, *Chinese Literature, 2: Nature Poetry* (New York: Columbia University Press, 1977), 22.

28. Wikipedia, s.v. "Tao Yuanming," citing Xiaofei Tian, "From the Eastern Jin through the Early Tang (317–649)," in *The Cambridge History of Chinese Literature*, ed. Kang-I Sun Chang and Stephen Owen, vol. 1, *To 1375* (Cambridge: Cambridge University Press, 2013), 221–22.

29. Stephen Owen, *The Great Age of Chinese Poetry: The High T'ang* (New Haven, CT: Yale University Press, 1981), xi, 6.

30. Su Shi, quoted by his brother Su Ziyou (1039–1112), as translated by J. Timothy Wixted, in *Classical Chinese Literature: An Anthology of Translations*, John Minford and Joseph S. M. Lau, 491 (New York: Columbia University Press, 2000).

31. Brian Patrick McGuire, *Friendship and Community: The Monastic Experience, 350–1250* (Ithaca, NY: Cornell University Press, 2010), 98. Like Ambrose before him, Fortunatus also wrote two majestically simple Latin hymns, "Pange lingua gloriosi" and "Vexilla Regis prodeunt," that are sung to this day in Catholic masses.

32. Alcuin, *Carmen* 21, *Poetarum Latinarum Medii Aevi* 1, ed. E. Dümmler (Berlin, 1881) 274–75; my translation in *Dark-Age Pastoral: The Poetry of Aldhelm, Bede, and Alcuin*, forthcoming.

33. Nora Chadwick, as quoted by Monica Weis, *Thomas Merton and the Celts: A New World Opening Up* (Eugene, OR: Pickwick Publications, 2016), 101. "Alcuin's first master, Colgu, had been Irish, as was his best friend, Joseph, who accompanied him to France and died beside him"; Thomas Cahill, *How the Irish Saved Civilization: The Untold Story of Ireland's Heroic Role from the Fall of Rome to the Rise of Medieval Europe* (New York: Nan A. Talese, Doubleday, 1995), 206.

34. Kuno Meyer, *Ancient Irish Poetry* (London: Constable & Co., 1913), 100. "The love of . . . birds is a strong motif in early Irish Christian literature"; Caitlin Matthews and John Matthews, *The Encyclopaedia of Celtic Wisdom: A Celtic Shaman's Sourcebook* (Rockport, MA: Element Books, 1994), 87. The poem is located on a margin of the late fourteenth-/early fifteenth-century *Leabhar Breac*, or *Speckled Book*, but is probably much earlier.

35. Alcuin, *Carmen* 23, *Poetarum Latinarum Medii Aevi* 1, ed. E. Dümmler (Berlin, 1881), 243–4; my translation in *Dark-Age Pastoral*, forthcoming.

36. Alcuin, *Letter to Ethelred, King of Northumbria*, Ep. 16; cf. Ep. 20: "Either this is the beginning of greater grief or the sins of those who live there have brought it upon themselves."

37. Joshua Davies, *Visions and Ruins: Cultural Memory and the Untimely Middle Ages* (Manchester: Manchester University Press, 2018), 36; discussing Alcuin, *De clade Lindisfarnensis monasterii* (On the destruction of the monastery of Lindisfarne), *Carmen* 9, *Poetae Latini aevi Carolini*, ed. E. Dümmler, 1, 229–35.

38. Owen, *The Great Age of Chinese Poetry*, 6.

39. Shuyuan Lu, *The Ecological Era and Classical Chinese Naturalism: A Case Study of Tao Yuanming* (Singapore: Springer, 217), xi.

40. By its focus on "leisure and deep stillness," Tao Qian's "Return to the Field" is to be distinguished from an earlier poem of the same title, also in the "Fields and Gardens" genre, by the Han poet Zhang Heng (78–139 CE). Here is an excerpt from Zhang's poem:

> I am like a dragon chanting on the moor
> Or a tiger roaring in the mountain.
> I gaze up and let loose the slender bowstring;
> Looking down, I fish in a long stream.

The loitering bird, struck by the arrow,
Drops from the clouds.
And the shark, hooked for greediness,
Is suspended in the watery abyss.

Wu-chi Liu, ed., *An Introduction to Chinese Literature* (Westport, CT: Greenwood, 1990), 54. Zhang is clearly involved in the bloody processes of nature, not liberated from them. Though Tao Qian talks in one of his poems of sowing beans and carrying a hoe, the dominant theme of his verse is that of the Buddhist-Taoist ideal, *wu wei* (nonaction).

41. Shuyuan Lu, *The Ecological Era and Classical Chinese Naturalism*, xi.

42. Anderson, *Passages from Antiquity to Feudalism*, 21, 22. Cf. 23:

In classical Greece, slaves were thus for the first time habitually employed in crafts, industry and agriculture beyond the household scale. At the same time, while the use of slavery became general, its nature correspondingly became absolute: it was no longer one relative form of servitude among many, along a gradual continuum, but a polar condition of complete loss of freedom, juxtaposed against a new and untrammelled liberty. For it was precisely the formation of a limpidly demarcated slave subpopulation that conversely lifted the citizenry of the Greek cities to hitherto unknown heights of conscious juridical freedom. Hellenic liberty and slavery were indivisible: each was the structural condition of the other, in a dyadic system which had no precedent or equivalent in the social hierarchies of the Near Eastern Empires, ignorant alike of either the notion of free citizenship or servile property.

43. I am associating Tao Qian with high monastic culture because of the Buddhist-Taoist praise of *wu wei* (nonaction) expressed in his poetry. He himself was not a monk, but he lived among Buddhists and is said to have befriended the important Chan (Zen) monk Hui-yüan.

44. "Man, in his moral nature, becomes, in his progress through life, a creature of prejudice, a creature of opinions, a creature of habits, and of sentiments growing out of them. These form our second nature, as inhabitants of the country and members of the society in which Providence has placed us." *Edmund Burke: Selected Writings and Speeches*, ed. Peter J. Stanlis (New York: Doubleday, Anchor, 1963), 494.

CHAPTER ELEVEN

1. The Yellow Turbans were led by Taoist priests, the Circumcellions by Christian priests later denounced by Augustine as Donatist. Leslie Dossey, *Peasant and Empire in Christian North Africa* (Berkeley: University of California Press, 2010), 2–4.

2. Dingxin Zhao, *The Confucian-Legalist State: A New Theory of Chinese History* (New York: Oxford University Press, 2015), 298.

3. Karen Armstrong, *Fields of Blood: Religion and the History of Violence* (New York: Knopf, 2014), 172, 166–67.

4. One might consider as an exception the reported slaughter of over one thousand British monks in prayer by the pagan Angle king of Bernicia, Æthelfrith (d. ca. 616), after a military victory. This slaughter of unarmed monks was the result (according to Bede) of their having "despised the [Roman Catholic] counsels of eternal salvation offered to them" (Bede, *Ecclesiastical History* 2.2).

5. Longdu Shi, "Case Studies of Three Persecutions of Buddhism, 444–846" (PhD diss., SOAS, London, 2016), 57.

6. Perry Anderson, *Passages from Antiquity to Feudalism* (London: Verso, 1978), 74; citing H. F. Jolowicz, *Historical Introduction to the Study of Roman Law* (Cambridge: Cambridge University Press, 1972), 337.

7. Theodoret, *Ecclesiastical History* 5.17: "The anger of the Emperor rose to the highest pitch, and he gratified his vindictive desire for vengeance by unsheathing the sword most unjustly and tyrannically against all, slaying the innocent and guilty alike. It is said seven thousand perished without any forms of law, and without even having judicial sentence passed upon them; but that, like ears of wheat in the time of harvest, they were alike cut down."

8. Simon Schama, *The Story of the Jews: Finding the Words 1000 BCE–1492 CE* (London: Bodley Head, 2013), 218–19; citing Gavin I. Langmuir, *Toward a Definition of Antisemitism* (Berkeley: University of California Press, 1990), 71.

9. Gratian, *Decretum*, C.2 q. 7 post c. 41, in Stanley A. Chodorow, "Magister Gratian and the Problem of 'Regnum' and 'Sacerdotium,'" *Traditio* 26 (1970): 376–77: "5. Sic et B. Ambrosius imperatorem excommunicavit, et ab ecclesia ingress prohibuit."

10. Brian Tierney, *The Crisis of Church and State, 1050–1300* (Toronto: University of Toronto Press, 2004), 20.

11. Socrates Scholasticus, *Historia Ecclesiastica* 5.17, http://www.ccel.org/ccel/schaff/npnf202.ii.ix.xix.html.

12. Armstrong, *Fields of Blood*, 166–74.

13. At the time Theodosius yielded to Ambrose in 390, he had defeated a challenge from the Roman emperor Maximus in Trier, but he still was sharing power with the Roman emperor Valentinian II in Vienne.

14. Having matured through the writing of this book, I now want to take issue with this earlier hope that divided power has prevailed politically over unitary power. It is now clear to me that lasting progress is never assured on the political level (the letter of legal order), only the cultural level (the spiritual level). On the contrary, over the course of time in any mindset, the letter eventually killeth, only the spirit giveth life. (Cf. 2 Corinthians 3:6).

15. Katherine Fischer Drew, *Magna Carta* (Westport, CT: Greenwood, 2004), 100. Medieval politics being volatile, Pope Innocent soon backed John against Stephen Langton, declared Magna Carta invalid, and released John from his obligations under it. However, Magna Carta was reissued (with alterations) in 1216, 1217, and 1225 and eventually served as the foundation for the English system of common law.

16. Ralph Turner, *Magna Carta: Through the Ages* (London: Routledge, 2003), 138.

17. J. G. A. Pocock, *The Ancient Constitution and the Feudal Law: A Study of English Historical Thought in the Seventeenth Century* (Cambridge: Cambridge University Press, 1987), 228.

18. The former was largely drafted by Sir Edward Coke.

19. The "Glorious Revolution" led to the end of the royal family's monopoly of the slave trade, and the consequent trebling of the number of English slave voyages in just four decades (William A. Pettigrew, *Freedom's Debt: The Royal African Company and the Politics of the Atlantic Slave Trade, 1672–1752*, [Chapel Hill, NC: University of North Carolina Press, 2013], 12).

20. Ron Grossman, "Trump and the Magna Carta," *Chicago Tribune*, February 15, 2019, https://www.chicagotribune.com/columns/ct-met-magna-carta-trump -20190215-story.html.

21. Isidore of Seville, *Sententiae* 3.51.1.

22. Julianna Grigg, "Aspects of the Cáin: Adomnán's *Lex innocentium*," *Journal of the Australian Early Medieval Association* 1 (2005): 41–50, https://www.academia .edu/5817305/Aspects_of_the_Cain_Adomnans_Lex_Innocentium.

23. *Cáin Adamnáin*, trans. Kuno Meyer (New York: AMS Press, 1989), 23–25.

24. Frederick S. Paxton, "History, Historians, and the Peace of God," in *The Peace of God: Social Violence and Religious Response around the Year 1000*, ed. Thomas Head (Ithaca, NY: Cornell University Press, 1992), 21.

CHAPTER TWELVE

1. Jacques Aillagon, ed., *Rome and the Barbarians: The Birth of a New World* (London: Thames & Hudson, 2008), 175.

2. Peter Brown, *Through the Eye of a Needle: Wealth, the Fall of Rome, and the Making of Christianity in the West, 350–550* AD (Princeton, NJ: Princeton University Press, 2014), 294–95.

3. Sam Moorhead and David Stuttard, *AD410: The Year That Shook Rome* (London: British Museum Press, 2010), 131–33.

4. Edward Jay Watts, *City and School in Late Antique Athens and Alexandria* (Berkeley: University of California Press, 2006), 197. A great deal of mythology, both ancient and modern, surrounds the murder of Hypatia. Catholics may wish to check what I have written against the entry for "St. Cyril of Alexandria" in the *Catholic Encyclopedia* (http://www.newadvent.org/cathen/04592b.htm), in which the role of Christian violence is even more prominent. (Cyril was only canonized as St. Cyril in 1882, by Pope Pius IX.)

5. Watts, *City and School*, 198–99; citing [seventh-century bishop] John of Nikiu, *Chronicle*, trans. R. Charles (Oxford: William & Norgate, 1916), 84, 97–102.

6. Karen Armstrong, *Fields of Blood: Religion and the History of Violence* (New York: Knopf, 2014), 161–62; citing Peter Brown, *The Making of Late Antiquity* (Cambridge, MA: Harvard University Press, 1978), 88–90; Migne, *Patrologia Graeca* 65.332a, 352cd.

7. Armstrong, *Fields of Blood*, 162; citing Peter Brown, *The Body and Society: Men, Women, and Sexual Renunciation in Early Christianity* (New York: Columbia University Press, 1988), 215.

8. "Christi ego miles sum: pugnare mihi non licet"; Sulpicius Severus, *Life of St. Martin*, 4, http://www.users.csbsju.edu/~eknuth/npnf2-11/sulpitiu/lifeofst.html. In this as in other respects Martin represented the traditions of preconciliar Christianity. St. Justin Martyr (d. ca. 165 CE) had said, "Christianus sum; non possum militari" (I am a Christian; I cannot make war), a statement repeated by St. Maximilian of Tabessa (d. 295 CE).

9. For example, in the *Vita St. Martini* 14.28 we find "virtutem edidit" (he performed a miracle), "ita virtute Martini" (such were Martin's powers), and "virtus illud divina dirueret" (might be destroyed by divine power).

10. F. R. Hoare, trans. and ed., *The Western Fathers, Being the Lives of Martin of Tours, Ambrosius, Augustine of Hippo, Honoratus of Arles, and Germanus of Auxerre* (New York: Harper & Row, 1965), 3.

11. Ernest-Charles Babut, *St. Martin de Tours* (Paris: H. Champion, 1912).

12. Babut, *St. Martin de Tours*, 14.

13. E.g., Jacques Fontaine, "Sulpice Sévère témoin de la communication orale en latin à la fin du IVe siècle gallo-romain," *Médiévales* 25 (1993): 17–32.

14. Hoare, *The Western Fathers*, 5: "Sulpicius did not, as Babut suggests, 'create' St. Martin, though he certainly exploited him. There was an immense popular devotion to St. Martin before Sulpicius had published a line about him."

15. Stancliffe, *St. Martin and His Hagiographer: History and Miracle in Sulpicius Severus* (Oxford: Clarendon Press, 1983), 167.

16. Hilary Powell, "'Once upon a Time There Was a Saint . . . ': Re-evaluating Folklore in Anglo-Latin Hagiography," *Folklore*, July 5, 2010, 171–89, https://www.ncbi.nlm.nih.gov/pmc/articles/PMC3672990/#R11.

17. Charles Bayet, in Ernest Lavisse, *Histoire de France depuis les origines jusqu'à la Révolution* (Paris: Hachette, 1900–11), 16; translated and quoted by Paul Halsall, in *Internet Medieval Sourcebook, Gregory of Tours (539–594): History of the Franks: Books I–X, Introduction*, https://sourcebooks.fordham.edu/basis/gregory-hist.asp#halsall.

18. Hoare, *The Western Fathers*, 40; citing Hippolyte Delehaye, "Saint Martin et Sulpice Sévère," *Analecta Bollandiana* 38 (1920).

19. Jerome, *Vita Malchi, praefatio* (Migne, *Patrologia Latina*, 1846), 23, 55.

20. Walter Goffart, *The Narrators of Barbarian History (A.D. 550–800)* (Princeton, NJ: Princeton University Press, 1988), 227.

21. Stancliffe, *St. Martin and His Hagiographer*, 16; citing Gennadius [late fourth century], *De viris inlustribus* 19. Pelagius like Sulpicius was an extended correspondent of the wealthy Paulinus of Nola (Sulpicius's closest friend), who as part of his conversion to Christianity renounced all of his properties (see below).

22. Gregory of Tours repeated a rumor that Brice had fathered an illegitimate child by a seamstress, a charge refuted when Brice made the infant, miraculously, deny it. Cf. Andre Mertens, *The Old English Lives of St Martin of Tours* (Göttingen: Universitätsverlag Göttingen 2017), 32: "Brice's episcopacy was not a

glorious one at first. He was often criticized for his tepidity, and when finally a nun gave birth to a child and rumour had it that Brice was the father, he had [temporarily] to abdicate."

23. Henry Mayr-Harting, *The Coming of Christianity to Anglo-Saxon England* (University Park: Pennsylvania State University Press, 1991), 97.

24. Technically, Ligugé was an Egyptian-style *laura* or collection of hermitage cells, as was Martin's later foundation at Marmoutier. Coenobial monasticism was standardized by St. Benedict and Pope Gregory I, but "when Benedict destroyed the old temple of Apollo at Montecassino, he built a shrine dedicated to Martin of Tours on it"; Brother Cyprian, "Martin of Tours," New Camaldoli Hermitage, https://www.contemplation.com/martin-of-tours/.

25. Megan Hale Williams, *The Monk and the Book: Jerome and the Making of Christian Scholarship* (Chicago: University of Chicago Press, 2006), 32; quoted in Brown, *Through the Eye of a Needle*, 261.

26. Brown, *Through the Eye of a Needle*, 76: "Not unlike the Buddhism that entered so dramatically into the somewhat stolid world of imperial China (between the fifth and seventh centuries A.D.), Christianity was a religion 'avid for the incommensurable'"; loc. cit., 75–76; citing Jacques Gernet, *Buddhism in Chinese Society: An Economic History from the Fifth to the Tenth Centuries* (New York: Columbia University Press, 1995), 141.

27. Wikipedia, s.v. "Ambrose."

28. Sulpicius Severus, *Vita St. Martini* 10.

29. Hugh G. Evelyn White, introduction to *Ausonius* (New York: Heinemann, 1919), 1, xiii.

30. Rutilius Namatianus, *De Reditu Suo* 1.445–46, trans. G. F. Savage-Armstrong (London: Bell, 1907).

31. Brown, *Through the Eye of a Needle*, 192–93, 208–16, 220–23.

32. Augustine, *Civ. Dei* 1.7:

All the spoiling, then, which Rome was exposed to in the recent calamity—all the slaughter, plundering, burning, and misery—was the result of the custom of war [consuetudo bellorum]. But what was novel [novo more], was that savage barbarians showed themselves in so gentle a guise, that the largest churches were chosen and set apart for the purpose of being filled with the people to whom quarter was given, and that in them none were slain, from them none forcibly dragged; that into them many were led by their relenting enemies to be set at liberty, and that from them none were led into slavery by merciless foes.

33. Paulinus of Nola, *Letter* 5.21, quoted in Brown, *Through the Eye of a Needle*, 220.

34. Brown, *Through the Eye of a Needle*, 215.

35. Brown, *Through the Eye of a Needle*, 215.

36. Sulpicius Severus, *Dialogues* 1.26, emphasis added, https://www.catholicculture.org/culture/library/fathers/view.cfm?recnum=2101. Stancliffe confirms that "the majority of Gallic bishops tended to feel hostile towards Martin's strict asceticism, with its implicit criticism of their own comfortable lives"; Stancliffe, *St. Martin and His Hagiographer*, 311. Cf. my discussion of Charles Freeman in the introduction.

37. Brown, *Through the Eye of a Needle*, 51; citing J. F. Matthews, *Western Aristocracies and Imperial Court, A.D. 364–425* (Oxford: Clarendon Press, 1975), 145–59:

> Martin ... is found rescuing from devastation the estates in central Gaul of an ex-prefect, Auspicius, and saving from an epidemic the family of Lycontius, who had held a vicariate. Whatever the literal basis in truth of these stories, the fact of Martin's contacts with such people seems impossible to doubt; and their importance is that, in making these contacts, Martin was moving among men whose support and co-operation was of great importance to evangelist bishops like himself, in their forays against the paganism of the Gallic countryside" (Matthews, *Western Aristocracies*, 156; relying in turn on Sulpicius, *Dialogues* 3.4, 3.14; Hoare, *The Western Fathers*, 129–30, 138–39)

38. Brown, *Through the Eye of a Needle*, 520.

39. Babut, *St. Martin de Tours*, 7.

40. Sulpicius had described how, "in destroying a tower dedicated to pagan cult, Martin prays during the night and in the morning (*Dial.* 3.8.7 *mane*) a storm brings it to the ground." In Fortunatus the single word *mane* becomes "when a new morning was spreading dawn over the earth and Phoebus was extending his saffron garment (*croceum . . . amictum*) among the clouds [Venantius Fortunatus, *Vita Sancti Martini*] (4.221–22); . . . cf. Ovid, *Ars Amatoria*, 3.179: *croceo velatur amictu*; Virgil, . . . *Aeneid*, 4.585, 9.460." Michael Roberts, "The Last Epic of Antiquity: Generic Continuity and Innovation in the *Vita Sancti Martini* of Venantius Fortunatus," *Transactions of the American Philological Association* 131 (2001): 268–69.

41. Brian Patrick McGuire, *Friendship and Community: The Monastic Experience, 350–1250* (Ithaca, NY: Cornell University Press, 2010), 98.

42. Fortunatus, Poem 11.6, to Agnes. *Venantius Fortunatus: Personal and Political Poems*, trans. Judith George (Liverpool: Liverpool University Press, 1995), 52.

43. Marilyn Dunn, *The Emergence of Monasticism: From the Desert Fathers to the Early Middle Ages* (Oxford: Blackwell, 2000), 62.

44. "St Martin of Tours (1) 316–397: Patron of France," CatholicIreland.net, https://www.catholicireland.net/saintoftheday/st-martin-of-tours-316-397-patron-of-france. For the Irish devotion to St. Martin after Patrick, see Michael Richter, *Ireland and Her Neighbours in the Seventh Century* (New York: St. Martin's, 1999).

45. Sulpicius Severus, *Dialogues* 2.13, http://www.newadvent.org/fathers/35033.htm.

46. Augustine, *Civ. Dei* 14.28.

47. Letter of 417 to Bonifacius, governor of Africa.

48. Perhaps a poet will be allowed to comment that, in a broad sense, the "arc of the moral universe" that "bends toward justice" can be traced through Martin, to his namesake Martin Luther (baptized on St. Martin's Day), to *his* namesake Martin Luther King Jr.

49. For the considerable influence of Martin on Irish monasticism, see Richter, *Ireland and Her Neighbours*. Richter cites the early ninth-century *Book of Armagh*, a manuscript containing three distinct groups of material: a complete text of the New Testament, a dossier of materials on St. Patrick, and almost all the writings on St. Martin by Sulpicius Severus.

50. Richard Woods, "The Spirituality of the Celtic Church," *Spirituality Today* 37, no. 3 (1985): 243–55.

51. Bede, *Ecclesiastical History of the English Nation*, 3.5, https://sourcebooks .fordham.edu/basis/bede-book3.asp. Cf. *Ecclesiastical History*, 3:28: "So Ceadda, being consecrated bishop, began . . . to apply himself to humility, self-denial, and study; to travel about, not on horseback, but after the manner of the Apostles, on foot." These monks studiously avoided being the stereotypic monk criticized by Sulpicius, "who had previously accustomed to travel on foot, or at most to ride on the back of an ass, must needs now ride proudly on frothing steeds" (*Dialogues* 1.21).

52. Columbanus, for example, was welcomed to Frankish Burgundy by King Gontram and to Lombardy by King Agilulf.

53. J. Campbell, "Bede [St Bede, Bæda, known as the Venerable Bede] (673/4–735)," *Oxford Dictionary of National Biography*.

54. For example, the two Anglo-Saxon monks, both called Hewald, who traveled without protection to the Saxons in western Münsterland: "White Hewald they slew outright with the sword; but they put Black Hewald to lingering torture and tore him limb from limb in horrible fashion, and they threw their bodies into the Rhine" (*Hist. Eccl.* 5.9).

55. The civilizing role of these monastics was not confined to missionary work. As we saw in the last chapter, Adomnán of Iona, ninth abbot of Iona after St. Columba, secured passage at the Synod of Birr (697) of the Cáin Adamnáin (Law of Adomnán), also known as the Lex Innocentium (Law of Innocents). It provided for the protection in warfare of women and noncombatants, extending the Law of Patrick, which had protected monks.

56. "By the year 1000 the legal category of slave had been replaced by that of serf or villein. Whether the actual living conditions improved in the change from one status to another is a matter of some uncertainty because serfs were still unfree in many important respects"; Daniel Donoghue, "Lawman, Bede, and the Context of Slavery," in *Reading Laȝamon's Brut: Approaches and Explorations*, ed. Rosamund Allen, Jane Roberts, and Carole Weinberg (Amsterdam: Rodopi, 2013), 198. However, the most oppressive feature of serfdom, the serf's being tied to the land, did not appear until about 1200.

57. Anderson, *Passages from Antiquity to Feudalism* (London: Verso, 1978), 128, 131.

58. Wickham, *The Inheritance of Rome*, 530.

59. Thomas Cahill, *How the Irish Saved Civilization: The Untold Story of Ireland's Heroic Role from the Fall of Rome to the Rise of Medieval Europe* (New York: Nan A. Talese, Doubleday, 1995), 193–95, 206.

60. Matteo Nicolini-Zani, *Christian Monks on Chinese Soil: A History of Monastic Missions to China*, trans. Sophia Senyk and William Skudlarek (Collegeville, MN: Liturgical Press, 2016).

61. David Marshall Lang, *Lives and Legends of the Georgian Saints* (London: Allen & Unwin, 1956), 81–83.

62. Alberto Ferreiro, ed., *The Visigoths: Studies in Culture and Society* (Boston: Brill, 1999), 81n.

63. Cahill, *How the Irish Saved Civilization*, 191.

64. Thomas Kinsella, trans., *The Táin: From the Irish Epic Táin Bó Cualinge* (Oxford: Oxford University Press, 2002), 132–33. I see in this charitable detail of forgiveness a reflection of contemporary accounts of saints' *virtutes* (miracles), as in this firsthand anecdote from Gregory of Tours (d. 594):

> It happened once that I was journeying to visit my aged mother in Burgundy. And when passing through the woods on the other side of the river Bèbre we came upon highwaymen. They cut us off from escape and were going to rob and kill us. Then I resorted to my usual means of assistance and called on St. Martin for help. And he came to my help at once and efficiently, and so terrified them that they could do nothing against us. And instead of causing fear they were afraid, and were beginning to flee as fast as they could. But I remembered the apostle's words *that our enemies ought to be supplied with food and drink, and told my people to offer them drink.* They wouldn't wait at all, but fled at top speed. (Gregory of Tours, *De Virtutibus Sancti Martini* 1.36, emphasis added)

65. Kinsella, *The Táin*, 186.
66. Brown, *Through the Eye of a Needle*, 400–401.

CHAPTER THIRTEEN

1. Peter Brown, *Augustine of Hippo: A Biography* (Berkeley: University of California Press, 1969), 62.

2. Brown, *Augustine of Hippo*, 61–62.

3. Thomas A. J. McGinn, "Concubinage and the *Lex Julia* on Adultery," *Transactions of the American Philological Association* 121 (1991): 343–44.

4. Brown, *Augustine of Hippo*, 41.

5. Matthew 22:37; quoted in Augustine, *De Doctrina Christiana*, 2.7.10. Cf. Deuteronomy 6:5.

6. I am quite certain that a remarkable poem attributed to St. Augustine, "In Praise of Dancing," is in fact not by him. But it too speaks of achieving a focused mental balance:

> Dance is a transformation of space, of time, of people,
> who are in constant danger of becoming all brain, will, or feeling.
> . . .
> Dancing demands a freed person, one who vibrates
> with the balance of all his powers

Brendan O'Malley, *Lord of Creation: A Resource for Creative Celtic Spirituality* (Harrisburg, PA: Morehouse Publishing, 2008), 43.

7. An allusion to Moses on Mount Nebo; Deuteronomy 32:49.

8. In the opinion of Paul Johnson, "Next to Paul . . . [Augustine] did more to shape Christianity than any other human being." Paul Johnson, *A History of Christianity* (New York: Atheneum, 1976), 112.

9. J. J. O'Meara, "Augustine's *Confessions*: Elements of Fiction," in *Augustine: From Rhetor to Theologian*, ed. Joanne McWilliam (Waterloo, Ont.: Wilfrid Laurier University Press, 1992), 77; citing Pierre Courcelle, *Recherches sur les Confessions de Saint Augustin* (Paris: E. de Boccard, 1950), 188–202.

10. Herbert H. Yeames, "The Tragedy of Dido. Part I," *Classical Journal* 8, no. 4 (1913): 142.

11. Roy Pascal, *Design and Truth in Autobiography* (Cambridge, MA: Harvard University Press, 1960), 22.

12. Czeslaw Milosz, "The Importance of Simone Weil" (1960), in *To Begin Where I Am: Selected Essays* (New York: Farrar, Straus & Giroux, 2001), 247–48; discussion in Peter Dale Scott, *Ecstatic Pessimist: Catastrophe and Hope in the Poetry of Czeslaw Milosz* (Lanham, MD: Rowman & Littlefield, 2023), 20–21, etc.

13. Czeslaw Milosz. *Native Realm: A Search for Self-Definition* (New York: Farrar, Straus & Giroux, 1968), 247; discussion in Scott, *Ecstatic* Pessimist, 5, 24, 232–33.

14. Milosz, "The Importance of Simone Weil," 248.

15. Brown, *Augustine of Hippo*, 296.

16. Max Simon Nordau, *The Interpretation of History* (New York: Moffat, Yard, 1911), 64–65; citing Robert Flint, *The Philosophy of History in France and Germany* (Edinburgh: Blackwood, 1874), 21–22: "These are the leading propositions of what we may call in a lax and general way the Augustinian philosophy of history, which was substantially the only one known in medieval Europe. . . . Its assertion of the existence, power, and wisdom of the First Providential Cause, although admirable in itself, is unsupported by adequate proof, that being only attainable by the investigation of secondary causes, which are neglected."

17. Cf. St. Paul's condemnation of money as "the root of all evil" (1 Timothy 6:10) and Virgil's "auri sacra fames" (*Aeneid* 3:57).

18. Augustine, *Civ. Dei* 3.17; quoting Sallust, *Historiae Fragmenta* 1.11.

19. Augustine, *Civ. Dei* 3.14; quoting Sallust, *Bellum Catilinae* 2.2.

20. Augustine, *Civ. Dei* 10.27; quoting Virgil, *Eclogues* 4.13ss.

21. Augustine, *De Doctrina Christiana* 3.32; cf. *Civ. Dei* 18.49: "In this situation, many reprobates are mingled in the Church with the good."

22. Ola Sigurdson, *Heavenly Bodies: Incarnation, the Gaze, and Embodiment in Christian Theology* (Grand Rapids, MI: Eerdmans, 2016), 593; citing Augustine, *Civ. Dei* 18.49, 16.25, 19.13.

23. Augustine, *Civ. Dei* 19.14.

24. W[illiam] Cunningham, *S. Austin and His Place in the History of Christian Thought* (London: C. J. Clay, 1886); quoted in John Neville Figgis, *The Political Aspects of St. Augustine's City of God* (London: Longmans, 1921), 23.

25. Augustine rejected however Origen's doctrine of apocatastasis, the belief that ultimately all free moral creatures—angels, men, and devils—will share in the grace of salvation. For Augustine this deprived of significance the dialectic of history and Christ's promise of redemption.

26. F. B. A. Asiedu, "The Song of Songs and the Ascent of the Soul: Ambrose, Augustine, and the Language of Mysticism," *Vigiliae Christianae* 55, no. 3 (2001): 300.

27. Alcuin Blamires, *The Case for Women in Medieval Culture* (Oxford: Clarendon Press, 1997), 113.

28. See Stephen Jay Gould, *Ontogeny and Phylogeny* (Cambridge, MA: Belknap, 1977).

29. This was analogous to the Thai practice of offering food at the shrines of local spirits, or *phi* (discussed in chapter 12).

30. Brown, *Augustine of Hippo*, 42–44.

31. Gillian Clark, introduction to *Confessions. Books I–IV*, by Augustine, ed. Gillian Clark (Cambridge: Cambridge University Press, 1995), 18; citing Augustine, *Confessions* 7.9.13, 8.2.3.

32. James Carroll, *Constantine's Sword: The Church and the Jews; A History* (Boston: Houghton Mifflin, 2001), 217, 219.

33. Paula Fredriksen, "Augustine and 'Thinking with' Jews: Rhetoric Pro- and Contra Iudaeos," *Ancient Jew Review*, February 13, 2018, https://www.ancientjewreview.com/read/2018/2/3/augustine-and-thinking-with-jews-rhetoric-pro-and-contra-iudaeos.

34. Ora Limor and Guy G. Stroumsa, eds., *Contra Iudaeos: Ancient and Medieval Polemics between Christians and Jews* (Tübingen: J. C. B. Mohr, 1996), 22.

35. "The sabbatical millennium . . . first appeared in Christian texts in the early second century" (in the Judaizing *Epistle of Barnabas*). Richard Landes, "The Fear of an Apocalyptic Year 1000: Augustinian Historiography, Medieval and Modern," *Speculum* 75, no. 1 (2000).

36. Cf. Acts 4:32: "The group of those who believed were of one heart and mind, and no one said that any of his possessions was his own, but everything was held in common" (Multitudinis autem credentium erat cor unum, et anima una: nec quisquam eorum, quæ possidebat, aliquid suum esse dicebat, sed erant illis omnia communia).

37. For a study of the monk-bishop in the Byzantine Church, see Andrea Sterk, *Renouncing the World Yet Leading the Church: The Monk-Bishop in Late Antiquity* (Cambridge, MA: Harvard University Press, 2004).

38. "Saint Hilary of Arles," *Faith: The Magazine of Catholic Diocese of Lansing*, n.d., https://faithmag.com/saint-hilary-arles.

39. Celestine, Letter 4, *Patrologia Latina* 50.430–31, 434; quoted in Brown, *Through the Eye of a Needle: Wealth, the Fall of Rome, and the Making of Christianity in the West, 350–550 AD* (Princeton, NJ: Princeton University Press, 2014), 426.

Brown dates this letter as of 428. In 431 the same Pope Celestine consecrated a monk, St. Palladius, as the first missionary bishop to Ireland (which did not yet have a local clergy). Palladius is said to have later presided over a monastic community in Scotland.

40. Nevertheless, the Rule of St. Benedict incorporated elements from the rules of St. Augustine for his monks at Hippo and also St. John Cassian (d. ca. 435), an Abbot close to the monks of Lérins. Gregory, ironically, was the first ex-monk to become pope.

41. E.g., Karin Schlapbach, "Giambattista Vico (1668–1744)," in: K. Pollmann/W. Otten (eds), *Oxford Guide to the Historical Reception of Augustine* (Oxford: Oxford University Press, 2014):

V[ico]'s use of the notion of the "city" (e.g. "the great city of the nations, founded and governed by God," paragraph 1107) is influenced by the "earthly city" of *civ[itas Dei*, City of God] (*New Science* xxii). The strong emphasis on providence throughout also betrays his indebtedness to Aug[ustine].

42. I would now say, "the Roman Meta-System, for reasons I hope to develop elsewhere."

43. Brown, *Augustine of Hippo*, 70.

44. Jennifer V. Ebbeler, "Religious Identity and the Politics of Patronage: Symmachus and Augustine," *Historia: Zeitschrift für Alte Geschichte* 56, no. 2 (2007): 230–42, 231.

45. Brown, *Augustine of Hippo*, 71.

46. Augustine, *Confessions* 8.6.14.

47. A. H. M. Jones, J. R. Martindale, and J. Morris, *The Prosopography of the Later Roman Empire*, vol. 1 (Cambridge: Cambridge University Press, 1971), 715: "Ponticianus *agens in rebus* (West) 386–87: African, Christian, served for a time in the imperial court in Trier, presumably as *agens in rebus* since two *agentes in rebus* are described as his *contubernales*, then served at court at Milan ('*praeclare in palatio militans*'), where he met Augustine and Alypius to whom he told the story of St. Anthony Aug. *Conf*. VIII 6. 14–15."

48. Augustine, *Confessions* 8.6; Brown, *Augustine of Hippo*, 107.

49. Erika Hermanowicz, *Possidius of Calama: A Study of the North African Episcopate in the Age of Augustine* (Oxford: Oxford University Press, 2008), 37; citing Possidius, *Vita S. Augustini*, 3.3–5: "Augustine's sermon 355 offers no clue as to the identity of the acquaintance who prompted Augustine to leave Thagaste for Hippo. The *Vita* identifies him as an *agens in rebus* and adds the brief detail that he was 'bene Christianus Deumque timens': a good Christian who feared God. I wonder if this brief description of a nameless bureaucrat who pops out dramatically from the narrative constitutes a kind of inside joke, the story of how Possidius once vacillated before his expectant mentor. Many readers of the vita have commented that Possidius maintains a low profile in the biography. . . . Possidius also anointed himself protector and heir of Augustine's literary heritage. In his own anonymous way, Possidius always claims his proper credit, and the understanding that he likes to write himself into Augustine's biography—we shall see more of this later—propels my assertion that this *agens in rebus* may be no other than Possidius himself." Cf. Brown, *Augustine of Hippo*, 136.

50. Augustine, *Confessions* 9.8; Brown, *Augustine of Hippo*, 126.

51. Matthew Bunson, *Encyclopedia of the Roman Empire* (New York: Facts on File, 2012), 221. Cf. Christopher Kelly, *Ruling the Later Roman Empire* (Cambridge, MA: Harvard University Press, 2006), 206–7: "For the distinguished Antiochene orator Libanius [d. ca. 392] . . . *agentes* were the ubiquitous 'eyes of the emperor,' interminable 'snoopers' who, instead of seeking out genuine misconduct, terrorized provincials, These were the 'sheep-dogs who had joined the wolf pack,' [who] 'would plant evidence of magical practices on those who were completely innocent.' . . . For the most part, the reality was more prosaic. . . . It is unlikely that these officials could ever have functioned effectively as a 'secret service or internal police force.'"

52. In 383, no less than five men claimed to be Roman emperor: two in the East (Theodosius and his son Arcadius) and three in the West (Valentinian II, Gratian, and the pretender Maximus). But there was greater stability and continuity at the bureaucratic level.

53. Eusebius Pamphilus, Socrates Scholasticus, and Evagrius Scholasticus, *The History of the Church from Our Lord's Incarnation, to the Twelfth Year of the Emperor Mauricius Tiberius, or the Year of Christ 594* (London: J. M. for Awnsham and John Churchill at the Black Swan in Pater-Noster Row, 1709), 3.15: "Further, when Constantine saw the mischief increase daily, he solved upon convening a General Council of Bishops, that thereby he might restore peace to the Church. In order thereto he dispatch'd right away the *Veredarsi* [?] (Coursers) and *Agentes in Rebus* (Messengers of the Emperor) throughout all the Provinces, who might call together the Bishops to Nicaea of Bithynia."

54. Brown, *Through the Eye of a Needle*, 95.

55. W. H. C. Frend, *The Donatist Church: A Movement of Protest in Roman North Africa* (Oxford: Clarendon Press, 1971), 164; citing Augustine, *Psalmus contra Partem Donati, Patrologia Latina* 43, col. 27; Jerome, *De Viris Illustribus*, 93: "paene totam Africam decepit."

56. Hermanowicz, *Possidius of Calama*, 31.

57. Brown, *Through the Eye of a Needle*, 330. In like fashion, the former *agens in rebus* Evodius, after joining Augustine as a monk in Hippo, left to become the monk-bishop of Uzalis, a city in modern Tunisia where "the main church or cathedral (*ecclesia*) had been in the possession of the Donatists, ostensibly an indication of their once dominant position in the city." Giselle de Nie and Thomas F. X. Noble, eds., *Envisioning Experience in Late Antiquity and the Middle Ages: Dynamic Patterns in Texts and Images* (Farnham: Ashgate, 2012), 126.

58. James J. O'Donnell, "Augustine's Unconfessions," in *Augustine and Postmodernism: Confessions and Circumfession*, ed. John D. Caputo and Michael J. Scanlon (Bloomington: Indiana University Press, 2005), 229. This synod approved a Christian biblical canon that corresponds closely to the modern Catholic one.

59. John H. Beck, "The Pelagian Controversy: An Economic Analysis," *American Journal of Economics and Sociology* 66, no. 4 (2007): 681–96, 685.

60. Peter Brown, *The Ransom of the Soul: Afterlife and Wealth in Early Western Christianity* (Cambridge, MA: Harvard University Press, 2015), 95. Jacob Viner quotes a similar thought from St. Jerome: "It is not without reason that the Gospel calls the riches of this earth 'unjust riches,' [Luke 16:11] for they have no other source than the injustice of men, and no one can possess them except by the loss and the ruin of others"; Viner, *Religious Thought and Economic Society* (Durham, NC: Duke University Press, 1978), 36.

61. Augustine, Letter 156; quoted in Brown, *Through the Eye of a Needle*, 361; Brown, *Ransom of the Soul*, 95–96.

62. Brown, *The Ransom of the Soul*, 96. In his book *Reichstumskritik und Pelagianismus: Die pelagianische Diatribe de divitiis: Situierung, Lesetext, Übersetzung, Kommentar* (Freiburg: Universitätsverlag Freiburg Schweiz, 1999). Andreas Kessler contends that "expressions like 'Pelagian criticism of riches' or 'Pelagian

social criticism' have become commonplace among scholars [but] largely unwarranted. Significantly, his book is not entitled 'Pelagian criticism of riches,' or similarly, but rather 'Criticism of Riches *and* Pelagianism.' The two issues, according to Kessler, should not be seen as doctrinally connected, but as two separate historical phenomena, albeit closely related"; Josef Lössl, review of *Augustine through the Ages: An Encyclopedia*, ed. Allan D. Fitzgerald, *Journal of Theological Studies* 51, no. 2 (2000): 739.

63. Brown, *Through the Eye of a Needle*, 331. Cf. Beck, "The Pelagian Controversy."

64. Beck, "The Pelagian Controversy," 689; citing Augustine, Letter 157.

65. "Pelagius," *The Catholic Encyclopedia* (New York: Encyclopedia Press, 1913), 607.

66. Brown, *Augustine of Hippo*, 358.

67. Gerald Bonner, *St. Augustine of Hippo: Life and Controversies* (Philadelphia: Westminster Press, 1963), 340–45.

68. Brown, *Augustine of Hippo*, 362. Such crass bribes in the service of holy dogma were by no means unknown in the *corpus permixtum* of the fifth-century Catholic Church. In 431, "St. Cyril of Alexandria bribed the emperor's court with gold and ostrich eggs (and much more) to confirm the banishment from the church of the Nestorians, many of whom sought refuge in Persia and China. By analogous maneuvers the African Donatists were also excluded, explaining their later swift conversion to Islam"; Peter Dale Scott, note to poem "Secular Prayer," in *Mosaic Orpheus* (Montreal: McGill-Queen's University Press, 2009), 178; citing Charles Freeman, *The Closing of the Western Mind: The Rise of Faith and the Fall of Reason* (New York: Knopf, 2003), 215–16, etc.

69. "Pelagius," *The Catholic Encyclopedia* (New York: Encyclopedia Press, 1913), 607.

70. Beck, "The Pelagian Controversy," 684; quoting Paul Tillich, *A History of Christian Thought* (New York: Simon & Schuster, 1968), 128.

71. Beck, "The Pelagian Controversy," 685; citing Jaroslav Pelikan, *The Christian Tradition: A History of the Development of Doctrine*, vol. 1, *The Emergence of the Catholic Tradition (100–600)* (Chicago: University of Chicago Press, 1971), 308.

72. Czeslaw Milosz, *The History of Polish Literature* (Berkeley: University of California Press, 1983), 377–78.

73. Augustine, *Civ. Dei* 4.4.

74. Czeslaw Milosz, *The Witness of Poetry* (Cambridge, MA: Harvard University Press, 1983), 14, 114.

CHAPTER FOURTEEN

1. There are, of course, major similarities as well as differences between the two traditions. See my forthcoming book, *Dark-Age Pastoral: The Poetry of Aldhelm, Bede, and Alcuin.*

2. "In *Medieval Cities*, Pirenne describes the revival of trade in tenth-century Europe as sweeping 'like a beneficent epidemic' from Venice." Peter Brown, "'Mohammed and Charlemagne,' by Henri Pirenne," *Daedalus* 103, no. 1 (1974): 32.

3. The shift from a yin-dominated to a yang-dominated ethos is well illustrated by this shift in meaning of the word *historia*, from "story" (for Gregory) to "history" (today). What was undoubtedly a welcome gain in objectivity was quietly offset by a corresponding loss in recognition of moral efficacy.

4. Gregory of Tours, *History of the Franks*, bk. 2, preface, https://sourcebooks .fordham.edu/basis/gregory-hist.asp#book2.

5. Walter Goffart, *The Narrators of Barbarian History (A.D. 550–800)* (Princeton, NJ: Princeton University Press, 1988), 220.

6. Goffart, *The Narrators of Barbarian History*, 217–18.

7. Goffart, *The Narrators of Barbarian History*, 174; quoting Erich Auerbach, *Mimesis* (Princeton, NJ: Princeton University Press, 1953), 79.

8. Erich Auerbach, *Mimesis* (Princeton, NJ: Princeton University Press, 1953), 79.

9. Gregory of Tours, *History of the Franks*, 9.19. Cf. Auerbach, *Mimesis*, 67–82.

10. Auerbach, *Mimesis*, 484.

11. Peter Brown, *Through the Eye of a Needle: Wealth, the Fall of Rome, and the Making of Christianity in the West, 350–550 AD* (Princeton, NJ: Princeton University Press, 2014), 491; citing Gregory of Tours, *Historia Francorum* 2.23.

12. Gregory of Tours, *Historia Francorum* 2.22; Migne, *Patrologia Latina* 71.217. Gregory does not see fit to mention that Sidonius Apollinaris was a poet, one who has been considered "the single most important surviving author from fifth-century Gaul"; Eric J. Goldberg, "The Fall of the Roman Empire Revisited: Sidonius Apollinaris and His Crisis of Identity," *Essays in History* 37 (1995), https://web .archive.org/web/20090902221243/http://etext.lib.virginia.edu/journals/EH/EH37/ Goldberg.html.

13. Gregory of Tours, *Historia Francorum* 2.23; Migne, *Paetrologia Latina* 71.217–20.

14. Goffart, *The Narrators of Barbarian History*, 232; citing Christopher Dawson, *The Making of Europe: An Introduction to the History of European Unity* (London: Sheed & Ward, 1932), 98; Edward Gibbon, *The History of the Decline and Fall of the Roman Empire*, ed. J. B. Bury (London: Methuen, 1909–1913), 4:150. Gibbon's actual words, often misquoted, were "the triumph of barbarism and religion."

15. Goffart, *The Narrators of Barbarian History*, 187; cf. Augustine, *Civ. Dei* 20.8–13.

16. Gregory the Great, *The Dialogues of Saint Gregory . . . Translated into our English tongue by P. W. and printed at Paris in MDCVIII*, ed. Edmond G. Gardner (London: P. L. Warner, 1911), 173–74, http://www.tertullian.org/fathers/gregory_03 _dialogues_book3.htm.

17. Goffart, *The Narrators of Barbarian History*, 250.

18. Modern historians tend to agree that Bede gives the Synod of Whitby a dramatic significance it does not deserve. The Irish churches had been debating the Easter issue for half a century, and many Irish clergy had already accepted the Roman calculation.

At Whitby, the Roman advocate, Bishop Wilfrid, "had pushed triumphantly against an open door"; Peter Brown, *The Rise of Western Christendom: Triumph and Diversity, A.D. 200–1000* (Oxford: Blackwell, 2003), 361.

19. Brown, *The Rise of Western Christendom*, 363. Cf. Henry Mayr-Harting, *The Coming of Christianity to Anglo-Saxon England* (University Park: Pennsylvania State University Press, 1991), 69: "One of the major puzzles of Bede's *Ecclesiastical History* is . . . that though Bede was a supporter of the Roman Church order it is the Irish missionaries who have made the overwhelming impact on the imagination."

20. Bede, *The Ecclesiastical History of the English Nation*, trans. J. E. King, in *Baeda Opera Historica*, Loeb Classical Library (Cambridge, MA: Harvard University, 1930), 4.3; henceforward *Hist. Eccl.* Cf. Bede's account of St. Aidan (*Hist. Eccl.* 3.5).

21. Cf. Brown, *The Rise of Western Christendom*, 351: "Bede went out of his way to create a new unity. He viewed Britain as a whole [and] was the first author to speak of the disparate groups of settlers . . . as a single *gens Anglorum*, a single 'nation of the English.'"

22. Bede, *Hist. Eccl.*, 5.23: "And both the beginning and the course thereafter of [King] Ceolwulf's reign have been filled with so many grievous commotions and withstanding troubles, that it may not yet be known what should be written of them, or what end they will severally have." Bede's *History* also recorded a letter from his mentor Abbot Ceolfrid (d. 716), foreseeing "the redemption of the whole world" (redemptionem totius mundi; op. cit., 5:21).

23. Colin Kidd, *Subverting Scotland's Past: Scottish Whig Historians and the Creation of an Anglo-British identity, 1689–c. 1830* (Cambridge: Cambridge University Press, 1993), 22.

24. "Characterising the language of Bishop Gregory of Tours, the French scholar M. Bonnet wrote 'Hardly a line of it could have been written in the classical age.'" Peter Rickard, *A History of the French Language* (London: Hutchinson, 1974), 10–11.

25. Henri Pirenne, *Mohammed and Charlemagne* (New York: Barnes & Noble, 1958), 45.

26. This is the so-called "Frankish view" of the Donation of Pepin's importance, summarized by the French historian Halphen when he called the donation the "foundation charter" of the Papal State; Louis Halphen, "Les origins du pouvoir temporal de la papauté," in *A Travers l'histoire du moyen age* (Paris, 1950), 39. For a Catholic response, see Thomas F. X. Noble, *The Republic of St. Peter: The Birth of the Papal State, 680–825* (Philadelphia: University of Pennsylvania Press, 1984), xxxii.

27. Leopold Ranke, *History of the Reformation in Germany*, trans. Sarah Austin (London: Longman, Brown, Green, and Longman's, 1845), 1:5.

28. There was papal precedent for resorting to forced conversion. "For pagans, [Pope Gregory I] generally considered sterner measures more appropriate. The pagan slaves of Corsica were to be chastised by beating and torture so that they might be 'brought to amendment'; the pagan peasants of Sardinia were to be burdened with a rent which would make them 'hasten to righteousness'"; Mayr-Harting, *The Coming of Christianity*, 146.

29. *Capitulatio de partibus Saxoniae*, no. 8 [782 CE?], in *Selections from the Laws of Charles the Great*, ed. Dana Carleton Munro, vol. 2 (Philadelphia: Department of the University of Pennsylvania, 1900).

30. Robert Ellsberg, *Blessed among Us: Day by Day with Saintly Witnesses* (Collegeville, MN: Liturgical Press, 2016), 286. Cf. Rolph Barlow Page, *The Letters of Alcuin* (New York: [Forest Press], 1909), 52–53; citing Alcuin, *Epistola* 111: "Alcuin deplores this policy [of beheading those refusing to convert] and ventures to suggest to Charles that he entreat the barbarians gently as 'the first fruits of the earth,' teaching them and encouraging them with words of advice and comfort."

31. Steven Stofferahn, "Staying the Royal Sword: Alcuin and the Conversion Dilemma in Early Medieval Europe," *The Historian* 71, no. 3 (2009): 461–80, https://www.thefreelibrary.com/Staying+the+royal+sword%3A+Alcuin+and+the+conversion+dilemma+in+early...-a0209404378.

32. The economic importance of the European slave trade increased after the installation of the Abbasids as caliphs in 750 CE. The Abbasids, in contrast to the Umayyads before them, shifted from an imperial policy of rapid expansion to one of defending the territorial limits already achieved. Thus, their economy, which had become adapted to the rapid influx of slaves from conquest, now had to maintain that level through purchase from non-Muslim sources.

33. Michael McCormick, "New Light on the 'Dark Ages': How the Slave Trade Fuelled the Carolingian Economy," *Past & Present* 177, no. 1 (2002): 49–50.

34. McCormick, "New Light on the 'Dark Ages,'" 53–54: "Slave trading was by no means the sole cause of the far-reaching changes . . . but it was a central part of these changes. [It contributed to] the run up to the eleventh and twelfth centuries, with their impressive trading fleets, emergent cities and merchant practices." Cf. Michael McCormick, *Origins of the European Economy: Communications and Commerce, A.D. 300–900* (Cambridge: Cambridge University Press, 2001).

35. Roger Wright, *A Sociophilological Study of Late Latin* (Turnhout: Brepols, 2002); quoted in Gregory Hays, "Review of Wright, R., *A Sociophilological Study of Late Latin*," *Catholic Historical Review* 93, no. 4 (2007). Emergent Romance languages like Old French now acquired their own distinct spelling, as first exemplified in the Strasbourg Oaths of 842 ("Pro Deo amur et pro Christian poblo et nostro commun salvament").

36. French education in particular has remained highly centralized to the present day.

37. Alcuin, *Letter to Ethelred, King of Northumbria*, Ep. 16; cf. Ep. 20: "Either this is the beginning of greater grief or the sins of those who live there have brought it upon themselves."

38. Page, *Letters of Alcuin*, 62; summarizing Alcuin, Epp. 9, 16, 109, 130.

39. Earlier in the eleventh century, forced conversions of Jews, by the French king Robert II the Pious (d. 1031), the Norman duke Richard II the Good (d. 1026), and the Holy Roman emperor St. Henry II (d. 1024), had been quashed, on the authority of St. Augustine, by the Roman Catholic Church. See Salo Wittmayer Baron, *Social and Religious History of the Jews*, vol. 4 (New York: Columbia University Press, 1957). Forced conversions of Jews would be revived in the thirteenth century.

40. See introduction.

41. We think of artificial intelligence as the cutting edge of Silicon Valley, but many of us may not be aware that, as Kate Crawford has written, "exploitative forms of work exist at all stages of the AI pipeline, from the mining sector . . . to the software side, where distributed workforces are paid pennies per microtask." Kate Crawford, *Atlas of AI: Power, Politics, and the Planetary Costs of Artificial Intelligence* (New Haven, CT: Yale University Press, 2023), as quoted by Sue Halpern, "The Human Costs of AI," *New York Review of Books*, October 21, 2023. See also Jenny Chen, Mark Selden, Ngai Pun, *Dying for an iPhone: Apple, Foxconn, and the Lives of China's Workers* (Chicago: Haymarket Books, 2020).

42. Steven Sofferahn, "Staying the Royal Sword: Alcuin and the Conversion Dilemma in Early Medieval Europe," *The Historian* 71, no. 3 (2009): 461–80.

43. "For the Love of Learning," *Christian History Magazine*, no. 108 (2014), https://christianhistoryinstitute.org/magazine/article/charlemagne-for-the-love-of-learning.

44. Chris Wickham, *The Inheritance of Rome: A History of Europe from 400 to 1000* (New York: Penguin, 2009), 411.

45. Manuel Giménez Fernández, "Fray Bartolomé de Las Casas: A Biographical Sketch," in Juan Friede and Benjamin Keen (eds.), *Bartolomé de las Casas in History: Toward an Understanding of the Man and his Work.* (DeKalb, IL: Northern Illinois University Press, 1971), 67–126.

46. Part of Luther's leadership ability was his skill at composing words and music for hymns, some now part of the Lutheran liturgy.

47. Lord Acton, introduction to *Il Principe*, by Niccolò Machiavelli, ed. L. A. Burd (Oxford: Clarendon Press, 1891), 52.

48. See, for example, Maurizio Viroli, "The Revolution in the Concept of Politics," *Political Theory* 20, no. 3 (1992): 32: "Machiavelli had altered the traditional meaning of prudence, transforming it from a moral ethic of action and politics into a method of pure political effectiveness justified by civic needs, otherwise known as 'reason of state.'"

49. At a private dinner in March 1944, Rotblat heard General Leslie Groves, director of the Manhattan Project, say words to the effect that the real purpose in making the bomb was to subdue the Soviets. Joseph Rotblat, "Leaving the Bomb Project," *Bulletin of the Atomic Scientists* 41, no. 7 (1985): 16–19.

50. Boris Altshuler, *Sakharov and Power: On the Other Side of the Window* (Hackensack, NJ: World Scientific Publishing, 2022). Altshuler attributes these facts to newly declassified documents of the Soviet Politburo.

51. Sidney D. Drell and George P. Shultz, *Andrei Sakharov: The Conscience of Humanity* (Palo Alto, CA: Hoover Institution Press, 2015).

52. Albert Einstein, "Science and Religion," Panarchy.org, May 19, 1939, https://www.panarchy.org/einstein/science.religion.1939.html.

CHAPTER FIFTEEN

1. Czeslaw Milosz, *The Witness of Poetry* (Cambridge, MA: Harvard University Press, 1983), 57; see also *The Land of Ulro* (New York: Farrar, Straus & Giroux, 1985), 93–96, 122.

2. Rorty's critique of American intellectuals, for prioritizing knowledge over hope, can be restated, in terms of this book, as faulting their excess of yang theorizing at the expense of yin dreams. See *Achieving Our Country* (Cambridge, MA: Harvard University Press, 1999), 94ss.

3. Walter Scheidel, "The Only Thing, Historically, That's Curbed Inequality: Catastrophe," *The Atlantic*, February 21, 2017, emphasis added, https://www.theatlantic .com/business/archive/2017/02/scheidel-great-leveler-inequality-violence/517164/. Cf. Walter Scheidel, *The Great Leveler: Violence and the History of Inequality from the Stone Age to the Twenty-First Century* (Princeton, NJ: Princeton University Press, 2017).

4. Graham Allison, "Can China and the United States Escape Thucydides's Trap?," *The Atlantic*, September 24, 2015, https://www.theatlantic.com/international/archive /2015/09/united-states-china-war-thucydides-trap/406756.

5. Barbara Tuchman, *The March of Folly* (New York: Random House, 2014), chap. 1, https://www.penguinrandomhouse.ca/books/180852/the-march-of-folly-by -barbara-w-tuchman/9780345308238/excerpt.

6. Thomas Piketty, *Harvard Gazette*, March 3, 2020, https://news.harvard .edu/gazette/story/2020/03/pikettys-new-book-explores-how-economic-inequality -is-perpetuated/. Cf. Thomas Piketty, *A Brief History of Equality* (Cambridge, MA: Belknap, 2022).

7. Reuters, June 24, 2020, https://www.deccanchronicle.com/business/in-other -news/240620/trump-threat-to-decouple-us-and-china-hits-trade-investment-reality .html.

8. Allison, "Can China and the United States Escape Thucydides's Trap?" The subtitle to a companion Allison essay in *Foreign Policy* was more open-ended: "When One Great Power Threatens to Displace Another, War Is Almost Always the Result— But It Doesn't Have to Be." Graham Allison, "The Thucydides Trap," *Foreign Policy*," June 9, 2017, https://foreignpolicy.com/2017/06/09/the-thucydides-trap/.

Allison did not include in his list of sixteen, but very plausibly could have, the American War of Independence against Great Britain (https://www.belfercenter .org/thucydides-trap/case-file). This war should be cited as a fifth exception to the "Thucydides trap." Public opposition led the British House of Commons to vote in 1783 against further war in America, paving the way for the Second Rockingham Ministry and the 1783 Peace of Paris.

9. *South China Morning Post*, May 21, 2020, https://www.scmp.com/news /china/diplomacy/article/3085321/destined-conflict-xi-jinping-donald-trump-and -thucydides-trap. Like most men in power, Xi can speak in conflicting voices.

10. Robert Levering, "How Anti-Vietnam War Protests Thwarted Nixon's Plans and Saved Lives," WagingNonViolence.org, November 12, 2019, https:// wagingnonviolence.org/2019/11/anti-vietnam-war-moratorium-mobilization-nixon.

11. The Catholic Church played an even more prominent role in the essentially nonviolent coalition that helped overthrow President Ferdinand Marcos in the People Power Philippine Revolution of 1986. (Catholic and Protestant clergy, along with Jewish rabbis, also contributed to the success of the U.S. civil rights movement, and later of the antiwar movement that grew out of it.)

12. Because of his opposition to the Mexican-American War, Thoreau in 1846 refused to pay his poll tax, spent a night in jail in consequence, and when released explained his tax resistance in his lectures on "The Rights and Duties of the Individual in Relation to Government."

13. Quoted in John Bauldie's sleeve notes for *The Bootleg Series Volumes 1–3 (Rare & Unreleased) 1961–1991*. In the lines, "Yes 'n' how many times must a man turn his head / Pretending he just doesn't see?" the critic Michael Gray has detected an echo of Ezekiel 12:1–2: "Son of Man, thou dwellest in the midst of a rebellious house, which have eyes to see and see not; they have ears to hear and hear not."

14. Cf. Noah Adams, "The Inspiring Force of 'We Shall Overcome," NPR, August 28, 2013, https://www.npr.org/2013/08/28/216482943/the-inspiring-force-of-we -shall-overcome. "It has been a civil rights song for 50 years now, heard not just in the U.S. but in North Korea, in Beirut, in Tiananmen Square, in South Africa's Soweto Township. But 'We Shall Overcome' began as a folk song, a work song. Slaves in the fields would sing, 'I'll be all right someday.'" It was adapted for use in the civil rights movement by Zilphia Horton at the Highlander Folk Center.

15. Quoted in Stephen D. Snobelen, "'God of Gods, and Lord of Lords': The Theology of Isaac Newton's General Scholium to the Principia," *Osiris* 16, "Science in Theistic Contexts: Cognitive Dimensions" (2001), 169.

16. G. Smith, "Newton's *Philosophiae Naturalis Principia Mathematica*," Stanford Encyclopedia of Philosophy, https://plato.stanford.edu/entries/newton-principia.

17. Czeslaw Milosz, "Traktat moralny," in Milosz, *Wiersze*, vol. 2 (Kraków: Wydawnictwo Znak, 2002), 100; translated and discussed by Peter Dale Scott, *Ecstatic Pessimist: Czeslaw Milosz, Poet of Catastrophe and Hope* (Lanham, MD: Rowman & Littlefield, 2023), 117.

18. Milosz, *Wiersze*, 2:89; Scott, *Ecstatic Pessimist*, 112.

19. Milosz, *Wiersze*, 2:98–99; Scott, *Ecstatic Pessimist*, 112; cf. 155–78.

20. See Scott, *Ecstatic Pessimist*, 81–89.

21. See chapter 14.

22. John Adams, *The Works of John Adams* (Boston: Little, Brown, 1956), 10:85; quoted in Jonathan Schell, *Unconquerable World: Power, Nonviolence, and the Will of the People* (New York: Metropolitan Books, 2003), 160. Schell also quotes on the same page from p. 180 of the Adams volume: "The revolution was in the mind of the people, and in the union of the colonies, both of which were accomplished before the hostilities commenced."

23. Adam Michnik, "The Montesinos Virus—Democracy, Dictatorship, Peru, Serbia, Poland," *Social Research*, Winter 2001.

APPENDIX

1. In my trilogy *Seculum*, I recall my discomfort with "the reasonableness of my dons // and their political science textbooks / proving *prophetic wisdom is harmful* / impeding *the application // of the piecemeal methods of science / to the problems of social reform* / appeals to openness // I would not now cavil with." Peter Dale Scott, *Listening to the Candle: A Poem on Impulse* (New York: New Directions, 1992), 50; citing Karl Popper, *The Open Society and Its Enemies* (New York: Routledge, 1945), 5.

2. Sidney Hook, "From Plato to Hegel to Marx," *New York Times*, July 22, 1951, https://www.nytimes.com/1951/07/22/archives/from-plato-to-hegel-to-marx-plato -hegel-and-marx.html.

3. Walter Kaufman, "The Hegel Myth and Its Method," in *From Shakespeare to Existentialism: Studies in Poetry, Religion, and Philosophy* (Boston: Beacon Press, 1959), https://www.marxists.org/reference/subject/philosophy/works/us/kaufmann .htm; reprinted in Jon Stewart, ed., *The Hegel Myths and Legends* (Evanston, IL: Northwestern University Press, 1996), 82–83.

4. I hope to deal elsewhere with my mixed reaction to the achievements and short-comings of the work abroad of the Open Society Foundations of George Soros (quite beneficial in Hungary, a country he knows well, but much less so, in my opinion, in more alien cultures like Thailand).

5. See Scott, *Listening to the Candle*, 43–45.

6. Gilbert Ryle, in *Mind: A Quarterly Review of Psychology and Philosophy* 56, no. 222 (1947): 169.

7. See Karl Popper, *Objective Knowledge: An Evolutionary Approach* (1982) and *The Open Universe: An Argument for Indeterminism* (1982).

8. For a scholarly documentation of U.S. assistance to the massacre, see Bradley R. Simpson, *Economists with Guns: Authoritarian Development and U.S.-Indonesian Relations, 1960–1968* (Stanford, CA: Stanford University Press, 2008). For my own treatment of U.S. involvement in the massacre, see Peter Dale Scott with Freeman Ng, *Poetry and Terror: Politics and Poetics in "Coming to Jakarta"* (Lanham, MD: Lexington Books, 2017), 207–26.

9. Scott, *Listening to the Candle*, v.

10. Peter Dale Scott, *Minding the Darkness: A Poem for the Year 2000* (New York: New Directions, 2000), 11.

11. Peter Dale Scott, *Deep Politics and the Death of JFK* (Berkeley: University of California Press, 1993), 22; quoted in Jason Boulet, "'I Believe in Enmind-ment': Enlightenments, Taoism, and Language in Peter Dale Scott's *Minding the Darkness*," *University of Toronto Quarterly* 75, no. 4 (2006): 925.

12. Jack Foley, "'No More Inhibitions': Philip Lamantia (1927–2005)," *Poetry Flash*, May 2021; referring to Matthew Fox, *Original Blessing: A Primer in Creation Spirituality Presented in Four Paths, Twenty-Six Themes and Two Questions* (New York: Jeremy P. Tarcher/Putnam, 2000), 139.

13. David Colquhoun, "The Age of Endarkenment," *Guardian*, August 15, 2007, https://www.theguardian.com/science/2007/aug/15/endarkenment: "The

enlightenment was a beautiful thing. . . . The past 30 years or so have been an age of endarkenment. It has been a period in which truth ceased to matter very much, and dogma and irrationality became once more respectable."

14. Paul Thagard, "Endarkenment and 'The Secret,'" *Psychology Today*, May 7, 2010, https://www.psychologytoday.com/us/blog/hot-thought/201005/endarkenment -and-the-secret:

> Symptoms of Endarkenment, the contemporary resurgence of magical, superstitious, and religious ideas.
>
> Endarkenment is the opposite of Enlightenment, which was the philosophical and scientific movement of the seventeenth and eighteenth centuries that challenged mysticism, traditional theology, and autocratic government. . . . Today, endarkenment comes in various forms: religious, spiritual, and philosophical.

15. Both *enmind* and *enmindment* are nonetheless gaining currency. Cf. Christian de Quincey, "Stories Matter, Matter Stories," *IONS Noetic Sciences Review*, June–August, 2002, 11: "What is needed now . . . is to find a way to restore a sense of the sacred to science and to the world—to embody mind and to 'enmind' matter."

Index

Abraham, 61, 305n75

Aeneid (Virgil), 19, 38, 61, 90, 102, 106, 129–30, 133, 138, 140, 141–43, 145, 147–49, 226, 227

Aeschylus, *Persae*, 78, 79

Agens in rebus (secret agent), 233–35

Aidan, Saint, 24, 171, 215, 245–46, 316n37

Alcuin, 19, 94, 131, 162, 181–82, 189, 194, 239; "De Luscinia" (To a Nightingale), 184–87; educational reforms of, 246–49; influence of noncoercive power and, 252–55; reurbanization of Europe and, 249–50

Alexander the Great, 94–95, 105, 231; as cusp ruler, 19, 89, 170

Alexandria: flourishing of, 89; founding of, 78; Greco-Judaean-Egyptian culture of, 101–2; imperial patronage in, 96; Judeo-Hellenic-Egyptian culture of, 108; leisure in, 125; noetic class in, 90–91; noetic cusp and, 19; *Sibylline Oracle* and, 139–40; status of Jews in, 103–5; status of women in, 105–7; urban Christian violence in, 202; yin and yang fusion and culture of, 76, 91–93. *See also*

Plotinus; post-Socratic poets; Song of Songs

Algeria, 7, 212

Allison, Graham, 257–59, 260

alterity, 16, 33, 56, 59, 80–81; dialectic of ethogeny and, 59; escape to, 568; as otherness, 16; religion and, 33; Second Pivotal Moment and, 56; sophists and, 80–81. *See also* otherness

Ambrose, Saint, 193; Arianism and, 156; Augustine and, 228–29, 231, 233; as bishop, 155, 193, 208; as culture shaper, 207–8; imperial events and, 156–57, 193, 234, 252–53, 311n7, 321n13; as minder, 22; Monica and, 229–30; Paulinus of Nola and, 209; wealth of, 208, 209

American Revolution, 15, 199, 263

Analects (Confucius), 53, 54

anti-Semitism: in Christian Europe, 42, 251, 288n37, 335n39; in early Christian era, 231; in Egypt, 123; in Muslim Spain, 251; of Nazi Germany, 251; in United States, 7

apocalyptic moments: apocalyptic change, 48–51; apocalyptic resistance in the Far East, 52–53; in Confucian China, 53–54; martyrdom

341

Eclogues (Virgil), 19, 126, 130–31;
ambiguous prophecy in, 141–42;
criticisms of, 145–46; *Eclogue* 4,
134–36, 149, 260; historic context
to *Eclogue* 4, 136–38; prophetic
tradition and *Eclogue* 4, 138–41;
urbanity and rusticity in, 132–34
Ecstatic Pessimist (Scott), 1, 6
ego, moreness and, 8
Egypt, religious tensions in, 7
Eisenstadt, S. N., 34
Elijah, 171
Eliot, T. S.: on culture, 4; inspiration
from Eastern religions,
30; inspiration from social
circumstances, 78; "The Moot"
(Christian discussion group), 3–4;
*Notes towards the Definition of
Culture*, 4; notion of history, 287n23;
urbanity and, 131; *The Waste Land*,
4, 64
Ellsberg, Daniel, role model of, 261–63
Emerson, Ralph Waldo, 260
emotions: evolution of, 38, 52. *See also*
ethogeny
empowerment, status quo and, 55–56
enchantment, 40–41
endarkenment, 340n14; as healthy
phase, 263; modern forms of, 340;
recognizing, 162; usage of term,
267–68; yin or "Dark" ages of,
167. *See also* Dark Ages; disruption
enforcement, 53, 145, 179, 193, 195,
197, 199, 200; empowerment and,
199, 200
enlightenment: Buddha and, 33;
decomposition of, 13–14; four Places
of Enlightenment, 157; searches for,
8; spiritual, 82, 200, 261; as yang
term, 7, 74; as yin term, 7
the Enlightenment: Catholic Church
and, 121; contempt for poetry and
religion, 267; creative momentum
of, 267; decay of values of, 238;
division of culture from religion by,

214; endarkenment and, 340n14;
Fifth Pivotal Shift and, 18, 57; Freud
as child of, 39; Hegel and Nietzche
on, 93–94; inspiration of Zeno and
Epicurus on, 98; left-hemisphere
mindset and, 261; moving beyond
attitudes of, 266; postmodern
challenge to, 81; rationalism of, 2, 5;
right-hemisphere mindset and, 261;
spirit of inquiry of, 25; yang legacy
of, 163; yin inspiration and, 20
enmindment: deeper progress toward, 8;
defined, 2; third nature and, 8
environmental disasters, role in social
change, 16
epics, 38, 66; as "spine" of high
culture, 38. *See also Aeneid* (Virgil);
Argonautica (Apollonius); *Comedy*
(Dante); *Iliad* (Homer); *Odyssey*
(Homer)
epicurean ideal, 126
Epicureans, 90, 93, 95
Epicurus, 76, 90, 98, 102
episteme, 3, 7, 13, 143, 199, 200, 210,
266, 279n35
Erdoğan, Recep Tayyip, xi
erotic love: in Song of Songs, 24;
spiritual versus, 219
Essenes, 51
ethical decline, 226–27
ethogeny, 5, 8, 14, 16, 17–19, 22,
41; definition of, 5, 8, 14, 228;
dialectical pattern of, 5, 14;
disruptive moments in, 17–18;
ethosphere and, 22; evolution of
persuasive power and, 22; moreness
and, 8; prayer and, 16, 40–41
ethologists, 8
ethos (normative, otherworldly, yin),
10–11, 181, 237, 250–51; bottom-up
ethos, 218; as dialectical, 13, 144,
181; evolution of, 13, 15, 38, 92,
160, 181, 218; global ethos, 9–10,
11–14, 42, 75, 197; grace and, 237;
nonviolence and, 250; second nature

About the Author

Peter Dale Scott was a Canadian diplomat and later a professor in the UC Berkeley English Department from 1966 to 1994. He was also a cofounder of the Peace and Conflict Studies Program at UC Berkeley. In 2002 he received the Lannan Poetry Award.

Scott's books of poetry include his trilogy *Seculum*: *Coming to Jakarta* (1989), *Listening to the Candle* (1992), and *Minding the Darkness* (2000). The poet and critic John Peck said of his trilogy that "Scott's Seculum is one of the essential long poems of the past half century" (John Peck, "Seeing Things as They Are," *Notre Dame Review* 31 [Winter/Spring 2011]: 239–52). Of *Coming to Jakarta*, James Laughlin wrote, "Not since Robert Duncan's Groundwork and before that William Carlos Williams' Paterson, has New Directions published a long poem as important as Peter Dale Scott's."

For five years in the 1960s Peter Dale Scott translated Polish poetry with Czeslaw Milosz and with him produced two important books, *Post-War Polish Poetry* (1964) and *Zbigniew Herbert: Selected Poems* (1968).

He is also the author of books on American deep politics (a term he coined), including *The Road to 9/11* (2007) and *The American Deep State* (2014, revised 2017). Roger Morris, former NSC staffer, wrote of *The Road to 9/11* that "Peter Dale Scott is one of that tiny and select company of the most brilliantly creative and provocative political-historical writers of the last half century. . . . As in his past work, Scott's gift is not only recognition and wisdom but also redemption and rescue."

ESPRIT DE L'ESCALIER

[Belated response to Marv Engel, who asked me to give, in one sentence, the message of my forthcoming book, *Reading the Dream*]

"This is the word of the Lord unto Zerubbabel, saying, Not by might, nor by power, but by my spirit, saith the Lord of hosts."

—Zechariah 4:6

—why didn't I simply say

people like us here
        at this Chanukah table
    should not just talk about politics

which let's face it
        we can do nothing about
    we should talk about culture

preparing people's minds
        for tomorrow's revolution
    and if pain like Blake's

in the left foot forces us
        to be poets who mind
    we can turn to the black windshield

in front of our eyes
        smeared by journalists academics
    and worst of all our friends

with the grime of facts
        and clean it a bit with hope
    hope powerful because

it has always been there
        in the minds of those most healthy
    while we wait for the great poet

on whose shoulder
        that eagle flying
    above and ahead of us

in the darkness
will come down briefly to rest

—Berkeley, December 7, 2023

www.ingramcontent.com/pod-product-compliance
Lightning Source LLC
Chambersburg PA
CBHW022259280326
41932CB00010B/916

* 9 7 8 1 5 3 8 1 8 1 5 2 2 *